LIBRARY OF HEBREW BIBLE/
OLD TESTAMENT STUDIES

724

Formerly Journal for the Study of the Old Testament Supplement Series

DRESS HERMENEUTICS AND THE HEBREW BIBLE

"Let Your Garments Always Be Bright"

Edited by
Antonios Finitsis

t&tclark

LONDON • NEW YORK • OXFORD • NEW DELHI • SYDNEY

T&T CLARK
Bloomsbury Publishing Plc
50 Bedford Square, London, WC1B 3DP, UK
1385 Broadway, New York, NY 10018, USA
29 Earlsfort Terrace, Dublin 2, Ireland

BLOOMSBURY, T&T CLARK and the T&T Clark logo are trademarks of
Bloomsbury Publishing Plc

First published in Great Britain 2022

A catalogue record for this book is available from the British Library.

Library of Congress Control Number: 2022933771

ISBN: HB: 978-0-5677-0268-5
ePDF: 978-0-5677-0269-2

Series: Library of Hebrew Bible/Old Testament Studies, volume 724
ISSN 2513-8758

Typeset by Newgen KnowledgeWorks Pvt. Ltd., Chennai, India

To find out more about our authors and books visit www.bloomsbury.com
and sign up for our newsletters.

To everyone who appreciates dress as communication and to the memory of Konstantinos Finitsis and Christos Passalis for impressing upon me the social and communicative aspects of dress from a young age

CONTENTS

FIGURES AND TABLES

FOREWORD

Martina Weingärtner
Collège de France

Symbolic language provides new possibilities of expression when ordinary language reaches the end of the thread. It is capable of clothing profound emotions when, otherwise, there would be only silence. It also exposes unspeakable, even unbearable, injustices imposed by oppressive powers. Dress and clothing, being closely attached to the body and the self, actualize symbolic expression. The expressive details that biblical texts can articulate by this seemingly mute object are illustrated in the present volume, *Dress Hermeneutics and the Hebrew Bible: "Let Your Garments Always be Bright,"* which should be viewed in continuity with the previous publication, *Dress and Clothing in the Hebrew Bible: "For All Her Household Are Clothed in Crimson."*

In that first volume the contributions emphasized a wide range of the productive or destructive dimensions of power communicated by dress. While that volume requires further interpretation in the different attempts to harness power, the book at hand testifies to the achievement made possible by the research group's continued studies and robust analyses.

The contributions in this volume put forward a more detailed and interdisciplinary examination. The research is based upon the widely accepted notion that dress and dressing are not only incidental or functional acts but also acts communicating dynamic, symbolic, yet meaningful significations. The contributors examine and discuss the rapidly growing field of dress and clothing studies in biblical and cognate texts, showing the potential of a promising academic debate. They perceive and review the discourse in social, psychological, and linguistic approaches which underlines the enriching interdisciplinary work.

The present volume explores further the necessity of the phenomenon of power communicated by dress by weaving together two essential patterns. First, focusing on the dynamic aspects of power, the notion of agency as an ability to alter plays an essential role. It has been stated in various contexts that dress communicates in its signs differentiation and distinction—before any verbal interaction. Most prominently, we talk about social distinction because dress declares a certain role or status. As the process of ascribing social standing reveals, one should not think of status as a static attribution, firmly fixed. Dress metaphors design dynamic forms of agency. Biblical texts, in a parallel manner, push the idea of a public self that must not be purely determined by alterity but can be the configuration of autonomous activity, which can mean manipulative or distorted action by the subject. The emphasis on the powerful agency in or with dress brings the ethical dimension of communication into sharp relief. Integrating the notion of dress in a concept of agency, or answerability, accents the individual's capacity and responsibility for decorating one's own dressed body. The representations of such configurations in this volume create awareness of agency's ability to disguise as well as the fact that it can never be neutral.

Second, and closely related to the aspect of alteration, this study displays through varying contexts how the effects of power define distinctions, construct barriers, and create hierarchies. In its communicative power, dress is analogous to language, and in each specific framework it can be unraveled into its constituent parts and its signs. Linguistic analysis and phonetic or semiotic approaches reveal the surplus of meaning while investigating the differences between particular signs, between sentences, and between parallel texts. These philological and intertextual studies provide the reader with new perspectives and lead to stimulating interpretations. The intertextual work, within biblical discourse, following postbiblical reception history, or bringing words and artifacts into dialogue, goes beyond a mere collection of comparable dress motifs. The interweaving of tropes and motifs that these comparative detailed analyses bring to light holds intriguing hermeneutic potential. In this way, new narrative arcs are stretched, and thus, not infrequently, innovative patterns are discovered that always reveal a transitory potential before a unilaterally determining function. Furthermore, the interwoven traditions highlight the display of a polysemic language that is characteristic to such metaphoric and symbolic, maybe parabolic, texts. The polysemic and deeply ambivalent and thus most challenging character of each chapter encourages the reader to interact with the texts. Given this observation, it is not surprising that many chapters in this volume dive into linguistic and philological studies, including cognate Semitic languages or Greek translations, offering a great surplus to the interpretation of the texts.

Dress makes a difference. This volume demonstrates the differentiating power of dress in two ways. It overcoats the stigmatizing tendencies of differentiation and focuses on the conducive dynamics in alterity processes and accessory modulation in political and societal interactions. As a result, it highlights the great potentiality of dress in its signs and symbols—an achievement of the editor and the authors, who may be warmly congratulated at this point.

The potential of diversity of meaning provokes a lively interpretative process between expectations and realization, between articulation and reception. The textual and iconographic approaches uncover the potential for a variety of life-encouraging views and engender new possibilities in self-perception and interactive relationship.

ACKNOWLEDGMENTS

A big part of the work in this book was completed under extraordinary circumstances globally. Contributors had to wrestle with the specters of the Covid-19 pandemic, social upheavals, and environmental crises, among others. Focusing on this research came with a set of unforeseen challenges. Thus, I want to present an additional note of sincere gratitude to all participants for making the time and space to contribute to and engage with one another productively. We all improved because of this generous collaboration and indomitable passion for the subject matter.

Of course, one has also to be mindful of the distinctive struggles involved. Sara, Carmen, Jen, and S. J. were the first to join this second round of research on Dress and as such faced bravely the dread of seeing their initial idea change drastically from one year to the next. Brady, Scott, and Selena came on board during our second year of work and confronted with poise a salvo of sustained and daunting feedback from more seasoned participants. Heather, Susy, and Ellie were the last to join and proved that they were as intellectually nimble as they were swift in completing successive rounds of editing with tight deadlines. They all met their respective challenges admirably and deserve credit for it. I consider myself fortunate to have worked with such excellent scholars.

The Pacific Northwest chapter of the Society of Biblical Literature and American Academy of Religion functioned once more as our "research headquarters." Hence, I have to recognize all our regional colleagues who lent their support and scholarly curiosity to our research project.

We would also like to thank our reviewers for offering constructive criticism and for motivating us to put forward a more polished and nuanced version of our work.

Personally, I would like to acknowledge: Martina Weingärtner for her interest in our work and for her collegiality; Alicia Batten for being a delightful friend and for producing inspiring work on Dress; Carmen Joy Imes and Selena Billington for their attention to detail and their precise editorial suggestions; Agnes Choi for her earnest friendship and constructive feedback; and my Religion Department colleagues at Pacific Lutheran University for their encouragement and camaraderie.

ABBREVIATIONS

AB	Anchor Bible
ABC	Anchor Bible Commentary
ABD	*Anchor Bible Dictionary*
AJA	*American Journal of Archaeology*
AJP	*American Journal of Philology*
ARA	*Annual Review of Anthropology*
ATA	*Alttestamentliche Abhandlungen*
AUSS	*Andrews University Seminary Studies*
AYBRL	The Anchor Yale Bible Reference Library
BA	*Biblical Archaeologist*
BBR	*Bulletin for Biblical Research*
BCOT	Baker Commentary of the Old Testament
BDB	Francis Brown, S. R. Driver, and Charles A. Briggs, *A Hebrew and English Lexicon of the Old Testament* (Oxford: Clarendon Press, 1907)
BHS	Biblia Hebraica Stuttgartensia
Bib	*Biblica*
BibInt	*Biblical Interpretation*
BJS	*Brown Judaic Studies*
BSOAS	*Bulletin of the School of Oriental and African Studies*
CAJ	*Cambridge Archaeological Journal*
CANE	*Civilizations of the Ancient Near East*, 4 vols., edited by J. Sasson (New York: Charles Scribner's Sons, 1995)
CBQ	*Catholic Biblical Quarterly*
CBR	*Currents in Biblical Research*
CDPS	*Current Directions in Psychological Science*
Com	*Communio*
ConBOT	Coniectanea biblica: Old Testament Series
COS	*The Context of Scripture*, 3 vols., edited by W. W. Hallo (Leiden: Brill, 1997–)
CTRJ	*Clothing and Textiles Research Journal*
DCH	*Dictionary of Classical Hebrew*, edited by David J. A. Clines (Sheffield: Phoenix, 1993)
ESV	English Standard Version
FAT	*Forschungen zum Alten Testament*
FRLANT	*Forschungen zur Religion und Literatur des Alten und Neuen Testaments*
FS	*Feminist Studies*
FT	*Folia theologica*
HALOT	Ludwig Koehler and Walter Baumgartner, *The Hebrew and Aramaic Lexicon of the Old Testament*, translated and edited by M. E. J. Richardson (Leiden: Brill, 2001)

HeBAI	*Hebrew Bible and Ancient Israel*
HR	*History of Religions*
HTR	*Harvard Theological Review*
HUCA	*Hebrew Union College Annual*
JAAR	*Journal of the American Academy of Religion*
JAMT	*Journal of Archaeological Method and Theory*
JAOS	*Journal of the American Oriental Society*
JBL	*Journal of Biblical Literature*
JBQ	*Jewish Bible Quarterly*
JFSR	*Journal of Feminist Studies in Religion*
JNES	*Journal of Near Eastern Studies*
JPS	The Jewish Publication Society
JSNTSup	*Journal for the Study of the New Testament, Supplement Series*
JSOT	*Journal for the Study of the Old Testament*
JSOTSup	*Journal for the Study of the Old Testament, Supplement Series*
JSP	*Journal for the Study of the Pseudepigrapha*
JSS	*Journal of Semitic Studies*
JTISup	*Journal of Theological Interpretation Supplement*
JTS	*Journal of Theological Studies*
KJV	King James Version
KUB	*Keilschrifturkunden aus Boghazköi*
LDiff	*lectio difficilior*
LHBOTS	Library of the Hebrew Bible, Old Testament Studies
LSTS	Library of Second Temple Studies
LXX	Septuagint
MT	Masoretic Text
NASB	New American Standard Bible
NEA	*Near Eastern Archaeology*
NET	New English Translation
NICOT	New International Commentary on the Old Testament
NIDOTTE	Willem A. VanGemeren (ed.), *New International Dictionary of Old Testament Theology and Exegesis*, 5 vols. (Grand Rapids, MI: Zondervan, 1997)
NIV	New International Version
NIVAC	New International Version Application Commentary
NJB	New Jerusalem Bible
NLT	New Living Translation
NSRV	New Revised Standard Version
OBO	Orbis biblicus et orientalis
OEAE	*Oxford Encyclopedia of Ancient Egypt*
OG	Old Greek
OIP	Oriental Institute Publications
OTE	Old Testament Essays
OTL	Old Testament Library
PAM	*Polish Archaeology in the Mediterranean*
RSV	Revised Standard Version
SBJT	*Southern Baptist Journal of Theology*

SBS	*Stuttgarter Bibel-Studien*
SCS	Septuagint Cognate Studies
SJOT	*Scandinavian Journal of the Old Testament*
STDJ	*Studies on the Texts of the Desert of Judah*
TDOT	G. J. Botterweck and H. Ringgren (eds.), *Theological Dictionary of the Old Testament*, 17 vols. (Grand Rapids, MI: Eerdmans, 1974–2018)
TLB	The Living Bible
TLOT	*Theological Lexicon of the Old Testament*, 3 vols., edited by E. Jenni, with assistance from C. Westermann, translated by M. E. Biddle (Peabody, MA: Hendrickson, 1997)
TynBul	Tyndale Bulletin
UF	*Ugarit-Forschungen*
VC	*Vigiliae Christianae*
VT	*Vetus Testamentum*
WBC	*Word Biblical Commentary*
ZA	*Zeitschrift für Assyriologie und Vorderasiatische Archäologie*
ZDPV	Zeitschrift des Deutschen Palästina-Vereins

INTRODUCTION: "LET YOUR GARMENTS ALWAYS BE BRIGHT"

Antonios Finitsis

There is comfort in wearing something familiar. This might be the reason why I decided to convene a research group to work on a subsequent volume on the topic of dress and the Hebrew Bible.[1] Then again, it might have been the positive experience of having worked in a community of mutually encouraging scholars who shared a passion toward a common goal. The contents of this volume are the outcome of a follow-up, distinct research team who worked together for the better part of three years supporting and inspiring one another. Regardless of the motivation, our return to the topic of dress approximately two years after our first publication comes with distinct advantages. First, as a field of inquiry, dress has captured scholarly interest and generated numerous engaging and insightful publications over the past two years. Essays and monographs on dress and the Bible keep appearing with rapid frequency. Second, our sophomore attempt at investigating this particular topic aspires to be a bit more nuanced and discerning. On the one hand, we have learned much from our conversation partners who probed deeper and wider with their research. For that we are grateful. On the other hand, because we continued working on the same topic, we have tried intentionally to sharpen our questions and push our investigation. For this goal, we require your feedback to determine whether we have been successful or not. In the meantime, we are content that we have had the opportunity to try this research topic on for size one more time.

Toward a Dress Hermeneutic

Our return to the topic of dress came with a responsibility: that of developing some guidelines that would define our approach and delineate the means by

---

1. For our first volume, see Antonios Finitsis, ed., *Dress and Clothing in the Hebrew Bible: "For All Her Household Are Clothed in Crimson,"* LHBOTS 679 (New York: T&T Clark, 2019).

which we would produce meaning. Thankfully, we have had a wealth of research available on the study of dress and have profited enormously from it. Sound methodology requires that we start with a definition. Precise definitions allow for better assessments, generate productive conversations, and create value for the field of inquiry beyond their ability to provide accurate descriptions. Specifically, we could lean on the foundational work of our colleagues in the social sciences who have made impressive advances on this front. Thus, we turned to the work of Sharron J. Lennon, Kim K. P. Johnson, and Nancy A. Rudd. They specify: "Dress as a verb refers to all the behaviors undertaken to create an appearance or to modify the body in some way."[2] As such, dress is a broad category that encompasses both clothing and adornment. However, dress is both verb and noun. "Dress used as a noun is defined as the assemblage of body modifications and body supplements worn by an individual at a specific moment in time."[3] As a noun, it is what is done to the body, and dress as a verb is how it is done. The implication here is that research ought to be alert both to the "what" and to the "how" questions. Lennon, Johnson, and Rudd conclude: "Dress is both a product and a process."[4] Thus, any attempt to investigate and uncover the valence of the verb and the noun ought to examine both the modus operandi and the outcome. Utilizing and reflecting on several decades worth of research on dress enabled us to delineate our approach.

Epistemology in the field of biblical studies has emphasized the importance of questions that scholars pose. In the wake of the classic and structured methods of interpreting text (i.e., source, form, rhetorical criticism, etc.) came approaches (i.e., sociological, feminist, iconographic, queer, etc.) that drew attention not to the merit of the procedure but to the significance of the questions raised. Awareness of our positionality allows us to perceive our blind spots and thus put under scrutiny details and assumptions that were previously left unchecked.[5] Biblicists

---

2. Sharron J. Lennon, Kim K. P. Johnson, and Nancy A. Rudd, eds, *Social Psychology of Dress* (New York: Fairchild, 2017), 3.

3. Ibid., 2. Lennon et al. cite here the seminal work that Roach and Eicher published in 1973. M. E. Roach and J. Eicher, *The Visible Self: Perspectives on Dress* (Englewood Cliffs, NJ: Prentice Hall, 1973). They continued their investigation in 1992. M. E. Roach-Higgins and J. Eicher, "Dress and Identity," *CTRJ* 10 (1992), 1–6. They culminated their work in 1995 with their influential publication with Johnson. M. E. Roach-Higgins, J. Eicher, and K. Johnson, *Dress and Identity* (New York: Fairchild, 1995).

4. Lennon et al., *Social Psychology of Dress*, 4. Here they cite Eicher and Evenson. J. Eicher and S. Evenson, eds, *The Visible Self: Global Perspectives on Dress, Culture and Society*, 4th ed. (New York: Fairchild, 2015).

5. Garcia-Ventura cautions that applying contemporary theoretical proposals to the past is a controversial practice since they entertain the danger of understanding the past just as we understand our present. In her view, however, the scholarly debate should focus on the unstated assumption that one ought to study the past employing exclusively a modern theoretical framework "and, more specifically positivism." This assumption is problematic because positivism supports the hegemonic principles of modernity. Agnès Garcia-Ventura,

have realized that all knowledge is situated.[6] Dress hermeneutics stem from this realization. In biblical studies discovery of new material is rare since we mostly deal with a closed canon. Correspondingly, dress evidence was always there; it was simply a matter of subjecting it to scrutiny. Biblical research of dress came under the influence of the rapidly developing interdisciplinary field of dress, and strong ties exist between the field of biblical studies, as a primarily text-focused discipline, and dress studies.[7] Shahidha Bari explains the connecting seams as follows: "The word *text* itself retains the memory of a lost materiality, connected to 'textile' and deriving from the Latin *texere* 'to weave.'"[8] Put differently the connection is intrinsic; it was just a matter of time, cultural progress, and/or viewpoint for the inquisitive scholar to be able to raise her questions on dress and the Hebrew Bible.

Having determined that both process and product ought to be investigated, a dress hermeneutic also needs to address the type of information one would hope to discover. As Batten observes, "References to dress are plentiful throughout ancient literature … by using dress as a lens for reading … we notice things that previously may have gone under the radar, for presumably the authors included every reference to dress for a reason."[9] We may systematize in three broad categories the meaning dress can help us construct: first as an artifact, second as a mentifact, and third as a sociofact.[10] I will describe these categories in turn below. For researchers

"Postfeminism and Assyriology: An (Im)possible Relationship?" in *Studying Gender in the Ancient Near East*, ed. Saana Svärd and Agnès Garcia-Ventura (University Park, PA: Eisenbrauns, 2018), 183–4. She concludes her discussion of why proposals from postmodernism are better suited than those of modernity when trying to engender Assyriology by quoting Knapp: "There is no ultimate explanation but, rather, an array of interpretive approaches that can provide a better understanding of past environments, social processes, cognition, and human agency" (185).

6. Haraway used the term "situated knowledge" to explain that all research is always biased and conditioned by the context in which it is produced. DonnaHaraway, "Situated Knowledges: The Science Question in Feminism and the Privilege of Partial Perspective," *FS* 14.3 (1988), 575–99.

7. For example, Lennon et al. divide their book (*Social Psychology of Dress*) in three sections according to the disciplinary approach they undertake to examine dress. Chapters 4–9 adopt a psychological/social psychological approach, chapters 10–12 employ a sociological perspective, and chapters 13–14 use an anthropological one. Similarly, dress studies have thrived in classics, philosophy, history, and many other disciplines. For an extensive annotated bibliographical guide to dress studies in the biblical field, please consult: Alicia Batten and Antonios Finitsis, "Clothing," in *Oxford Bibliographies in Biblical Studies*, ed. Christopher Matthews (New York: Oxford University Press, 2020), 1–35.

8. Shahidha Bari, *Dressed: A Philosophy of Clothes* (New York: Basic Books, 2020), 19.

9. Alicia J. Batten, "Foreword," in Finitsis, *Dress and Clothing in the Hebrew Bible*, x.

10. Lennon et al. credit Sir Julian Sorell Huxley (1880–1975), an English evolutionary biologist, with coining the terms "mentifact" and "sociofact" in his effort to explain the nonmaterial aspects of culture. Lennon et al., *Social Psychology of Dress*, 11.

of the past, dress is first and foremost valuable as an artifact. In the past, such items had tremendous material value. In the present their material value can hardly be understated, yet it is their informational value that is incalculable. They are a tangible piece of evidence left for us and have intrinsic value as survivors of a world that no longer exists. In a sense, they are an eyewitness offering a first-hand account for a cold case that an investigator wants to crack. Archeological studies of artistic remains become particularly essential when one considers the highly ideological nature of most of the ancient sources about dress.[11] Given the fact that much of the evidence biblical scholars have is literary, one has to examine how language relates to artifact. The examination of this relationship can be uniquely illuminating. Additionally, an artifact should be studied in terms of its material property, form, method of construction, signification, and use.[12] Museums regularly respond to this need by producing lavish publications that display elegantly dress artifacts that enchant the senses and enhance our understanding of the lives of the people who interacted with them.[13]

Second, dress is significant as a "mentifact." Mentifacts are "facts" of the mind such as guiding beliefs, values, attitudes, goals, traditions, aesthetics, and worldviews. They function as "the guiding principles of groups of people and of individuals."[14] As such they shed light into a group's ideology and help us to understand the decision-making of group members. They also assist in comprehending a group's concepts and symbols about the sacred and the profane as well as their beliefs about the relationship between the two.[15]

11. Alicia Batten and Kelly Olson organize their examination of dress under three topics: methods, materials, and meanings. Under the topic of materials, they present seven essays that explore the *realia* of dress. Alicia J. Batten and Kelly Olson, eds, *Dress in Mediterranean Antiquity: Greeks, Romans, Jews, Christians* (London: T&T Clark, 2021), 53–155.

12. Lennon et al., *Social Psychology of Dress*, 11.

13. Batten clarifies that the study of dress in the ancient world began primarily as a topic of interest for museum curators such as François Bouche, antiquarians such as Alfred Rubens, and artists such as Maurice Leloir and Carl Köhler. Batten and Finitsis, "Clothing," 4. Most recently, Verduci assessed the metal jewelry from twenty-nine sites in the southern Levant, the Aegean, and Cyprus, resulting in the creation of the first multiregional typology of metal jewelry for the Iron Age I-IIA Eastern Mediterranean shedding new light on the understanding of the Sea Peoples. Josephine A. Verduci, *Metal Jewellery of the Southern Levant and Its Western Neighbours: Cross-Cultural Influences in the Early Iron Age Eastern Mediterranean*, Ancient Near Eastern Studies Supplement 53 (Louvain, Belgium: Peeters, 2018).

14. As examples of two major worldviews, they offer independence and interdependence. They observe that many Western cultures hold a worldview of independence while many Asian and African cultures hold one of interdependence. Ibid., 11–12.

15. Lennon et al. consider ideology a universal of culture and specify that "ideology refers to the principle beliefs and values of a culture, a group, or a social movement." They

Third, dress is consequential as a "sociofact." Sociofacts are facts of the social organization, including social status, gender, government, politics, family, economy, instruction, law, purity/impurity, myth, and ritual.[16] As such, they help us to understand institutions, the articulation of relationships, and the construction of hierarchies both in the physical and in the metaphysical plane. The three types of information dress can help us discover, underscore the wide range of information one may recover and the advantages of this research. I shall attempt to demonstrate such a discovery in the last part of my introduction.

Dress as an artifact, mentifact, and/or a sociofact brings to the forefront another important consideration. For a complete hermeneutical approach, we further need a delineation of the steps necessary to produce meaning. A thorough engagement of the study of dress requires the examination of at least four different dimensions. First, we need to consider the setting and examine the evidence in context. For archeological artifacts this means a close investigation of how the artifact reflects actual lived experience.[17] For literary evidence, setting includes attention to genre, rhetorical goal, and broader literary and sartorial affinities.[18] For example, dress evidence found in a ritual setting ought to be treated differently from dress evidence in monumental architecture and/or royal annals. Second, we need to take into account the historical time frame since the same "artifact" can communicate differently in different time periods.[19] In biblical studies time

offer as an example "social justice," which "is a social and political ideology that supports the equal distribution of goods and opportunities to all members of a social system regardless of any arbitrary factors such as race, ethnicity, or gender." Ibid., 12.

16. Ibid.

17. For example, Baadsgaard shows that the mortuary attire of three females in the Ur Royal Cemetery indicates the existence of a distinct royal, feminine fashion whose embodiment was essential for the emergence of female rulers at Ur. Aubrey Baadsgaard, "All the Queen's Clothes: Identifying Female Royalty at Early Dynastic Ur," *NEA* 79.3 (2016), 148–55. Fletcher-Jones provides another illustration. He argues that ancient Egyptians wore jewels not only for their aesthetic and socio-material value, but also because they served another fundamental purpose: its wearers saw it as a means to absorb positive magical and divine powers—to protect the living and the dead from malignant forces. Nigel Fletcher-Jones, *Ancient Egyptian Jewelry: 50 Masterpieces of Art and Design* (Cairo: American University in Cairo Press, 2020).

18. For example, LeMon and Purcell argue that "the conceptual blending of royal warrior images and viticultural imagery creates a composite image of renewal that serves the larger rhetorical goals of Third Isaiah." Joel M. LeMon and Richard A. Purcell, "The Garments of God: Iconographic Case Studies from Isaiah 6:1; 59:17; and 63:1-6," in *Clothing and Nudity in the Hebrew Bible*, ed. Christoph Berner, Manuel Schäfer, Martin Schott, Sarah Schulz, and Martina Weingärtner (London: T&T Clark, 2019), 284.

19. Livneh has shown, for example, that the Maccabean author transformed the "robe of righteousness" in Isa. 61:10 into "garments of war" on the basis of a *gezerah shava* (equal category/argument by analogy) reading with Isa. 59:17. The biblical metaphor of "being clothed with shame" in 1 Macc. 1:28, on the other hand, refers to the "putting on

frame is further complicated when one considers the chronological differences between the various redactional layers of a biblical text. Third, we need to address the particular social circumstances in which the evidence is located, that is, urban, rural, royal/monarchical, imperial, priestly, scribal, exilic, postexilic, and so on. Dress is a crucial component of social interactions and critical in ascribing identity.[20] The circumstances influence the way we understand the transmission and meaning of the evidence in relationship to roles, groups, and structures. Finally, we need to consider the relationship dress evidence creates or the goal it is trying to reach. Dress is an embodied practice that partakes in its own discourse.[21] One has to examine the objective of this discourse analyzing the interconnections between its visual, somatic, and semantic aspects. This is important because it allows us to ask questions that our evidence may have taken for granted or was not concerned to reflect upon. As Bari astutely remarks, "Dress, in its fullest range, intimates something of the diversity and delicacy of the lived experience, to which words only falteringly reach."[22] The steps outlined earlier are not exhaustive. There are more dimensions to consider in the study of dress. However, the four suggested steps guarantee a thorough examination of the context in which we find the evidence and, thus, lead to a more complete understanding.

---

of mourning dress"—a practice also alluded to in 1 Macc. 1:26. Atar Livneh, "Garments of Shame, Garments of War: Clothing Imagery in 1 Maccabees 1:25–28, 14:9," *VT* 69.4–5 (2019), 670–81.

20. Van Oorschot comments that "humans who are naked are not fully human. Likewise, differentiation of human society is linked to having clothes." Jürgen van Oorschot, "Nudity and Clothing in the Hebrew Bible: Theological and Anthropological Perspectives," in *Clothing and Nudity in the Hebrew Bible*, ed. Christoph Berner, Manuel Schäfer, Martin Schott, Sarah Schulz, and Martina Weingärtner (London: T&T Clark, 2019), 239.

21. Serova remarks that "having the ability to convey symbolic meaning, apparel and adornment are often staged to communicate and express gender, age, ethnic identity, power, and also emotions." Dina Serova, "Stripped Bare: Communicating Rank and Status in Old Kingdom Egypt," in *Clothing and Nudity in the Hebrew Bible*, ed. Christoph Berner, Manuel Schäfer, Martin Schott, Sarah Schulz, and Martina Weingärtner (London: T&T Clark, 2019), 163. Bauks provides another example: she asserts that when Noah's sons cover their father with a garment in Genesis 9 their deed "represents an act of social rehabilitation, showing Noah respect despite their shame over their drunken and uncontrolled father." Michaela Bauks, "Clothing and Nudity in the Noah Story (Gen 9:18-29)," in *Clothing and Nudity in the Hebrew Bible*, ed. Christoph Berner, Manuel Schäfer, Martin Schott, Sarah Schulz, and Martina Weingärtner (London: T&T Clark, 2019), 385.

22. Bari, *Dressed*, 19. She adds: "In dress, we impart some mysterious thought, quality, mood, or aspect, only inadequately conveyed by any other means." Moreover, her book "comes from the conviction that there may be in clothes that which language cannot contain, and something else in language, too, that might realize the life of clothes that is otherwise left unspoken" (19–20).

Last, no dress hermeneutic would be complete were it to omit the interdisciplinary nature of the undertaking. Interdisciplinarity is integral to the genealogy that enabled the study of textiles. As a discipline the study of textiles requires in equal measure the cooperation of natural sciences, social sciences, and humanities.[23] In turn, the study of textiles broke the ground and set the stage for the development of dress studies. Furthermore, one can hardly overestimate the importance of theories, models, and perspectives that all these other disciplines bring to biblical studies. Because biblical studies is a relative latecomer to this type of investigation, the interdisciplinary insights prove valuable in many ways. They allow us to cover the communication gap between the past and the present and to observe the dynamics in which our evidence is immersed. Dress studies are reaching a critical mass of scholarly attention, and the field offers exciting opportunities for further advancement.

"Let Your Garments Always Be Bright"

Dress is primarily communicative.[24] Elizabeth Grosz argues that the body should be "understood as a surface for social inscription and as the locus of lived experience."[25] Dress as the assemblage of body modifications and body supplements worn by an individual is a surface of social inscription. In this capacity, it can exchange information about gender, class, status, role, group affiliation, and relationships, among others. Dress, as a verb referring to all the behaviors undertaken to create an appearance or to modify the body in some way, shapes the locus of lived experience. As such it highlights the bilateral relationship between humans and dress. Dress is a human creation, and yet it re-creates human

23. Barber, for example, combines various fields, including archeology, paleobiology, and linguistics, to demonstrate the significance and all-consuming nature of the ancient textile industry, and she underlines to what extent women were at the center of this work. Elizabeth J. Wayland Barber, *Prehistoric Textiles: The Development of Cloth in the Neolithic and Bronze Ages with Special Reference to the Aegean* (Princeton, NJ: Princeton University Press, 1991). See also Elizabeth J. Wayland Barber, *Women's Work: The First 20,000 Years. Women, Cloth, and Society in Early Times* (New York: W.W. Norton, 1994).

24. See, for example, Entwistle, who examines how dress communicates bodily, sexual, and gender identities in the modern context. Joanne Entwistle, *The Fashioned Body: Fashion, Dress and Modern Social Theory* (Cambridge, UK: Polity, 2000). Olson argues that clothing functioned as part of the process of communication by which male elite influence, masculinity, and sexuality were made known and acknowledged, and furthermore that those concepts interconnected in socially significant ways. Kelly Olson, *Masculinity and Dress in Roman Antiquity* (London: Routledge, 2017).

25. Elizabeth Grosz, "Bodies and Knowledges: Feminism and the Crisis of Reason," in *Feminist Epistemologies, Thinking Gender*, ed. Linda Alcoff and Elizabeth Potter (New York: Routledge, 1993), 188.

experience. It places humans in relationship with their body and affects, among others, their emotions, disposition, behavior, and interactions. The subtitle of our volume is meant to communicate this dual aspect of dress. The following chapters explore in various ways the communicative aspects of dress.

The book begins with a chapter by Brady Alan Beard. He reviews descriptions of headgear in the Hebrew Bible and compares such headgear to iconographic and material remains of headgear from Egypt, the Levant, and Mesopotamia. His goal is to provide a context for references to YHWH's glorification and splendor and the metaphors of such terminology. This information highlights the social importance and (re)presentation of headdresses throughout the ancient Near East. He concludes by suggesting that YHWH's glorification of Zion and the people of Judah may reflect the material realities of headdresses and especially those of mural crowns.

In Chapter 2, Heather A. McKay first analyzes and categorizes the functions of dress and then explains how the manipulation and distortion of those functions permit dress to be used as a vital constituent of deceptions in biblical narratives. Her work calls attention to the ways dress communicates assumed social identities and redefines the situation for both the victims of the planned deception and any observers or witnesses.

In Chapter 3, Sara M. Koenig surveys the reception history of Eve and Adam's clothing in Genesis 3. Despite the relatively simple sequential description in Genesis 3 where Eve and Adam realize their nakedness, clothe themselves with garments made from fig leaves, and then are clothed by God in garments of skin, interpreters throughout the millennia understand their clothing in various diverse ways. These differences include the timing of their nakedness as well as the timing of being clothed, the style of the fig-leaf attire, the type of skin used for their garments, and the significance of their outfits. Koenig approaches Eve and Adam's clothing through the lens of social perception and perceiver variables as a way to account for the differences in perceptions of their dress.

In Chapter 4, Scott R. A. Starbuck proposes a generative reading of Gen. 2:4b–3 by placing the clothing acts in this passage in the locus of lived experiences. He argues that the double act of clothing in the narrative communicates two helpful trajectories of textual insight and healing. The sewing of fig leaves in Gen. 3:7 may encourage reflection upon attempts of those in post-traumatic states to camouflage their vulnerability rather than take steps toward healing. The divine clothing act in Gen. 3:21 can be read as an invitation to inhabit violated bodies that are also clothed in skin to better face retraumatizing events. As such, this text may provide an opening for those who have suffered trauma to embrace their own skin and experience a recovery of their traumatized body.

In Chapter 5, Jennifer M. Matheny shows that in the stories of Tamar and Ruth articles of dress communicate desire and provide a provocative pathway toward a future inheritance. As marginalized women, their unique prowess uncovers bodies along with future of possibilities. Scandalous negotiation in the areas of communication and identity will raise the name of the dead, generating potent stories of redemption. Matheny investigates how dress is the means of (mis)communication and moves the narratives of Tamar and Ruth forward, enabling each of these marginalized women to negotiate a familial inheritance. She demonstrates that dress becomes a powerful medium of seeking an ethical response, a response of answerability.

In Chapter 6, Ellena Lyell explores the use of clothing in narratives about the Benjaminites. She traces the thread of Benjaminite dress from Benjamin himself to the time of the judges, the time of the monarchy, and into the postexilic period. Dress offers insights into the characteristics of the tribe of Benjamin and links the tribal line in Judges with the royal Benjaminites in Samuel and Esther. More specifically, Lyell argues that certain items of clothing and adornment reflect the warrior-like and deviant characteristics associated with the line of Benjamin and, ultimately, reflects the cyclical rise-and-fall pattern of the key men of Benjaminite heritage, commenting on the suitability of their prerogative to reign.

In Chapter 7, Carmen Joy Imes considers dress metaphors in the Hebrew Bible's imprecatory psalms in light of their literary and historical-cultural contexts, with a view to their theological implications. Given the role of dress as the surface of social inscription, it is not surprising that Psalms 35 and 109 include clothing metaphors. Dress metaphors are fitting because clothing is publicly conspicuous and identity forming. When an offense involves unwarranted public disgrace, the psalmist petitions God to administer the public shaming of the perpetrator. Imes demonstrates that dress metaphors are not only the means whereby the psalmists accomplish the public shaming but they are particularly apt for doing so.

In Chapter 8, Susannah Rees explains how dress is used to construct and perform gender and status. She shows that a number of items in the list of dress and adornment worn by the Daughters of Zion in Isa. 3:16-24 are reserved elsewhere in the Hebrew Bible for men in positions of power. By reading Isa. 3:16-24 in the context of Isaiah 3 and considering the well-attested prophetic trope of inversion, she argues that the Daughters of Zion are performing masculine identities and roles through their dress and thereby subverting the natural world order in the minds of the biblical author(s) and redactor(s).

In Chapter 9, S. J. Parrott investigates the investiture of dress by YHWH on personified Jerusalem in Ezek. 16:1-14. She concludes that YHWH's investiture of dress on Jerusalem constitutes her new identity as a royal and 'holy' representative of the deity. Without that dress, Jerusalem has no such identity and her relationship to YHWH remains unclear, which helps elucidate the motif of nakedness in Ezekiel 16. Dress therefore serves once more as the locus of social inscription. It functions as a differentiating choice with an intended result.

In Chapter 10, Jennifer Brown Jones examines Joshua's high-priestly garments in Zechariah 3. Situating a lexical and intertextual analysis of Joshua's clothing in Zechariah within dress theory and nonverbal communication theory, she concludes that the high priest Joshua's garments are best understood as communicating a coded critique of his priestly role. She argues that Joshua's purification should be read as warning him to hold closely to the ways of YHWH, rather than be viewed as the bestowal of validating vestments that affirm or expand the priestly role in the postexilic community.

Selena Billington provides the concluding chapter. She illustrates that the motif of cloth and clothing is used in Esther as a literary device that provides narrative structure, identifies social standing, and illuminates the relationship between characters. She demonstrates that the ironic reversals, for which the book of Esther is known, are exemplified via clothing throughout the narrative. Furthermore, clothing, as a fundamental motif, is associated with each of the five main characters in the book and is used to highlight each character's agency.

The innovation presented here is not the emphasis on the communicative properties of dress. Scholars have studied these properties for several years in many disciplines. Beyond adding to this conversation, the chapters in this volume are also intended to focus attention on the Hebrew Bible and the world of the ancient Near East. Conducting research on the social dynamics and/or the nature of the lived experience of a world we know only through meticulous study of text and archeological discoveries remains a daunting task. We believe that dress provides a lens that may assist us in this endeavor in ways that we have not yet anticipated. Sometimes it is the selection of the appropriate instrument that allows a researcher to succeed in discovering meaning.

Dress, Aesthetics, and Socialization in the Ancient Near East and the Hebrew Bible

The bilateral relationship between humans and dress received its due appreciation in the ancient Near East. Moreover, it seems that the ancient world was acutely aware of the ways in which dress re-creates the human experience. An Akkadian poem from the late Bronze Age period (thirteenth to twelfth century BCE) wisdom tradition offers the relevant evidence. The poem entitled "The Date Palm and the Tamarisk" belongs to a subgenre of Mesopotamian wisdom literature known as debate or disputation compositions. In this genre, one finds two protagonists who are trying to outwit each other by declaring their individual superiority. The main thrust of each argument is to prove each contestant's usefulness for humanity.[26] For this poem, there are six preserved exchanges. In the third exchange (v. 35'), we read the case Tamarisk makes for itself: "I am a weaver, I s[pin] thread, [I clothe the c]rowd, and make the king all bright."[27]

---

26. Cohen explains that the disputations were the products of scribal schools, and they served a didactic purpose. This poem seems to explore the economic, religious, cultural, and symbolic value of the date palm and the tamarisk trees. Each debate/disputation ends after the contestants have stated their respective cases and are brought to the judgment of god. The end is missing for this particular composition so we cannot know which tree won. Yoram Cohen, *Wisdom from the Late Bronze Age*, ed. Andrew R. George (Atlanta: Society of Biblical Literature, 2013), 177–8.

27. Cohen transcribes the Akkadian text of this verse as follows: "išparākuma qê a[maḫḫaṣ ulabbaš u]mmānamma unammar šarra." "The Date Palm and the Tamarisk, Exchange III:35," in ibid., 184.

Tamarisk's exclamation, that it is also a weaver, implies "by way of metonymy that the Tamarisk's wood provides part of the loom that is responsible for spinning thread to clothe people and royalty alike."[28] This metonymical connection sheds light on dress as an artifact. More important for our purpose is the claim that Tamarisk provides more than the means with which to make clothes for the people; it also assists in enhancing the appearance, splendor, and quite possibly the mood of the king by making him all bright.[29] With this observation we are transitioning from an artifact to a mentifact consideration of dress. The people, who give voice to the merits of the Tamarisk in this contest of wits, put forward for us their guiding beliefs.

The same conviction is put forth in the literature of ancient Egypt. The Egyptian "Harpers' Songs of King Intef" is preserved in two New Kingdom copies (between the sixteenth and the eleventh century BCE).[30] They receive their name because they were accompanied by the image of a harper who was singing them. These songs are haunted by the suspicion that the hope to win immortality was at best beset by uncertainties and at worst futile. Thus, they exhort one to enjoy life in view of human mortality. In the second part of the song, we read:

> So rejoice your heart!
> Absence of care is good for you;
> Follow your heart as long as you live.
> Put myrrh on your head,
> Dress yourself with fine linen,

28. Ibid., 194.

29. Both Wilcke and Streck, who have studied this text in detail, translate the last part of this verse: "und lasse den König erstrahlen" (and make the king shine). Claus Wilcke, "Die Emar-Version von "Dattelpalme und Tamariske—ein Rekonstruktionversuch," *ZA* 79 (1989), 180. Michael Streck P., "Dattelpalme und Tamariske in Mesopotamien nah dem akkadischen Streitgersprach," *ZA* 94 (2004), 256.

30. The first is found on the Ramesside Papyrus Harris and the second was carved on a wall of the tomb of Paatenemheb from Saqqara. The song's introductory line states that it reproduces a song inscribed in the tomb of a king Intef. This name was borne by several kings of the 11th and 17th Dynasties. However, Lichtheim notes that "since the two New Kingdom copies reproduce a genuinely Middle Egyptian text, we need not doubt that an original text, carved in a royal tomb of the Middle Kingdom, existed." Miriam Lichtheim, "Harpers' Songs: The Song from the Tomb of King Intef," 1:30 *COS*, ed. William W. Hallo and K. Lawson Younger Jr. (Leiden; Boston: Brill, 2003), 48. Simpson asserts that "the actual origin of Harper song is uncertain, but they do provide an interesting insight into the attitudes of ancient Egyptians toward the balance of life and death." William Kelly Simpson, *The Literature of Ancient Egypt: An Anthology of Stories, Instructions, Stelae, Autobiographies, and Poetry* (New Haven: Yale University Press, 2003), 330.

Anoint yourself with the exquisite oils
Which are only for the gods.[31]

According to this song, essential elements of human delight are adornment and clothing. More to the point, from the Egyptian point of view fine dress connects humans not just to royalty but also to divinity. That is to say, humans have the opportunity to affect positively both their lived and religious experiences through their choices of dress. This helps us gain a nuanced understanding of ancient Egyptian ideology around death, the afterlife, and mortal life.

This argument is picked up in the Hebrew Bible in the book of Qoheleth that also reflects on mortality. Even though this text is much later than the previous two, it carries on with the same train of thought.[32] In 9:8 we read: "Let your garments always be bright[33]; do not let oil be lacking on your head."[34] Wright cites Crenshaw's observations about this passage (9:7-10): "The advice to enjoyment is expanded in detail: eating bread, drinking wine, dress and appearance, love of one's spouse, and full engagement in work and other activities."[35] However, Leo

31. The translation here is by William Kelly Simpson. Simpson, *The Literature of Ancient Egypt*, 333. Miriam Lichtheim notes that the literal translation of the last verse would be: "with the genuine marvels that belong to a god." Lichtheim, "Harpers' Songs," 49.

32. Dates proposed for Qoheleth range from the Persian to the Hellenistic period. For example, Seow proposes a date "between the second half of the of the fifth and the first half of the fourth centuries B.C.E." (Seow, *Ecclesiastes*, 38), while Kruger offers a date of composition "in the second half of the third century B.C.E." (Thomas Kruger, *Qoheleth*, Hermeneia [Minneapolis, MN: Fortress, 2004], 19).

33. Qoheleth 9:8. I chose to translate the Hebrew word לָבָן as "bright" instead of its more traditional translation "white" to convey better the idea of cheerfulness and joy that the Hebrew text wants to convey and to avoid racial-cultural connotations that white clothing has in the modern American context. Cf. William Gesenius, *BDB*, 526; and Koehler-Baumgartner, *HALOT* 2: 517. See also Seow who comments that the meaning of the verse is "let your garments be fresh and bright." He adds further "clean garments indicate a good life (so 'white/ bright garment' symbolizes the good life in the *Tale of Sinuhe* [Text B 153]." Choon-Leong Seow, *Ecclesiastes*, The Anchor Bible, Vol. 18C (New York: Doubleday, 1997), 301.

34. Scholars have noticed the connection between the book of Qoheleth and the Epic of Gilgamesh. A tablet reportedly from Sippar (*ca.* 1800 BCE) offers an Old Babylonian variant in which Gilgamesh speaks with the tavern-keeper Siduri. The text it holds runs parallel to parts of tablets IX–X of the standard version of the epic. One of the notable differences is Siduri's speech in column iii 10a where she says: "Let your clothes be clean, let your head be washed, may you bathe in water." As Seow observes, "It is remarkable that this passage from Gilgamesh contains not only the same elements that we find in Qoheleth's call for enjoyment, but the items appear in the same order (1) feasting, (2) fresh clothing, (3) washing one's head, and (4) family." Seow, *Ecclesiastes*, 30–56.

35. Addison G. Wright, "Ecclesiastes 9:1-12: An Emphatic Statement of Themes," *CBQ* 77.2 (2015), 251. In his commentary, Crenshaw attributes the emphasis on this particular

Perdue misses completely the importance of dress in his analysis; according to him four things provide the potential of joy for human living: labor, eating and drinking, the lover, and youth.[36] I want to rectify this omission. The importance of adornment and cosmetics can hardly be underestimated for its contributions to the quality of life.[37] Additionally with this passage and his exhortation to pleasure and action in view of death (9:1-10), Qoheleth sheds light into a notable sociofact. In 9:4 we read: "A living dog is better than a dead lion." The implied construction of the hierarchy comes from the juxtaposition of a dog over against a lion.[38] In life, a lion was admired while a dog was despised.[39] The lion's death, however, reverses this particular power structure. Qoheleth seems to argue that in death all is gone. In life, however, there are possibilities, and dress enhances these otherwise elusive possibilities for meaning. Furthermore, I wish to underline another crucial detail regarding the type of clothing preferred. The sources discussed highlight the importance of fine quality and brightness of clothes.[40] These details communicate

choice of dress to environmental considerations. He writes: "The value of white clothes in a hot climate was widely known, and the frequent application of oils to combat the deleterious effect of dry heat on skin was widely practiced by those who could afford it." James L. Crenshaw, *Ecclesiastes: A Commentary*, OTL (Philadelphia, PA: Westminster, 1987), 163.

36. Perdue explains that "wealth, possessions, honor, numerous offspring, and longevity have no intrinsic value or worth if one does not experience joy." Leo G. Perdue, *The Sword and the Stylus: An Introduction to Wisdom in the Age of Empires* (Grand Rapids, MI: William B. Eerdmans, 2008), 254.

37. Manniche explains, "Perfumed oil provided moisturisation for the body and protection from the sun, as well as deodorization, particularly important in a hot climate." L. Manniche, *Sacred Luxuries: Fragrance Aromatherapy, and Cosmetics in Ancient Egypt* (Ithaca, NY: Cornell University Press, 1999), 144. Quick adds, "The popularity of cosmetics in ancient Palestine is attested by the wealth of archaeological material related to beauty and beauty treatments, including numerous tools for application of cosmetics, as well as storage containers for powders, creams and oils, perfume bottles, and polished mirrors." Laura Quick, "Decorated Women: A Sociological Approach to the Function of Cosmetics in the Books of Esther and Ruth," *BibInt* 27 (2019), 357. Indeed, perfume bottles were discovered in large numbers at a burial tomb at Ketef Hinnom in Jerusalem dating from the seventh to the sixth century BCE. M. Dayagi-Mendels, *Perfumes and Cosmetics in the Ancient World* (Jerusalem: Israel Museum, 1989), 127.

38. Crenshaw believes that the dog in this verse is a metaphor "for a contemptible or worthless person, whereas 'lion' designated a prince or person of great worth." Crenshaw, *Ecclesiastes*, 161.

39. Seow explains that "dogs were among the most despised of creatures in the ancient Near East. Together with the pig, they were not offered as sacrifice. Rather, they were regarded as scavengers." Seow, *Ecclesiastes*, 301. He adds that "the use of the use of the dog as a metaphor for the living is ironic ... since dogs may have been associated with death and the underworld" (ibid.).

40. In contrast, Michael V. Fox recounts a series of rabbinic interpretations of Qoheleth 9:8 that deflect attention from the importance of dress. He writes: "Rashbam says that

the ability of dress to change human life. Andrew J. Elliot and Markus A. Maier call attention to the fact that "every visual stimulus processed by the human perceptual system contains color information."[41] They add that "different colors are presumed to have different associations, and viewing a color is thought to trigger psychological responses consistent with these associations."[42] They argue that the specific meanings that colors can carry are grounded on learned associations.[43] The ancient Near Eastern sources associate brightness with happiness and enjoyment. This literature uses clothing as the catalyst that brings about the association and the concomitant psychological response. Put differently, the cultural context of the ancient Near East taught consistently that bright clothes could generate a sense of joyfulness. Thus, when people wore bright clothes, they were also inclined to exhibit this joy in their behavior and attitude.

Returning to the four dimensions necessary for a thorough examination of dress we can draw the following conclusions. In terms of the context and the historical timeframe, for the most part of a thousand years, give or take a century, one finds the belief that dress matters in tangible and intangible ways. In the literature of the entire geographical range of the ancient Near East this opinion remains constant. Regarding the social circumstances, at least the scribal circles, who produced these texts, and their audience seem to believe that the choice of dress is a choice of life and possibly a choice that connects humans to the divine. Lastly, the rhetorical goal that the three texts examined here are trying to reach is that dress directly affected the lived experience. We can only hope that the research present in this volume will also affect scholarly discourse.

these actions represent purity in behavior. Rabbi Juda ha-Nasi that the clean clothes and oil represent good deeds and Torah, whereby we keep ourselves morally ready for God's 'banquet' on the day of our death (Koh. R.). Ibn Ezra, more plausibly, identities all these actions as physical luxuries, which he considers inadequate." Michael V. Fox, *Ecclesiastes*, The JPS Bible Commentary (Philadelphia, PA: Jewish Publication Society, 2004), 63.

41. Andrew J. Elliot and Markus A.Maier, "Color and Psychological Functioning," *CDPS* 16.5 (2007), 250.

42. Ibid.

43. Ibid., 251. Elliot and Maier list the core premises "of the model of color and psychological functioning: 1) colors can carry specific meanings; 2) color meanings are grounded in two basic sources, learned associations and biologically based proclivities; 3) the mere perception of color evokes evaluative processes that help discern whether a stimulus is hostile or hospitable; 4) the evaluative process evoked by color stimuli produce motivated behavior; 5) color typically exerts its influence on psychological functioning in an automatic fashion without conscious intention or awareness; 6) color meanings and effects are contextual" (ibid.).

Chapter 1

WHAT TO LOOK FOR IN A HEADDRESS: פאר AND תפארה IN MATERIAL CULTURE AND ICONOGRAPHY SIGNIFICANCE AND SIGNIFICATION

Brady Alan Beard

Introduction

When examining lists of clothing, jewelry, and other ornamentation throughout the Hebrew Bible (HB), one often comes across the terms פְּאֵר (pəʾēr or headdress) and עֲטֶרֶת תִּפְאָרֶת (ʿăṭêrêt tipʾaret or crown of glory). Metaphorically, these words can refer to features and achievements that bring a person honor.[1] Included among the ritual dress of the priests (Exod. 39:28), as well as the dress of non-ritual actors (Ezek. 24:23) and royal persons (Ezek. 44:18), the headdress poses an interpretive challenge.[2]

The root פאר appears nominally fifty-one times and occasionally relates to the root כבד, "glory." This relation suggests the headdress "adorns" or "glorifies" the wearer or perhaps sets them apart for a cultic ceremony. In certain poetic texts, YHWH's glory, תִּפְאָרֶת, denotes his ability to deliver his people (Ps. 71:8; Isa. 60, 62). Ultimately, YHWH's פְּאֵר signifies his salvific acts toward Zion and, by extension, Israel. For instance, in Prov. 28:12, the triumph of righteousness leads to "glory," תִּפְאָרֶת. Likewise, wisdom and signs of wisdom, such as gray hair, bestow

---

1. In the ancient Mediterranean world, honor is a phenomenon distinct from glory. Though, as pointed out by Richard Rohrbaugh, honor can be both ascribed and acquired, it is at once an innate and obtained trait. According to Rohrbaugh, "Ascribed honor came first of all from family, because an honorable birth was the foundation on which a good reputation rested … Acquired honor, however, came as a result of good behavior. It accrued to those who lived in accord with community values and was considered a public reward for virtuous behavior." Richard L.Rohrbaugh, "Honor," in *The Ancient Mediterranean Social World: A Sourcebook*, ed. Zeba A. Crook (Grand Rapids, MI: Eerdmans, 2020), 64.

2. I use "dress" here as a term meant to be inclusive of any additions to the body whether through modification of the body or the adornment of the body with cloth, paint, jewelry, and so on.

glory.[3] In several places, the word also refers more generally to the "glory" or "adornment" of someone or something. For instance, in Ps. 78:61, God's "glory," תִּפְאֶרֶת, and power, עֹז, go into exile.

Regularly, YHWH's glory functions as a personal attribute. Psalms 78:61 and 96:6 parallel God's תִּפְאֶרֶת with God's majesty, הוֹד.[4] תִּפְאֶרֶת especially relates to YHWH's work, promises, and relationship with Zion. For instance, YHWH treats Israel and Jerusalem as the glory of the nations, the crowning achievement as it were, in Ps. 149:4. In another passage, YHWH himself is the "glory" of Zion (Isa. 60:9, 19, 21) and Zion is the house of YHWH's glory (Isa. 60:7). Verbal forms, like that in Psalm 149, also reveal this conceptual connection between adornment and deliverance.

As a verb, פאר appears thirteen times in the HB in the *hitpaʿel* and *piʿel* forms. Nine of the thirteen times it occurs in Trito-Isaiah. In these cases, the root reflects YHWH's activity to redeem, deliver, and restore Israel.[5] Through such acts, YHWH is glorified and glorifies his house (Isa. 44:23; 49:3; 55:5; 60:7, 9, 13, and 21; 61:3). The breadth of the root's meaning complicates interpretations of the word within specific passages. The relation between the nominal and verbal forms of the root is especially perplexing in lists of clothing, jewelry, and other dress.

In this chapter, I propose that attention to iconographic representations of headdresses can instruct interpretation of the phrases. In other words, when faced with the challenge of interpreting a word with complex, multivalent, or even contradictory contextual meanings, material culture could shed light on the ideas, beliefs, and values conveyed in texts. Ultimately, iconographic investigation can shed light on the relationship between the nominal form of the root as it pertains to a particular item of dress and YHWH's acts, which "glorify" the recipient.

To accomplish this task, I examine three typologies of headdresses because of their overlap with the major meanings connected to the root פאר. Then, I examine iconographic and textual depictions of ritual (i.e., dress worn by a king or other priestly figure as he offers sacrifices or performs adoration before an image of a deity) headdresses.[6] Finally, I examine mural crowns that, I suggest, may instruct

---

3. J. Hausmann, "פאר," *TDOT* 11: 464.

4. For a thorough study of YHWH's clothing, see Shawn W. Flynn, "YHWH's Clothing, Kingship, and Power: Origins and Vestiges in Comparative Ancient Near Eastern Contexts," in *Dress and Clothing in the Hebrew Bible: "For All Her Household Are Clothed in Crimson,"* LHBOTS 679, ed. Antonios Finitsis (London: T&T Clark, 2019), 11–28. In this piece, Flynn notes that the communicative nature of dress is also applied to dress of divine beings in art and literature of the ancient Near East. YHWH's aniconic presence makes identifying his dress difficult. For another study of YHWH's dress, see Joel M. LeMon and Richard A. Purcell, "Iconographic Case Studies from Isaiah 6:1; 59:17; and 63:1–6," in *Clothing and Nudity in the Hebrew Bible*, ed. Christoph Berner, Manuel Schäfer, Martin Schott, Sarah Schulz, and Martina Weingätner (New York: Bloomsbury, 2019), 269–87.

5. D. Vetter, "פאר to Glorify," *TLOT* 2: 963.

6. I do not include processional scenes in this category.

interpretations of Jerusalem as Israel's glory in Persian Period prophetic literature. I conclude by suggesting that the divine realm, references to YHWH's glory, or his glorification of someone else relates to the material realities of finery, jewelry, and crowns or headdresses. Thus, this chapter attempts to demonstrate the theological and cultural importance of the root פאר within the HB by examining ancient Near Eastern (NE) visual cultures.

Headdresses in the Hebrew Bible and the Ancient Near East

The question of whether the Hebrew root פאר shares cognates with other ancient NE languages is a debated one.[7] Despite these complications, scholars generally agree that a clear connection exists between the nominal and verbal forms of the root. In other words, the act of glorification relates closely to the notion of adorning oneself with a headdress. It is possible that this meaning relies on associations between the head (the top of the body), the top (as a location), pride, boasting, and the glory of one's wealth expressed in fine dress and jewelry.[8] More importantly, however, the root is used in both ritual and non-ritual domains. In the following sections, I examine three uses of the term in the HB. I categorize these uses as ritual, adornment, and political. In each section, I examine headdresses in their material and iconographic forms.[9]

7. Koehler-Baumgartner, for instance, suggests that פאר comes into Hebrew as an Egyptian loanword; *HALOT* 3: 90 and Benjamin J. Noonan, *Non-Semitic Loanwords in the Hebrew Bible: A Lexicon of Language Contact* (University Park, PA: Eisenbrauns, 2019), 169–70. Thomas Lambdin does not include פאר in his study of Egyptian loanwords in the HB—"Egyptian Loan Words in the Old Testament," *JAOS* 73.3 (1953), 145–55. J. Barth, for instance, suggests a Syriac cognate, while W. J. Gerber suggests that the verbal root is a denominative verb from the word and Zorrell associates it with an Arabic cognate from *fḫr* meaning "to boast"; for a full bibliography, see D. Vetter's entry in *TLOT* 2: 936.

8. Wordplay like this is known from associations that accompany other words with similar semantic ranges such as גאה and גבה.

9. In the study of ancient NE iconography, "minor art," in contrast to "monumental art," is the category of small, portable, or wearable art and visual media. By contrast, the term "monumental art" refers to wall-reliefs, obelisks, and other statuary. As a category, minor art usually includes stamps, scarabs, and cylinder seals, the latter being rarer in Israel/Palestine than stamp seals and other jewelry. These items often contain abbreviated forms of motifs, scenes, and representations found in the monumental art of the major empires of the ANE. Because of its size, transferable and portable minor art indicates what could be known by the non-elite. Like signatures, seals identified families and persons and in the owner's absence could represent him in a variety of circumstances. Since a strong record of monumental art is virtually nonexistent in Israel/Palestine, minor art remains the best way to understand the visual cultures of Israel/Palestine.

Headdresses in Ritual Context

Dress was an important feature of ritual participation in the ancient Near East. Distinct clothing and adornment, or lack thereof, demarcated priests and kings as particular ritual actors and often indicated their relationship to the gods and temple precincts.[10] Images of nonroyal ritual actors are scarce in the minor art (stamp seals and jewelry) of Israel/Palestine. Those that do exist demonstrate the remarkable impact that Egyptian and Egyptianizing iconography had on the region. Images of the pharaoh in ritual participation are relatively common in Egyptianizing motifs. For instance, in the Late Bronze Age (1426–1400 BCE) cache from Tell el-Ajjul near Gaza, south of Ashkelon, an oval plate depicts the king in the blue crown offering bread before an image of Re.[11] As usual in such motifs, the king wears no special headdress other than his customary crown with the uraeus band, which symbolized the gods' protection over and guidance of him.

Another Egyptian example, from a limestone stele slightly earlier than the above plate, demonstrates how common the aforementioned motif was.[12] In this image, the king, possibly Thutmoses III, makes a wine offering before an image of Amon.[13] He wears the blue crown (recognizable by its distinct shape), with a uraeus, and raises two vessels before the god. This motif, depicting the king as a ritual actor who demonstrates his love and loyalty to the gods, was also common throughout temple walls and on other royal stelae. In return for the king's ritual participation, the gods grant life and loyalty to him.

In contrast to the headdresses of the king, Egyptian priests wore no headgear, instead going before the deity bareheaded, as depicted in the 19th Dynasty

---

10. Michael D. Swartz, "The Semiotics of the Priestly Vestments in Ancient Judaism," in *Sacrifice in Religious Experience*, ed. Albert I. Baumgarten, Studies in the History of Religions 93 (Leiden: Brill, 2002), 77. The term "ritual" is, of course, fraught in the study of religion and the HB. In this chapter, by ritual headdress I refer to an item worn by ritual actors in distinctly cult-related ritualization, essentially the headgear of priests and other ministers responsible for maintaining the sacrificial system of Israel. For more on the notion of ritualization and the difficulties of identifying something as ritual or not, see Catherine Bell, *Ritual: Perspectives and Dimensions* (New York: Oxford, 2009). For the purposes of this chapter it remains necessary to denote when the root refers to a specific piece of the high-priestly garment and when it refers to a garment worn outside of a cultic role.

11. To view the oval plate, see the Bibel + Orient Datenbank Online (BODO) (number 15712): http://www.bible-orient-museum.ch/bodo/details.php?bomid=15712.

12. To view the stele, see BODO (number 33912): http://www.bible-orient-museum.ch/bodo/details.php?bomid=33912.

13. In Egypt, the pharaoh was the priest and, in this role, he mediated between the gods and mortals; Othmar Keel, *The Symbolism of the Biblical World: Ancient Near Eastern Iconography and the Book of Psalms*, trans. Timothy J. Hallett, reprint (Winona Lake, IN: Eisenbrauns, 1997), 127.

(1292–1279 BCE) limestone stele from Thebes.[14] This image illustrates one of the key differences between the king and the priests as ritual participants. They were marked, not only in terms of role but also in terms of dress. The priests and monarchs participated not only in the lives of the gods by making offerings but also in distinct dressing rituals of the images of the gods. Such rituals were common in both Mesopotamia and Egypt, and the former had distinct rituals to dress the statues and images of the gods (e.g., the *mīs pî* and the *lubuštu*).[15] Attention to the proper garments then extended beyond the human participant and necessarily engaged aspects of divine dress as well. Specifications surrounding the priestly garments occupy much of the descriptive imagination of the priestly garments in both Exodus and Leviticus.[16]

The fundamental texts that describe the Israelites' priestly dress in Exodus 28 and 39 and Leviticus 8 present a rather different picture than the Egyptian examples. Like the headdresses in the ritual settings of other NE cultures, the Israelite headdress is also heavily symbolic and denotes a certain kind of relationship between the wearer and God. Unlike their Egyptian counterparts, Israelite priests wore a wrap, with additional decoration, around their head. Descriptions of this headgear come from Second Temple Literature. Josephus describes the rich symbolic elements of the dress.

In *Antiquities*, Josephus describes the headdress as a cap to which was added a blue embroidery and three-tiered gold crown.[17] Similarly, the *Az be-ʾEn Kol*, an anonymous rabbinic era text, identifies the headdress as a "holy diadem."[18] Interpretations of the priestly dress vary widely. Josephus and Philo view the priest's garments as a model of the cosmos. Other Second Temple sources view these garments as the same items worn by Adam in Eden.[19] Sophisticated Midrashic exegesis not only establishes the connection between the priestly dress

14. To view the stele, see BODO (number 33922): http://www.bible-orient-museum.ch/bodo/details.php?bomid=33922.

15. Kiersten Neuman, "Gods among Men: Fashioning the Divine Image in Assyria," in *What Shall I Say of Clothes? Theoretical and Methodological Approaches to the Study of Dress in Antiquity*, ed. Megan Cifarelli and Laura Galinski (Boston, MA: Archaeological Institute of America, 2017), 5–15; M. B. Dick, "Pīt Pî und Mīs Pî," in *RlA* 10: 580–5.

16. This difference also distinguishes the Israelite priestly attire from Egyptian attire. See Carmen Joy Imes, "Between Two Worlds: The Functional and Symbolic Significance of the High Priestly Regalia," in *Dress and Clothing in the Hebrew Bible "For All Her Household are Clothed in Crimson,"* ed. Antonios Finitsis, LHBOTS 679 (New York: T&T Clark, 2019), 38–41. Notably, the priests go bareheaded before the god. Removing bodily hair and going without a headdress indicated their ritual purity and holiness. See Keel, *Symbolism of the Biblical World*, 124.

17. Josephus, *Jewish Antiquities, Volume 1: Books 1–3*, trans. H. St. J. Thackeray, LCL 242 (Cambridge, MA: Harvard University Press, 1930), 3:172.

18. Swartz, "The Semiotics of the Priestly Vestments," 77.

19. Ibid., 64.

and primordial Adam but also demonstrates the connection between the dress and light.[20]

In Exod. 28:2, the תִּפְאָרֶת specifically connects to the "glory" (כבד) of Aaron and his sons and, therefore, the Levitical priesthood. In this passage, YHWH commands Moses to make sacred garments of glory for his brother Aaron וְעָשִׂיתָ בִגְדֵי־קֹדֶשׁ לְאַהֲרֹן אָחִיךָ לְכָבוֹד וּלְתִפְאָרֶת.[21] In addition to the glorification of the wearers, the item may index the glory and beauty of the sanctuary, of which the high priest and other ritual actors were considered an integral part.[22] These passages suggest that תִּפְאָרֶת ought to be understood as an attribute and accoutrement of certain persons. As a type of dress, they reflect the person's glory and honor and can parallel other attributes such as strength, honor, and majesty. That dress may convey immaterial qualities, principles, or even morals is not surprising. By design, dress communicates multiple qualities about an individual's standing within any given society.[23] Thus, Ps. 96:6 may give a glimpse into YHWH's own cultic appearance, which filled his sanctuary with these items.[24]

The symbolic nature of dress is not lost on the rabbis who describe the priests' dress as a system that explicates Israel's sins.[25] While the precise identification of the headdress may remain something of a mystery, despite Second Temple and

---

20. See Sara Koenig's chapter in this volume.

21. Hausmann makes this point explicit. See "פאר," 464.

22. Ibid.

23. Terence S. Turner, "The Social Skin," *HAU: Journal of Ethnographic Theory* 2.2, reprint (2012): 487.

24. Hausmann, "פאר," 464; and A. A. Anderson, *Psalms*, NCBC 2 (1972), 683. Hossfeld and Zenger suggest that the items in question are members of YHWH's court not elements of his dress; Frank-Lothar Hossfeld and Erich Zenger, *Psalms 2*, Hermeneia (Minneapolis, MN: Fortress, 2005), 465. The aniconic nature of YHWHism continues as a highly charged debate within the study of ancient Israelite religion. One need only consider the debates around Kuntillet Ajrud. At most, it seems best to say that the Deuteronomist, as well as other central theologians in the HB, demands the aniconic worship of YHWH; however, it remains plausible, if not probable, that the worship of YHWH involved at least in some form his representation or representations of his symbols. I should add here, however, that identifying a representation of YHWH remains difficult short of clearly identifiable accompanying inscriptions. On the nature of the debate of aniconism in YHWH, see Christoph Uehlinger, "Anthropomorphic Cult Statuary in Iron Age Palestine and the Search for YHWH's Cult Image," in *The Image and the Book: Iconic Cults, Aniconism, and the Rise of Book Religion in Israel and the Ancient Near East*, ed. Karel van der Toorn (Leuven: Peeters, 1997), 97–155; on Kuntillet Ajrud, see Brent A. Strawn and Joel M. LeMon, "Once More, YHWH and Company and Kuntillet 'Ajrud," *Maarav* 20 (2015), 83–114; pl. VI–VII; on YHWH's symbolic representatives, see Joel M. LeMon, *Yahweh's Winged Form in the Psalms: Exploring Congruent Iconography and Texts*, OBO 242 (Fribourg: Academic, 2010).

25. Swartz, "Semiotics of the Priestly Vestments," 69–72.

later rabbinic suggestions that it was a metal or gold frontlet, the symbolic importance of this piece of dress cannot be ignored. The פארי המגבעת formed one part of a larger system of dress that provided ritual meaning and signaled information about the wearer and the community. It functioned as one part of a whole meant to represent Israel before God.[26]

The noun פְּאֵר refers to a headdress limited to certain officeholders that is distinct from other headgear, including the turban, מצנפת. Such is the case in Exod. 39:28 where Aaron and his sons receive instructions about and description of their priestly attire.[27] In this setting, the פְּאֵר wraps around an individual's head and the turban. Both are made of the same "fine linen," שש. Interpreters suggest that the phrase indicates a type of ritual cap worn on top of the priestly turban used by priests during their ritual duties. Thus, possible translations include "a cap of glory," "cap of the headdress," or "high-hat headwear."[28]

The LXX simplifies the phrase: τὴν μίτραν when the phrase stands parallel to the "turban," τὰς κιδάρεις.[29] It remains unclear what precisely the priestly פְּאֵר was made of, because of the complex syntax and context, but the LXX suggests that the headdress was understood as a metal ringlet, a diadem.[30] Thus, in at least some places, the LXX envisions a headpiece constructed of metal that was worn in addition to a turban or headwrap.[31] Other LXX texts (Exod. 39:28; 28:40; 29:9; and

---

26. Ibid., 78.

27. Hausmann, "פאר," and C. John Collins, "פאר," *NIDOTTE* 3: 574. Though many have identified it as a turban; see, for instance, Phillip J. King and Lawrence E. Stager, *Life in Biblical Israel*, Library of Ancient Israel (Louisville, KY: Westminster John Knox, 2001), 275.

28. John I. Durham, *Exodus* 3, WBC (Waco, TX: Word Books, 1987), 492.

29. According to Liddell-Scott, this is either a Persian headdress or a "turban of Jewish high priest." Henry George Liddell and Robert Scott, *A Greek-English Lexicon*, 6th ed. (Oxford: Clarendon, 1871), 950b. For another study of this Persian headdress, see Alison Salvesen, "כֶּתֶר (Esther 1:1; 2:17; 6:8): Something to Do with a Camel?" *JSS* 64 (1999), 35–46. Elsewhere in the LXX (Exod. 29:6), the word μίτρα is used for מצנפת and indicates a type of metal diadem, נזר. The diadem likely featured a rosette pattern, which, Joshua Joel Spoelstra suggests, likely held apotropaic functions. See Joshua Joel Spoelstra, "Apotropaic Accessories: The People's Tassels and the High Priest's Rosette," in *Dress and Clothing in the Hebrew Bible: "For All Her Household Are Clothed in Crimson,"* ed. Antonios Finitsis, LHBOTS 679 (New York: T&T Clark, 2019), 68.

30. While it may be difficult to discern whether the LXX Greek traditions are working from a framework informed by their own styles of dress and traditions of understanding this term, it remains clear that the headdress is distinct from the turban and cloth headgear worn by priests. Undoubtedly the Greek traditions struggle to identify this term apart from the other headgear mentioned in this catalog.

31. For an in-depth description of Aaronide priestly dress in relation to its ancient NE context, see Imes, "Significance of High Priestly Regalia," *Dress and Clothing in the Hebrew Bible: "For All Her Household Are Clothed in Crimson,"* LHBOTS 679, ed. Antonios Finitsis (New York: T&T Clark, 2019), 29–62.

Lev. 8:13) suggest instead a cloth headdress perhaps in the style of Persian or early Jewish garb.[32] Two options then appear: a cloth cap on top of the high priest's turban or, when read with the Septuagint, a cloth wrap or perhaps a metal ringlet. Regardless of the traditional interpretations, pinpointing the precise nature of the headdress remains quite troublesome.

Headdresses in "Secular" Context

As a non-ritual item, the פְּאֵר may adorn individuals, including women, on a variety of occasions (Isa. 61:3, 10). In Ezek. 24:17, 23, people are commanded to leave the headdress on despite the usual expectations for mourning the dead.[33] These usages demonstrate that the פְּאֵר has a broad application and can be worn in any number of contradictory circumstances.

In the "jewelry catalogue" of Isa. 3:18-23, תִּפְאָרֶת refers to a collection of materials that are associated with specific offices. Elizabeth Platt suggests that the term refers to all the elements of fine dress via synecdoche.[34] Thus, this collective noun refers to the insignias of office, worn by women and men, indicated by a crown or other headdress.[35] Like the פְּאֵר, the תִּפְאָרֶת encircles the head by being wrapped around or set upon it.[36]

In Isaiah 3, תִּפְאָרֶת describes the list of finery in the chapter. Within the context of Isaiah, the inclusion of תִּפְאָרֶת emphasizes that YHWH's judgment stems from the people's haughtiness and ill-gotten gains. In a flash of poetic justice, the women of Jerusalem are left bald in rags and the men die at the hands of the invaders.[37]

---

32. This troublesome dichotomy also appears in Hebrew, where the root refers to a linen פאר (Ezek. 44:18). On the Greek meaning, see Liddell-Scott, *A Greek-English Lexicon*, 950 and 1798.

33. The fact that clothing, especially within religious contexts, may indicate, signify, and communicate is well known. For a treatment on the performative nature of dress and clothing, see Mary Ellen Roach-Higgins and Joanne B. Eicher, "Dress and Identity," *Clothing and Textiles Research Journal* 10 (1992), 1–8. See also Antonios Finitsis, "For All Her Household Are Clothed in Crimson," in *Dress and Clothing in the Hebrew Bible: "For All Her Household Are Clothed in Crimson*," LHBOTS 679, ed. Antonios Finitsis (New York: T&T Clark, 2019), 2–3. For an example of the narrative significance of dress in the HB, see Lyell's chapter, "Dressing Benjaminites, Defining Kingship: Dress as a Royal Prerogative for the Tribe of Benjamin," in this volume. As Lyell notes, "Clothing is crucial in the construction and communication of power, and in the case of the Benjamin tribe, dress offers insights into the characteristics of an Israelite king, and presages the success of their reign."

34. Elizabeth E. Platt, "Jewelry," *ABD* 3: 830–1.

35. Ibid.

36. In other words, the headdress encloses the head. For a theoretical investigation of dress that encircles the body, see Roach-Higgins and Eicher, "Dress and Identity," 2.

37. On the inversion of dress and subsequent divine judgment in Isaiah 3, see the chapter "'Women Rule over Them': Dressing for an Inverted World in Isaiah 3" by Susannah Rees in this volume.

YHWH is the one who snatches their finery and expensive dress. The result is the humiliation of captivity. No longer do they wear jewelry around their hands, arms, and necks but ropes and bonds of captivity.

Often treated as a collective noun, תִּפְאָרֶת refers to items of personal adornment and the dress of honored positions.[38] The rest of the catalogue in Isaiah 3 indicates general items of jewelry such as bracelets, necklaces, and nose rings and earrings.[39] Such materials were often made of gold, other precious metals, precious stones, faience, and glass. In Mesopotamia, gold was worn by men, women, children, the gods, and even mythical, hybrid creatures (*mischwesen*).[40] Gold was often selected for its malleability but also because of its associations with the divine realm. In his 1949 study "The Golden Garments of the Gods," Leo Oppenheim explores the golden clothing worn by the gods, which is described in literary accounts. One of the terms, *aiaru*, refers to a golden ornament in the form of a rosette.[41] Another type of golden rosette, *air pâni*, refers to the "front rosette," worn on a type of miter or headband. Many divine beings and kings are depicted with this headdress.[42] Humans too wore headdresses made of gold and decorated with rosettes.

For instance, consider the headdress from the early New Kingdom, 18th Dynasty (1550–1295 BCE). Made of gold, gesso, carnelian, jasper, and glass, an elite woman, possibly one of Thutmose III's wives, likely wore this headdress. The headdress contains an incredible amount of gold rosettes that fall in neat rows down the sides and back of the head.[43] Within the Egyptian iconographic system, jewelry, such as crowns and pectorals, displayed royal power and reinforced the monarch's authority within the cosmic order by drawing on images and materials associated with the gods and the divine realm.[44]

---

38. Platt, "Jewelry," 831.

39. Another example can be found in Ezek. 16:12, where YHWH bestows to Jerusalem a "crown of glory," עטרת תפארת, among other items of jewelry: nose rings and earrings. Later, Jerusalem removes these gold and silver items, referenced collectively as תִּפְאָרֶת, and turns them into "male images" and acts promiscuously with them, וַתַּעֲשִׂי־לָךְ צַלְמֵי זָכָר. Isaiah also imagines Jerusalem as wearing such items and refers to the cities as "garments of glory," בִּגְדֵי תִפְאַרְתֵּךְ.

40. Zainab Bahrani, "Jewelry and Personal Arts in Ancient Western Asia," *CANE* 3: 1635. One of the most important finds for understanding Mesopotamian jewelry is the Royal Cemetery of Ur excavated by Sir Leonard Woolley.

41. A. Leo Oppenheim, "The Golden Garments of the Gods," *JNES* 8.3 (1949), 173.

42. Ibid., fn. 4.

43. See the holding at the Metropolitan Museum of Art (number 26.8.117), https://www.metmuseum.org/art/collection/search/548677.

44. Gay Robbins, *The Art of Ancient Egypt*, rev. ed. (Cambridge, MA: Harvard University Press, 2008), 114. Jewelry was, in fact, accessible to many people and Egyptians wore jewelry. Carol Anderson, *Ancient Egyptian Jewellery* (London: Trustees of the British Museum, British Museum Press, 1990), 101. In fact, no laws are known from Egypt that limited the wearing of any material for the elite. Yvonne J. Markowitz, "Jewelry," *OEAE* 2: 204.

Headdresses in the ancient world communicated key features about the wearer. For instance, Egyptian royal crowns, which involved fine cloth and precious metals, connected the wearer to the gods by virtue of shape, material, and shimmer.[45] By relating the wearer to the realm of the divine, the headdress suggested a sense of importance that could not be known apart from the emblematic features of gold, silver, gemstones, and other precious materials. Thus, to wear crowns, royal clothing, and other fine dress was, for Egyptian royalty, to participate within the divine realm.[46] Importantly, such items also symbolized the wearer's relationship to his or her society.

Crowns and other royal accoutrements conveyed information about the wearer's earthly status and, in the case of monarchs, implicitly shaped their political identity. It did so by using precious materials that came from and were representative of the kingdom. By incorporating elements from the far reaches of the empire, the monarch, through his dress, became a map of the boundaries of the kingdom and, therefore, representative of the kingdom. As a result, the monarch's body symbolized the close relationship between the realm of the gods and the realm of humans. Put another way: "Leaders in political structure like a monarchy take on public identities as representatives of their state when they present themselves in rituals with robes, crowns and scepters."[47]

Jewelry decorated with rosettes is also known in Israel/Palestine. One of the most prominent finds comes from the tombs at Megiddo. First excavated in 1903 and 1905, the Megiddo site has been at the center of many debates about biblical archeology and life in Israel during the Late Bronze and Early Iron Age periods. The influence of Egypt on the region during this period cannot be overstated. Minor art especially reflects a distinct Egyptian influence on the artistry and material culture of the area during that period.[48] Later strata reveal the Assyrian influence over Megiddo when it became the capital of the Assyrian province Magiddu.[49] The importance of this site is, no doubt, due in large part to its location on major trade routes through the Levant between Egypt and Syria on the Via Maris. Thus, the jewelry of Israel/Palestine often reflects the motifs and skills of Mesopotamian and Egyptian artisans.[50]

---

45. In Egypt, gold was "the flesh of the gods" while silver was known as "the bones of the gods." Beyond their malleability and recyclability, precious metals were highly valued for their symbolism and glint that recalled associations with astral bodies, especially the sun. Markowitz, "Jewelry," 201; and Katja Goebs, "Crowns," *OEAE* 1: 322.

46. Oppenheim, "The Golden Garments of the Gods," 172–93.

47. Roach-Higgins and Eicher, "Dress and Identity," 6.

48. David Ussishkin, "Megiddo," *OEANE* 3: 463–4.

49. Ibid., 467.

50. The tomb itself dates to the first part of the Middle Bronze Age and contains objects that seem to have been intrusions from later periods. The materials from this tomb contain several stamp rings, beads, and objects made of faience, glass, and stone. The plaques themselves are of gold foil with etched decoration and rosettes. Hugh Tait, ed., *Seven*

The Megiddo tombs are of interest for this chapter because of the amount of jewelry collected from them.[51] Tomb 39 reveals several sheet gold frontlets among the items.[52] A wearer could tie a frontlet to his head with straps attached through bored holes on the frontlet. The frontlets are decorated with rosettes.[53] Rosettes play a significant role in the iconography of the ancient Near East. Prominent in dress and in stamp seals, the rosettes provided a connection between the royal house and solar imagery.[54] As late as the Persian Period Yehud, rosettes connected the elite to the divine realm by means of solar connotations.[55]

To summarize, the root פאר functioned in three essential ways when related to dress. First, the ritual headgear, likely an addition to the priestly headwrap, was worn by a ritual actor in a cultic context. Second, the same term indicated a headdress worn in a non-ritual, "secular," context. The removal of this item expressed a sense of mourning. And finally, the term can be used collectively to refer to jewelry or individual materials that made up a person's dress. The items could be tangible elements of dress or intangible symbols. This resulted in the ascription of "glory" or beauty to the wearer, which could also be symbolically applied to a city of some importance such as Jerusalem. Because of the way that Jerusalem is considered YHWH's glory, mural crowns, which combine elements from the previous two categories and apply them to both the realm of the divine and the realm of cities, are particularly insightful.

Thousand Years of Jewellery (London: Trustees of the British Museum, British Museum Publications, 1986), 3.

51. See the study of dress in mortuary contexts by Josephine A. Verduci, "Early Iron Age Adornment within Southern Levantine Mortuary Contexts: An Argument for Existential Significance in Understanding Material Culture," in *What Shall I Say of Clothes? Theoretical and Methodological Approaches to the Study of Dress in Antiquity*, ed. Megan Cifarelli and Laura Galinski (Boston, MA: Archaeological Institute of America, 2017), 25–46.

52. P. L. O. Guy and Robert M. Engberg, *Meggido Tombs*, OIP 32 (Chicago, IL: University of Chicago Press, 1938), 118–19.

53. On jewelry, see Tait, *Seven Thousand Years of Jewellery*, 31. Other Sumerian headdresses utilized gold rosettes, singular or double, looped onto strings of beads. Such rosettes were often inlaid with precious stones such as lapis lazuli. For specifics of the Meggido finds, see Guy and Engberg, *Meggido Tombs*, pl. 165.

54. Izaak J. de Hulster and Brent A. Strawn, "The Power of Images: Isaiah 60, Jerusalem, and Persian Imperial Propaganda," in *Iconographic Exegesis of the Hebrew Bible/Old Testament*, ed. Izaak J. de Hulster, Brent A. Strawn, and Ryan P. Bonfiglio (Göttingen: Vandenhoeck and Ruprecht, 2015), 202. This system eventually replaced the *lmlk* seal impressions. Ido Koch and Oded Lipschits, "The Rosette Stamped Jar Handle System and the Kingdom of Judah at the End of the First Temple Period," *ZDPV* [1953–], 129.1 (2013), 56.

55. Izaak J. de Hulster, *Iconographic Exegesis and Third Isaiah*, FAT 2 36 (Tübingen: Mohr Siebeck, 2009), 192.

Headdresses in Political Context: The Mural Crown

In addition to wraps and frontlets, mural crowns, headdresses in the shape of city walls or a city façade, conveyed significant meaning in Mesopotamian royal attire. Monarchs, both men and women, were depicted wearing mural crowns, and these items, combined with other elements of the monarch's dress, could demonstrate the close relationship between the monarch and the city. Gods also wore mural crowns in their visual depictions.[56] In the relatively few depictions of Neo-Assyrian queens, the queen carries the symbol of the political domain, represented by the crown, on her person. Such representation suggests that queens were "deeply involved" in the running and governing of the state because of their roles in the royal households.[57] Mural crowns also gained significance as they personified cities and referenced other aspects or attributes such as power and prestige.[58]

Mural crowns are especially pertinent to the discussion of פְּאֵר in the HB because of their ability to emphasize the close relationship between the gods, the royal families, and the city or empire. Two of the most well-known mural crowns come from Neo-Assyrian reliefs of queens. The first relief, on a heavily damaged stele of Assurbanipal's (668–627 BCE) queen Libbali-Šarrat, depicts the queen, seated with her right arm raised and the left grasping an unknown item. On her right wrist she wears a bracelet in the shape of a rosette. On her head, she wears a mural crown of a walled city with three towers topped by battlements.[59]

In the well-known Banquet Scene relief (645–35 BCE) from Assurbanipal's North Palace at Nineveh, Assurbanipal relaxes with the queen, perhaps Libbali-Šarrat.[60] As in the stele, the mural crown is quite striking when compared to the rest of the queen's dress. This crown contains several towers with battlements and is distinct from the rest of the headgear worn by the other figures in the scene. Her hair, visible above and below the crown, is orderly, coming to distinct rows of curls at the base of her neck. In addition to the crown, the queen wears bracelets

---

56. Divinities also wore mural crown, and quite often a city's titular or patron deity wore the mural crown on their head. As Keel puts it, "The first unambiguous attribute of city goddesses is the mural crown." Othmar Keel, *Goddesses and Trees, New Moon and Yahweh: Ancient Near Eastern Art and the Hebrew Bible*, JSOTSup 261 (Sheffield Academic, 1998), 52. See also Othmar Keel, *Deine Blick sind Tauben: zur Metaphorik des Hohen Liedes*, SBS 114/115 (Stuttgard: Katholisches Biblewerk, 1984), 32–9, figs 5–8.

57. Sanna Svärd, "Political Leadership," in *The Oxford Encyclopedia of the Bible and Gender Studies*, ed. Julia O'Brien (Oxford: Oxford University Press, 2014), 20.

58. Amy C. Smith, "Personification in Art," in *The Oxford Encyclopedia of Ancient Greece and Rome*, ed. Michael Gagarin and Elaine Fantham (Oxford: Oxford University Press, 2010), 225–6.

59. The stele is available in the online catalog of the Vorderasiatisches Museum, Staatliche Museen, Berlin (number VA 08847): http://www.smb-digital.de/eMuseumPlus?service=ExternalInterface&module=collection&objectId=1744005&viewType=detailView.

60. A full image of this relief is on view at the British Museum's online catalog (number 124920): https://www.britishmuseum.org/collection/object/W_1856-0909-53.

decorated with rosettes, earrings, and a collar containing disks. Circles, likely indicating metal or gold applique, perhaps rosettes, cover her ornate robe.[61]

The king's crown, a thick band above his hairline decorated with disks, is simpler than that of the queen. His bracelets, like the queen's, depict rosettes, balanced carefully on the band. His short-sleeved tunic is decorated with circular applique. He also wears a bedcover, a *dappastu*, which covered the gods in the temples.[62] By virtue of their appliques, material, and headdresses, the king and queen clearly communicate their close relationship to the divine realm. The elite and the gods wore clothing that was much the same.[63] Not only were the kings and queens the highest level of social class, they were distinct in their relationships with the gods and crossed over into the divine realm, sometimes during their lifetimes and sometimes after death.

Within the iconographic traditions, mural crowns allowed for the artist to personify capital cities as a consort of the king. This signification emphasized the king's role to care for and protect the city as he would his own consort or wife. When the king wore the mural crown, the image depicted the king's own body as one with the city's body.[64] In other words, the use of mural crowns, by representing the queen and city as one, depicted the body politic by referencing the special relationship between the king and the city.[65]

61. Golden appliques are well known in extant materials from Assyria and Babylon. Salvatore Gaspa, "Gold Decorations in Assyrian Textiles: An Interdisciplinary Approach," in *Prehistoric, Ancient Near Eastern and Aegean Textiles and Dress: An Interdisciplinary Anthology*, ed. Mary Harlo, Cécile Michel, and Marie-Louise Nosch (Philadelphia, PA: Oxbow Books, 2014), 228, 230.

62. Ibid., 230–1.

63. Ibid., 227; Benjamin Sass, "Jewelry," *OEANE* 3: 238. Artisans were highly valued, and the best goldsmiths were sought after by wealthy patrons. Jack Ogden, *Ancient Jewellery*, Interpreting the Past (Berkeley: Trustees of the British Museum and the University of California Press, 1992), 56–7.

64. Dieter Metzler, "Mural Crowns in the Ancient Near East and Greece," in *Yale University Art Bulletin, An Obsession with Fortune: Tyche in Greek and Roman Art*, ed. Susan B. Matheson (New Haven, CT: Yale University Art Gallery, 1994), 77. Kings occasionally wore images of cities on their own clothing, and Darius I even wears a crown with pinnacles, which Christl Maier describes as a variant of the mural crown, on his own head. Christl M. Maier, "Daughter Zion as Queen and the Iconography of the Female City," in *Images and Prophecy in the Ancient Eastern Mediterranean*, FRLANT 233, ed. Martti Nissinen and Charles E. Carter (Göttingen: Vandenhoeck & Ruprecht, 2009), 150. Likewise, in Sargon II's reliefs from Khorsabad male attendants bring what appear to be mural crowns to the king. And Assurnasirpal II (883–859 BCE) wears a mural crown on a glazed tile. Christoph Uehlinger, *Jerusalem: Texte, Bilder, Steine* (Göttingen: Vandenhoeck & Ruprecht, 1987), 157, fig. 7.

65. Maier, "Daughter Zion as Queen and the Iconography of the Female City," 148.

At times, the biblical writers pick up on the broader ANE symbolism of mural crowns and apply it to Jerusalem as YHWH's consort (Isa. 54:11-13; 62:1-5; Jer. 13:18-21; Lam. 5:16-18). In Isa. 54:11-13, for instance, YHWH says to Jerusalem, "I will make your pinnacles of rubies, your gates of jewels, and all your walls of precious stones." Jeremiah, describing the crowns as תִּפְאֶרֶת, writes: "Take a lowly seat for your beautiful crown has come down from your head. The towns of the Negeb are shut up with no one to open them; all Judah is taken into exile, wholly taken into exile."

In Isa. 61:3, Jerusalem receives a headdress, פְּאֵר, instead of "ashes," אֵפֶר. Moreover, those who live and mourn in Zion will glorify, לְהִתְפָּאֵר, YHWH because he has redeemed them. This imagery continues into chapter 62 where the prophet describes redeemed Jerusalem as a "headdress of beauty," עֲטֶרֶת תִּפְאֶרֶת, in YHWH's hand and a "royal diadem," צָנוֹף מְלוּכָה.[66] This imagery has already been recognized as a potential description derived from the mural crowns of the ancient Near East.[67] Mark Biddle, while arguing that the use of mural crowns does not indicate the deification of a city, a suggestion that seems open to debate, claims that passages such as Isaiah 61 and 62 contain allusions to mural crowns with the appropriate "modifications."[68] Darr, by way of Biddle's work, argues that the traditions around mural crowns in the ancient Near East inform YHWH's relationship to and redemption and rebuilding of Jerusalem in Isaiah. In other words, for these authors, the related claims that Jerusalem will be redeemed and become YHWH's glory cannot be separated from the mural crowns. Anderson takes this relationship one step further and argues that the פאר is not only a reference to the mural crowns but a pun that relies on wedding headdresses.[69] Isaiah 62 reinforces this reference when it imagines Jerusalem's redemption in terms of a wedding ceremony, thus becoming YHWH's consort.[70]

66. On the use of עֲטֶרֶת in Persian period texts, see Jason M. Silverman, *Persian Royal-Judean Elite Engagements in the Early Teispid and Achaemenid Empire: The King's Acolytes* (New York: T&T Clark, 2019), 156.

67. Katheryn Pfisterer Darr, *Isaiah's Vision and the Family of God*, Literary Currents in Biblical Interpretation (Louisville, KY: Westminster John Knox, 1994), 200. Darr notes that this correlation was expressed with Muilenburg's work in 1956 and Westermann's shortly thereafter (1969).

68. Mark Biddle, "The Figure of the Lady Jerusalem: Identification, Deification and Personification," in *The Biblical Canon in Comparative Perspective*, ed. Bernard Frank Batto, William W. Hallo, and K. Lawson Younger (Lewiston, NY: Mellen, 1991), 182.

69. Darr, *Isaiah's Vision*, 202.

70. See McKay's discussion of the role of dress in constructing identities in her chapter "Dress Deployed an Agent of Deception in Hebrew Bible Narratives" in this volume. See also the recent work by Laura Quick, *Dress, Adornment, and the Body in the Hebrew Bible* (New York: Oxford University Press, 2021).

Conclusion

In conclusion, it may be beyond the prerogatives of this brief chapter to identify the precise nature of the פְּאֵר headdress in the HB. However, iconographic considerations reveal a range of instructional features that especially reveal the symbolic function of headdresses as able to connect the wearer to the divine realm via material, engraving, and the dynamic relationship between item and wearer.

Emic descriptions of ritual headgear of Israel/Palestine are essentially limited to textual resources. Iconographic depictions of ritual actors from Israel/Palestine are rare, but, in accordance with trends in minor art from the period, Egyptian and Egyptianizing art will likely continue to demonstrate that no special headdress was worn aside from what an individual's social or ritual responsibilities would require. Thus, Egyptian priests would go bareheaded according to their practice and the king would continue to wear his crown in ritual settings. Such a setting, however, would be largely unhelpful when considering the role of פְּאֵר in relation to YHWH. He is not, after all, generally depicted as one who offers sacrifices. Thus, one might need to look to another aspect of this term.

The second way that this term might be inflected comes through its connection to jewelry or other finery made of precious metals such as gold. The LXX translations of the pertinent terminology in Exodus and Leviticus, rabbinic interpretation, images of the gold frontlets like those at Megiddo, and the use of rosette patterns in ancient NE jewelry may suggest that YHWH's glorification and splendor, his פְּאֵר and תִּפְאֶרֶת, rely on the metaphorical meaning of fine items. Moreover, the fact that rosette patterns were closely connected to solar imagery may shed light on the use of such terminology in certain passages like Isaiah 60, which rely on distinct solar qualities to express YHWH's splendor.

Finally, when it comes to YHWH's glorification of Zion and his people, the mural crown may be of some importance. This suggestion has been made by many others, but it certainly seems to be a viable option for understanding why פְּאֵר would be associated with the glorification and crowning of Jerusalem, YHWH's city and sometimes consort. Each of these areas could, and should, be explored more closely. While this is only a starting place, the close connections and the wordplay between YHWH's פְּאֵר and תִּפְאֶרֶת and the terms as they relate to ancient dress cannot be denied.

Chapter 2

DRESS DEPLOYED AS AN AGENT OF DECEPTION IN HEBREW BIBLE NARRATIVES

Heather A. McKay

Introduction

When Joseph's ten travel-weary brothers arrive at the court of Pharaoh to beg to purchase grain to take back to Canaan, they are met by a richly garbed and highly important member of that court, someone second only to Pharaoh himself. They do not encounter their brother Joseph. That brother is highly and effectively disguised from both their sight and their perception. The official speaks only in Egyptian and converses with them through an interpreter. By pretending to regard them as spies, he learns much of their current situation. He secretly plans to have his revenge upon them for their ruthless treatment of him in years long past. And how can he effect this plan? By hiding himself in plain sight, in Egyptian clothes and regalia, in Egyptian speech, and in his vastly superior social, well-nigh royal, standing in Pharaoh's court. His dress effectively provides him with a long-desired opportunity to turn the tables on those ten brothers.[1]

This chapter will begin by explaining what may be regarded as deception in interpersonal relations. Thereafter follows an analysis and categorizing of the functions of dress, going beyond the basic functions of protection and modesty and identifying dress as an assumed interface which can be chosen in such a way as to display multiple types of information about the wearer albeit either honestly and truthfully or with intent to manipulate what be perceived by both close and distant observers.

Then follows an account of the role of dress in skilled manipulators' creations of false scenarios that lead their protagonists to acceptance of the manipulators' undeclared intentions and goals, usually not to the protagonists' advantage.

Dress can also be accorded to the wearer by others and may, willingly or unwillingly, limit or constrain the wearer in a variety of ways and circumstances: weaponry, modest attire, and royal insignia provide simple examples.

---

1. Genesis 42–45; see later for a full discussion of this long-playing encounter between estranged siblings.

The latter part of the chapter will explain how the managing, manipulation, and, even, distortion of any, or all, of those functions permit dress to be used as a vital—if not the main—constituent of deceptions practiced by one character on another in biblical narratives.[2]

Identifying Deception

It is easy to recognize deception by a person who is involved in:

- hiding wrongdoing by masking the evidence of it;
- theft of some description or regaining rights previously denied: time, service, assurance of patrimony, genetic material, disguised eavesdropping;
- hiding shame or embarrassment or from personal danger by assuming a mask of anonymity; or
- telling a contrived tale to change the mind of another.

Considerations of motive, intentionality, and audience further complicate the determination of deception.[3] For example, is "deception" the appropriate word if a person uses dress to raise an unconsidered option in another's mind by aiming to redefine herself in a new role by changing out of her everyday dress into clothing suited to that new, as yet unassumed, role?

And how should those situations be regarded where a person misreads the actions or motives of another through ignorance or inexperience of life outside their own circle? Were they deceived, or did they deceive themselves? Of course, such could be the case for modern-day readers of the narratives as much as for the characters portrayed in those narratives.

It is important also to consider the possible types of characters that might be deceived in the narratives: those participating in the events, attending court officials, family members, other observers, or any passersby who see or hear only part of the action.

Furthermore, readers also become subject to the chance of being deceived about the true nature of the stories, whether, again, by lack of experience or wisdom

---

2. I wish to present my sincere thanks to Antonios Finitsis, who provided substantial editing to my contribution, which distils into one chapter the accumulation of twenty-six years of output on the many "faces" and functions of dress in the Hebrew Bible; also to David Clines for a meticulous reading of the near-final manuscript.

3. Perhaps the images conjured up by a group playing poker provide a familiar cultural analogy. The bewildered beginner or loser may well mistrust the others, but we realize that the difficulty is due to inexperience and not any unreliable qualities in the others. They are being as reliable as they can—at being successful poker players. The beginner's mistrust is no more than a measure of the others' superior skill.

about human life, by their youth, or their cushioning from the harsher realities of life in a well-supplied and secure, but restricted, home life.

The Functions and Powers Resident in Dress

Absence of Dress

In many cultures nakedness in humans carries no shame for only the very young and the insane members of that society.[4] Main characters in a story are rarely depicted as naked;[5] and the body is never *described* in its unclothed state.[6] The raptures in the Song of Songs remain vague in terms of carnal detail; much is communicated by allusion or innuendo. There is always discretion concerning all the circumstances in which a person may be unclothed; only in the morning after consummating his first marriage did Jacob discover that his first bride was Leah.[7] And Noah's sons went to great lengths to protect his genital privacy.[8]

Dress as Declaratory Interface

In the Hebrew Bible various types of dress and adornments are referred to for men and women for different activities and occasions, and, although not mentioned in every book of the Hebrew Bible, dress is considered important enough to be

---

4. Several essays addressing nudity in all its locations and complexity are presented in Christoph Berner, Manuel Schäfer, Martin Scholl, Sarah Schulz, and Martina Weingärtner, eds, *Clothing and Nudity in the Hebrew Bible* (London, UK: Bloomsbury T&T Clark, 2019). Particularly, the contributions of Anna-Katharina Höpflinger, "Between Regulation, Identification and Representation: Clothing and Nudity from the Perspective of the Study of Religion" (5–18); Agnès Garcia-Ventura, "Clothing and Nudity in the Ancient Near East from the Perspective of Gender Studies" (19–32); Lars Allolio Näcke, "Clothing and Nudity from the Perspective of Anthropological Studies" (33–49); and several further essays throughout the substantial and well-illustrated volume provide useful background material in great detail. It is worth noting that many discussions about shame are included alongside discussions of nudity. In this chapter, however, I will focus on a completely different topic. I will examine in detail the motives of the deceptions through dress and the means of manipulation.

5. Excepting the case of Saul prophesying naked in 1 Sam. 19:24; see discussion in Ora Horn Prouser, "Suited to the Throne: The Symbolic Use of Clothing in the David and Saul Narratives," *JSOT* 71 (1996), 27–37 (32–3).

6. There is no biblical data about, for example, whether night attire was worn or not, and such references as there are to the bodies of the beloved ones in the Song of Songs tend to the metaphorical rather than the purely physical and anatomical.

7. Gen. 29:21-25.

8. Gen. 9:20-27. See also Michaela Bauks, "Clothing and Nudity in the Noah Story (Gen. 9:18-29)," in Berner et al., *Clothing and Nudity in the Hebrew Bible*, 379–87.

frequently described and is sometimes crucial in the narrative. Items of dress can have an indispensable function in the biblical "plot."

This crucial function is exercised through the part played by dress and insignia in both the creation and the description of biblical "characters."[9] Main characters are rarely depicted as naked, and the clothes create, extend, or alter every character's sphere of influence and give them their role, status, and means to act.[10]

I wish to go further and claim for dress a more proactive role. I see in dress not only a second skin or psychosocial "face," by means of which human beings—or human characters—are made present to their "audience"[11] but also a declaratory interface which communicates to others, at some distance and in advance of any meeting, information vital to the ensuing interactions between them. As a corollary to that relatively innocent role, dress can also have a constraining effect whenever the forms of dress available to a person are restricted by rules or conventions of society, or by the person's poverty, or their physical size, or their social role, by the mores of their family, or the pressures of their peer group. Getting dressed could rarely be a simple matter.

In the Hebrew Bible several basic dress items are named for both genders in the same terms. The materials used were wool, linen, and animal skins, mainly sheep, goat, and camel.[12] A garment in general and unspecified as to nature or style was named a *beged* or *simlah*. When clothes were described in more detail, people are depicted wearing an under-tunic, *ketonet*, and a more voluminous over-tunic, a *me'il*, perhaps including sleeves. However, distinctions between the different garments are hard to pin down, and the garments of each sex have to be distinguished by other means or inferred from the prohibition on cross-dressing in Deut. 22:5—for none are stated—or regarded as being added by type of fabric, color, patterning or ornamentation, or additions such as jewelry. Notwithstanding

---

9. I have adopted the understanding of "characters" as readerly constructs and of the characterization process as occurring in the nexus of author, narrator, and active reader as set forth in Heather A. McKay, "Only a Remnant of Them Will Be Saved: New Testament Images of Hebrew Women," in *The Hebrew Bible in the New Testament*, ed. A. Brenner, *A Feminist Companion to the Bible*, vol. 10 (Sheffield: Sheffield Academic Press, 1996), 32–61 (40–3).

10. See also Höpflinger, "Between Regulation, Identification and Representation," 6.

11. See Erving Goffman, "The Mentally Ill and Management of Personal Front," in *Dress, Adornment and the Social Order*, ed. Mary Ellen Roach and Joanne Bubolz Eicher (John Wiley, 1965), 266–8.

12. Animals are clad only very rarely in the Hebrew Bible; only the fasting beasts of Nineveh in Jon. 4:7-9, 11 wear sackcloth to exemplify the city's mourning. See "Violence with Humour: Is This Possible in the Hebrew Bible?," in *Violence in the Hebrew Bible: Between Text and Reception. Papers Read at the Joint Meeting of the Oudtestamentisch Werkgezelschap, the Society for Old Testament Study, and the Old Testament Society of South Africa, Groningen 2018*, Old Testament Studies 79, ed. Jacques van Ruiten and Koert van Bekkum (Leiden: Brill, 2020), 42–63.

the lack of visually clear descriptions of the dress of the characters in the stories, the biblical narrators make it plain that the other characters in their stories could easily "read" what the dress implied.

But dress can also be put to the use of the wearer in other ways than providing shelter from the elements; different articles of dress can be used to create a different persona and to provide misdirection in the minds of any observers of the altered person. Moreover, the different, or disguised, person can alter the significance of any interaction undertaken and control the outworking of the newly created situation in ways unavailable to their original self in their own, usual, dress.

Materiality of the Declaratory Interface

While listing and delineating dress items might seem to be a simple, straightforward task, a close study of the list below will prove that not to be the case. Dress items consist of:

- enclosures of the body—wrapped, suspended, pre-shaped, or some combinations of these; and
- attachments to body enclosures—inserted, clipped, or adhered;

and how these may be categorized by their:

- color,
- volume and proportions,
- shape and structure,
- surface design,
- texture,
- odour (whether of scented oils or the person's sweat),[13] or
- sound;

and further classified according to:

- general body locus, for example, head, neck, trunk, arms, and legs, or
- more specific locus, for example, face, ears, hands, feet, and trunk, including breasts and genitals.

Material Manifestations of the Declaratory Interface

Similarly, a close study of the list below will prove that the material manifestations of dress are equally complex:

---

13. I maintain that it was of key importance that Isaac recognize Esau's body odor on the garments currently worn by Jacob (Gen. 27:15-27).

- personal identity: female/male, slave/free, spurned messenger;[14]
- social status (wealth, influence, likely future): landowner, employer;
- sociopolitical status: king or queen;
- enjoying success, or undergoing some threat, or at war;
- social role, including benefits or drawbacks;
- sexual availability: wife, bride, widow, prostitute;[15]
- familial role: son/oldest son, daughter/virgin daughter, wife, proven mother (i.e., likely source of heirs);
- social hierarchy: master, mistress, servant, widow; and
- magico-religious status.[16]

The wide range of material signals amenable to change or distortion by those invested bestow on dress an enormous power to declare truth or falsehood, aspiration, conformity, submission to or defiance of the person's interlocutors or observers. Even so, the perpetrator of any deception must have finely tuned knowledge of the target's normal expectations in order to achieve exactly the planned effect by choosing a disguise that will perfectly attune the target's mind and expectations to the path planned by the perpetrator.[17]

The Creation and Function of False Scenarios

As Erving Goffman has shown,[18] many human interactions take place *within* acts of courtesy or courtship, but these may be of genuine or deceptive *intent*. With ambiguity built into them, these interactions can provide *slippage* from innocent friendliness to a hidden seeking to take advantage of the interlocutor; hence, they can be planned in deceptive mode by the would-be manipulator/s and "read" and reacted to as if genuine by the intended victim. There is always an uncertain

14. The envoys of David to Hanun were degraded and returned to him in shame. So Hanun seized David's envoys, shaved off half the beard of each, cut off their garments in the middle at their hips, and sent them away (2 Sam. 10:4).

15. See also the discussion by Jennifer M. Matheny in "Tamar and Ruth: Dress as (Mis) Communication and Inheritance Preservation" in this volume.

16. See also the discussion by S. J. Parrott in "'Because of My זְנוּת I Set upon You': Transformation through Dress in Ezekiel 16:1-4" in this volume.

17. See further the discussion by Carmen Joy Imes in Chapter 7 of this volume. In particular the discussion of "social validation theory" is applicable, which sequences the stages in the publicly accepted acquisition of an assumed persona or role. The person, or in this case, character, adopts the dress and behavior of the assumed role or persona and, if adequately proficient, succeeds in being accepted as presented. The discussion on "expectancy violations theory" is not precisely relevant in regard to disguise as I discuss it, but it can be useful in considering the deceived person's reaction when the disguise is uncovered.

18. Erving Goffman, *Frame Analysis* (New York: Harper & Row, 1974), 43–4.

distinction between civility expressed in courtesy and courting another's attention to seek a favor or other benefit. The recipient of the courtesy is constrained by expected reciprocal courtesy to accept the situation as genuine, but there is always a possibility of a slight gap in the courter's intentions such that they *should* be, but are not, read wisely and with caution; they may be, in fact, *misread* as sincere. An enterprising interlocutor can slide a request for more than was seemingly at stake through that gap—between assumed straight dealings and what is actually going on. The deceiver can set up an assumed social identity by eschewing her/his "normal" personal front for the purposes of the false scenario s/he has planned. This deceptive self-presentation, then, functions to define the situation for those who observe the performance, in this case the victims of the planned deception and any attendant observers or witnesses.

Another superb analyst of the creation of false scenarios is William Beeman, who worked as a university teacher in Iran in the 1960s and gathered much information about how language functioned in the social interactions of that society,[19] aided both by the complexity of grammar in the Farsi language and by his knowledge of sociolinguistics and cultural anthropology. He traveled widely through the society, involved in university and nationally funded projects which enabled his interaction with local people in many aspects of public and private life. His many and varied insights into the use of language in both private and public settings, from business meetings to betrothal arrangements, shed significant light on similar situations portrayed in Hebrew Bible narratives, which I have found to be of great benefit in many areas of my research. He identified the ways in which adroit speakers can make their status in a societal hierarchy obvious, their familiarity or distance from others evident, their dominance in negotiations plain, and their willingness to help subordinates—within clearly defined limits— similarly clear. These characteristics can be readily recognized even in biblical characters, and Beeman's insights have rendered them more readily identifiable.

Moreover, other analyses have shown that the deceiver manipulates both the quality and quantity of the information passed on to the victim/s during the scenario.[20] Any number of lies may be transmitted plus a subtle restricting of the truth to convey false impressions. Even more effective is the telling of those lies in a family situation where truth and reliability should always be the norm.[21]

Because the observers and interlocutors "enter" the false scenario and behave in it as if they were participating in, or watching, a real situation, they accept the falsity as reality and react to it in the way planned for by the deceiver.

19. William O. Beeman, *Language, Status and Power in Iran*, Advances in Semiotics (Bloomington: Indiana University Press, 1986). Beeman also declares himself to be a follower of Goffman's work (xiv).

20. S. A. McCornack, "Information Manipulation Theory," *Communication Monographs* 59:1 (1992), 1–16.

21. Irma Kurtz, *The Lying Game*, BBC Radio 4, April 26, 2003.

Dress as a Powerful Means of Human Discourse

Dress presents a public "self." As such, it defines the situation for those who observe the performance. It further reveals or conceals emotions, and as such it manipulates both the quality and quantity of the information presented.[22] Dress represents a means of:

- the public creation of a "self;"[23]
- the definition of a person's social role in the community, including indication of wealth, and of political, religio-ritual standing and sexual status;[24]
- the facilitation of social rituals, with concomitant reinforcement of traditional beliefs, custom, and values;[25] or,
- by corollary, the intended disruption of those same social rituals, with concomitant disregard of traditional beliefs, custom, and values.

As such, dress allows the deceiver a powerful means by which to stage-manage the discourse of the false scenario. The target's expectations are carefully orchestrated by the manipulator at the beginning of the interaction, and if the manipulator works smoothly toward executing the plan, no jarring notes will caution the target to be hesitant and alert to other, less favorable, matters proceeding beneath the apparent.

Dress as a Discourse Participant

However, dress is not merely a passive means to an end. Its unique qualities allow it to participate in discourse in remarkable ways. Ronald Schwarz, resisting the typical scholarly response of reticence about identifying the human emotions underlying the wearing of dress, treats extensively the symbolic or rhetorical power of dress.[26] He claims that dress is an important indicator of emotion, revealing, or

---

22. In addition, dress renews and confirms group harmony and articulates aspects of the symbolic universe, including relationships between humans and the "supernatural." Also in each of these discursive arenas sexual politics supplies a subplot to the main narrative of power distribution in society. See also the discussion by Susannah Rees in "'Women Rule over Them': Dressing for an Inverted World in Isaiah 3" in this volume.

23. Goffman, "The Mentally Ill and Management of Personal Front," 266–8.

24. See also the discussion by Jennifer Brown Jones in "Coded Critique, Validating Vestments: Joshua's Garments in Zechariah 3" in this volume.

25. Mary Ellen Roach and Joanne Bubolz Eicher, "The Language of Personal Adornment," in *The Fabrics of Culture: The Anthropology of Clothing and Adornment*, World Anthropology, ed. Justine M. Cordwell and Ronald A. Schwarz (The Hague: Mouton, 1979), 7–22; see also their earlier analysis in Roach and Eicher, *Dress, Adornment and the Social Order*, 6–7.

26. Ronald A. Schwarz, "Uncovering the Secret Vice: Towards an Anthropology of Clothing and Adornment," in Cordwell and Schwarz, *The Fabrics of Culture*, 23–46. See

sometimes concealing, a person's desires, ambitions, and emotions, in both cases making the exercise, or abrogation, of authority easier.

Schwarz recounts how a Benin "village chief wears one hat when acting in his capacity of chief, another when performing his duties as head of a lineage group, and another when acting as head of his family."[27] The hat functions as a material indicator both to the chief and to his villagers that he has the authority to carry out a particular role in the community and that he is now about to do so. They express publicly his status and rank, silently and assertively, and both reduce his self-doubt and nonaggressively underscore his authority.[28] The different hats *enable* him differently to execute his different roles in the community.[29]

Conversely, younger, or less powerful, males use dress to indicate their unwillingness to challenge tribal leaders. For example, young males among the North African Tuaregs tie their head veils in particular ways that indicate whether the wearer is a bold, brash, immodest fellow, or an impeccable, would-be military man, or courtier.[30] In these ways the head veils reduce anxiety in low-ranking group members by expressing publicly their current lack of pretensions to status, rank, and authority, and thereby reducing the chance of their being perceived as a serious threat by persons of high status.[31]

Dress *does* more than it appears to do: on the one hand, it describes the social order in a symbolic way and, on the other, it modulates and alters societal interactions, indeed does so more effectively than any other material product.[32] The most powerful members of society, and their would-be successors, are males and are identified in these roles by their attire. After all, visual communication occurs before verbal interaction takes place,[33] and, generally speaking,[34] identifies

also Mary Shaw Ryan, *Clothing: A Study in Human Behaviour* (New York: Holt, Rinehart & Winston, 1966).

27. Schwarz, "Uncovering the Secret Vice," 28.

28. See also the discussion by Brady Beard in "What to Look For in a Headdress: פאר and תפארה in Material Culture and Iconography Significance and Signification" in this volume.

29. See also Henry JohnDrewal, "Pageantry and Power in Yoruba Costuming," in Cordwell and Schwarz, *The Fabrics of Culture*, 189–230 (199), where masks are seen as essential facilitators of those dancing in Yoruba cultic ritual ceremonies.

30. See also the discussion by Carmen Joy Imes in "Just Clothing? The Function of Dress Metaphors in Imprecatory Psalms" in this volume.

31. Also, by controlling and expressing both shame and attraction (see further discussion below).

32. Schwarz, "Uncovering the Secret Vice," 31; some might suggest that money has similar or, even, more power.

33. Ruth Barnes and Joanne B. Eicher, eds, *Dress and Gender: Making and Meaning in Cultural Contexts*, Cross-Cultural Perspectives on Women, vol. 2 (Providence: Berg, 1992), back cover, 1. See also Roberta Gilchrist, *Gender and Material Culture: The Archaeology of Religious Women* (London: Routledge, 1994).

34. It has been suggested that the Scottish Highlander's kilt may be (mis)identified at a distance as a garment signaling a female.

gender distinctions at a distance.[35] It is a commonplace to say that a person's dress displays their position in the social order, but it is nonetheless true; kings are rarely mistaken for paupers, nor are midwives confused with courtesans.[36]

Furthermore, several biblical scholars have identified various narrative significances in the wearing, making, giving, receiving, and displaying of garments.[37] The value of dress items as tokens of respect and favor between men,[38] pledges as to future actions,[39] markers of social role,[40] and evidence[41] has been explored, as has the effect of the exchange of items on the relationship between donor and recipient.

These effects show that societal barriers are not always impenetrable, particularly where an *achieved* quality is concerned. If the societal barrier is *permeable*, naturally gifted persons may honorably join the elite. But even if the barrier is not permeable, it may yet be successfully transcended by some *deception*, and a verbally adroit person,[42] while remaining scrupulous in all other aspects of life, may gain the advantageous inclusion they strive to achieve by sleight of speech. And the skillful choice of dress can achieve the same success. Marginal people *can* succeed by applying artifice, for example, the employment of a *disguise* of fine clothing, or an assumed voice or accent, or a false claim to highly valued experience. They can *disguise* themselves so that they appear to belong to—or to merit a place in—the elite group.

Much more rarely, central figures may disguise themselves in anonymous dress, as in the folktale image of a king traveling freely through his realm disguised as a humble citizen. Saul attempts to disguise himself for his visit to the medium of Endor but fails to deceive her for she recognizes him partway through their encounter.[43] Similarly, the disguise adopted by Jeroboam's wife is readily seen through by the purblind Ahijah.[44]

35. Barnes and Eicher, *Dress and Gender*, 2.

36. Gender is discussed in several essays in Berner et al., *Clothing and Nudity in the Hebrew Bible*: see again Höpflinger, "Between Regulation, Identification and Representation; and Garcia-Ventura, "Clothing and Nudity." See also Marilyn E. Burton, "Robed in Majesty: Clothing as a Metaphor for the Classical Hebrew Semantic Domain of *kabod*," 289—300, and Stefan Fischer, "Women's Dress Codes in the Book of Proverbs," 544–56.

37. Phyllis A. Bird, "The Harlot as Heroine: Narrative Art and Social Presupposition in Three Old Testament Texts," *Semeia* 46 (1989), 119–39; Richard Coggins, "On Kings and Disguises," *JSOT* 50 (1991), 55–62 (56-57); Victor H. Matthews, "The Anthropology of Clothing in the Joseph Narrative," *JSOT* 65 (1995), 25–36.

38. Nelly Furman, "His Story versus Her Story: Male Genealogy and Female Strategy in the Jacob Cycle," *Semeia* 46 (1989): 141-9.

39. Bird, "The Harlot as Heroine," 123, referring to Tamar in Genesis 38.

40. Furman, "His Story versus Her Story," 145.

41. Ibid., 142.

42. Beeman, *Language*, 28.

43. 1 Sam. 28:5-12; Holger Gzella, "Nudity and Clothing in the Lexicon of the Hebrew Bible," in Berner et al., *Clothing and Nudity in the Hebrew Bible*, 217-35, esp. 225-6.

44. 1 Kings 24; see also Table 2.2.

Situations in Which Changed Dress Can Be Used to Signal That a/the Desired
or Hoped For Change Has Occurred or Is Possibly About to Occur

In one case the person removes one set of clothes, followed by ablutions, and
then dons a fresh set of clothes—of the same type: Mephibosheth had not taken
care of personal hygiene between David's departure and his safe return, which
is celebrated in this way.[45] And David himself washed and changed his clothes
to signify the return to normal life after seven days of fasting and mourning the
death of his first son with Bathsheba.[46] Such bodily cleansing and assumption of
clean dress were also required to prevent illness or impurity,[47] or when changing
religious loyalties, as when Jacob brought his family back to Bethel,[48] and when
Moses prepared the people for the Sinai theophany.[49]

In the other case the person removed one set of clothes, followed by ablutions/
anointings, and then donned a fresh set—of a different type. Ruth is directed by
Naomi who plans a rearrangement of Boaz's priorities: "Now wash and anoint
yourself, and put on your best clothes and go down to the threshing floor."[50]

Women were also obliged to change their clothes upon marriage, or following
capture—which seems to have amounted to much the same thing—and to
adopt the dress designated by the culture of their husband.[51] Even a betrothal
led to significant changes in apparel, for Abraham's servant presented Rebekah
with jewelry and clothes as betrothal gifts[52] and Esther spent six months being
beautified with oil of myrrh and six months with spices and ointments before she
was maritally joined with Ahasuerus to become not merely a royal favorite but
Queen Esther.[53] Change of sexual availability was indicated by a change of dress.[54]

On the other hand, disheveled or torn female dress was *always* regarded as
evidence of a woman's illicit sexual experience and, hence, of female shame
because, in the world of the text, such occurrences were generally associated
with loss of virginity outside marriage[55] or with the aftermath of unlawful sexual

45. 2 Sam. 19:24.
46. 2 Sam. 12:15-23.
47. Exod. 29:4; 30:19-21; 40:12, 30-32; Lev. 11:25, 28, 40; 13:6, 34; 14:8, 9; 47; 15:5-8,
10-11, 13, 16-17, 21-22, 27; 17:15-16; Num. 19:7-8, 10, 19, 21.
48. Gen. 35:2.
49. Exod. 19:10, 14.
50. Ruth 3:3.
51. Deut. 21:13; see also Selena Billington, "Social Standing, Agency, and the Motif of
Cloth and Clothing in Esther," in this volume.
52. Gen. 24:(22), 53.
53. Est. 2:12; see also the discussion by Sara Koenig in "Styling Eve and Adam's
Clothes: An Examination of Reception History" in this volume.
54. See also the discussion by S. J. Parrott in "'Because of My הדר I Set upon You':
Transformation through Dress in Ezekiel 16:1-14" in this volume.
55. Deut. 22:14, 17.

encounter, as in the mysterious matter of Dinah's excursion and encounter with Shechem,[56] or rape, for example, Tamar[57] and the unnamed woman of Exod. 22:16-17.

But more interesting yet than the role of dress in the accounts of women's assumption of new status and gender roles[58]—whether beneficial or deleterious—is the description of the *exactly* parallel process for Joseph.[59] In Canaan, Joseph's favored status as the firstborn son of Rachel was displayed by the gift of a "long coat with sleeves."[60] In Egypt, severed from his father, he received at first the short kilt of a servant in Potiphar's house.[61] Later, he gained his status and the legal exercise of his sexuality from Pharaoh, in the form of fine dress and a gold chain and a wife,[62] much as young women received theirs from a father or husband. Joseph's move from prison to Pharaoh's court and his rapidly ensuing marriage parallel Ruth's move from gleaner to proprietor's wife and Esther's move from female citizen to king's favorite wife. And all these changes are accompanied by significant, and recorded, changes of apparel.[63]

Dress Applies Subtle Controls by Constraining Bodily Movements and Attitudinal Poses

Sociologists, cultural anthropologists, and psychologists have realized that the overall inculturation and socialization of children "teaches" them many activities and movements that were formerly assumed to be inherited.[64] Marcel Mauss identified and described a range of these behaviors and named them "body techniques." They include methods of body care, eating, walking, and running—in fact, all those activities that we might, unthinkingly, class as "natural" or

---

56. Genesis 34.

57. 2 Samuel 13.

58. See also the discussion in McKay, "Only a Remnant," 40–3.

59. See also the discussion by Ellena Lyell in "Dressing Benjaminites, Defining Kingship: Dress as a Royal Prerogative for the Tribe of Benjamin" in this volume. See also Dina Serova, "Stripped Bare: Communicating Rank and Status in Old Kingdom Egypt," in Berner et al., *Clothing and Nudity in the Hebrew Bible*, 163–84.

60. Gen. 37:3; cf. Tamar's robe, denoting her status as a virgin daughter of King David in 2 Sam. 13:18.

61. Gen. 39:12. The white, wraparound, waist-to-knee kilts worn by Egyptian slaves are familiar from tomb art; see https://ancientegypt.fandom.com/wiki/Slavery (accessed April 7, 2021).

62. Gen. 1:14, 42, 45, 50.

63. See also Holger Gzella, "Nudity and Clothing in the Lexicon of the Hebrew Bible," 217–35, esp. 225–6.

64. M. Mauss, "Introduction," in *Sociology and Psychology: Essays by Marcel Mauss*, trans. B. Brewster (London: Routledge & Kegan Paul, 1979), 1–14.

"instinctive."[65] For Mauss, all these activities are *learned* activities, taught to the young by their elders.[66]

Furthermore, on reflection, we come to realize that the "body techniques" described by Mauss are seen by others as performed not by the naked body but through the enshrouding medium of dress. The external appearance of all bodily actions is mediated by clothes that muffle or, perhaps conversely, accentuate such postures and gestures.[67]

A powerful case has also been made that distinctive dress indicates one's standing in hierarchically ordered groups.[68] Younger males can use their dress to indicate whether they remain brash adolescents or have become biddable would-be member of the society of their elders.[69] Older established males wear different styles that indicate their higher position in the hierarchies of decision-making and authority. This differentiation shows us that males—as much as females—are gradually empowered by gradations of dress, and are also *gendered* by them, since maturity and dominance confer the sexual rights of marriage and procreation; though, to be sure, it seems, at first sight, that their clothes indicate no more than their social standing.

Dress Modifies a Person's Public Persona

By means of dress observers easily identify others' roles, functions, and activities. A particularly vivid illustration of this is provided by a consideration of the restricting ceremonial costumes of classical Japanese dance. American students found that until they were severely constrained by properly fitted and secured kimonos, they could not execute the complex, elegant movements required by the dances.[70] Once they were properly, that is, tightly, bound, the correct

---

65. An unexamined and, from Mauss's perspective, erroneous assumption might be that the typical variation in these activities among humans is produced *only* by the normal variations in size, weight, limb length, and fitness of the persons in question.

66. M. Mauss, 'Body Techniques,' in *Sociology and Psychology*, 95–123.

67. Jean-Claude Schmitt, "The Ethics of Gesture," in *Fragments for a History of the Human Body*, part 2, ed. Michel Feher with Ramona Naddaff and Nadia Tazi (New York: Urzone, 1989), 97–123.

68. Ronald A. Schwarz, "Uncovering the Secret Vice: Towards an Anthropology of Clothing and Adornment," in Cordwell and Schwarz, *The Fabrics of Culture*, 23–46 (28); the "secret vice" is that of "Big Men" when they indulge in the practice of "custom tailoring" that displays their social importance (23).

69. Ibid., 29.

70. Joann W. Keali'inohomoku, "You Dance What You Wear, and You Wear Your Cultural Values," in Cordwell and Schwarz, *The Fabrics of Culture*, 77–86 (77–8), where the author describes a summer school class for elementary school teachers at the University of Hawaii.

movements became relatively easy to perform.[71] The dress limited and therefore also choreographed the movements they could make.[72]

This admittedly extreme form of control of movement[73] and gesture by dress allows us to recognize the same phenomenon when it is more subtly expressed in everyday movements and gestures.

Dress Negotiates Gender and Status

In human life gender differentiation occurs quite largely by means of dress. First, the form and style of one's dress *shapes* most behavior, being particularly effective in making distinctions clear during walking and sitting or crossing one's legs when seated and in rendering those activities more visibly *gendered* activities.[74] Even from a distance it is easily possible to recognize the gender of people as they move and change position, speed, and stance.

The second aspect of the daily assumption of dress is *submission* to the control effected by dress.[75] For, although a person's choice of fresh dress is not totally free, being influenced by factors such as climate, or function, wearers can choose dress that—in their opinion—best represents them in the roles they follow. Each morning, as consciousness returns, humans reassume self-awareness and become situationally present again and begin the day by rebuilding what Goffman calls their "personal front," that is, the complex of dress, makeup, hairdo, and other surface decorations normal to daily life.[76] They plan—and then build—their persona for the day.

So, the consistent outcome of rising and dressing is that any society's definitions of its citizens are both internalized and reaffirmed every day. As they dress, people voluntarily reassume their *ascribed*[77] gender and social status and make that

71. Cf. similar results with Korean, Arabian, Pueblan, Samoan, and Burmese dancing (ibid., 78–9).

72. I have observed the same phenomenon in Bali at a performance of the Kecak dance where the main characters in the favorite story from the Ramayana, Rama and Sita are played by young women who are differently clad in order to emphasize either powerful swinging shoulder movements in the case of Prince Rama or supple, submissive hip movements in the case of Princess Sita.

73. For even more extreme forms of bodily control, consider the straitjacket.

74. Keali'inohomoku, "You Dance What You Wear," 80.

75. Mary Ellen Roach and Joanne Bubolz Eicher, eds, *Dress, Adornment and the Social Order* (New York: John Wiley, 1965), 1.

76. Goffman, "The Mentally Ill and Management of Personal Front," 266–8.

77. Those "barriers" put in place by society demand qualities that may be achieved or ascribed; H. F. Dickie Clark, *The Marginal Situation: A Sociological Study of a Coloured Group*, International Library of Sociology and Social Reconstruction (London: Routledge & Kegan Paul, 1966), 32–3, 43; see also Joanne B. Eicher and Mary E. Roach-Higgins, "Definition and Classification of Dress," in *Dress and Gender: Making and Meaning*, ed. Ruth Barnes and Joanne B. Eicher (New York: Berg, 1992), 8–28.

acceptance manifest to others by their clothes. Of course, for some people that freedom may be restricted or constrained by the dress codes adopted or, possibly, enforced by their family, ethnicity, creed, culture, or work role. Certain professions nowadays, such as nursing, prescribe a readily recognizable dress code and certain roles in the ancient world laid similar dress restrictions on their practitioners.[78]

Cross-Dressing

It should be noted that nowhere in the Hebrew Bible is cross-dressing described in a narrative. This may be because of the demand in Deut. 22:5: "A woman shall not wear a man's apparel,[79] nor shall a man put on a woman's garment; for whoever does such things is abhorrent to the Lord your God." Some possibilities occasioned by the wearing of clothing of the opposite gender spring to mind, such as:

- the altered outlines and body shapes presented could mislead the (probably) male observer,
- hence causing "wrong" imaginings of the underlying body and the wearer's social role, and, furthermore,
- "wrongly" aroused expectations of how the interaction might proceed, whether to arrange terms or evade an awkward or embarrassing situation.[80]

It may, however, be nothing other than an example of priestly antipathy to mixtures of any sort, in this case of the public appearance of the sexes.

Finally, as we have seen above, dress, as much through its fine control of human movements as its physical appearance, gives clear indications of a person's cultural location, so it will come as no surprise to discover that deceptive changes of dress accompany, facilitate, or even determine the achievement of some personal aim of the deceiver. However, in order to "work" deceptively, the particular dress assumed must play a key role in the creation of the "false scenario" necessary to allow the manipulation of the victim's subsequent words and actions.

78. Cf. especially priestly garb: Exod. 28:39-42; 39:1-31. See also the discussion by Brady Beard in "What to Look For in a Headdress: פאר and תפארה in Material Culture and Iconography Significance and Signification" in this volume.

79. Heather A. McKay, "Gendering the Body: Clothes Maketh the (Wo)Man," in *Theology and the Body*, ed. Robert Hannaford and Jan Jobling (Leominster: Gracewing, Fowler, Wright, 1999), 84–104.

80. Also, possible male reactions might include fear of a diminution of heterosexual congress and, hence, a risk of insufficient offspring to maintain tribal/clan numbers; loss of the widely purveyed sense of the unique delight, with attendant assurance of paternity of offspring, offered by a virgin bride to lusty young males; fear of misidentifying a male prostitute for a female prostitute with accompanying shame and/or horror.

Biblical Deceptions Achieved by Disguise

The nine deceptions outlined in Table 2.1 will be explored in turn based on the aim of the deception practiced. Table 2.2 lists other changes of dress that proved unsuccessful, or even unclear, in their purpose.

Motivations for the deceptions can be listed as follows:

- hiding wrongdoing by masking the evidence of it;
- theft of some description or regaining rights previously denied: time, service, assurance of patrimony, genetic material, information obtained by eavesdropping in plain sight but "disguised" as seemingly unable to understand what was being said;
- hiding shame or embarrassment or from personal danger by assuming a mask of anonymity;
- changing the mind of another person;
- raising an unconsidered option in another's mind;
- finding the self-confidence to tackle a daunting task or enterprise.

Hiding Wrongdoing

Adam and Eve had discovered the existence of nakedness, a concept previously unknown to them, and while intending to disguise their newfound knowledge, they actually succeeded in drawing attention to their shortcoming by overlaying their genitalia with a covering of leaves.[81] Viewed in one way, there is a nice example of irony here, or—even—of poetic justice if taken the other way.

Theft of Some Sort or the Regaining of Rights Currently Denied

Stealing something from someone who deserves better treatment always occasions disapprobation, and some of the following characters take the practice of manipulation to a fine art. Here the deceptions of Jacob against Isaac,[82] Laban against Jacob,[83] Tamar against Judah,[84] and Joseph against his brothers[85] will be explored.

---

81. See Jürgen van Oorschot, "Nudity and Clothing in the Hebrew Bible: Theological and Anthropological Aspects," 237–49 and Friedholm Hartenstein, "Clothing and Nudity in the Paradise Story (Gen. 2–3)," 357–78, in Berner et al., *Clothing and Nudity in the Hebrew Bible.*

82. Gen. 27:1-28:5.

83. Gen. 29:1-25.

84. Gen. 38:11-26.

85. Genesis 42.

Table 2.1 Changes of apparel that were successful disguises regardless of whether the ploy succeeded or not

Who was disguised	With what	By whom or at whose behest	Reference	As who/ what	Victim of deception	Reason/ purpose	Successful or unsuccessful outcome
Adam and Eve	Leaf aprons	Themselves	Genesis 3	Innocent selves	Yahweh	To hide disobedience	Unsuccessful
Jacob	Esau's clothes, etc.	Rebekah	Genesis 27	Esau	Isaac (purblind)	To steal Esau's blessing	Successful
Leah	Unclear/ darkness, perhaps veil	Laban	Genesis 29	Rachel	Jacob	To get Leah married and/ or extort more service from Jacob	Successful
Tamar	Veil, etc.	Herself	Genesis 28	Prostitute	Judah	To become impregnated by Judah	Successful
Joseph	Egyptian garb	Himself	Genesis 42	Egyptian overlord	Brothers	To lengthen time with them/exact pain as revenge	Successful
Saul	Other clothes	Himself	1 Sam. 28:8	Not King Saul	Medium of Endor	Possibly to hide his anxiety or shame	Unsuccessful
Ahab	Nonidentifying armor	Himself	1 Kings 22; 2 Chronicles 18	Not King Ahab	Enemy in battle	To hide his identity in battle	Successful in disguise but unsuccessful in saving life
Wise Woman of Tekoa	Widow's clothes	Joab	2 Samuel 14	Mourning widow	David	To persuade David to change his mind about Absalom's exile	Successful
Ruth	Best clothes	Naomi	Ruth 3	Would-be bride	Boaz	To give Boaz an unexpected option to consider	Successful

Table 2.2 Changes of apparel that were unsuccessful or unintended disguises

Who was disguised	With what	By whom or at whose behest	Reference	As who/ what	Victim of deception	Reason/ purpose	Successful or unsuccessful outcome
Wife of Jeroboam	Ordinary clothes	Jeroboam	1 Kings 14	Ordinary woman	Ahijah (purblind)	Unclear: perhaps to get a true answer to Jeroboam's query	

Jacob, ably aided and abetted by his mother Rebekah, is disguised bodily by wearing his brother's clothes and by having the skin of a kid on his arms so that he can chouse his purblind father Isaac out of the eldest son's blessing, thereby also cheating Esau of that valued portion of *his* birthright. Rebekah creates a fully-fledged false scenario that bemuses all of Isaac's functional senses; and the wearing of Esau's dress is a key part of that scenario. The cheating does not go smoothly. Jacob is forced to persist verbally in his deception and lie about his identity when his father doubts his voice—for he did not *sound* like Esau—and Jacob succeeds rather because his father recognizes the feel of Esau's arms and—I maintain—the feel and smell of Esau's clothes.[86] But is Isaac really deceived? Could any man's forearms be so similar to a kid's fleece? After all, Isaac does decide that the voice he heard belonged to Jacob while commenting the hands felt like Esau's, and by assessing Esau's clothes.[87] Perhaps, I suggest, Isaac wanted to give Jacob his blessing—those important words. However, because Jacob left the district shortly after, in fear for his life, readers are left uncertain as to what, if anything, Esau inherited.

Laban implicitly disguises Leah as her sister Rachel by presenting her to Jacob in marriage and leads Jacob to marry her sight unseen since she is veiled as a bride when he is conducted to her. The false scenario is patent: a wedding feast followed by the presentation of a veiled bride in bridal attire to her bridegroom. This deceit was perpetrated despite the fact that Laban had already had the benefit of seven years of service from Jacob as the bride price for Rachel. The following morning, Jacob realizes that he has been tricked and demands that he be allowed to marry Rachel, his original chosen, bargained for, and labored for bride. Laban agrees after demanding a token extra seven days—rather than years—of monogamy with Leah before the second wedding. Then Jacob is allowed to marry Rachel and began his second seven years of service to Laban. Laban effectively stole seven years of remunerated labor from Jacob.

Tamar effectively "steals" genetic material from Judah in order to generate issue for herself and the family that truly belongs within the family.[88] As a widow, Tamar found herself in a hopeless situation for she was required to wear distinctive garments that clearly declared her (lack of) marital status to the community.[89] She had been left a widow and as such was honor bound to preserve her chastity until her youngest brother-in-law was allocated to her as a spouse by her father-in-law, Judah. She, like Ruth, was trapped in one of the most marginal social situations depicted in the Hebrew Bible—that of a childless (i.e., in that society, sonless) widow. To change the situation, she must overcome the two disabling difficulties of

---

86. Gen. 27:24. I believe that finding and feeling the hands and arms would necessitate feeling and being very close to the clothes allowing Esau's body odor to overlie Jacob's; in Gen. 27:27, Isaac remarks on the smell of the fields on the clothes.

87. Gen. 27:22.

88. Genesis 38; Ruth 4:18-22.

89. See the implication of the identifiable nature of such garments in Deut. 24:17.

her condition, namely, her lack of sexual intercourse with an acceptable mate and her isolation in private living quarters. She can bypass both of these difficulties at one blow only by veiling her face,[90] sitting by the roadside, and, thereby, adopting the role of a prostitute.[91]

She could take the desperate sartorial step and so disguise herself to free herself from the control those widow's clothes exercised over her sexual availability.[92] She would also effect the regaining of privileges currently denied to her by the death of her first two husbands, also by Onan's famous "sin" that greatly diminished Tamar's chance of conceiving a son,[93] and by Judah's quasi-denial to her of marriage rights with Shelah by putting off the date of the wedding into a hazy future—he was admittedly quite young at the time of her second widowhood.[94] After some time spent in despair, Tamar took steps to create a convincing false scenario, one that would lead Judah to behave in the way she wished for.[95]

Tamar disguised herself as a prostitute in two ways, by sitting idly by the side of the road and by wearing a veil—and not wearing widows' clothes. She disguised only her identity and the constraints Judah had placed upon her; by wearing the dress of a prostitute she did not disguise her potential for motherhood. Judah did not penetrate her disguise but made use of her services. As a pledge against her future payment, she took three items of his personal insignia and later used them to save not only her honor but also his and her own life too. Without her (false) clothes and his (true) insignia—the story says—Tamar's wrong would never have been put to right. But she had to disguise herself—partially, at least—in order to operate in the public domain, to nudge events in the right direction.

Obviously, observers may be misled by disguise in several ways. First, the disguise may hide someone's face from the observers and so from the shame occasioned by being discovered in a place where that person should not have been. So, a veil proved useful to Tamar. Second, a disguise can conceal personal identity under a mask of anonymity—allowing the wearer's identity to "melt" into insignificance—as Tamar's did when she shed her widow's garb, dressed herself

---

90. Of parallel, but contrary, interest is the point made by Wolfgang Oswald in "Veiling Moses Shining Face (Exod. 34:29-35)," 449–57, esp. 457, in Berner et al., *Clothing and Nudity in the Hebrew Bible*, namely that Moses' face is not veiled for any of the usual reasons but to make "the radiance on his face invisible when there is no need for a sign of God's presence."

91. See also Martina Weingärtner, "The Symbolism of Vestimentary Arts in Gen 37, Gen 38, and 1 Sam 17," 403–16, esp. 409–10, in Berner et al., *Clothing and Nudity in the Hebrew Bible*.

92. Gen. 38:14, 19.

93. Gen. 38:6-10. During intercourse with his wife Tamar, Onan withdrew and ejaculated outside of Tamar's body to avoid siring a son that would belong to his deceased brother through his levirate marriage with Tamar. In those times, ejaculation within the woman's vagina was believed to be necessary for conception.

94. Gen. 38:11.

95. Gen. 38:12-14.

in other clothes, *and* added a veil. She used a cleverly constructed false scenario to yield to her the rights and privileges currently denied her. The different dress *enabled* her to carry out this outrageous maneuver.

Joseph, a spoilt and bumptious child, had been well bullied and more than paid back for his impertinence to his brothers by their selling him into slavery in Egypt.[96] However, he succeeds in creating a new life for himself there, rising to a position of high importance and power. He then wore Egyptian dress—clothes and accessories—given to him by Pharaoh[97] and could treat everyone—save Pharaoh—with well-nigh regal condescension and carelessness, and he made the most of that elevated position, making slaves of the whole population of Egypt.[98]

So, when his half brothers come into his power on their visit to Egypt to buy grain, he torments them by devising the most heinous of tricks to perpetrate upon them,[99] namely, lying to them—even if only by omission, that is, pretending he does not understand their speech—and cheating them who were, after all, his nearest of kin—other than Benjamin.[100]

And he does this by hiding in plain sight, eavesdropping on their nervous, secretive conversations, assuming an indifferent and apparently unknowing pose, all the while determined to generate the greatest amount of pain and self-doubt in them that he could stir up. He desperately wanted to see his younger, full brother Benjamin again and, even more deceitfully, perhaps self-deceitfully, masked that want as a bargaining chip to ensure his half brothers' acquiescence. Disguised in the dress, role, language, and demeanor of an Egyptian potentate, he forces them to agree to deceive and grieve their joint father in order to buy the grain necessary for survival.

It is quite evidently Joseph's usual dress as an Egyptian overlord that effectively disguises him as not-himself, as not-a-brother to them, and makes the creation of several extremely cruel false scenarios revolving around "stolen" money and a silver cup, as he danced them back and forward before him until they could be driven to organize his reunion with his full brother Benjamin. Then, and only then, did he break down in front of them—although he had already shed tears in private—and become truly *himself*, in the sense of *their* grieving but restored brother. His now less-than-pristine dress was no longer effective as a disguise.

---

96. Gen. 37:28-29; Reuben was not involved in the sale procedure.

97. Gen. 41:41-44.

98. Gen. 47:21.

99. See further, Heather A. McKay, "Lying and Deceit in Families: The Duping of Isaac and Tamar," where lying is exposed as the cardinal sin within the family circle, in *The Family in Life and Death: The Family in Ancient Israel*, ed. Patricia Dutcher-Walls (London: T&T Clark International, 2009), 28–41.

100. Genesis 42–45.

Hiding Shame or Embarrassment or from Personal Danger

Elsewhere in the Hebrew Bible, two kings adopt a disguise that led to their being (mis)taken for a less distinguished person. Ahab believed that, as king of Israel, his life would be sought with more determination than that of a common soldier, so he "disguised" himself as not-the-king.[101] He was nonetheless killed, though not by someone aiming to kill him particularly but rather by striking him by chance. Ahab's "disguise" worked partially; he was not recognized as the king and was not killed as the king. Nonetheless, the prophetic words of Micaiah ben Imlah came true, and readers may infer, therefore, that Ahab's assumption of a disguise could not hoodwink the deity.[102]

Saul, on the other hand, disguised himself to reserve to himself the privilege of breaking his own laws against mediums. By going to Endor he could visit a medium and by disguising himself as not-the-king he could consult her.[103] However, suddenly, the medium realizes who Saul is and names him to his face. The reader is left to infer that divine revelation—or her own observational skills—has given her this knowledge that instantly puts Saul to shame. She identifies him by his name—not as the king. It is not his role and position that are shamed, for they were disguised; it is Saul himself and it was his disguise of common dress that led to his feeling ashamed before the seer and, worse still, before a woman.

Changing King David's Mind

Joab's position vis-à-vis David was equivocal. Throughout the narrative he acted like David's alter ego or doppelgänger, providing the strength to do whatever was necessary when David was unwilling to act and to supply the cunning—behind the scenes if necessary, when David balked at the prospect.[104] But Joab knew just how dangerous it would be to approach David directly to try to persuade him to bring back Absalom. He was not himself in a position to approach the king as a lowly petitioner, self-deprecating and abject. His status in the army and as David's counselor was far too high for that. And yet, he was by no means the king's equal, able to tackle him face to face as Nathan had earlier on.[105] He had to devise an oblique attack. So, he employed a woman, someone from "outside the frame,"

---

101. 1 Kings 22; 2 Chronicles 18, leaving to one side the question of whether Ahab gave Jehoshaphat his royal robes to wear; cf. John Gray, *I & II Kings: A Commentary*, 2nd ed., OTL (London: SCM, 1970), 444–56 (447); cf. Coggins, "On Kings and Disguises," 56-57. 56-57).

102. Coggins, "On Kings and Disguises," 58.

103. Hans Wilhelm Hertzberg, *I & II Samuel: A Commentary*, trans. J. S. Bowden (Philadelphia, PA: Westminster, 1964), 215–21 (218); Coggins, "On Kings and Disguises," 56-7.

104. 2 Sam. 3:22-39, the killing of Abner; 11.1, Joab goes into battle in place of David; 11:6-25, the elimination of Uriah; and 18:5–19.8, the elimination of Absalom.

105. See 2 Samuel 12, where Nathan tells David the story of the Poor Man's Lamb.

someone who was so far beneath the king in status that she could present a petition and expect to be heard.[106]

Like Beeman's verbally adroit individuals,[107] Joab knew how to supply those elements that would create the scenes that they wished to have operative in the minds of others. He could effect at second hand the establishment of a believable and effective scenario and use it to gain the outcome he desired.[108] He described the role he wished the woman to perform: that of a longtime mourning widow whose misery stemmed from the fact that of her two sons, one was destined for death because he had killed his brother in a fight in the open air. Joab told her exactly how he wanted her to play the scene. He simply manipulated David by giving a convincing woman a convincing tale to tell,[109] which she did effectively by using polite and formal speech that alternated between abasing her own status and honoring that of the king.[110] But, of course, at first sight what David saw was a miserable-looking widow, and these images were created by her clothes and bodily attitude in them. Thereafter, although she acted as Joab's agent, this Wise Woman of Tekoa manipulated David's mind by filling out the details of the false scenario in which he may be depended on to act honorably. The woman she conjured up for him is of such a low social standing that the king would be sure to pity her and listen to her and without fear of coercion.[111] David had no fear of losing face in this scenario and while acceding to her request realized that he had been put in the position where he must also forgive Absalom. Too late, he recognized Joab's role in changing his mind.

Ruth was a completely marginal figure. She was a poor, childless, and sonless foreign widow with no access to resources or rights in Bethlehem. She had to walk from Moab, then begin her gleaning work at the edges of the fields.[112] Quickly,

---

106. 2 Samuel 14.

107. Beeman, *Language*, 66.

108. See also, Goffman, *Frame Analysis*, 43–4.

109. Beeman, *Language*, 67.

110. Ibid., 140: "One important strategy people use in dealing with others is to indicate elevation of the status of the other person in interaction, placing a positive value on the action of those others and to indicate depreciation and lowering of one's own status while placing a negative value on one's own action. Furthermore, all parties in interaction must be able to use ambiguous and subtle language that contains at least three elements: (1) other-raisin elements, (2) self-lowering elements, and (3) a variational structure that allows both sets of elements to be used simultaneously by all parties without logical contradiction."

111. Cf. Rizpah's clever use of a rock "wearing" a piece of sackcloth to emulate a mourner, in her bid to change David's mind, in Heather A. McKay, "Making a Difference, Then and Now: The Very Different Afterlives of Dinah and Rizpah," in *Making a Difference: Essays on the Bible and Judaism in Honour of Tamara Cohn Eskenazi*, Hebrew Bible Monographs, 49, ed. David J. A. Clines, Kent Harold Richards, and Jacob L. Wright (Sheffield: Sheffield Phoenix, 2012), 224–41.

112. It is important that readers envisage the body position necessary for gleaning, especially for many hours and while reaching into awkward corners.

however, the narrator moves her closer to the center of power, Boaz the landowner. She shared his lunch break and was thereafter allowed to move throughout the fields to glean. Physically she became more visible and central. But she was still excluded from participation at the higher level in society by her poverty and (wrong) ethnicity. Ruth trod a very narrow line indeed when she anointed and dressed and re-presented herself, even *recreated* herself as a (would-be) bride and confronted Boaz late one evening, at the threshing floor, in a situation where skirt "covering" and "uncovering" were quite feasible.[113] The darkness aided her partial disguise, and Boaz did not immediately recognize her. However, she had no need to be afraid for, luckily for her, everyone—Boaz included—knew what an "honest" woman she was.[114] Readers can almost hear the gnashed teeth of the disappointed Bethlehem gossips, the women of the town.

Setting to one side the question of where such a poverty-stricken young woman could find the means to anoint herself and acquire "best clothes" to put on, readers note that her finer attire and perfume allowed her to approach Boaz as more nearly his social equal and also signaled silently her desire to change to a new role—that of being his wife. At first, Boaz replied to this "speaking" silence in no more than a nonverbal utterance of untranslatable surprise at being thus awakened.[115] Then he asked who she was, and she replied: "I am Ruth, your servant; spread your cloak over your servant, for you are next-of-kin."[116] Boaz responded favorably and matters progressed as Naomi had hoped and planned for. Readers feel certain that her gleaner's dress could not have effected this drastic change of status quite so successfully!

Conclusions

A close examination of the variety of roles, functions, and messages—patent and subliminal—carried out by a person's dress, followed by a detailed study of the effects, motivations, and outcomes of a person changing their mode of dress, has led to the realization that, while dress can communicate quite clearly a range of matters about a person, let alone that person's mood, desires, and aims, the communication via dress offered by the wearer,[117] and effected in the mind of the interlocutor or observer, is often disparate and always likely to be highly slippery.

113. Ruth 3:9; cf. Deut. 22:30; 27:20; and Ezek. 16:8, where an undisturbed skirt functions as a circumlocution for sexual integrity.

114. Ruth 3:11.

115. R. Davidson, personal communication, *ca.* November1983; in class, the professor produced a growl of indrawn breath shading into a muffled shriek.

116. Ruth 3:9.

117. Sol Tax in General Editor's Preface to the collection of papers (mainly) from sessions of the IXth International Congress of Anthropological and Ethnological Societies and collected and published as: Cordwell and Schwarz, *The Fabrics of Culture*.

Furthermore, the readers of texts describing these matters also join the ranks of observers and are, hence, subject to misreading the clues contained in data about what the characters in the narrative are wearing or carrying. The readers' own understandings of human life and their awareness that the motivations, altruistic or otherwise to which humans are prone, along with the cultural, familial, financial, social, or religious constraints acting on a person's choices in every sphere throughout life, all these may yet be limited due simply to lack of experience in those aspects of life. Their remaining lack of insight and understanding may mislead them at numerous places within the narratives. Sustained reflection on the function of the material objects in a narrative becomes essential in order to arrive at an even more worthwhile reading.

The varied possibilities provided by adoption of different types of dress in the creation of false scenarios become evident. Moreover, a change of dress can actually enable or create a change of role and status. An adroit speaker, or rather, performer, can thus create situations or junctures in familiar scenarios where the targets can do little other that follow the paths laid before them *but* whether as gulled victims or wary protagonists remains a moot point.

Close readings of several biblical narratives have made plain the crucial role of dress in the creation of false scenarios devised with the intention of deception in mind.

First, the failed attempt of Adam and Eve to hide their wrongdoing by masking the evidence of it occurred because in their situation it was truly impossible to use their dress as a disguise.

Secondly, the various "thefts" perpetrated by Jacob—of Esau's birthright, by Tamar—of Judah's semen, by Laban—of years of Jacob's labor, and by Joseph—of his brothers' privacy in consultations, all these manipulations depended entirely on the use of deceptive dress or disguises while Saul's lack of success in his disguise before the medium of Endor and Ahab's similar failure on the battlefield allowed those two latter stories to show kings being put in their place for overweening self-pride. Similarly, David's amour propre received a knock when Joab's neat trap, which depended on the Wise Woman's disguise as a miserably bereft widow being successful, forced him to change his mind by her creation of a powerful and compelling false scenario.[118]

Ruth used a successful ploy when she raised the unconsidered option of marriage in Boaz's mind by presenting him suddenly with the idea of what her presence at his side could mean. Her success definitely depended on her improved appeal and scented and finely clad appearance. Ruth could envision herself *as a different* person and had the confidence in that role to keep calm when Boaz awoke startled and disorientated.

---

118. A method successfully applied against David also by Nathan (see unpublished conference paper: H. McKay, "Showing Respect through Deception: Nathan, Joab and Joseph," International Organization for the Study of the Old Testament, Helsinki, July 2010) and Rizpah (see McKay, "Making a Difference, Then and Now," 224–41).

Dressing a person differently certainly produces different reactions from both interlocutors and observers, including also the readers of biblical narratives. The different dress actually enables the "player" to keep confident and secure in foreshadowing the proposed new role as it did for Ruth.

Chapter 3

STYLING EVE AND ADAM'S CLOTHES: AN EXAMINATION OF RECEPTION HISTORY

Sara M. Koenig

In 2016 the Fitzwilliam Museum in Cambridge announced that Adam and Eve were unclothed again. Centuries after someone had painted a veil over the naked Eve and a loincloth over the naked Adam in an illustrated manuscript from the medieval period, a new technology had removed the artistic alterations, restoring the image of the biblical couple to its original state of nudity.[1] The prudishness of that anonymous artist notwithstanding, there are a surprising variety of interpretations about when exactly Adam and Eve were naked and clothed, especially given the clear sequential descriptions in Genesis 3: realizing that they are naked, the two cover themselves with fig leaves (Gen. 3:7), and are subsequently clothed by the LORD God in "garments of skin" (Gen. 3:21). In addition to the various answers about the timing of their nakedness and their covering, there is also a variety of biblical receptions about the nature of the "garments of skin." The "skin" has been interpreted literally as skin of different animals or even as human epidermis; that latter reception implies that before being clothed in skin the first humans were glorious, even celestial beings. "Skin" is also understood more metaphorically, signifying such things as sacrifice and protection, or mortality and shame.

This chapter will explore the reception history of the clothing of Adam and Eve, noting the diverse ways in which their clothing has been received throughout history. Reception history helps us see the manifold possibilities in the text—that there is no single meaning for any given biblical text and, in this case, there is no single possible meaning for Adam and Eve's clothing.[2] An

---

1. https://www.theguardian.com/artanddesign/2016/jul/25/adam-eve-naked-again-after-centuries-old-cover-up-fitzwilliam-museum (accessed August 4, 2018).

2. Drawing on French theorist Giles Deleuze's distinction between the "virtual" and the "actual," we can assert that an actual reception of a text at a certain time in history does not rule out other virtual possibilities. These terms are especially helpful in their capacity to account for new readings of texts insofar as the actual is that which exists in the world of our experience. The virtual, by contrast, refers to the conditions and capacities

admittedly deserved critique of biblical reception histories is that they resemble "scrapbooks of effects" that simply display what the author finds interesting, meaningful, or memorable.[3] If this reception history (inevitably) includes some elements of that, it will also account for two other important aspects in reception history: first, the active role of the person who receives the text, and second, the implications or consequences of such receptions. Though the word "reception" can sound passive, reception history is aware that those who receive the text play an active role in making it into something different.[4] Eric Ziolkowski uses an analogy from American football, where a "receiver" who catches a pass thrown by a quarterback must advance the ball down the field.[5] In order to highlight the role played by the receiver, this chapter will draw on the theory of social perception and perceiver variables from studies on dress from the field of social psychology. As noted above, implications of receptions are important to consider because receptions are not neutral.[6] In particular, this chapter will pay attention to theological and anthropological implications of the receptions of the humans' clothing. For example, when Gary A. Anderson explains that the type of clothing God gave Adam and Eve would help them survive outside the garden, this portrays God as one who cares for the humans even after they disobeyed

that generate the actual and allow it to transform. Giles Deleuze, *Difference and Reception* (New York: Columbia University Press, 1994), 212, 239, 245. Brennan Breed, in *Nomadic Text: A Theory of Biblical Reception History* (Bloomington: Indiana University Press, 2014), uses an analogy of the sky to explain,

> When one looks at the sky one experiences the current "actual" color of the sky. But we would be wrong to think that the current color of the sky exhausts the reality of the coloring power of the sky. On the contrary, the potential power of the sky to turn a wide variety of colors, even surprising or unusual ones, is just as real as the actual color that is manifest at any present moment. (121)

3. Rachel Nicholls, *Walking on Water: Reading Mt. 14:22-33 in the Light of Its Wirkungsgeschichte* (Leiden: Brill, 2006), 190.

4. In response to an article by Brennan Breed, in which he compares biblical texts to animals in a zoo escaping their cages, Nyasha Junior writes to clarify that texts do not have agency on their own, "Texts do not swim, slither, or run, and biblical scholars are not chasing them down wearing pith helmets and waving butterfly nets … Instead, texts are repurposed, corralled, and coerced into new contexts." Nyasha Junior, "Re/Use of Texts," http://www.atthispoint.net/editor-notes/reuse-of-texts/265/.

5. Eric Ziolkowski, "Webinar: Exploring the Bible and Its Impact with EBR Online," June 24, 2020.

6. Choon-Leong Seow refers to this process of paying attention to the implications of interpretations as the "history of consequences." He points out how receptions or interpretations are not always neutral but instead have consequences. Seow, *Job 1–21* (Grand Rapids, MI: Eerdmans, 2013), 184–5.

God.[7] When Church Father Origen interpreted human skin as punishment, such an interpretation can have the consequence of a functional gnosticism in understanding the human body.[8] To use another analogy, these receptions of the clothing of Adam and Eve are like rivers whose sources can be traced to the text of Genesis 3 but whose waterways branch out and divide into various channels and streams. Many of these streams flow independently, but others resemble braided rivers, those which flow as several interconnected streams of water. These multiple receptions and perceptions of Adam and Eve's clothing—and their nakedness—flow through the centuries in ways that matter for theology and anthropology.

Every biblical narrative contains gaps, and I contend that it is these lacunae in the text that inspire various receptions.[9] For example, though the text says that God clothed the humans in "garments of skin" (Gen. 3:21), neither the type of garments nor skin is detailed. Receptions fill the gaps by claiming the garment was an apron or a tunic; made from the skin of the serpent in Genesis 3 or a goat, as discussed below. But not all gaps are equal.[10] While some open up possibilities for different interpretations, others can lead to religious disagreements. In Scott R. A. Starbuck's chapter in this volume, he notes how reading the gaps in Genesis 3 as "initiation riddles" may promote stronger self-agency for one who has suffered from trauma, even of a religious sort.

Social Perception and Perceiver Variables

Social perception refers to the cognitive process by which one person uses information to form impressions of another. Within the field of the social psychology of dress, social perception accounts for how the perceiver selects cues from another's attire or appearance and then makes judgments based on those cues. This process can include "interpretive inference," when the perceiver infers traits to the one being perceived, typically on the basis of the selectively perceived

---

7. Gary A. Anderson, "The Garments of Skin in Apocryphal Narrative and Biblical Commentary," in *Studies in Ancient Midrash*, ed. James Kugel (Harvard: Harvard University Press, 2001), 110.

8. In other words, if physical skin—and the human body—is understood as a punishment, that idea can lead to a devaluing of the physical body.

9. See *Bathsheba Survives* (Columbia: University of South Carolina Press, 2018), 2–4.

10. Meir Sternberg explains that some gaps are simple elements that a reader can link automatically, while others are "intricate networks that are figured out consciously, laboriously, hesitantly, and with constant modifications in the light of additional information disclosed in later stages of the reading." Meir Sternberg, *The Poetics of Biblical Narrative* (Bloomington: Indiana University Press, 1987), 186. Moreover, Sternberg differentiates between a "gap" and a "blank," with the latter being a detail that is intentionally omitted and need not be filled in for the story to still signify (236).

cue(s) and the meaning that the perceiver associates with those cues.[11] For example, when I see a woman wearing a camouflage uniform, her uniform is the cue I select to infer that she is a member of the armed forces. Within the reception history of the clothing of Adam and Eve, social perception accounts for the process by which different interpreters take the textual clues about their clothing to infer theological or anthropological meaning.

Perceiver variables are those aspects of the perceiver that affect what she or he perceives. These can include physical traits such as the perceiver's visual acuity, personal traits such as goals or values, and cognitive structures such as memory or knowledge.[12] If a person varies her clothing—changing out of her military uniform into an evening gown, for example—the social perceptions of her will change. But perceiver variables account for why the same dress can receive different interpretations from different perceivers. In what sounds very similar to a hermeneutical focus on "the reader," Sharron J. Lennon and Leslie L. Davis write, "The sheer multitude of possible perceiver variables seems to suggest that much of perception could reside in the perceiver."[13] Instead of simply drawing on reader-response criticism to account for variations in receptions, I find these theories—social perception and perceiver variables—especially helpful because of their focus on clothing and dress. To echo Lennon and Davis, the sheer multitude of receptions about the clothing of Adam and Eve confirms that there is more than one way to receive their attire, and the reception is done by the receiver. There are also areas of surprising congruence, as between Christian and Jewish receptions of the clothing acts in Genesis, especially given the sharp disagreement of what each religion thinks happens in the Garden of Eden.

A Time to Dress: Being Naked and Clothed

The single word "clothing" in English carries a double meaning, as it can function as a noun or a verb.[14] This section will focus on Adam and Eve's clothing as a

11. W. John Lively and Dennis Basil Bromley describe a total of four stages in the process: after cue selection and interpretive inference, the third stage is "extended inference," and the fourth stage is "anticipatory set" of expected behaviors. W. John Lively and Dennis Basil Bromley, *Person Perception in Childhood and Adolescence* (New York: John Wiley & Sons, 1973).

12. Other perceiver variables would include the perceiver's mentifacts and sociofacts. Not only is dress itself significant as a mentifact and sociofact, as Antonios Finitsis explains in the Introduction, but these two categories could account for the guiding principles in the perceiver's mind and the facts of the perceiver's social organization (pp. 3–13).

13. Sharron J. Lennon and Leslie L. Davis, "Clothing and Human Behavior from a Social Cognitive Framework Part 1: Theoretical Perspectives," *Clothing and Textiles Research Journal* 7.4 (Summer 1989), 42.

14. Finitsis makes the same claim about "dress" in the introduction to this volume, explaining, "As a noun, it is what is done to the body, and dress as a verb is how it is done.

verb, noting the possibilities for the timing of that action. Gary A. Anderson comments, "This simple narrative progression of nakedness, leaves, and then garments is almost never handled in a simple fashion."[15] The receptions support Anderson's assertion, with at least three possible frames for when Adam and Eve were clothed: (i) in the garden before they ate from the fruit of the tree; (ii) with fig leaves after they ate the fruit; and (iii) when their fig-leaf couture was replaced with garments made of skin.[16] The medieval Apocalypse of Moses suggests a further variation for possibility (ii), in that Adam and Eve are not clothed at the same time: Eve first makes her "fig apron" before giving naked Adam the fruit. He apparently did not notice that she was wearing a garment made of fig leaves (Apocalypse of Moses, xx.5–xxi.5).[17] In the Genesis Rabbah—which does have Adam and Eve as being naked in the garden initially—there is a suggested timing change for the narrative:

> Why is the story [of the snake and the temptation] placed [after Gen. 2:25]? It should have been placed after the verse, "*And he made for Adam and his wife coats of skins and clothed them.*" Certainly the purpose was to inform you as to why the snake leapt upon them: he had seen them naked and making love in view of all and became attracted to her. (Gen. Rabbah 18:6)

There is the possibility that Adam and Eve were not clothed with garments of skin until after being expelled from the garden, as indicated by the late medieval image shown in Figure 3.1.

Most art, however, has Adam and Eve clothed leaving the Garden of Eden. The Italian rabbi, commentator, and physician Sforno (*ca.* 1475–1550) specifies that God "did not drive them out naked, lest they later dress themselves through their own efforts, and thereby believe that they had attained a higher status."[18] Sforno, like many commentators, ascribes motives to God's acts of dressing the humans, but a theological implication of his reception is that God's act of clothing the humans was a teaching tool, to remind them of their low status.

The implication here is that a research ought to be alert both to the 'what' and to the 'how' questions" (p. 2). In this section, I will also consider the "when."

15. Anderson, "The Garments of Skin," 104.

16. The different receptions do not always distinguish between the three possible moments of clothing but instead sometimes collapse them, such as when Rashi asserts that the events in Gen. 3:21 took place before the serpent encountered the humans. Radaq similarly reads the verbs as pluperfects, pertaining to earlier events. Ibid., 115.

17. https://www.newadvent.org/fathers/0828.htm.

18. A. J. Rosenberg, ed., *Genesis*, Mikraoth Gedoloth, Judaica Books of the Torah (New York: Judaica, 1993), 60.

Figure 3.1 "Adam and Eve Eating the Forbidden Fruit; The Expulsion from Paradise," unknown, about 1400–1410, Tempera colors, gold, silver paint, and ink on parchment. Leaf: 33.5 × 23.5 cm (13 3/16 × 9 1/4 in.), Ms. 33 (88.MP.70), fol. 5v. The J. Paul Getty Museum, Los Angeles.
Source: The J. Paul Getty Museum, Los Angeles: Open Content Program.

A Style to Dress: Royal and Priestly

That Adam and Eve were clothed in the garden before eating from the fruit of the tree is certainly not the most common reception. As mentioned above, they are predominantly depicted as naked in the garden, especially in Western iconography. Eastern traditions, however, suggest other possibilities, as in a fifth-century floor mosaic from Syria in which Adam is depicted regally sitting on a throne, fully clothed, and exercising dominion over the animals. Because the specific animals in this image include those typically understood to be predators—a winged griffon, a jackal, a bear, and a mongoose—Henry Maguire asserts, "The animals' tame demeanor indicates that the setting is the Earthly Paradise and that the time is before the Fall."[19] Maguire goes on to identify what he refers to as "one striking anachronism" in the mosaic:

19. Henry Maguire, "Adam and the Animals: Allegory and the Literal Sense in Early Christian Art," *Dumbarton Oaks Papers* 41 (1987), 368. Other Syriac mosaics and certain Russian icons depict Adam and Eve wearing decorative clothing in the garden. For example,

Adam is not naked, as the biblical account requires, but fully clothed. This is a certain clue that the designer of the mosaic did not intend us to read the story in its literal sense, for a fully clothed Adam, enthroned, and reading from a book, is no part of the account in Genesis. This Earthly Paradise can only be understood in the spiritual sense as allegory.[20]

Maguire here demonstrates his own perceiver variable: the assumption that a literal interpretation cannot also involve allegorical elements or vice versa. As we will see below, a number of receptions of the clothing of Adam and Eve will conflate the literal and allegorical. Such moves were quite common for centuries, as with Origen, and throughout the medieval "senses of scripture." The social perception of the unknown mosaic designer could have been that Adam was clothed before the Fall, when ruling over the animals.[21] Then again, perhaps a king—or other royalty—commissioned and paid for the art, and the image of Adam enthroned reflects the social perception of the patron, not that of the artist. Though we may not be able to definitively identify whose perception gets reflected, language about social perception must consider the perceiver.

While Adam's seat—a throne—in the Syrian floor mosaic suggests his robes are royal, the Midrash Abkir specifies that Adam wore priestly attire pre–fig leaf, saying, "God made high-priestly garments for Adam which were like those of the angels; but when he sinned, God took them away from him and he put on fig leaves."[22] Another midrash describes the elaborate wedding celebration of the first couple and includes the detail that "God Himself, before presenting her to Adam, attired and adorned Eve as a bride."[23] All these receptions share the relatively uncommon idea that Adam and Eve were clothed, not naked, before the Fall, but the variable is in the type of their clothing.

Other receptions have Adam and Eve dressed in glory before eating from the tree, though this need not be read as literal clothing. For example, in the Apocalypse of Moses, Eve asks the serpent, "Why have you done this to me, in that

Gary Anderson discusses an image from the Stroganov Icons titled "Creation of the First Humans and Expulsion from Eden." In the top half of the image, Adam is clothed, but in the bottom half—the expulsion—the two are topless, clad only in short skirt-like garments. Gary Anderson, *The Genesis of Perfection* (Louisville, KY: Westminster John Knox, 2001), 118.

20. Maguire, "Adam and the Animals," 368.

21. Another possibility is that the book from which Adam is reading is the legendary holy book of wisdom—the Sepher Ha-Razim ("the book of mysteries")—from God and the angels. If this is the book, however, the tradition gives two possibilities for the timing of it: in the Zohar, God directs the angel Raziel to give Adam this book while Adam is in paradise (1, 55b), but in another version of the legend, Adam receives the book after the Fall, in response to his prayer for knowledge and help. Louis Ginzberg and David Stern, *Legends of the Jews* (Philadelphia, PA: Jewish Publication Society, 2003), 89–90.

22. Ibid., 79; Anderson, "The Garments of Skin," 123.

23. Ginzberg and Stern, *Legends of the Jews*, 66.

I have been deprived of the glory with which I was clothed?"[24] As discussed above, the Apocalypse of Moses is the text that includes Eve making a fig-leaf apron for herself because she realized her nakedness, so the glory to which she refers in that narrative is most likely more symbolic than an actual glorious piece of clothing. A Lebanese Christian liturgical text (date uncertain) is not definitive about the glory as a physical garment but leaves open the possibility as it explains,

> With radiance and glory was Adam clothed at the beginning, before he sinned; the Evil one was envious, led Eve astray, and had Adam ejected from Paradise: he was then covered by fig leaves in place of the glory with which he had been clothed.[25]

Similarly, the Zohar reads, "Before the fall they were dressed in 'garments of light' ... after the fall in 'garments of skin,' which were useful only for the body, not for the soul" (1, 36b). The connection between light and skin is because of the Hebrew homophone אוֹר/ עוֹר ('ôr/'ôr), which I will discuss in more detail below as I review the various possibilities for the materials out of which their garments were made.

Reasons to Dress: Art and Sex

Why Fig Leaves?

According to Gen. 3:7, "The eyes of the two of them were opened, and they knew that they were naked, and they sewed together fig leaves, and made themselves coverings."[26] If the receptions agree that the material for these garments came from fig foliage, they offer variations in their reasons for that botanical material. A midrash explains that there was no other option, for Adam "heard one tree after the other say, 'There is the thief that deceived his Creator ... take no leaves from me!' Only the fig-tree granted him permission to take of its leaves. That was because the fig was the forbidden fruit itself."[27] Philo (*ca.* 20 BCE–50 CE) suggested more sexually oriented explanations for the choice of the fig leaves, noting that while the taste of a fig is sweet and pleasant, like sexual pleasure, its leaves are rough, like the pain that sometimes accompanies things surrounding sex, such as female menstruation and childbirth.[28] Twentieth-century German theologian Erik

24. https://www.newadvent.org/fathers/0828.htm.

25. Sebastian Brock, "Clothing Metaphors as a Means of Theological Expression in Syriac Tradition," in *Typus, Symbol, Allegorie bei den östlichen Vätern und ihren Parallelen im Mittelalter*, ed. Margot Schmidt and Carl Friedrich Geyer (Regensburg: Friedrich Pustet, 1981), 14; Anderson, "The Garments of Skin," 112–15.

26. All translations are my own.

27. Ginzberg and Stern, *Legends of the Jews*, 72.

28. Stephen N. Lambden, "From Fig Leaves to Fingernails: Some Notes on the Garments of Adam and Eve in the Hebrew Bible and Select Early Postbiblical Jewish Writings," in

Peterson connected the fig leaves with that "tree to which the Son of God went when hungry, only to find it unfruitful and its leaves withered."[29] Some sixteen centuries earlier, Ephrem the Syrian also connected that cursed fig tree (Mt. 21:18-22) with the material worn by the first humans, in Ephrem's baptismal liturgy, as will be noted below.

The Hebrew word for their garment, חגרת (*ḥăḡōrōṯ*), has been translated into English as "aprons," "loincloths," "girdles," "sashes," and even "breeches."[30] Stephen N. Lambden notes that it is difficult to tell whether this first garment signifies a more or less adequate means of attire than the כתנת (*kĕṯōnet*) in 3:21,[31] though that latter piece of clothing gets translated as apparel that would cover more than the English words used in 3:7: "coats," "garments," "tunics," "robes," in addition to the more generic "clothes." Lambden himself eventually argues that the כתנת does cover more. He reasons that God demonstrates God's superior wisdom in making the humans coats of skin; the humans were foolish to think they could adequately cover themselves with "aprons."[32] In this argument, Lambden's theological and anthropological assumptions are clear—that God's knowledge and provision are greater than that of the humans. By contrast, Severian of Gabala, a late-fourth-century Syrian bishop, perceives an anthropological skill in the first humans. Severian comments on the "inventiveness of the artisans" making the garments of fig leaves, explaining, "Adam's first skill was sewing; before exercising any other skill he took fig leaves and stitched them together."[33] Yet another interpretation comes from contemporary author Friedhelm Hartenstein, who reflects on the change from Adam and Eve's previous condition of being together naked and unashamed (Gen. 2:25). Hartenstein suggests that they each separately made a garment for himself/herself, "in order not to be exposed to each other anymore."[34] As a result

A Walk in the Garden: Exegesis, Iconography and Literature, ed. P. Morris and D. Sawyer (Sheffield: Sheffield Academic Press, 1992), 84.

29. Erik Peterson, "A Theology of Dress," *Com* 20 (Fall 1993), 564.

30. In fact, the sixteenth-century Geneva Bible—one of the earliest complete translations of the Old and New Testaments into English, predating the King James version by some fifty years—is also known as the "Breeches" bible, based on its particular—and singular—translation of Gen. 3:7.

31. Lambden, "From Fig Leaves to Fingernails," 77.

32. Ibid.

33. Severian was supposedly involved in the downfall, exile, and eventual death of John Chrysostom. *Commentaries on Genesis 1–3: Severian of Gabala and Bede the Venerable. Commentaries on Genesis 1–3*, ed. Michael Glerup, trans. Robert C. Hill and Carmen S. Hardin, Ancient Christian Texts (Downers Grove, IL: InterVarsity, 2010), 81.

34. Friedhelm Hartenstein, "Clothing and Nudity in the Paradise Story (Gen. 2–3)," in *Clothing and Nudity in the Hebrew Bible*, ed. Christoph Berner, Manuel Schäfer, Martin Schott, Sarah Schulz, and Martina Weingärtner (London: T&T Clark, 2019), 369.

of Hartenstein's perceiver variable, the humans' fig-leaf garments are understood as cover and concealment against interpersonal connection.[35]

Materials to Dress

Plant Skins: Texture and Healing

Perhaps because Gen. 3:7 definitively states that the material used is "fig leaves," there is much more debate about the type of textile used for the garments in 3:21: "And YHWH God made for Adam and his wife garments of skin, and he clothed them." One, relatively infrequent reception, is that the "skins" are plant material. For example, the Syriac apocryphal "The Book of the Cave of Treasures" explains,

> God made for them tunics of skin which was stripped from the trees, that is to say, of the bark of the trees, because the trees that were in Paradise had soft barks, and they were softer than the byssus and silk wherefrom the garments worn by kings are made. And God dressed them in this soft skin, which was thus spread over a body of infirmities.[36]

Two aspects of this reception are worth highlighting: first, this reception may share some social perception with those receptions that understand Adam to have had a royal role in Eden, as it connects the tree-bark tunics with those garments worn by kings. Second, the motive given to God for this act makes God sound like a healer, dressing a wound.[37] The theological implication is that God cares for the "infirm" humans. R. Joḥanan did not definitively state whether the skins were animal or plant, but rather than being made of skin, he understood them to be those worn nearest to the skin. He said they were "like the fine linen garments which come from Bethshean."[38]

Animal Skins: Death, Sin, and Punishment

Most understand the skin to come from animals, but within kingdom Animalia, a variety of vertebrate possibilities are given. R. Eleazar argued that they were made

---

35. In this volume, Heather A. McKay offers the explanation that Adam and Eve clothe themselves in the fig-leaf garment to hide their wrongdoing (see pp. 46–7, 54.).

36. *The Book of the Cave of Treasures*, trans. Sir E. A. Wallis Budge (London: Religious Tract Society, 1927), 65, https://www.sacred-texts.com/chr/bct/bct04.htm.

37. G. Brooke Lester, private correspondence.

38. H. Freedman, trans., *Midrash Rabbah Genesis*, ed. H. Freedman and Maurice Simon (London: Soncino, 1983), 171. In the second century CE, Bethshean was known by the Greek name Sycthopolis and became one of the textile centers of the Roman Empire, likely because of its famed linen.

of goat's skin, while R. Joshua said they came from the skin of hares (Gen. Rabbah 20:12). A Jewish legend has God using the skin stripped from the hapless serpent as the material for the garments. Not only would this action punish the serpent further but this legend specifies God's motivation for this as being "full of pity for Adam and his wife."[39] R. Samuel b. Naḥman understood "garments of skin" to refer to that which comes off of the skin, namely, "the wool of camels and the wool of hares." Resh Laḳish identified the wool as specifically "Circassian" sheep wool, connected with the type of clothing worn by those who performed sacrifices before the priests.[40] The same late medieval manuscript that depicted Adam and Eve clad in fig leaves has them wearing woolly garments while Adam works the land and Eve attends to young Cain and Abel, after they have been expelled from the garden (Figure 3.2).

Interpreters' social perception led them to make different interpretive inferences about the specific type of material used for the garments. Church Father Jerome, for example, understood things made of animal products as bad insofar as they were a sign of death.[41] The Pythagoreans believed that wool in particular contrasted with linen. Second-century philosopher Apuleius of Madaura referred to linen as *purissimum velamentum* for divine things, coming from the most pure seed of one of the best plants earth produces, which was why it was used by Egyptian priests for their vestments, but he described wool as "the excretory product of a sluggish body taken from an animal."[42] Reformer John Calvin writes that the reason he thinks they were clothed with garments of skin is

> because garments formed of this material would have a more degrading appearance than those made of linen or of woolen. God therefore designed that our first parents should, in such a dress, behold their own vileness, just as they had before seen it in their nudity, and should thus be reminded of their sin. [43]

39. Ginzberg and Stern, *Legends of the Jews*, 76–7. God's pity is contrasted with the callous response from the moon, the only created being that did not grieve with Adam and Eve.

> When the serpent seduced Adam and Eve, and exposed their nakedness, they wept bitterly, and with them wept the heavens, and the sun and the stars, and all created beings and things up to the throne of God. The very angels and the celestial beings were grieved by the transgression of Adam. The moon alone laughed, wherefore God grew wroth, and obscured her light. Instead of shining steadily like the sun, all the length of the day, she grows old quickly, and must be born and reborn, again and again. (Ibid.)

40. Genesis Rabbah, 171.

41. Johannes Quasten, "A Pythagorean Idea in Jerome," *The American Journal of Philology* 63.2 (1942), 207–15.

42. Ibid., 209–10.

43. John Calvin, *Commentary on Genesis, Volume 1*, ed. and trans. John King (Edinburgh: Banner of Truth Trust, 1965), 182.

Figure 3.2 "Adam and Eve Working; The Sacrifice of Cain and Abel," unknown, about 1400–1410, Tempera colors, gold, silver paint, and ink on parchment. Leaf: 33.5 × 23.5 cm (13 3/16 × 9 1/4 in.), Ms. 33 (88.MP.70), fol. 6. The J. Paul Getty Museum, Los Angeles. *Source*: The J. Paul Getty Museum, Los Angeles: Open Content Program.

Martin Luther has a similar take, but his language is slightly milder than Calvin's, as he says,

> God Himself gave Adam and Eve clothes to remind them of their wretched Fall. As often as they put them on, they were to think how sorely they had fallen from the greatest blessedness into the deepest misery … God clothed them with the skins of slain animals to remind them that they were in mortal and lived in constant danger of death.[44]

Calvin also admonishes those who desire to wear anything more than simple garments, explaining, "When immoderate elegance and splendor is carefully sought after, not only is that Master despised, who intended clothing to be a sign of shame, but war is, in a certain sense, carried on against nature."[45] For Calvin, God's clothing signifies punishment and shame. In contrast, Anderson, who

44. Martin Luther, *Luther's Commentary on Genesis: Volume I*, trans J. Theodore Mueller (Grand Rapids, MI: Zondervan, 1958), 85.

45. Calvin, *Commentary on Genesis*, 182.

understands the garments of skin as made from animals and therefore superior to those made from the fig leaves, credits God with positive motives, writing, "God graciously condoned to provide man with the garments he would need to survive the vagaries of lie outside the Garden."[46]

Additionally, Calvin asserted that God did not create the garments of skin, "as if God had been a furrier, or a servant to sew clothes."[47] Instead, he argues that God directed Adam and Eve to kill the animals in order to cover themselves with animal skins.[48] Calvin's own language is somewhat sarcastic, but Severian imagines a taunt from "the allegorists," who say, "Surely [God] did not slaughter oxen and sheep, open a tannery and perform the work of a tanner?"[49] While Calvin's solution is to make Adam and Eve the creators of the garments, Severian's reply to the mocking allegorists is:

> [God] produced the animal fully grown, without breeding, without copulation. He made what did not exist: surely he is not incapable of making part of what does exist? ... I hear of blood in Egypt and look for the way he turned the Nile into blood, the great number of animals he slaughtered. The river turned into blood, and no animal was slaughtered; there were two skins, and ... in that case as well there was skin without an animal.[50]

Both receptions include a theological assumption: Calvin understands God as above the act of sacrificing the animals or tailoring garments for the humans, while Severian perceives God's creative power as extending to creating animal skins that did not come from an animal.

Human Skin: Radiance and Corporeality

Another reception of the "garments of skin" in Gen. 3:21 is that the "skin" God provided was neither animal nor plant but human epidermis. In other words, the eating of the fruit of the tree led to God clothing human beings with skin. Previously, Adam and Eve were celestial beings, and they were made human by God covering their forms with skin. In a Talmudic debate about the origins of human life, Rabbi Yehoshua b. Hanina cites Gen. 3:21 and explains, "This text teaches us that the Holy One—blessed be He—does not make skin for a man unless he has been [bodily] formed" (b. Nid. 25a). According to Christian rhetorician

---

46. Anderson, "The Garments of Skin," 110.

47. Calvin ascribes any confusion about this matter to "Moses" (Calvin's understood author of Genesis) because Moses writes "in a homely style" (*Commentary on Genesis*, 181).

48. Ibid.

49. Severian of Gabala, *Homilies on Creation and Fall*, trans. Robert C. Hill, *Ancient Christian Texts: Commentaries on Genesis 1–3*, ed. Michael Glerup (Downers Grove, IL: IVP Academic, 2010), 81.

50. Ibid.

Procopius of Gaza (465–530 CE), the human material body only came into being as a result of the Fall and God clothing Adam and Eve in skins; they had radiant bodies before the Fall.[51] Anderson asserts, "To be clothed in skin is to become human," noting that the Hebrew phrase could be translated as "'skinlike garments' or even 'skin [acting] as garment.' In this understanding, normal human skin is conceived to be a garment that adorns our inner-fleshly self."[52] While both Jewish and Christian receptions include this possible meaning for skin, its theological and anthropological implications become much more developed by the Christian church fathers, as will be discussed below.

Light: Divinity and Luminosity

One stream of reception, seemingly with Rabbi Meir at its headwaters, identifies the homonyms עוֹר (*'ôr*, "skin") and אוֹר (*'ôr*, "light") and reads God's fashion design as luminous clothing, "garments of light."[53] A Jewish interpretation that combines "skin" and "light" explains that the material used was the skin of Leviathan. Leviathan's fins are said to radiate such brilliant light that the sun is obscured by it, and after Leviathan's eschatological death "what is left of Leviathan's skin will be stretched out over Jerusalem as a canopy, and the light streaming from it will illumine the whole world."[54]

God's choice of light as the material for the clothing for humans might be connected with God's own clothing: Ps. 104:2 describes God as one "who wraps Godself in light as with a garment." Ehud Ben Zvi asserts, "Ps. 104:2 refers to the luminescent aspect of the presence of YHWH, not to anthropomorphic garments,"[55] but Pirke de Rabbi Eliezer takes that same verse to reason that God created the heavens "from the light of the garment with which [God] was robed" (PRE 3:7). If God wears light according to receptions of Ps. 104:2 and makes garments of light for the humans, this could be another way that God's creations bear God's image, in their attire.

Anne Catherine Emmerich (1774–1824), a Christian mystic from Westphalia, Germany, also perceived Adam and Eve as dressed in light, describing them in paradise before the Fall as "clothed with beams of light as with a veil."[56] But in

---

51. Anders Lund Jacobsen, "Genesis 1–3 as Source for the Anthropology of Origen," *VC* 62 (2008), 216.

52. Anderson, "The Garments of Skin," 111.

53. Genesis Rabbah, 171.

54. Ginzberg, *Legends of the Jews*, 28–9.

55. Ehud Ben Zvi, "Were YHWH's Clothes Worth Remembering and Thinking About among the Literati of Late Persian/Early Hellenistic Judah/Yehud? Observations and Considerations," in *Dress and Clothing in the Hebrew Bible: "For All Her Household are Clothed in Crimson,"* LHBOTS 679, ed. Antonios Finitsis (London: T&T Clark, 2019), 167.

56. Anne Catherine Emmerich, *The Life of Jesus Christ and Biblical Revelations from the Visions of Blessed Anne Catherine Emmerich 1774–1824*, vol. 1, ed. Carl E. Schmoger (Charlotte, NC: TAN, 2001), EBL edition, chapter 3.

Emmerich's vision, in addition to their garments being made of beams of light, their very beings are also light: Adam and Eve are "like two unspeakably noble and beautiful children, perfectly luminous."[57] Light pours out from their features; "From Adam's mouth I saw a broad stream of glittering light," which represents the holiness of his spoken word before the Fall. She also sees their hair glittering and notes that the lack of incandescence of the average human hair today is because "our hair is the ruined, the extinct glory." Emmerich even saw that "from the hands and feet of Adam and Eve, shot rays of light."[58] It could be that the blurred line between Adam and Eve's shining clothing and their shining bodies ties back to the Hebrew homonym; it could also be a shared social perception between perceivers. The church fathers also highlighted the theme of the clothing of light and the glory of the first humans' bodies, discussed below.

Fingernails: Adornment, Impurity, and Holiness

A Jewish stream of interpretation compares the Gen. 3:21 garments to human fingernails. Isaac the Elder, for example, described the clothes God created for the humans as being "as smooth as a fingernail and as beautiful as a jewel."[59] Pirke de Rabbi Eliezer understood fingernails as the material of the primal garment before the humans ate from the tree, writing:

> What was the dress of the first man? A skin of nail, and a cloud of glory covered him. When he ate of the fruits of the tree, the nail-skin was stripped off him, and the cloud of glory departed from him, and he saw himself naked.[60]

Anderson reflects on reasons why these interpreters chose fingernails as the material for the garments and suggests the possibility that fingernails are translucent, "for if Adam's flesh was resplendently effulgent the presence of a fingernail-like covering would allow that effulgence to shine forth."[61] Note here how Anderson, with other perceivers, infers that Adam's body is "light." Anderson also explains that fingernails provide a shield from heat, connecting the "stones of fire" mentioned on the holy mountain of God in Ezek. 28:14 to the idea that those stones were present in Eden. He writes, "If the surface of Eden was nothing

57. Ibid.
58. Ibid.
59. Gen Rabbah, 171.
60. *Pirke De Rabbi Eliezer*, trans. and annotated by Gerald Friedlander (New York: Benjamin Blom, 1971), 98.
61. Anderson, "The Garments of Skin," 118. In ANE iconography of the sun disk, a sun is partly obscured by a cloud. This imagery represents both the presence of the deity as well as its transcendence, partially covered with opaque material. Humans created in the image of God can signal the presence of the deity, but covered in translucent fingernails can still represent God's transcendence. Lester, private correspondence.

other than a swarming cauldron of fiery stones, then some sort of asbestos like shield would have been necessary for its human denizens."[62] Lambden offers other implications for the fingernail material, including that the garments were "smooth, tight-fitting, pearly, translucent and luminous."[63]

According to the Zohar, forces of impurity are connected to fingernails, especially the part that extends beyond the finger and can be cut off;[64] fingernails can attract demons or darkness (3:70a). Orthodox Jews burn their fingernails because of the Talmudic saying, "The righteous bury their nails, the pious burn them, and the wicked carelessly discard them" (Mo'ed Katan 18a and Niddah 17a). But fingernails are also things through which one can access holiness and light, as in the rite at the *Havdalah* (the moment that marks the end of the Sabbath and return to ordinary time), when the faithful are to gaze at their fingernails to remind them of that primordial clothing.[65] The literal, physical covering on the ends of human hands is interpreted as symbolic of what has been lost and might be regained.

Priestly Garments: Power, Nature, and Gender

A common stream of reception, mostly in Jewish sources, connects the clothing with priestly garments, as previously mentioned with the Midrash Abkir. Sebastian Brock notes that the phrase "robe of glory" appears in the Peshitta of Sirach 50:11 to refer to the attire of the priest.[66] There is a tradition that Adam functioned as a priest before the Aaronic or Levitical priesthood. Lambden writes that by about the first century CE, "Adam came, in certain circles, to be seen as a royal, kingly, angelic or divine figure who manifested something of the divine 'glory' (כבוד, δόξα) and who exercised primordial priestly functions."[67] There are different receptions about the material of the garment, or even its timing—as mentioned

---

62. Anderson, "The Garments of Skin," 118. Anderson seems to be quite generous regarding a fingernail's ability to protect from fire, given that a fingernail is composed of keratin, which can melt in the heat.

63. Lambden, "From Fig Leaves to Fingernails," 89.

64. Apparently, this belief relates to instructions for how to cut fingernails; not in sequential order from one's little finger to the thumb, written by Rashi's student Rabbi Simchah ben Shmuel of Vitry, because it can bring forgetfulness, poverty, and premature death of one's children. See Shulchan Aruch, Orach Chaim 260:1; Shulchan Aruch ha-Rav, Orach Chaim 260:3; Mishnah Berurah 260:8.

65. Lambden, "From Fig Leaves to Fingernails," 89; Anderson, "The Garments of Skin," 118. The Rema (OC 298:3) quotes the Zohar that when one makes the blessing on the candles during Havdalah on Motzai Shabbos one should look at the nails of their right hand with the hand curled inward and the thumb tucked away out of sight.

66. Brock, "Clothing Metaphors," 14. The "robe of glory" is also worn by the angel who speaks to Daniel in Dan. 10:5 and 12:7.

67. Lambden, "From Fig Leaves to Fingernails," 78.

above, some have Adam wearing priestly garb before eating from the fruit, while others have him receiving priestly garments after[68]—but they share the same final perception that Adam acts as a priest.

These various receptions do not clarify if Adam's priestly role is because he wears the garments or if the garments connect with the priesthood because of their material. According to Pirke de Rabbi Eliezer, the clothes of skin had their own power (PRE 24). Rabbi Jehudah explained that the "garments of skin" God made for Adam and Eve were with Noah in the ark and were passed down to Ham, Cush, and eventually Nimrod.

> These garments had a wonderful property. He who wore them was both invincible and irresistible. The beasts and birds of the woods fell down before Nimrod as soon as they caught sight of him arrayed in them, and he was equally victorious in his combats with men. The source of his unconquerable strength was not known to them. They attributed it to his personal prowess, and therefore they appointed him king over themselves.[69]

The above interpretation mentions Adam as king, not as priest, and seems to indicate that Adam is only successful while wearing the garments. However, Carmen Joy Imes argues that the high-priestly regalia is both symbolic of the role of the priest and also constitutive of that role.[70] Adam's garments may function similarly: symbolic of various meanings and also constituting aspects of Adam's nature. Although God clearly clothes both Adam and Eve in Gen. 3:21, the receptions which refer to Adam's garments as priestly do not mention Eve wearing priestly clothing; she does not act as a priestess. But this lacuna is not surprising, especially when we consider how social context affects social perception: the lack of women in priestly roles during these historical times makes it very unlikely that the perceivers would view Eve in such a position.

Garments of Glory: Sovereignty and Glory

Social perception of these garments as made of light, discussed above, may have included the idea that they are glorious, and some of the descriptions of the robes as priestly also carry the connotation of glory. Several Aramaic Targumim insert

---

68. Midrash Abkir, for example, has Adam wearing priestly garments before he sinned, but in the Targum of Ezekiel, the description of Adam in Eden has him wearing robes adorned with the same jewels that are on the priestly breastplate. Cf. G. K. Beale, "Adam as the First Priest in Eden as the Garden Temple," *SBJT* 22.2 (2018), 10–11.

69. Ginzberg and Stern, *Legends of the Jews*, 161. One legend explains that Ham had stolen the garments, while Pirkei de Rabbi Eliezer has Noah giving them to Ham.

70. Carmen J. Imes, "Between Two Worlds: The Functional and Symbolic Significance of the High Priestly Regalia," in *Dress and Clothing in the Hebrew Bible: "For All Her Household is Clothed in Crimson,"* LHBOTS 679, ed. Antonios Finitsis (London: T&T Clark, 2019), 30.

the direct description of "glory" into their translations of Gen. 3:21: "The Lord God made for Adam and his wife garments of glory for/over the skin of their flesh."[71] The Peshitta for Ps. 8:6 suggests something similar as it says, "You created humans a little less than angels: in honor and glory did you clothe him."[72] *The Book of the Cave of Treasures* describes Adam's clothing as follows:

> [Adam] was arrayed in the apparel of sovereignty, and there was the crown of glory set upon his head, there was he made king, and priest, and prophet, there did God make him to sit upon his honourable throne, and there did God give him dominion over all creatures and things.[73]

Here, Adam's clothing relates to his role as king, priest, and prophet. As with Emmerich's vision, both Adam's apparel and his visage are glorious in *The Book of the Cave of Treasures*; when the angels look at Adam, they see "the image of his face burning with glorious splendour like the orb of the sun, and the light of his eyes was like the light of the sun, and the image of his body was like unto the sparkling of crystal."[74] As with other receptions, it is not entirely clear if these descriptions are literal or metaphoric. To return to the idea of receptions as streams, it could be that different currents run within the common riverbed of "glory." To draw on the theory of social perception, it could be that glorious clothing has the perceiver infer that those wearing that clothing are, themselves, glorious.[75]

Garments of Salvation: Jesus as the Second Adam and Immortality

Several church fathers make connections between the garments of skin, the garments of glory, and the incarnation, including Origen (184–253), Ephrem the Syrian (306–373), Gregory of Nyssa (*ca.* 335–395), and Augustine (354–430). Origen is not terribly clear, as evidenced by the scholarly debates about what he meant.[76] In a passage from his *Homilies on Leviticus*, Origen contrasts

71. Anderson, "Garments of Skin," 120ff. These Targumim vary regarding their prepositions: Onkelos has "The Lord God made for Adam and his wife garments of glory *over* the skin of their flesh," while Neophyti has "The Lord God made for Adam and his wife garments of glory *for* the skin of their flesh." Anderson writes, "It is important to note that all Targumim preserve a double interpretation of the כתנת עור. They understand the Hebrew phrase to refer to both the 'garments of glory' (לבושין דיקר) and 'fleshly skin' (משך בשרא)" (121).

72. Brock, "Clothing Metaphors," 15. Both the MT and the LXX for Ps. 8:6 have "crown" instead of "clothe."

73. *Cave of Treasures*, 53.

74. Ibid., 52.

75. See the discussions by Brady Beard on p. 29 and S. J. Parrott on pp. 203–7.

76. Cf. Anders Lund Jacobsen, "Genesis 1–3 as Source for the Anthropology of Origen," *Vigiliae Christiane* 62.3 (2008), 213–32; and Alexandra Pârvan, "Genesis 1–3: Augustine and Origen on the 'coats of skin,'" *VC* 66.2 (2012), 56–92.

Aaron's priestly garments—"clothes of faith" (*fidelibus indumentis*)—with the "clothes of unhappiness" (*infelecia indumenta*) that Adam and Eve receive after sinning; those are the skin coats. His main idea is that the "skin coats" refer to the mortal corporeality of humans, and he never assigns a positive connotation to them. Alexandra Pârvan argues that Origen does not want to interpret the "skin coats" literally, but neither does he fully quite approve of them as symbolizing immortality.[77] In places, Origen seems to think that they denote a physical body, but elsewhere it seems as if they connect to mortality.[78] According to Anders Lund Jacobsen, Origen "suggests at the very least that the skin coats have something to do with the fall of the soul leading to its being clothed in a body."[79] If none of Origen's perceptions of the "skin coats" are positive, the (too) easy implication could be that the human corporeal form is something negative. Even such subtle gnosticism, which denigrates the physical body in favor of the immortal soul, can have harsh consequences for our theological anthropology. Starbuck's chapter in this volume demonstrates how God's act of clothing humans in skin can be read not as overly literal or simplistic—something the allegorically minded Origen would appreciate—but as God's empowering act of investiture for humans after their rebellion. In Starbuck's reception, humans can embrace their bodies with awareness of their vulnerability, as well as the belief that those bodies have been created in the image of God and clothed in skin by God.[80]

Ephrem wrote about the imagery of clothing in his "Hymns on Virginity," explaining, "Christ came to find Adam who had gone astray, to return him to Eden in a garment of light."[81] In one of Ephrem's nativity hymns, the symmetry between the fall of Adam and the life of Christ is highlighted by using clothing imagery:

All these changes did the Merciful One make,
stripping off glory and putting on a body;
for He had devised a way to reclothe Adam
in that glory which he had stripped off.
He was wrapped in swaddling clothes,

77. Pârvan, "Genesis 1–3," 77–8.

78. Ibid., 92.

79. Jacobsen, "Genesis 1–3 as a Source for the Anthropology of Origen," 224. Again, while Origen's use of Gen. 3:21 is not entirely clear, Origen primarily draws on Gen. 1:26 to assert that the inner human—the immaterial soul—is what has been created in God's image and resembles the Logos, the son of God, who is God's image (231). Cf. Margaret M. Watzek, "The Theological Anthropology Developed in Origen's Interpretations of Genesis 1:26-30 and Genesis 2:4-9," master's theses (1986), 3493, https://ecommons.luc.edu/luc_theses/3493.

80. Scott R. A. Starbuck, "The Divine Clothing of Adam and Eve and the Hermeneutics of Trauma Recovery," p. 97.

81. Brock, "Clothing Metaphors," 68.

corresponding to Adam's leaves,
He put on clothes in place of Adam's skins;
He was baptized for Adam's sin,
He was embalmed for Adam's death,
He rose and raised Adam up in His glory.
Blessed is He who descended,
put Adam on and ascended.[82]

In this passage, both God's act of (re)clothing the new Adam and the clothes themselves perform a salvific function. Ephrem even perceives Jesus's cursing of the fig tree in Mt. 21:20-21 through the lens of this clothing salvation history typology, writing:

> When Adam sinned and was stripped of the glory in which he had been clothed, he covered his nakedness with fig leaves. Our Savior came and underwent suffering in order to heal Adam's wounds and provide a garment of glory for his nakedness. He dried up the fig tree, in order to show that there would no longer be any need of fig leaves to serve as Adam's garment, since Adam had returned to his former glory, and so no longer had any need of leaves or garments of skin.[83]

For Gregory of Nyssa, a created body could not be negative because it was a (good) creation of God. Instead, Gregory locates the limiting aspects of mortality in the skins that clothed Adam's body in Gen. 3:21. In reference to God's command that Moses remove his sandals in Exod. 3:5, Gregory explained:

> Sandaled feet cannot ascend that height where the light of truth is seen, but the dead and earthly covering of skins, which was placed around our nature at the beginning when we were found naked because of disobedience to the divine will, must be removed from the feet of the soul.[84]

Abraham Malherbe explains that the phrase "placed around our nature" is important for Gregory's anthropology in that "the real self is something other than the fleshly existence."[85] Because Adam did have a body in Eden, the "garments of skin" that come later are not just bodily existence per se. Instead, they represent other things added to the human nature made in the image of God: the passions, sexuality, and mortality.[86]

---

82. Ibid., 69.

83. Ibid.

84. Gregory of Nyssa, *Life of Moses*, trans. Abraham J. Malherbe and Everett Ferguson (New York: Paulist, 1978), 59.

85. Ibid., 160.

86. Ibid.

Baptismal Garments and Ritual Symbolism: Restoration,
Resurrection, and Eschatology

Christian practices of baptism hold together the various possibilities for the garments—as skin, as glory—in their rituals. Brock explains the different stages in Syriac incarnation typology: first, the original Adam loses the robe of glory at the Fall. Then, the second Adam—Christ—puts on the body of the first Adam in the incarnation. This is done so that the robe of glory can be restored to all humans in their baptism, which is the third stage: the Christian puts on "the new self" (Eph. 4:24) or "Christ" (Rom. 13:14; Gal. 3:27) at baptism. A final, eschatological stage makes this garment exchange permanent, when at the resurrection of the dead, the just will reenter the heavenly paradise clothed in robes of glory.[87] Some baptismal liturgies included the nakedness of the one being baptized, a nudity that symbolically—and positively—represented new life.[88] Other baptismal liturgies included the taking off of garments made of goat skin and stomping on those garments, before going into the water. Augustine identifies the goatskin in the Tabernacle (Exod. 26:7) as a reminder of sins, and therefore the trampling on the goatskin in the ritual of baptism may be an allusion to the treading on sin in Gen. 3:15.[89]

Though Augustine's allegory of the "garments of skin" is related to Origen's,[90] his is more complicated. For Augustine, the skins are bad because of their connections with sin and mortality, but they are also good because of the incarnation; Jesus wore human skin and did so with humility. Even though Augustine approved of the ritual of trampling on goatskin during baptismal rites, he also urges catechumens, "clothe yourselves in goatskin" (*induite vos cilicio*).[91] Pârvan discusses the metaphorical implications of this command:

> It is not a skin that the catechumen has to put on so that he may take it off later in the ceremony, but repentance and humility ... skin means sin and mortality, but

87. Brock, "Clothing Metaphors," 16.

88. Jonathan Z. Smith notes that while nudity often represented something negative in Christianity, there are a number of Christian images of nudes that are types of the resurrection: Jonah emerging from the mouth of the big fish, Daniel emerging from the lion's den, and the resurrected bones in Ezekiel's vision. Smith argues that such nudity as a symbol of new life promised in the resurrection, when appearing in connection with baptism, signifies sacramental rebirth. Jonathan Z. Smith, "The Garments of Shame," *HR* 5.2 (Winter 1966), 221–2.

89. Smith, "The Garments of Shame," 229.

90. A number of studies point out parallels between Augustine and Origen, such as Roland J. Teske's "Origen and St. Augustine's First Commentaries on Genesis," *Origenia quinta* (1992), 179–85. György Heidl argued for a direct influence of Origen's writing on Augustine's exegesis in *Origen's Influence on the Young Augustine: A Chapter in the History of Origenism* (Louiaze: Notre Dame University and Georgias Press, 2003).

91. Pârvan, "Genesis 1–3," 65.

also repentance, humility, and rebirth. As such, the coats of skin represent our condition of intermediateness not only inasmuch as they denote our acquired fallen state which requires to be surpassed, but also inasmuch as they could be the precisely the means for this surpassing.[92]

Erik Peterson also allegorizes the clothing and nakedness of the first humans into the rituals of baptism, explaining that before the Fall,

> supernatural grace covered the human person like a garment. Man did not simply stand in the light of the divine glory; he was actually clothed with it. But, through sin, man lost this divine glory, and when we see him now, we see a body without divine glory: naked in the sense of the purely physical, stripped down to what is merely functional; a body lacking nobility, now that the divine glory which had enveloped and ultimately dignified it was no more.[93]

Peterson continues, affirming that by putting on "the baptismal garment," a person removes "the clothing that he wore after the fall: the clothing made from the leaves of the barren fig tree, from the skins of dead animals symbolizing our mortality,"[94] and in the baptismal "garment," the baptized person receives back the glorious clothing that humans once wore and lost in the Fall. Peterson also extends the ritual of baptism into eschatology. He explains,

> The unclothing of baptism is consummated in the "unclothing," the stripping of death, when we are naked for judgment. And what the white baptismal garment has already bestowed on us (cf. Col 3:3ff) will also be visibly completed when we are clothed with the risen body, with the "garment that will not decay" ... this clothing, which was given us in baptism and which at the resurrection will be fetched from the treasure house of heaven (cf. 2 Cor 5:1), is one which, in St. Basil's words, "has extinguished death in the flesh and swallowed up mortality in the garment of immortality." This clothing will never be lost, for it is not the glory that clothed the "unclothed" nature of the first Adam but the glory of the second Adam, who assumed "stripped" human nature into his divine Person and so "swallowed up mortality in the garment of immortality."[95]

92. Ibid. Augustine's allegory of the "garments of skins" also extends to the "skin of scripture"; in Book 13 of *The Confessions* Augustine combines the description in Ps. 104:2 of God stretching out the heavens like a skin with Gen. 3:21, writing, "You know, O Lord, how you clothed men with skins when by sin they became mortal. In the same way you have spread out the heavens like a canopy of skins, and these heavens are your Book." The heavenly canopy, for Augustine, becomes the manuscript of scripture stretched taut as a shelter over God's people. Augustine explains how both "the skin and the vault" can be taken figuratively and literally.

93. Peterson, "A Theology of Dress," 561.

94. Ibid., 565–6.

95. Ibid., 566–8.

Peterson understands the prelapsarian humans to have been without any physical clothing but argues that they were still not naked in the metaphysical sense that they belonged to God and were covered by God's supernatural grace and glory.[96] Hartenstein reads nakedness differently, but also in a positive manner, connecting it with the lack of shame mentioned in Gen. 2:25. He writes, "The first couple may be 'naked' specifically inasmuch as they do not clothe each other in 'dishonor' and do not 'robe' each other with disgrace through words and looks."[97] Both of these interpretations of nakedness—being clothed with God's grace and glory or being in a situation of safety and honor with other humans—sound appealing, and if nakedness signifies such a state, who would not want to be naked again?

Conclusion

Indeed, this reception history of Adam and Eve's clothing demonstrates that what matters most is not clothing—and nakedness—in themselves but rather what those things signify. Social perception is powerful and accounts for how inferences are made based on appearance, including dress. The theological and anthropological implications of those inferences are also powerful. To reiterate with an allusion to Qoheleth, there is a time to dress, and the loss or covering of clothing can be perceived as punishment or protection. There is a type of dress: when the garments are perceived as royal, the humans exercise dominion over the animals; if priestly, the humans serve a mediating role between God and the rest of creation. There are materials to dress, with the leaves of the fig tree perceived to be connected with sex, whereas the "skin" from certain trees is perceived to heal. Garments made from animal skin mostly imply punishment for sin, but when skin is perceived as radiance or light, the implication is that humans are glorious. Undoubtedly, my own perceiver variables affect my examination of the reception of Adam and Eve's clothing. Then again, given the breadth of possibilities for meaning in these two relatively simple verses—Gen. 3:7 and 3:21—we might all be encouraged to be aware of our individual perceiver variables and examine our perception of any given biblical text.[98]

96. In Peterson's words,

Before the Fall man belonged to God in such a way that the body—albeit not dressed in any clothes—was still not "naked." This "non-nakedness" of the body, along with its unclothedness, is explained by the fact that supernatural grace covered the human person like a garment. Man did not simply stand in the light of the divine glory; he was actually clothed with it. But through sin, man lost this divine glory. (Ibid., 561)

97. Hartenstein, "Clothing and Nudity in the Paradise Story," 369.

98. I am so very honored to participate in this project with such a wonderful group of colleagues. In particular, Jen Brown Jones, Serena Billington, and Carmen Joy Imes each gave astute and generous feedback on earlier versions of this chapter. None of us could have done our work without the help of Tony Finitsis, with his matchless ability to guide a group of academics. Thank you, Tony!

Chapter 4

THE DIVINE CLOTHING OF EVE AND ADAM AND THE HERMENEUTICS OF TRAUMA RECOVERY

Scott R. A. Starbuck

Introduction

The first act of clothing in the Hebrew Bible occurs in Gen. 3:7 when the man and the woman sew together fig leaves and make girdles for themselves. The second act of clothing occurs soon thereafter in Gen. 3:21 when YHWH makes tunics of skin and clothes the primordial couple. These two successive acts of clothing bracket a confrontation and cursing by YHWH, each occurring at liminal transitions in the origin story of Gen. 2:4b–3. Although an act of clothing may often signify a change in social status, in Gen. 2:4b–3, especially since the movement is from nudity to being clothed, identity formation is also at stake.[1] Whereas the two acts of clothing are regularly noted by commentators on Gen. 2:4b–3, few studies consider the acts of clothing as essential to character development in the story or view the two acts of clothing as movement from traumatic response to healing and support for the man and the woman. Because of this, an all too common reading of Gen. 2:4b–3 pursues the motif of disobedience and punishment—a reading of the text that not only misses the thread of post-traumatic healing within the narrative but can itself be retraumatizing. Recognizing that a close reading of the text raises significant theological questions and exposes processing gaps within the narrative, one may use the clothing acts in Gen. 2:4b–3 pastorally as ways of engagement for the healing of trauma.[2] Building upon insights from dress studies, trauma studies, reader-response criticism, narrative criticism, and historical criticism, this chapter attempts a fresh reading of Gen. 2:4b–3 that understands its narrative to

---

1. See Agnès Garcia-Ventura, "Clothing and Nudity in the Ancient Near East from the Perspective of Gender Studies," in *Clothing and Nudity in the Hebrew Bible*, ed. Christoph Berner, Manuel Schafer, and Martin Schott (Edinburgh: T&T Clark, 2019), 22.

2. I intend these reflections and suggestions to be theologically suggestive rather than clinical. I write them from the point of view of an interpreter of scripture who has pastoral contact with post-traumatic individuals who have shared their struggles and processes engaging Gen. 2:4b–3.

be akin to a *rite of intensification*[3] for the postexilic community. As such, it holds the possibility of being read pastorally in modern contexts as a reflective narrative in support of the healing of individual and collective trauma.

Reading the Text Centered on Two Acts of Clothing

Gen. 2:4b–3 is widely accepted as a narrative unit that is part of a larger story that continues into Genesis 4. Reading the text informed by dress studies, one notes that a double act of clothing occurs in Genesis 3 at verses 7 and 21. Recognizing that clothing connotes both mentifacts and sociofacts and also that changes in dress reflect societal norms and expectations,[4] it is fruitful to pursue the narrative development with an eye to shifted states of dress.

At first, and for a prolonged period, neither Adam nor Eve is clothed. Being a human origin story, it makes empirical sense that the primordial couple would begin naked and later be clothed. All human beings begin their life naked. In Hebrew society, being subsequently clothed was the societal expectation. Considering that outside of the garden nakedness was often a shame creator,[5] it is noteworthy that in Gen. 2:25 the narrative states that the man and the woman were naked and *without* shame (וַיִּהְיוּ שְׁנֵיהֶם עֲרוּמִּים הָאָדָם וְאִשְׁתּוֹ וְלֹא יִתְבֹּשָׁשׁוּ). To be unclothed, naked, was a source of shame often inflicted upon captives and indicated a loss of status and extreme vulnerability.[6] However, this is the only occurrence of the lemma בּוֹשׁ (shame) in the entire Genesis narrative.

The primordial couple is comfortable in or unaware of their nakedness. Yet the two will not remain naked for long because, after eating of the fruit of the tree of discernment and their eyes being opened to their naked status, the man and the woman immediately invent an act of clothing (Gen. 3:7).[7] Sewing together fig leaves, they make girdles *ḥăḡōrōṯ* (חֲגֹרֹת) for themselves. Although it is often presumed that they do this to cover their nakedness now knowing the emotions of shame, the text itself does not indicate this explicitly. Rather, whatever specific clothing item the man and the woman make, it is somehow related to their subsequent act of hiding from YHWH in the midst of the trees of the garden (Gen. 3:8). It is not immediately clear why the couple hides. Are they hiding their

3. Serena Nanda and Richard L. Warms, *Cultural Anthropology*, 12th ed. (London: Sage, 2020), 287.

4. See the introduction to this volume by Antonios Finitsis (pp. 3–6).

5. See Friedhelm Hartenstein, "Clothing and Nudity in the Paradise Story (Gen. 2-3)," in Berner et al., *Clothing and Nudity*, 370–2.

6. See Andrea Beyer, "Nudity and Captivity in Isa: 20 in Light of Iconographic Evidence," in Berner et al., *Clothing and Nudity*, 496.

7. Since "dress places humans in relationship with their body and affects among others their emotions, disposition, behavior, and interactions" (p. 8 of this volume), this act of clothing signals a psychological if not metacognitive shift for the characters.

nakedness from the divine? This is unlikely since previously in the narrative the man and the woman are routinely in the presence of God naked, and the deity expresses not a hint of displeasure with their nudity. Although a reader might likely infer feelings of shame upon the couple, the text itself is silent.

Rather than *shame*, the narrative connects the primordial couple's act of clothing to *fear*. In Gen. 3:10 Adam defends his actions before the deity, explaining that he was afraid because he could see that he was naked and out of this *fear*, he attempted to hide himself in the garden. Not only is the man apparently unmotivated by shame, there is no indication in the narrative that Adam felt aggrieved for violating the commandment. Instead, he reacts out of a sense of his own preservation. The shift from nakedness to girding fig leaves in the midst of the trees was to hide from YHWH, not out of shame but fear.[8]

Moreover, the deity, inattentive to Adam's fear (after all the deity could have said "do not fear," but does not), fixates on the newly uncovered *knowledge* of Adam—that he *knows* he is naked, not that he *is* naked. Perhaps rhetorically, YHWH queries if he was told by someone (the serpent?) that he was naked? Then, specifically, the deity interrogates Adam to discern if he violated the commandment and ate from the tree of discernment.

Instead of answering the deity's question directly, "Yes, I ate from the tree," Adam blames his wife: "The woman whom you gave to be with me, she gave me fruit from the tree, and I ate." Turning to the woman, the deity now interrogates her actions. She, too, adopts a circuitous answer and blames the serpent for "tricking her" into eating the fruit. Although both the man and the woman blame and dodge, it is not evident in the text that they do this motivated by shame. Fear, itself, of their own vulnerability before the deity, is the narrative's overt contextual explanation.

Why is the couple afraid after eating the fruit when earlier they were not? Prior to and between the two acts of clothing, the narrative emphasizes the deity's command. In Gen. 2:16, YHWH commands the man to refrain from eating from the tree of discernment (וַיְצַו יהוה אֱלֹהִים עַל־הָאָדָם). In YHWH's interrogation of Adam in Gen. 3:11, the same lemma (*ṣāwāh* צָוָה "to command") is emphasized (אֲתָה הֲמִן־הָעֵץ אֲשֶׁר צִוִּיתִיךָ לְבִלְתִּי אֲכָל־מִמֶּנּוּ אָכָלְתָּ). Then, pointedly, in the chiasmus of the curses the commandment violation is invoked, "because you have listened to the voice of your wife, and have eaten of the tree about which I commanded you (צָוָה), 'You shall not eat of it,' cursed is the ground because of you" (Gen. 3:17). In terms of characterization the deity repeatedly chooses the language of command much like a parent, or a human sovereign, or even a despot. Because the couple, each alone and in turn, refuses to take responsibility for violating the divine

8. Note this trauma reflex is not necessarily normative. In Lam. 1:9, the exposed and stained persona (mother Jerusalem) wants *to be seen* in her misery. See Anne Letourneau, "The Stain of Trauma: The Skirts of Jerusalem in Lam. 1:9" (forthcoming). Letourneau's observation leads one to posit the following question: "Is there a sense that the primordial couple wants to be found out at some level in their psyche despite hiding?"

command and pass blame (itself a fear response), the narrative illustrates subterfuge in the face of accountability rather than bodily shame. At first glance, accountability seems to be emphasized by the deity in the form of various etiological punishments in verses 14–19.

The man and the woman are not exiled out of the garden until verses 23–24. Prior to being expelled, Adam names the woman Eve anticipating that she will be the mother of all the living, and God clothes the man and the woman. This is the second act of clothing in the narrative. Whereas in Gen. 3:7, the primordial couple makes girdles (חֲגֹרֹת) and then hides, in Gen. 3:21, YHWH makes "tunics of skin," *kātǝnwōṯ ʿwōr* (כָּתְנוֹת עוֹר), and with them, clothes the man and the woman. However, in verse 22, fearing the primordial couple might eat from the Tree of Life and live forever (v. 22), the deity decides to drive them out of the garden.

Why does the deity reclothe the man and the woman before driving them away from the garden?[9] Perhaps a better way of phrasing this question is what intention lies behind the act of creating tunics of skin and then clothing the primordial couple (כָּתְנוֹת עוֹר וַיַּלְבִּשֵׁם) *after* the etiological punishments? As noted, YHWH does this in the narrative prior to his decision to drive them out of the garden. Yet that decision, in a sense, has already been made with the curses. Thus, God clothes the man and the woman in response to the curses and anticipatory of life to be lived ahead banished from the garden. The curses themselves circumscribe a life that is opposite of the Edenic existence. It is a difficult life, a suffering life, a conflictual life, and a mortal life for "you are dust, and to dust you shall return" (v. 19). In other words, the tunics of skin will not protect Adam and Eve from death: they must serve another function of linking the clothed with the clothier.

The second act of clothing occupies a liminal space within the narrative between being mortally human inside the garden and being banished as mortals outside the garden, with no possible recourse to the Tree of Life.[10] In neither realm are fig-themed attachments needed or helpful. The tunics of skin are, it would appear, necessary or at least desirable in both realms—to face the consequences of

---

9. Gary Anderson observes that "this simple narrative progression of nakedness, leaves, and then garments is almost never handled in simple fashion." See Gary Anderson, "The Garments of Skin in Apocryphal Narrative and Biblical Commentary," in *Studies in Ancient Midrash*, ed. James Kugel (Cambridge: Harvard University Center for Jewish Studies, 2001), 104. The progression of being naked without shame, to being fearful, hiding, and "girded" with fig leaves, to being cursed, to being clothed by God, does not neatly fit either the human maturation hermeneutic or the original sin/fall hermeneutic.

10. In the Gilgamesh Epic, Enkidu is clothed by a female (harlot), and in the story this act of clothing functions as a liminal indicator of moving from the realm of the animals to the realm of the city state. Perhaps, then, it is more significant who clothes the primordial couple than the fact that clothing occurs as a liminal indicator in Genesis 2–3. See John A. Bailey, "Initiation and the Primal Woman in Gilgamesh and Genesis 2-3," *JBL* 89.2 (1970), 138.

individual mortality. In other words, the tunics of skin are needed, according to the narrative, whether Adam or Eve is to remain in the garden with God or if they are banished from the garden away from the presence of God.

YHWH makes כָּתְנוֹת, or shirt-like tunics. The deity makes them from "skin" (עוֹר). This can indicate either the skin of an animal or the skin of a person.[11] Rather than precise and focused, this act of clothing is suggestive and open. It is, in a word, multivalent[12] and exhibits a long and varied reception history.[13] On the one hand, the literal "surface" meaning of the term suggests that animal skins are intended. These would be more durable than woven cloth and provide some needed protection. This interpretation would suggest that the self-made girdles were insufficient for the harsh realities brought about by the curses.[14] If so, then the primordial couple is not only cursed by God but is also equipped to face the curses by God.

On the other hand, a garment made to be worn next to human skin could also be understood as the final gift of *divine immanence* given to the couple. In a sense, the clothing made by God and then put on the couple by God preserves a divine embrace, skin to skin.[15] The fact that this "skin" takes the shape of a tunic means that it also shares in the sacerdotal lexicon of the priests.[16] If so, then one might reasonably conclude that the primordial couple will have "priestly" access to the deity despite the severity of the etiological curses. Even more, once they are cast outside of the garden, they will not be barred from the ability to approach God. This would lead one to conclude that this quasi-liturgical action is both in response to the preceding curses and anticipatory of life to be lived ahead while physically banished from Eden, the primordial garden of God.

This divine act of creating clothing and then bestowing said clothing can be understood as an empowering act of accompaniment and investiture,[17] such as

---

11. If animal skin, this would be the only reference in the Hebrew Bible to clothing made only from animal skin. See Wolfgang Zwickel, "Fabrication, Functions, and Uses of Textiles in the Hebrew Bible," in Berner et al., *Clothing and Nudity*, 193.

12. See the chapter by Sara Koenig, "Styling Eve and Adam's Clothes: An Examination of Reception History," in this volume.

13. See Gary A. Anderson, *The Genesis of Perfection: The Man and the Woman in Jewish and Christian Imagination* (Louisville, KY: Knox, 2001), 117–34.

14. Friedhelm Hartenstein points out that this is the first act of autonomy or agency in the story. See Friedhelm Hartenstein, "Clothing and Nudity in the Paradise Story (Gen. 2-3)," in Berner et al., *Clothing and Nudity*, 373.

15. See Sara Koenig's discussion in "Styling Eve and Adam's Clothes: An Examination of Reception History" in this volume (pp. 69–70).

16. See Carmen Joylmes, "Between Two Worlds: The Functional and Symbolic Significance of the High Priestly Regalia," in *Dress and Clothing in the Hebrew Bible: "For All Her Household Are Clothed in Crimson,"* ed. Antonios Finitsis (London: Bloomsbury, 2019), 35.

17. See Hartenstein, "Clothing and Nudity in the Paradise Story," 373.

Hannah's act of clothing the boy Samuel.[18] Understood this way, the divine act is one of empowerment through extended (hypostatic) presence that allows and demands agency on the part of the primordial couple. As such, it signals character development within the narrative. Furthermore, it portrays a divine being "with," more than doing something "to" or "for." This becomes clear when this clothing act is compared to the act of clothing the man and the woman attempted earlier in the story.

Immediately upon realizing that they were naked (and, hence, vulnerable), the couple created a "body supplement" as a way to compensate for a perceived weakness. Technically, the man and the woman sew together fig leaves making belts or girdles (חֲגֹרֹת), a term most commonly used for military preparedness. However, its composition of fig leaves is at odds with the context of weaponry, and it is elusive to imagine how the leaves were sown together, and when sown together, how much of the body was actually covered. Perhaps the purpose was to create a covering for retraction, defense, flight, and distraction. Since the man and the woman hide in the midst of the trees of the garden (בְּתוֹךְ עֵץ הַגָּן), the intent most clearly is one of camouflage, a type of defensive weaponry. If so, their hope would have been to fade into the background and to disappear. In other words, when their eyes were opened and they saw themselves, their response was to obscure their vulnerable visage before God. The attempt does not work; it was feeble and fallible. The narrative does not allow using dress as a means to hide before the divine.

Read this way, the text will not allow human hiding from vulnerability, failure, confusion, and hurt. In the end, YHWH finds the couple, curses them, and then drives the humans from the garden while fortifying the garden against any attempted reentry. At the same time, they are exiled while clothed with "skin" by YHWH. They leave with each other. They leave together. Most importantly, upon being exiled by God, yet clothed by God, they discover a new type of knowledge: "Now the man *knew* his wife Eve (הָאָדָם יָדַע אֶת־חַוָּה אִשְׁתּוֹ), and she conceived and bore Cain, saying, 'I have produced a man with the help of the LORD'" (Gen. 4:1). They are no longer traumatized in their own perceived vulnerability. Rather, they know each other and they themselves create with YHWH a future generatively. They have discovered a new agency that enables them to face a harsh world in their own human/divine skin in *communitas*—the sense of sharing and intimacy experienced by people facing new and daunting circumstances together.

It is this sense of togetherness that might shed light on the appeal of the narrative. Regardless of its original compositional context, repetition of this narrative could reinforce communal identity. From an anthropological lens the two acts of clothing could function akin to a rite of intensification, "directed toward the welfare of the group or community rather than the individual. These rituals are structured to

---

18. See Neville L. A. Tidwell, "Linen Ephod: 1 Sam 2:18 and 2 Sam 6:14," *VT* 24.4 (1974), 506.

reinforce the values and norms of the community and to strengthen group identity. Through rites of intensification, the community maintains continuity with the past, enhances the feeling of social unity in the present, and renews the sentiments on which cohesion depends."[19] Despite the shared harsh realities of agrarian society, despite any number of command violations, despite the desire to become more than mere mortals, and despite an ever-present transcendent God, the community was bound together in their being dressed in skin by their God, equipped through skin to have access to God, even and despite divine punishment, and to create generatively so that the community, itself, lived on despite banishment from the Tree of Life.[20]

Reading the Text Situated by Exilic and Postexilic Generational Trauma

Although it is difficult if not impossible to locate Gen. 2:4b–3 in its original compositional context, increasingly scholars find it fruitful to situate it among the literature of the postexilic community of literati. It is in this community that earlier origin myths and ancestral tales were collected, combined, and read as *scripture*, perhaps for the first time. The community of the literati was also post-traumatic survivors.[21] It is likely that the impetus for burgeoning scriptural creation and collection sprung from attempts to make sense of their shared trauma but not in unilinear ways.

In his work on the multigenerational legacy of trauma, Yael Danieli notes that "massive trauma shapes the internal representation of reality of several generations, becoming an unconscious organizing principle passed on by parents and internalized by their children."[22] This would certainly hold true for the postexilic generations of Yehud literati. If exilic trauma can be an unconscious organizing principle, it seems wise to revisit the compilation and reading of biblical texts through the lens of trauma. In fact, it is likely that the preexilic core composition of Genesis 3 was preserved and reread as a narrative response to trauma accepted

---

19. Nanda and Warms, *Cultural Anthropology*, 287.

20. Significantly, directly following the curses, Adam names Eve, indicating that she will be the mother of all future living, another etiology but skillfully placed in the narrative. She will bear children, but she will need to do this with Adam. They are in this together, despite the curse of pain in childbirth. In other words, she must face, rather than avoid, what could be trauma inducing. That is her name, her call. She will need to find her agency.

21. See Kathleen M. O'Connor, *Smyth & Helwys Bible Commentary: Genesis 1-25A* (Macon: Smyth & Helwys, 2018), 3, note 2.

22. Yael Danieli, "Conclusions and Future Directions," in *International Handbook of Multigenerational Legacies of Trauma*, Plenum Series on Stress and Coping, ed. Yael Danieli (New York: Plenum, 1988), 670.

by a collective group in view of the horrendous destruction, dislocation, and post-traumatic stress of the exile and post-annihilated Jerusalem.[23]

In this section I will focus on how a post-trauma hermeneutic might open up the reading of the text, especially among the postexilic community in light of the exile. In the final section of the chapter I will suggest a modern reading of the text that might accompany trauma recovery. Although references to trauma are ancient,[24] trauma studies are based on multidisciplinary theory and praxis among modern scholars. As such, in order to explore a post-traumatic reading of Gen. 2:4b–3 among the ancient literati, modern paradigms must hermeneutically inform the narrative.

Overall, modern trauma studies suggest key steps to healing trauma are that the survivor must (i) find his or her agency, (ii) stop blaming themselves for the trauma (which means no longer covering up for bad parenting or other abuse), (iii) inhabit their violated bodies, and (iv) reprocess stored and hidden trauma memory as experiences no longer to be feared.[25] Robert Schreiter notes that in the healing of trauma "language has to be recovered as a vehicle for processing experience, the tyranny of past events that freezes us in an unending past and that blocks out the present and the future must be overcome, and a sense of meaning and a framework for right behavior must be restored."[26] Narrative, itself, much like the story of Gen. 2:4b–3, can be particularly effective in such restoration but only if it allows for the discovery of self-agency. In their article "Defining 'Trauma' as a Useful Lens for Biblical Interpretation," Christopher Frechette and Elizabeth Boase describe individual and collective efforts of narrative creation in response to trauma:

23. O'Connor, *Genesis 1-25A*, 71–3. While clear redactional evidence of postexilic tampering with the text remains elusive, Mettinger, for example, reads the text as informed by Deuteronomistic theological perspectives. See Tryggve N. D. Mettinger, *The Eden Narrative: A Literary and Religio-historical Study of Genesis 2–3* (Winona Lake, IN: Eisenbrauns, 2007), 133–6. Carr, on the other hand, sees a likely critique of late preexilic and exilic wisdom traditions operative in the narrative of Gen. 3:1ff. See David Carr, "The Politics of Textual Subversion: A Diachronic Perspective on the Garden of Eden Story," *JBL* 112 (1993), 577–93.

24. Eve-Marie Becker, "Trauma Studies and Exegesis: Challenges, Limits, and Prospects," in *Trauma and Traumatization in Individual and Collective Dimensions: Insights from Biblical Studies and Beyond*, ed. Eve-Marie Becker, Jan Dochhorn, and Else Kragelund Holt (Göttingen: Vandenhoeck & Ruprecht, 2014), 17–18.

25. Peter Levine, *The Healing Trauma Summit: Volume 1: Transform Trauma with Advances in Neuroscience, Spiritual Psychology, and Embodied Approaches to Healing*, 2019 Original Audible Audiobook; and Bessel A. Van der Kolk, *The Body Keeps the Score: Brain, Mind, and Body in the Healing of Trauma* (New York: Penguin, 2015), 202ff.

26. Robert J. Schreiter, "Reading Biblical Texts through the Lens of Resilience," in *Bible through the Lens of Trauma*, Semeia Studies 86, ed. Elizabeth Boase and Christopher G. Frechette (Atlanta, GA: SBL, 2016), 196.

In individual trauma, it is the unease felt by the survivor that motivates engagement in the challenging process of reinterpretation of the traumatic experience necessary to create a narrative of the trauma. In a collective, it is a shared sense of suffering felt by the collective that motivates certain groups to propose narratives to name and account for the suffering and that also moves the collective to accept a given narrative.[27]

While Gen. 2:4b–3 read as a trauma narrative may not be one of the dominant interpretations of this passage, its inclusion in a developing collection of scripture and its engagement among postexilic literati make such a *Neuinterpretation* likely. It is worth considering, then, if the core composition of Genesis 3 is preexilic, the text itself could well have been read, if not preserved, as a narrative response to trauma, accepted by a collective group, in view of the horrendous destruction, dislocation, and post-traumatic stress of the exile and post-annihilated Jerusalem.[28]

Christopher Frechette draws attention to the likelihood that the "survivors of the massive Judean traumas of the 580s BCE internalized core beliefs about lacking dignity of self and lacking safety in relationships with others and with YHWH"[29] and that "these core beliefs were likely passed on to their children."[30] If so, and if Gen. 2:4b–3 was likely read as a primary origin myth among the literati of Yehud, then we would expect to find indications of trauma response as well as openings for recovery. Trauma studies suggest this possibility as they "affirm the importance of creating a trauma narrative, a coherent narrative capable not only of processing past trauma but also fostering resilience against further traumatization."[31] Key to any recovery from trauma is for the traumatized to reclaim self-agency over one's life.

It would be impossible to offer a single trauma-sensitive reading of Genesis 3 as paradigmatic. Rather, I would like to highlight key openings in the text that make a trauma reading possible, if not likely. Many of these openings could function as interpretive opportunities offering openness of engagement necessary for a reader's

27. Christopher G. Frechette and Elizabeth Boase, "Defining 'Trauma' as a Useful Lens for Biblical Interpretation," in Boase and Frechette, *Bible through the Lens of Trauma*, 9.

28. O'Connor, *Genesis 1-25A*, 71–3.

29. Christopher G. Frechette, "Daughter Babylon Raped and Bereaved (Isaiah 47): Symbolic Violence and Meaning Making in Recovery from Trauma," in Boase and Frechette, *Bible through the Lens of Trauma*, 76.

30. Ibid.

31. Frechette and Boase, "Defining Trauma," 15. In particular,

whether or not a text originated in a historical context of trauma, a hermeneutics of trauma inquires into how appropriation of biblical text might have a capacity to affect individuals and collectives as they survive the effects of trauma or face ongoing (potentially) traumatic situations … such narratives serve to construct identity and solidarity in ways that can restore healthy assumptions about the self in relation to the world. (14–15)

self-agency. When these openings are exposed, it becomes clear that narrative, itself, resists a solipsistic disobedience/punishment explanation,[32] despite the fact that many a postexilic reader might find temporary solace in such a reading.

In fact, one can imagine that it would be nearly impossible for a postexilic generation to read Gen. 3:11 without connecting it to the threat of curses in Deut. 28:15: "But if you will not obey the LORD your God by diligently observing all his commandments and decrees, which I am commanding (צוה) you today, then all these curses shall come upon you and overtake you." Having lived through the disruption, dislocations, and the cultural tearing of the exile, how would generations of literati be able to read these texts without triggering a post-traumatic response? The man and the woman are caught red-handed, and their response to hide and then blame (plead) is completely understandable as a fear response associated with one's guilty deeds being uncovered.

It is reasonable, then, to conclude that at least one trauma narrative emerged that exonerated the deity and placed the entire blame on generational covenant violations, mythically expressed in Genesis 3 but historically detailed throughout the Deuteronomistic writings and numerous prophets.[33] A culturally dominant reading would likely tend to read the text in terms of law and order, but also blame the victim. According to this reading of the narrative, the lived-reality that the curses describe is a result of human failure (Gen. 3:14-19), rather than a divine overreaction or overcorrection.[34] We would expect this interpretation to evidence itself in traumatized communities, like the children of the exile, because, as Frechette notes, "long after the events of the trauma (itself), feelings of fear, anxiety, helplessness may occur in connections with beliefs about the self as utterly abandoned, worthless, and somehow deserving of being violated as the perpetrator."[35] Thus, the trauma of the exile was "their" fault entirely, they deserved it, they deserved all of its dehumanization and should even understand it as divinely sanctioned. In other words, this reading offers postexilic generations control by reading the narrative simplistically in terms of cause and effect.

However, when read this way, there is no clear path for trauma recovery because ultimately the victim is blamed. Even more, much of what follows in Genesis has little to nothing to do with any fidelity to the Sinai covenant. In fact, the literary

---

32. See Ziony Zevit, *What Really Happened in the Garden of Eden?* (New Haven, CT: Yale University Press, 2013), 232; and Lyn M. Bechtel, "Genesis 2.4b–3.24: A Myth about Human Maturation," *JSOT* 20.67, 3–26.

33. See Louis Stulman, "Reading the Bible through the Lens of Trauma and Art," in Becker et al., *Trauma and Traumatization*, 185.

34. Tiffany Houck-Loomis demonstrates that the exilic trope of self-blame, though reflective of a survival mechanism, in the end "colludes with the perpetrator and disallows authentic mourning to transpire." See Tiffany Houck-Loomis, "Traumatic Narratives: When Biblical Narratives of Trauma Re-traumatize," *Sacred Space: The E-Journal of the American Association of Pastoral Counselors* 9 (2017), 58.

35. Frechette, "Daughter Babylon," 74–5.

context of Genesis 3 destabilizes such a theodic defense of the deity; it problematizes a binary opposition, in which YHWH is completely in the right and the man and the woman are completely in the wrong. This is an important observation. The remainder of Genesis does not allow for a hegemonic Deuteronomistic reading of Genesis 3. That is, the remaining epic tales in Genesis are hardly driven by the stipulations of covenantal obedience.[36] Mark S. Smith has observed, "Genesis 3 does not characterize the eating of the fruit as evil or a sin or a transgression or a matter of guilt. Scholars characterize the act as disobedience or rebellion, but that language also is missing from Genesis 3."[37]

Rather, key interpretive openings occur both within the narrative and after a meta-consideration of its message. Greater attention to the subtleties of the text might lead to the pondering of a series of failures among all characters, including that of the deity. The text invites many questions that begin to undermine the rush to divine command judgment. For example, would the man and the woman have understood that they were doing something wrong prior to eating from the tree and gaining the knowledge of the discernment between good and evil? In other words, how would they know that it was better to obey than it was to pursue an independence of action and growth? Even if they intuited or guessed this was the case, could they possibly have anticipated the life-altering, life-alienating, trauma-inducing consequences spelled out in the divine curses and the subsequent expulsion from the garden? How does one account for the unequal power dynamics in the text? Both the deity and the serpent are privileged and presumably should adopt a protective stance vis-à-vis the younger, less-sophisticated couple. It is the deity who leaves the human couple alone and unsupervised in the garden while in the presence of the snake. The serpent, although it does not technically lie to the woman, does play the role of the instigator and begins to raise the cognitive possibility that the deity is withholding goodness from the man and the woman. The serpent's suggestion, in and of itself, though likely incorrect, must place within the mind of Eve the desire for an agency that would allow her to live into her created reality, that is, to live out what it means to be created like God in the image of God (Gen. 1:26) if one might extend a literati reading of a collected text to include the first creation story.

36. In Hellenistic Second Temple receptions of Genesis 2-3, the "fall" aspect of an overly Deuteronomistic reading is muted if not removed altogether in Ben Sira, Book of Jubilees, and 1 Enoch. See Michaela Bauks, "Text- and Reception-Historical Reflections on Transmissional and Hermeneutical Techniques in Genesis 2-3," in *The Pentateuch: International Perspectives on Current Research*, ed. T. B. Dozeman, K. S. Schmid, and B. J. Schwartz (Tubingen: Mohr Siebeck, 2011), 155–65.

37. Mark S. Smith, "Before Human Sin and Evil: Desire and Fear in the Garden of God," *CBQ* 80.2 (2018), 216–17. Helpfully, Smith notes that "Genesis 3 is complex and primal, arguably more so than the traditional interpretation of this biblical chapter understood as a narrative of disobedience, sin, and punishment. The chapter names fundamental terms of the human constitution: desire, knowledge, fear ... and difficulty" (219).

Even more pressing questions arise from a meta-consideration of its message. Why would God not want this too? Does God not want her and her partner to share "likeness" as divine images? When she looks at the withheld tree, she sees as God sees, that it is "good" and "to be desired" (Gen. 3:6). In fact, she discovers that the tree is "good for eating" (Gen. 3:6), as are all the other trees of the garden (Gen. 2:9). As the woman acts, at least within the narrative of the text, in godlike ways, she understandably wants to live into her image fully. To do this, she abandons the commandment of an increasingly suspect suzerain, an assuredly all-too-common lived-experience of many within the ancient Near East. Her husband trusts the one with him, the one given to be with him, rather than the commanding deity who is absent. In other words, the man acts within his divinely appointed "circle of security."[38]

Read this way, then, verses 14–19, the so-called curses, render divine judgment in the form of a series of etiologies describing the suffering (and trauma affecting) world of *every* common ancient person, but especially to surviving generations of the exile condemned to agrarian futility. Due to the violation of the (seemingly incongruous and arbitrary) command not to eat of the tree of discernment (and in the case of the snake to not protect the tree and its fruit), the protagonists are rendered crippled and will face famine, enmity and violence, painful childbirth (pain unto death?), marital conflict and exploitation, crop failure, malnutrition, and death. It is quite a list of curses for a single command violation! It is a violent reaction that is uncompromisingly out of proportion to the subtleties defining the initiating event. It is, in fact, cruel. Even more, the curses themselves describe the *actual* experienced world of the ancient person on a daily basis. All of the curses are trauma inducing, which is to say that the man and the woman will leave the garden traumatized to face even more traumatic events.

Frechette and Boase note that "texts witness to trauma through their encoding of *the not yet fully known or fully assimilated memories* that are present in the form of absences, gaps, and repetitions. Texts become representations of trauma as much through what is unspoken as through what is spoken."[39] In Genesis 3, there are significant unspoken and unresolved questions or gaps. For example, why does God ignore Adam's fear in Gen. 3:10? On the one hand, is it because Adam's fear is appropriate and not worth attending to? On the other hand, is the deity more urgently concerned with a boundary crossing involving the prohibited tree? Does God's question reveal a divine vulnerability, a lack of control or preparedness? Even after cursing the man and the woman to agrarian servitude within the garden, why does God subsequently drive them out from it, banishing them forever? Is the divine motivated by fear in ways similar to the primordial

---

38. A psychological term of art in attachment theory and therapy. See Amber Yaholkoski, Kylee Hurl, and Jennifer Theule, "Efficacy of the Circle of Security Intervention: A Meta-Analysis," *Journal of Infant, Child & Adolescent Psychotherapy* 15.2 (2016), 95–100.

39. Frechette and Boase, "Defining Trauma," 11; emphasis added.

couple in their attempt to separate from the deity through clothed camouflage? These questions and others press themselves upon the reader in a close reading of the text but may not even be noticed if the narrative is read primarily as one of disobedience and punishment. Importantly, these questions arise out of cognitive gaps in the narrative itself.

As such, the literati might intuit the following progression in the narrative consonant with the four general steps for healing trauma as well as a post-traumatic reading of the text. Below I will attempt to illustrate these steps. The man and the woman exhibit initial agency when they sew together fig leaves and hide. This is their initial reaction to an overwhelming sense of vulnerability. For the literati, this might recall any number of ways that they had to "fit in" and not stand out within Babylonian and Persian societies and structures. This attempt to blend in was fear motivated and proved ultimately ineffective since it did not work with their God. The divine still saw them as they were, however hidden in whatever cultural accommodation they might have attempted. Nevertheless, it was the first awkward step toward healing and is signaled in the narrative by the first act of clothing. Within the narrative, it is ultimately ineffective in terms of a flight or fight response, but it is never judged or ridiculed by YHWH.

The second general step of healing trauma is to stop blaming. In the narrative, the man and the woman do not stop blaming each other and YHWH until after the poetic curses, naming, bestowal of divine clothing, and expulsion from the garden. One can imagine the literati of Yehud reading the text and immediately recognizing the human currency of blame, especially when caught in what we recognize as a fear response. Yet, blaming in no way helps the couple. YHWH will not enter into the dance of blame, even when named as perpetrator by the man: "the woman *whom you gave to be with me*, she gave me fruit from the tree, and I ate" (Gen. 3:12). The fact that the attempts at blame turn up an empty husk illustrates the vital importance of abandoning blame in a post-traumatic way forward.[40] In other words, if the instinct to blame might be seen as akin to the first act of clothing, then to stick one's head in the sand, as it were, is insufficient.

The third general step for healing trauma is to embrace the violated traumatic body. The second act of clothing by the divine enables Adam and Eve to inhabit their violated bodies—a violation that is poetically voiced in the curses. Being clothed in divinely fashioned skin allows the primordial couple to advance in a post-garden world full of agrarian, political, and relational trauma. That the couple

---

40. P. D. Hanson makes this point when commenting on Isaiah 65, a text coterminous with the literati of Yehud and reflective of the processing of trauma: "If there was to be a restoration to health, denial had to be replaced with an honest acknowledgment of responsibility. Not God's indifference but the people's rebellion caused the nation to stumble and fall. The evasive tactic of blaming God, which was only hastening the disintegration of community." See Paul D. Hanson, *Isaiah 40–66*, Interpretation, a Bible Commentary for Teaching and Preaching (Louisville, KY: Knox, 1995), 241.

is able do this is clear in their mutually knowing and creating signaled in Gen. 4:1. This, then, is the third general step of healing trauma.

The fourth step in healing trauma is to reprocess traumatic memories and triggers. This fourth step is not evident in the narrative itself, but it can be found, as I have attempted to show in the transmission of the story, its interpretation, and the making of meaning. Roughly coterminous with the postexilic literati is the vision of Isa. 65:17-25, a poem that may not be intertextually connected to Gen. 2:4b–3 yet it clearly invokes Gen. 2:4b–3[41] with the aim of healing and restoration.[42] In Isa. 61:10 (though not intertextual with Gen. 2:4b–3) the postexilic and post-traumatic community is clothed by YHWH with "garments of salvation" and "the robe of righteousness," terms signaling an anticipation of empowerment, legitimacy, divine approval, dramatic social change, and an alternate path in post-traumatic Yehud to holiness.[43] Since there are only a handful of passages that

41.

The idea of a return to the first creation, to the paradisal existence of Eden, is present marginally in the allusion to the snake in the scribal addition in 65:25, as it is in the LXX and Targum glossing of the tree as the Tree of Life in v 22, and obliquely in the longevity theme in v 20. These and other allusions to motifs from the primeval history—Eden the garden of God (51:3), Noah and the flood (54:9)— demonstrate the currency at the time of writing of these narrative themes and traditions.

See Joseph Blenkinsopp, *Isaiah 56-66: A New Translation with Introduction and Commentary*, vol. 19B, Anchor Yale Bible (New Haven, CT: Yale University Press, 2008), 287. 42.

Chapter 65 ended with a picture of creation restored to its God-intended wholeness. All of God's creatures would live in harmony, and the place chosen by God for communion with humankind would display to the world the security and blessing that was God's intention for all people: "They shall not hurt or destroy on all my holy mountain, says the LORD" (65:25). The vision at the end of chapter 65 reaffirmed for a people torn by political turmoil and economic hardship the goal toward which they were moving as a pilgrim people ... the beleaguered human spirit stands in need of being uplifted through fresh visions of divine creativity. But visions take a turn quite opposed to encouraging courageous engagement if they become invitations to escape from involvement in the realities of life. At that point religion becomes an opiate as powerfully able to induce apathy and resignation as any narcotic. It is one of the marks of the Isaianic tradition that the eschatological vision of God's reign is repeatedly related to the realities of everyday life. (See Hanson, *Isaiah 40-66*, 247–8)

43. See Scott R. A. Starbuck, "Disrobing an Isaianic Metaphor," in Finitsis, *Dress and Clothing*, 143–59.

remember YHWH clothing human beings,[44] the connection between Gen. 3:21 and Isa. 61:10 is likely illustrative of an ongoing theological process of healing, through an "internal representation of reality" and by "fostering resilience against further retramautization" in the postexilic period.

Reading the Text Pastorally for Post-traumatic Healing

If a postexilic post-traumatic reading of Gen. 2:4b–3 illuminates the textual narrative, such a reading might also be helpful as a transformative intersection between modern post-traumatic individuals, their communities, and the biblical text. Readers would have to be guided in this direction, because this alternative reading is clearly not a majority reading in many religious traditions. Such guidance would honor the gaps and openings in the text to encourage hermeneutical engagement with a view to the lived-reality before the interpreter. Pastoral care must be given, however, because in many modern contexts a common reading of Gen. 2:4b–3 through a solipsistic hermeneutic of disobedience and punishment not only impedes trauma recovery but often drowns out the discomfort, if not full-blown triggering, of those post-traumatic, and can, itself, be retraumatizing.

One can describe trauma in terms of being rendered helpless in ways that arouse intense fear, loss of control, and threat of annihilation. Within the narrative the divine reaction to the violation of the command could easily render readers helpless while at the same time arousing fear, a sense of deep loss of future and eventual annihilation. Judith Herman points out that "traumatic events destroy the victim's fundamental assumptions about the safety of the world, the positive value of the self, and the meaningful order of creation."[45] A pastoral reading of Gen. 2:4b–3 would best be sensitive to the possibility of such reactions, that is, feelings of helplessness, depression, and lack of safety in front of the text.

It should be recognized that initial readings of the text that could be characterized as "blaming the victim" are, themselves, indicative of a trauma response. As Kathleen O'Connor points out, "Catastrophe stories … present causes for the violent events that place responsibility on the humans in some fashion. Some portray God as the punisher who brings on the disaster. Such theology enables survival."[46] But to move, in a modern pastoral context, from survival to healing, it is equally important to realize that "this theology is not acceptable today.

---

44. See Ehud Ben Zvi, "Where YHWH's Clothes Worth Remembering," in Finitsis, *Dress and Clothing*, 177.

45. Frechette, "Daughter Babylon," 74. See also Judith Lewis Harman, *Trauma and Recovery: The Aftermath of Violence—From Domestic Abuse to Political Terror*, rev. ed. (New York: Basic, 1997), 51–114.

46. See Kathleen M. O'Connor, *Smyth & Helwys Bible Commentary: Genesis 1–25A* (Macon: Smyth & Helwys, 2018), 47. Note, especially, O'Connor's observation that "taking responsibility, even if wrongly, helps people go forward because it ascribes cause and effect to past suffering" (72).

It takes a historically conditioned ancient view and freezes it as if it were a full and permanent insight into God's very being."[47] From a modern post-traumatic perspective, it is possible one might begin to even envision the deity as an abuser. For those who suffer domestic abuse, fear of the more powerful abuser often leads to pleading, blaming, and hiding before secondary reflections of shame settle.

Described thus far, the post-traumatic reading of the text is trauma-trigger sensitive but does not yet point to personal "agency" and "reembodiment" necessary for trauma recovery. Agency and accompaniment will be needed if recovery is to be had. Again, key steps to healing trauma are that (i) the survivor must find his or her agency, (ii) stop blaming themselves for the trauma (which means no longer covering up for bad parenting or other abuse), (iii) inhabit their violated bodies, and (iv) reprocess stored and hidden trauma memory as experiences no longer to be feared.

A close reading of the text that points out its narrative gaps and questions can aid a personal reconsideration such as whether Adam and Eve are completely to blame, if their punishment is in any way proportional to their transgression, and if the misery of the curses is, indeed, the best that God offers. A reading of the text as parabolic rather than descriptive may help those in trauma recovery discover the agency of their own voice over a hegemonic "blame the victim" motif. Read as a trauma narrative, the reader is invited to reflect upon the complexity and vulnerability of the divine–human relationship. For example, both the primordial couple and the divine seem to act out of fear. For Adam and Eve, their fear-filled girding is ultimately unsuccessful. This raises questions whether the banishment of Adam and Eve from the garden is successful for God.

When the narrative is approached this way, the text renders more questions than answers. Yet, it is in the unfrozen cognitive state of puzzlement that a reader is provided the opportunity to discover self-agency and come to terms not only with the harsh and traumatizing realities the text triggers but also with an increasing sense of personal embodiment. From the standpoint of reader response, these and other unanswered cognitive "gaps" in the text can,[48] in their silence, encourage the reader to begin to develop self-agency critical of what might be described as bad divine parenting.[49]

A close reading of the text that explores the double-act of clothing in the narrative uncovers two helpful trajectories of textual insight and healing. Both of them are historically situated. However, one is ancient while the second is modern. First, I have attempted to demonstrate that the postexilic post-traumatic

47. Ibid., 7.

48. To the extent that gaps help to trigger the brain to envision new perspectives and solutions, gaps help the emotional and intellectual immobilization of sections of the brain through detachment, derealization, depersonalization, and dissociative amnesia. See Becker, "Trauma Studies," 22.

49. In my own pastoral experience, some trauma survivors when in the process of healing are able to question perceptions of the deity, especially in terms of "good/bad parenting."

literati who gathered and read the scriptural text would likely understand it akin to a rite of intensification, a story inviting generative healing among the wider community and closeness to the divine. Second, in present-day scripture-valuing communities, I have tried to show how the narrative could be read in a way that accompanies the healing of the post-traumatic process, rather than in a way that could retraumatize or blame the victim.

In fact, a trauma-sensitive close reading of the double act of clothing in Gen. 2:4b–3 may encourage reflection upon attempts of those post-traumatic to camouflage their vulnerability and pain rather than taking steps toward healing. For this to happen, however, the text must be rescued from eisegetical body-shame interpretative traditions. If so, the narrative may likely be healing, connective, and generative for victims of trauma. The divine clothing of Adam and Eve in Gen. 3:21 can be helpfully read as an invitation to inhabit violated bodies that are also so clothed in skin as one embarks on a life certain to hold retraumatizing events. Here is an opening for those who have suffered trauma to embrace their own skin,[50] and being in their divinely made 'skin', experience a recovery of their traumatized body as holy and given agency by and connection to God apart from any religious functionary.

---

50. See Bonnie Badenoch, *The Heart of Trauma: Healing the Embodied Brain in the Context of Relationships* (New York: W.W. Norton, 2018), 59ff.

Chapter 5

TAMAR AND RUTH: DRESS AS (MIS)COMMUNICATION AND INHERITANCE PRESERVATION

Jennifer M. Matheny

Introduction

Dress research in the Hebrew Bible can vary methodologically from archeological "finds/pieces" of materiality to social scientific inquiries, and even areas of ethnographic approaches. In one sense, dress is strictly a material object and agency belongs to the person wearing the clothing items and/or bodily accessories (i.e., perfume, jewelry). The relationship between persons and dress is "more complex than has often been assumed in biblical scholarship."[1] Any person involved in picking out clothing before a job interview will quickly attest that there is more to clothing than just the covering of a body. There are social, religious, and political dimensions to dress, which when highlighted invoke a desired awareness and even a response in certain situations. Dress utilized in the biblical narratives is artistic and intentional. Descriptions are often rare in the Hebrew Bible and alert the reader that when dress is mentioned, it plays a significant role in the story and alters the trajectory of the story if the intended communicative effects of the desire and motivation of bodily adornments meet as intended.

Clothing change, within a narrative, can signal to the reader that a character is constructing or reconstructing one's identity.[2] The description of dress and physical characteristics is scant in Hebrew narrative and signals the reader

---

1. Bethany Joy Wagstaff, "Redressing Clothing in the Hebrew Bible: Material-Cultural Approaches," PhD dissertation, University of Exeter, 2017, 16.

2. Saul proves to be an example of dress shaping identity and shaping a story, especially with clothing related to battle. Sean E. Cook demonstrates how clothing in the Saul narrative depicts him as a foreigner, and through clothing and armor, "he is portrayed to look and act like a foreigner" and ultimately rejected by YHWH as king. See Cook, "Is Saul Among the Philistines? A Portrayal of Israel's First and Flawed King?" in *Dress and Clothing in the Hebrew Bible*, ed. Antonios Finitsis (New York: T&T Clark, 2019), 109–24.

to pay attention. In the modern discussion on gender, dress has become an important aspect in exploring markers of identification. In the Hebrew Bible, what is uncovered and covered on a body has the capacity to elicit provocative responses. Dress enters the conversation of desire and interaction, offering a voice that seeks to be heard and understood in a particular way. Similar to current trends in this clothing conversation that "violate social norms," the possibility for misunderstanding and miscommunication can have unfortunate results, such as alienation and rejection, even violence and abuse. Attention to clothing facilitates an intertextual dialogue with Ruth and Tamar (Gen. 38). Themes of irony weave between these two narratives: death and life; barrenness and pregnancy; empty and full; foreign and familial; recognition and nonrecognition; house of the father and house of the mother; levirate fulfillment by a male relative who is not a brother. This creative rereading seeks to explore intertextual connections through dress and identity within the story of Ruth and Tamar (Gen. 38). Intertextual readings provide the dialogic space to create new meanings, new possibilities.

Tamar is directly referenced in Ruth 4:12, as the elders and people of Bethlehem praise Tamar as a body of fecundity. Each woman's body represents society and what is hoped for in a social context. This blessing of social fecundity is pronounced upon Ruth, in hopes that through her body, life will birth forth new life and redeem the family inheritance, similarly to Tamar. Seed and fertility weave a narrative of hope for a future. Clothing and dress becomes the crux, signaling an outward momentum of initiation toward future possibilities of נחלה (inheritance, possession, property). The outcome of this risk-taking embodies individual agency that impacts Israel's ultimate future as a nation.

Tamar and Ruth: Evaluating Risk and Reward

The concept of the unified self will assist in framing this chapter and bringing together multiple themes, evidenced through this intertextual reading of Tamar (Gen. 38) and Ruth, highlighting the agency each woman exhibits that violates social systems yet contributes to Israel's ultimate future/s. Pioneering psychologist William James described the components of the self as separated into different spheres that collectively make up the unified self. The three main parts of the self are described as: (i) its constituents, (ii) the feelings and emotions they arouse, and (iii) the actions to which they prompt ("Self-seeking and Self-preservation").[3] James allocates four areas that make up the constituents of the self; these include: (i) the material self, (ii) the social self, (iii) the spiritual self, and (iv) the pure ego. This chapter will use the first three parts of the constituents of the self (material, social, and spiritual) to organize the critical intertextual themes found in the stories of Tamar and Ruth (dress,

---

3. William James, *The Principles of Psychology* (New York: Henry Holt, 1890), 292.

desire, seduction-reproduction, gender-ethnicity-identity, answerability, and inheritance possession).[4]

The focus of these three aspects of self (material, social, spiritual) will unveil in greater detail the risk each woman took as an individual foreign woman for the sake of the dominant community and the ultimate concerns for a future inheritance. The material self of Tamar and Ruth encompass the themes of dress, most notably observed in the function of items on the body, which create a future possibility within a specific situation. The social self extends from the materiality into the areas of seduction, reproduction, along with gender, ethnicity, and identity of Ruth and Tamar. A key factor within this social self is the idea of an invitation for an ethical response of answerability from another person, namely, Judah and Boaz. Finally, the spiritual self involves the individual's relation to key values. The driving factor here is the ultimate response of each woman to advance Israel's inheritance through pregnancy, in order that this family will have a continual inheritance and their memory will continue through generations.

One theme I want to focus on within the social self is the concept of answerability.[5] This concept was introduced by Mikhail Bakhtin and encompasses the ethical response of another within the dialogic encounter, embodying words, actions, and the esthetics of accountability. Translator Vadim Liapunov chose the English term "answerability" (from Bakhtin's Russian manuscripts) because it captures "the root sense of the term-answering; that point to bring out the 'responsibility'" involves the performance of an "existential dialogue."[6] This theme is critical to the unified self within its social location in the Tamar and Ruth stories as they negotiate their futures through dress. Their agency and desired outcomes within a contextual social system is connected to the ethical response of Judah and Boaz. Answerability embodies the potential response of life and death for these two women.

Dress is interpreted in the story as communicating deeds, identity, and advocacy. Interpretation of clothing becomes a provocative form of communication and

4. These basic foundational categories will be useful in this intertextual reading of the Tamar (Gen. 38) and Ruth stories. As readers, we are not given insights into their interior worlds, but James's concepts are useful in navigating their social worlds and social identity constructions (as they utilize dress and agency). It is important to note that James's work has been noted to be "steeped in patriarchy," yet there is also research showing "promising features," which has already demonstrated its influence with the work of women scholars (i.e., Edwina Barosa and Amy Oliver). "James emphasizes fringes and horizons, he appreciates fluidity and vagueness, and he values plurality and concrete experiences." See Erin C. Tarver and Shannon Sullivan, eds, *Feminist Interpretations of William James* (University Park: Pennsylvania State University Press, 2015), 2–3.

5. Mikhail M. Bakhtin, *Art and Answerability: Early Philosophical Essays by M.M. Bakhtin*, University of Texas Press Slavic Series 9, ed. Michael Holquist and Vadim Liapunov, trans. Vadim Liapunov (Austin: University of Texas, 1990).

6. Barbara Green, *How Are the Mighty Fallen? A Dialogical Study of King Saul in 1 Samuel* (England: Sheffield Academic, 2003), 226.

miscommunication, resistance and opportunity, ultimately moving the narrative forward. Texts and readers create this dialogic space and continued possibilities that resist finalization.[7] Bakhtin demonstrated the power of becoming through dialogic encounters (which influenced Julia Kristeva), showing how multiple voices (polyphony) and perspectives placed in dialogue enable new possibilities to emerge and remain open for more future possibilities (unfinalizability).[8] Not to be confused with dialectic, which can privy one voice over another, dialogue in Bakhtin's thought resists privilege and closure. Interpretation of dress contributes an intertextual voice within the dialogic interaction in the narrative.[9] Tamar (Gen. 38) and Ruth are related through intrinsic intertextual connections, along with shared motifs, and reveal how articles of dress communicate identity and action, advocating for narrative desire.

Tamar (Genesis 38)

Tamar is the type of woman in the Hebrew Bible that has been interpreted as a bold woman breaking social conventions and moral high ground by portraying herself as a prostitute.

Alongside her troubled identity within reception history, Genesis 38 has been historically understood as a problematic chapter within the Joseph cycle. Ironically, her portrayal in the Hebrew Bible suggests a very different perception. This problem woman in a problem chapter has found new horizons of positive impact in the past twenty years. A closer look at this story of Tamar, along the character of Ruth, unveils a powerfully evocative intertextual interpretation of these women, embodying agency within their unified person (material, social, spiritual) at great personal risk for their communities' ultimate concerns for survival. This agency is rooted in complex social systems and practices, and these women model resilience

7. Mikhail Bakhtin, *Problems of Dostoevsky's Poetics*, ed. and trans. Caryl Emerson (Minneapolis, MN: University of Minnesota Press, 1984), 87–8.

8. Shelley Birdsong reveals how Bakhtin's polyphony is useful within intertextual work and understanding diverse portraits of characterization. Using Bakhtin's polyphony as part of her multi-critical approach, Birdsong illuminates the diverse characterizations of Zedekiah/Sedekias in the Hebrew and Old Greek versions of Jer. 37(44):1–40(47):6 (i.e., the more compassionate king in the Hebrew and the manipulative portrait in the Greek). See Shelley L. Birdsong, *The Last King(s) of Judah: Zedekiah and Sedekias in the Hebrew and Old Greek Versions of Jeremiah 37(44):1–40(47):6*, Forschugen zum Alten Testament 2. Reihe (Tübingen, Germany: Mohr Siebeck, 2017).

9. Ellen van Wolde demonstrates that when texts are read together and placed in dialogue through synchronic intertextual readings, interpretive possibilities are enhanced. After reading each text independently, shared themes emerge, along with possible repetitions and analogies. Van Wolde notes that in the final step of comparing each text, there is the possibility of new meanings to emerge. Ellen van Wolde, "Texts in Dialogue with Texts: Intertextuality in the Ruth and Tamar Narratives," *BibInt* 5 (1997), 7 (1–28).

and adaptation within their environments as "both producers and products of social systems."[10]

The location of Genesis 38 has been misunderstood as a strange break in the Joseph cycle (Gen. 37–50) when these chapters are read chronologically. From Von Rad to Brueggemann, this chapter has been seen as one without connective tissue to the body of the Joseph material.[11] Conversely, Alter, paying close attention to the word choices and thematic elements, reveals the literary intentionality of this "interruption" chapter as a way to "build suspense" and demonstrate its purpose of insertion through intentional intertextual connections.[12] Through this lens, Genesis 38 becomes part of the intentional literary anatomy of the Joseph cycle and offers critical insights.[13] Fentress-Williams demonstrates that when Genesis 38 is read through the lens of chronotope, as a "play within a play," critical thematic elements emerge with greater clarity. The function of garments becomes more evident, as items that "conceal/deceive and reveal,"[14] material accessories functioning as a witness, demonstrating the provocative power of these dress items. Accessories left behind prove to be influencing objects of accusation and exoneration. In Genesis 39, the master's wife exploits the garments of Joseph to aid in her story of seductive deception and false accusation. Together, the garment and verbal cry provide a powerful pairing of propaganda.[15] In Genesis 38, ambiguity of

10. Agency can be misunderstood as activity outside of social systems, perhaps in the sense of "going rogue" that is often portrayed in literature and film. In detailing some of the key factors of agency within social cognitive theory, Albert Bandura, in *Self-Efficacy: The Exercise of Control* (New York: W.H. Freeman, 1997), writes,

Human adaptation and change are rooted in social systems. Therefore, personal agency operates within a broad network of sociostructural influences. In agent transactions, people are both producers and products of social systems … efficacious people are quick to take advantage of opportunity structures and figure out ways to circumvent institutional constraints or change them by collective action … this interplay involves agentic transactions between institutional functionaries and those who seek to accommodate to or change their practices." (6)

11. Von Rad describes this chapter as having "no connection," and Brueggemann sees it as "isolated" and as having "no connection to its context." See Gerhad Von Rad, *Genesis* (Philadelphia, PA: Westminster, 1972), 356–7. Walter Brueggemann, *Genesis* (Louisville, KY: Westminster John Knox, 1982), 307.

12. Robert Alter, *Genesis: Translation and Commentary* (New York: W.W. Norton, 1996), 217, n. 1. Alter highlights intertextual connections through verbs such as "went/brought down" which marks the beginning of the Judah (Gen. 38:1) and Joseph (Gen. 39:1) accounts.

13. See Ellena Lyell's chapter in this volume, "Dressing Benjaminites, Defining Kingship: Dress as a Royal Prerogative for the Tribe of Benjamin."

14. Judy Fentress-Williams, "Location, Location, Location: Tamar in the Joseph Cycle," in *Bakhtin and Genre Theory in Biblical Studies*, ed. Roland Boer (ed.) (Atlanta, GA: SBL, 2007), 67.

15. Ede writes,

identity is heightened by an initial false accusation of Tamar. The invitation to perceive identity is concealed until the end of the chapter, when Judah is invited to recognize material accessories: חתם (seal), פתל (cord), and מתתה (staff). The revealing of these items invokes a response of answerability. Will Judah respond as the Judah earlier in the story and shirk his responsibility of his daughter-in-law by sending her home, to the house of her father? Life and death stand before him in this final moment, similar to Joseph's final reveal with his brothers (Gen. 45). Before the final reveal, Joseph had intentionally hidden his identity through dress, as a נכר (foreigner), is "recognized as unrecognized," and more acutely stated, "active dis-recognition."[16] In the fields, Ruth expects to be dismissed because she is a foreigner. This moment involves a wordplay with wonder as she is shocked to be noticed, to be seen. Ruth proclaims astonishment that Boaz נכר (recognized) her, and she was a נכר (foreigner)![17] When Joseph allowed himself to be recognized, Joseph's brothers expect death and receive life. When Tamar's pregnancy is discovered, she is given a death sentence. Her only hope lies in the owner's recognition of three material items that will serve as witness—the cord, staff, and seal—to actively recognize them and respond to Tamar in life-giving answerability.

Tamar dramatically shifts the line of Judah from death to life through her agency. This strange story, often viewed as interruption to the Joseph narrative, breaks through to bring new beginnings to the story of Israel. Similar to the meaning of the name of her firstborn son, Perez פרץ (to break forth"), Tamar "breaks forth" through the waiting and the silence through a decision to act. This decision is marked by a change in dress which results in a misunderstanding of identity. Miscommunication in clothing will provide an opportunity for Tamar to take a risk of vulnerability and become an agent of change within a patriarchal society where women held limited agency.[18] This analysis will tease out this gap,

The seductress keeps the garment and calls upon the "men of her house" ... to whom she alleges that Joseph harassed her, while she raised her voice and cried (vv. 13–15). The cry signifies her non-consent to Joseph's alleged sexual approach and concords with the behavior required for a woman to go unpunished in the Deuteronomistic laws on rape such as Deut. 22:24, 27.

See Franziska Ede, "The Garment Motif in Gen. 37–39," in *Clothing and Nudity in the Hebrew Bible*, ed. Christoph Berner, Manuel Schäfer, Martin Schott, Sarah Schulz, and Martina Weingärtner (London: T&T Clark, 2019), 393.

16. Adi Ophir and Ishay Rosen-Zvi, *Goy: Israel's Multiple Others and the Birth of the Gentile* (New York: Oxford University Press, 2018), 26.

17. Ruth 2:10.

18. Sara Koenig, in her comparative analysis on "Tamar and Tamar: Clothing as Deception and Defiance" in Genesis, elevates the ambiguity of the decision to sleep with Judah. Koenig writes, "It is less clear *why* she does it" but "between the 'what' and the 'why' is Tamar's clothing, which becomes almost a character in itself." Koenig, "Tamar and Tamar: Clothing as Deception and Defiance," in *Dress and Clothing in the Hebrew Bible: "For*

highlighting how miscommunication through dress creates the opportunity for agency.

Beginning with Death

Death erupts early for three characters in Genesis 38—for Judah's wife and his two sons, Er and Onan. Er was married to Tamar, a woman whom Judah נשא אשה (lifted/carried) for his son. This idiomatic use to "lift/carry" a wife is used with only foreign women. The ethnicity of Tamar, though not explicit in the text, is probably Canaanite or Aramean. Tamar's name means date palm tree, and Frymer-Kensky connects the need for this tree to "be pollinated by direct human action," thus connecting Tamar's potential child-bearing fertility to the critical role of a levir.[19]

Er is considered evil in the Lord's eyes, and the Lord puts him to death (38:7). Tamar is now a widow, and Judah instructs his next eldest son, Onan, to act as a יבם (levir) and provide offspring, a child of inheritance, for his brother Er. In a twist of dark irony, the function of spilled seed outside of Tamar's body becomes a source of non-provision. Judah does not explicitly state that Onan was to marry Tamar. He instructs Onan to fulfill the duty of a brother-in-law as a levir, for his deceased brother as prescribed in Deut. 25:5-7. This same verb, יבם (levir), is used only here in Gen. 38:8 and Deut. 25:5, 7. Golka explains levirate duty:

> Genesis 38 and Ruth 4 are the only two narratives in the Bible that deal
> with the custom of levirate obligation, legally codified in Deut. 25.5-10.
> If a man
> dies without any male heirs, his brother is required to produce a son with the
> widow, which shall count as the dead man's son. The Hebrew word ... "to go to"
> does not mean "to marry" but "to have sex." Had Onan done his duty, the son
> would have counted as his brother's, and Tamar would have remained a widow.[20]

She is treated as a sexual object by Onan, used for purposes of pleasure and refused the possibility of progeny. Onan acted the part but spilled his semen on the ground (coitus interruptus) refusing to fulfill his duty because the child would not be his own (Gen. 38:9). The phrase "toward the ground" is not common in the Hebrew Bible and is used in Judg. 20:21 where the Israelites struck the Benjamites "towards the ground."[21] Along with this intertextual use in Judges, violence permeates this

---

All Her Household Are Clothes in Crimson," ed. Antonios Finitsis (New York: T&T Clark), 90–1; original emphasis.

19. Tikva Frymer-Kensky, *Reading the Women of the Bible: New Interpretations of Their Stories* (New York: Schocken, 2002), 266.

20. Friedemann W. Golka, "Genesis 37–50: Joseph Story or Israel-Joseph Story?" *Currents in Biblical Research* 2.2 (April 2004), 153–77.

21. Trent C. Butler, *Judges* (Grand Rapids, MI: Zondervan, 2009), 445.

phrase. One wonders if the *only* evil done to Tamar was coitus interruptus. With Judg. 20:21 in purview, perhaps rape or other acts of sexual violence characterize this story. Onan's actions are deemed רעע (evil), and he is struck down by YHWH (Gen. 38:10).

Judah instructs Tamar to return to the house of her father and "remain a widow" until his youngest son, Shelah, has grown up and can fulfill the levir duties (Gen. 38:11). Tamar obeys her father-in-law and returns to the house of her father. Alter points out that this was a "death sentence" against her and "a form of social disgrace in having to return to her father's house." Frymer-Kensky describes this moment as "Judah condemning Tamar to a living death."[22] Deciding not to wait out her death sentence, Tamar takes action. The change in dress will indicate a trajectory change for the narrative. Judah's last word to remain in the house of her father will not be the final word uttered. The symbolic move to change clothing on her own initiative is worth noting. Weingärtner reveals how vestimentary actions indicate symbolic meaning. Tamar's change in clothing not only signifies an outer shift in identity but also communicates an act of an "ethical struggle for righteousness."[23]

Covering and Uncovering: Provocative Redemption/Mistaken Identity

Tamar is wearing clothes that identify her as a widow. Zwickel notes that we do not have a description in the Hebrew Bible of the particular style, color, or fabric of the widow garments (Gen. 38:14, 19; Ruth 3:1-3; 2 Sam. 14:2).[24] What is clear about a widow's dress is its function. Gzella indicates that out of the two hundred instances of בגד (garment), the common term for garment, when it is in construct with another noun, it communicates the functionality of the clothing. One example is the garments of widowhood in Gen. 38:14.[25]

Tamar's identity as a widow is clear throughout the story, from the death of Er to the years that have passed as she remains in her father's house. Her garments of widowhood communicate her identity. A shift will be marked by the uncovering and recovering of her body with different items of dress. When Tamar "saw that Shelah had grown up," she realized that Judah was not keeping his promise to fulfill levirate duties. Tamar will remove her widow's garments in order to move her future forward. This is a very ambiguous scene as the narrative does not indicate

22. Frymer-Kensky, *Reading the Women of the Bible*, 280. Alter describes this as a "death sentence." See Robert Alter, *Genesis: Translation and Commentary* (New York: W.W. Norton, 1996), 219.

23. Martina Weingärtner, "The Symbolism of Vestimentary Acts in Gen. 27, Gen. 38, and 1 Sam. 17," in Berner et al., *Clothing and Nudity in the Hebrew Bible*, 412, n. 11.

24. Wolfgang Zwickel, "Fabrication, Functions, and Uses of Textiles in the Hebrew Bible," in Berner et al., *Clothing and Nudity in the Hebrew Bible*, 192.

25. Holger Gzella, "Nudity and Clothing in the Lexicon of the Hebrew Bible," in Berner et al., *Clothing and Nudity in the Hebrew Bible*, 229.

Tamar's motives. Does she want to confront her father-in-law? Does she desire for Judah to "remember" the promise he seems to have forgotten?

Fentress-Williams locates the use of clothing to reveal and conceal identity within the larger Joseph cycle:

> As is the case in the surrounding Joseph narrative, garments convey status, position, favor, or role. They also have the power to conceal or reveal identity. In the story of Joseph, the robe his father gives him is a visible sign of favor, and that same robe is used to deceive Jacob about his beloved son's death. Upon hearing of Joseph's demise, Jacob tears his clothes and replaces them with sackcloth, the garb of mourning. In Egypt, Potiphar's wife uses Joseph's robe to connect him to an offense he did not commit. When Joseph is restored in Pharaoh's house he receives a new wardrobe of fine linen, and Joseph's appearance keeps his identity hidden from his brothers when they encounter him years later.[26]

Tamar changes out of her widow garments to conceal her identity. This material self, presented through dress, indicates a "marker of status change."[27] This removal of widow's clothes suggests a suspension in her identity, with the possibility to be altered. Ironically, she will return to her garments of widowhood indefinitely.[28] As readers, we are aware her *intention* was to see Judah. We are not to privy to the information of her inner dialogue. Does she *want* to be noticed by Judah? The type of dress Tamar covers up her body with is the subject of much scholarly discussion. Along with dress, Tamar's location has been interpreted as indicating an intentional motive of Tamar to be seen as a prostitute.[29] This discussion often goes into three streams of interpretation: (i) Tamar intentionally dressed like a

26. Judy Fentress-Williams, "Location, Location, Location: Tamar in the Joseph Cycle," in *Bakhtin and Genre Theory in Biblical Studies*, ed. Roland Boer (Atlanta, GA: SBL, 2007), 64.

27. Gzella, "Nudity and Clothing in the Lexicon of the Hebrew Bible," 226.

28. Kang demonstrates the term אשה המת (wife of the dead) as a position in suspension, indicating that if a redeemer steps in, this position has the potential to shift. Though Tamar is not called אשה המת, her change of dress indicates a movement and shift of identity. In dialogue with Steinberg's analysis, Kang reveals the complexity of this term more fully, and this proves to possibly be another interesting place of Ruth and Tamar in dialogue, as the phrase אשה המת (wife of the dead) is found only in Ruth 4:5 and the levirate instructions in Deut. 25:5. See EunHee Kang, *The Dialogic Significance of the Sojourner, The Fatherless, and the Widow in Deuteronomy Through An Analysis of Chronotope Using Bakhtin's Reading Strategy*, dissertation, Graduate Theological Union, Berkeley, CA, 2009, 85; and Naomi Steinberg, "Romancing the Widow: Economic Distinctions Between the 'ALMANA, the 'ISSA-'ALMANA and the 'ESSET-HAMMET," in *God's Word for Our World*, JSOTSup 388, ed. Harold Ellens, Deborah Ellens, Rolf Knierim, and Isaac Kalimi (London: T&T Clark, 2004).

29. Heather A. McKay asserts this position in her chapter in this volume, "Dress Deployed as an Agent of Deception in Hebrew Bible Narratives."

prostitute to entice Judah, (ii) Tamar covered up in garments to conceal her identity and her motives remain concealed, and, finally, (iii) Tamar's location in town implies that she was a prostitute.[30] In this next section, I will demonstrate that a fourth possibility, and in my purview one more congruent with the text, is that Judah misidentifies Tamar for a prostitute on his own accord. Tamar was not intending for this scenario but in that moment, takes a risk for progenitive purposes and cooperates with Judah's false assessment.

Clothing change marks an identity shift for Tamar. Tamar סור (turns aside) her בגד אלמנות (garments of widowhood) and covers her face with a צעיף (wrapper/shawl/veil). Interpretations of Tamar concealing her face have led to the word choice of veil to describe the type of dress she uses. Many interpretations center around the identification of the צעיף as "veil" and associate it with the dress of a prostitute. This next section will demonstrate that the clothing and location of Tamar is intentionally ambiguous as a literary device. There is no direct correlation between dress or location that indicates Tamar was intentionally desiring to be seen and understood as a זנה (prostitute). This reading reveals the possibility that Judah's assumption was his own and not intentionally provoked by Tamar's dress or location. In order to make this claim, this next section will take into account the following three areas: (i) Where is צעיף translated as veil in the Hebrew Bible, and is this correlated with the dress of a זנה (prostitute)? (ii) If Tamar's clothing does not equate her with a prostitute, does her location make this a possibility? and (iii) If the clothing and location remain ambiguous in identifying Tamar as a prostitute, is there a possibility that Judah's assumption was his own and not intentionally provoked by Tamar's dress or location?

The use of a veil is limited in the Hebrew Bible and is only in reference to women. The other occurrence conveys a betrothal context, which is contrary to many interpretations that describe Tamar's use of the veil. Wolfgang Oswald observes that "there is no clear picture of the covering of one's head (or, more particularly, one's face) in ancient Israel."[31] Some interpretations conclude that Tamar's use of this clothing item indicates that she was attempting to play the part of a prostitute. The other occurrence of a woman covering her face is when Rebekah veils her face for betrothal (Gen. 24:65). The rarity of occurrences within the Hebrew Bible indicate that one must proceed with caution in immediately associating Tamar's use and function of clothing as one of an *intentional* prostitution. Middle Assyrian Laws detail extreme punishment for a prostitute wearing a veil. If a prostitute was caught wearing a veil, she was to be stripped of her clothing, beaten with "50 blows with rods" and, finally, "hot pitch" was to be poured over her head.[32] Veils were

30. Jennifer M. Matheny, *Judges 19–21 and Ruth: Canon as a Voice of Answerability*, dissertation, University of Kent, Canterbury, UK, 2018, 193.

31. Wolfgang Oswald, "Veiling Moses' Shining Face (Exodus 34:29-35)," in Berner et al., *Clothing and Nudity in the Hebrew Bible*, 456.

32. Martha T. Roth, *Law Collections from Mesopotamia and Asia Minor*, 2nd ed. (Atlanta: SBL, 1997), 167–8.

to be worn by wives, concubines, and widows. It becomes clear that the use of veil is limited in the Hebrew Bible and is not in connection to prostitution. In comparative literature, if a prostitute is caught wearing a veil, she will be severely punished.[33] Rather than veil, another possibility is that Tamar wore a wrapper, shawl, or scarf.[34] This misstep in the correlation of clothing communicating the vocation of prostitution has led to other interpretive possibilities. Location becomes the next possibility of Tamar conveying prostitute vibes to Judah.

Huddleston paints a portrait of Judah mistaking the identity of Tamar based not on dress but location. He also notes that Tamar's dress is "vague," and she is never explicitly called a "prostitute" but "the association is made by Judah the Hirah, and may have as much to do with her location and mannerism as her dress."[35] Frymer-Kensky alludes to this possibility with Judah when she writes, "He assumes that she is a prostitute because only a 'street-walker' would be hanging out in the open roadway."[36]

Conversely, the breadcrumb in the text does not associate her *location* with prostitution. The text leaves the connection solely in the mind of Judah. Judah "thought she was a prostitute, because she had covered her face" (Gen. 38:15). The verb used for this false assumption is השׁב, and it is "a word that can be used for false assessments."[37] Judah's false assumption most likely reveals not Tamar's motives and desires but Judah's. In my reading, I want to offer the possibility that the false assessment is solely made by Judah and not intentionally provoked by Tamar. Along with its use in Gen. 38:15, this verb (השׁב) describes Eli's false

---

33. This has been demonstrated by several scholars such as Tammi J. Schneider, Tikva Frymer-Kensky, and Sara M. Koenig.

34. Frymer-Kensky translates צעיף as "scarf." See *Reading the Women of the Bible*, 268.

35. J. R. Huddleston, "Divestiture, Deception, and Demotion: The Garment Motif in Genesis 37–39," *JSOT* 26.4 (2002): 47–62. Ede demonstrates that the location of Tamar "may be an indication of her profession" and this assumption "can be ascertained indirectly from passages such as Jer. 3:2 or Ezekiel 16:25, where sitting at the side of the road is associated with prostitution." See Ede, "The Garment Motif in Gen. 37-39," in Berner et al., *Clothing and Nudity in the Hebrew Bible*, 396. For this line of thought on location, see also Joan Goodnick Westenholz, "Tamar, *Qedesa, Qadistu*, and Sacred Prostitution in Mesopotamia," *HTR* 82 (1989), 245–66.

36. Frymer-Kensky, *Reading the Women of the Bible*, 270.

37. Koenig, "Tamar and Tamar: Clothing as Deception and Defiance," in *Dress and Clothing in the Hebrew Bible: "For All Her Household Are Clothed in Crimson,"* ed. Antonios Finitsis (New York: T&T Clark), 94. Koenig also uses the work of Maren Niehiff who shows the range of this term from "false assessment" to "thought" in "Do Biblical Characters Talk to Themselves?" *JBL* 111 (1992), 579. Another interesting use of this term is when Rachel and Leah utter it in a frustrated response to their father Laban, asking if there is any inheritance left in their father's house, proclaiming, "Are we not recognized by him as foreigners? For he has sold us and has indeed consumed our money" (Gen. 31:15).

assessment of Hannah as a drunken woman in 1 Sam. 1:13. The priest Eli falsely judges Hannah as a drunken woman when in reality she was praying fervently.

The ambiguity in this scene is intentional and a brilliant literary device, perhaps sparking more questions for the hearers. If prostitutes are forbidden to be veiled, this would heighten the focus on Judah's mistaken assessment and pulls the audience in to ask, "What will he do and what will happen next?" Scholars are quick to assume that Judah was in a celebratory mood because it was sheep-shearing time, a time of festivity.[38] Perhaps the joyous occasion increased his sexual desire. Often one sees what one wants, and perhaps Judah wants a prostitute. It could be as simple as that. What is clear in the text is that Tamar wants to conceal her identity. Confronting a father-in-law is not easy. The text conceals *why* Tamar wants to hide her identity. Perhaps she desires to assess the situation with her own eyes (i.e., Did Judah give Shelah to another woman? Should I discuss my death sentence of widowhood with Judah in person?). Schneider proposes that if veil is indeed the correct interpretation and is connected to a betrothal scenario (i.e., Gen. 24:65), perhaps "Tamar veils and rids herself of her widow garments because she plans on Judah taking her back to marry Shelah."[39] Judah misunderstands what he sees and mistakes her for a prostitute. Interpretations jump to this scene as a premeditated decision on Tamar's part to portray herself as a prostitute through dress. It is very likely that Tamar has other intentions in mind.

Mistaken identity creates a loophole of opportunity. Ironically, Judah is blind to her true identity. His import of desire shifts the narrative. Judah mistakes her for a זנה (prostitute) (Gen. 38:15). Miscommunication becomes the opportunity for Tamar to answer her death sentence of waiting. This reading proposes the possibility that Tamar was not *intending* to be noticed as a prostitute but with limited options as a woman in an ancient society, she took a risk to negotiate a future inheritance for the family. Judah avoided responsibility by sending her back home and dodges his familial duties a second time by not sending for Tamar when Shelah had grown up. He intentionally misguided Tamar by offering Shelah as levirate and avoided responsibility by sending her to the house of her family.

Tamar takes the leap and follows Judah's lead. She sleeps with Judah, allowing his false assessment to remain unchallenged. Thinking carefully, Tamar negotiates items of dress that belong to Judah to "secure a deposit" for what he imagines will be a later payment for her services. After Judah approaches Tamar and requests entry, Tamar asks what he will give her in exchange for the sexual encounter. Judah promises a kid from his flock, at a later date (another delayed promise!). Tamar insists on a deposit and Judah agrees to hand over his signet, cord, and staff. These items are personal, revealing, and recognizable. Tamar secures Judah's pledge in preparation to be recognized, and for Judah to be recognized. After she

---

38. Frymer-Kensky writes that Judah was in a "party mood." See *Reading the Women of the Bible*, 269.

39. Tammi J. Schneider, *Mothers of Promise: Women in the Book of Genesis* (Grand Rapids, MI: Baker Academic, 2008), 155.

has collected his pledge and he deposits his seed, Tamar is quick to return to her widow attire. Recognition will be held in a place of suspense.

When Judah later sends Hirah with the payment, he calls Tamar קְדֵשָׁה (consecrated woman).[40] This would indicate her possible association within a cultic community, rather than within a family system, where she would have a community identity and protection. Bird writes that זנה (prostitute) "is the defining term in this scene."[41] The reader is expecting the term זנה (prostitute) in the story and the introduction of Hirah using the term קְדֵשָׁה (consecrated woman) could indicate its common usage and understanding. Bird writes that this indicates a "'realistic' portrayal of a public exchange concerning a delicate matter for a patriarch."[42] Judah's personal possessions are now in the hands of an unknown woman. In an interesting turn of events, nobody remembers seeing this type of prostitute by the road at Enaim. This bit of information reinforces the fact that Judah wanted sex and imports desire into his false assessment of Tamar. He is the only witness. In small communities in the ancient Near East, it is difficult to imagine that nobody in town would remember a prostitute lurking in the open square during the day.

Ending with Life

Tamar will now uncover and cover once more. Taking off her clothing of concealment, Tamar places her garments of widowhood back on. Returning to the house of her father, Tamar waits. Through her material and social self, she is advancing the spiritual and existential concerns for an inheritance. Her risk pays off. Outwardly, her clothing functions to signify her identity as a widow, and inwardly, life is burgeoning. Though a product of a social system, she is at the same times a producer of bold initiative within it. Tamar refuses to remain a destitute widow with a death sentence.

After some time, Tamar cannot hide her pregnancy any longer. Her identity as a pregnant widow has reached the ears of Judah. Immorality and sin characterize her sentence. Without a chance to hear Tamar's side of the story, Judah sentences

40. This term has a long interpretive history. There are only five occurrences of the fem. noun קְדֵשָׁה (consecrated woman) in the Hebrew Bible (Gen. 38:21 (2x), 22; Hos. 4:14; Deut. 23:18). For a comprehensive study of קְדֵשָׁה (consecrated woman), see Phyllis A. Bird, *Harlot of Holy Woman? A Study of the Hebrew Qedešah* (University Park, PA: Eisenbrauns, 2019).

41. In the role of the קְדֵשָׁה (consecrated woman) in Genesis 38, Bird writes,

I conclude that its use in this passage assumes the existence of a class of women dedicated to cultic service, whose duties and duration of service remain unknown, but whose status as a single woman outside the family system placed them in the same general category as prostitutes and made them vulnerable to sexual exploitation, whether for the benefit of the cult or as a means of survival. (Ibid., 370)

42. Ibid., 367.

her to the fullest extent of punishment, burning (Gen. 38:24). Tamar refuses to be silent and her defense will be material accessories. She asks for Judah to נכר (recognize) these items. Articles of dress now become juridical advocates for righteousness. The function of these mute items is to symbolize their owner's identity. Tamar brings forward the evidence of her vindication: חתם (seal), פתל (cord), and מתתה (staff). The פתל was thought to be made from linen and could be dyed.[43] The signet or seal, cord, and staff belong to Judah. These accessories become a witness, an opportunity for answerability. They represent the identity of the one who has impregnated Tamar, and in this moment, they advocate for Tamar and her twin boys. The three would have died in the burning and these objects became accessories to life.

Ruth: Beginning with Death

Famine leads Naomi's family from Bethlehem to Moab. Ruth 1:1 literarily places this story in the "days the judges were judging." Violence and death loom in the background during this period and continue into the first chapter of Ruth. Early on, two Moabite women, Ruth and Orpah, enter into the family dynamics. Ruth and Orpah are נשא אשה (lifted/carried) as wives for the sons of Naomi. The men have not "taken" a wife, they נשא אשה (lifted/carried) wives for themselves (Ruth 1:4). The verb נשא means "to lift" or "to carry" and highlights the idea that Ruth and Orpah are *other*, as foreign women. This is the same verb used at the end of Judges where the Benjamite men "lift" and "carry" wives for themselves at the festival dance (Judg. 21:23). This was a mass kidnapping at the end of Judges. The use of the verb "taking" a wife is consistently used for foreign women in the Hebrew Bible. The more usual idiom is לקח (to take) an Israelite wife rather than נשא (to carry) a foreign one (see Gen. 24:4). This unusual verbal link, link "to take" a wife, in connection with the time period of Judges, creates an invitation of intertextual dialogue.

Ruth begins with the men being blown away like chaff from the harvest. This is almost a Jobian twist in reverse. Instead of children, the ones to *provide* this inheritance seed are removed. Ruth has oft been viewed as a "sweet little story," fairy-tale like and akin to Cinderella, where a woman in need is rescued by her prince. To the contrary, death hums through this story, with widows in the lead roles. Potential violence weaves through the Tamar and Ruth story, and their actions are bold and risky.[44] Opening scenes of mortality reveal that death as a motif invites intertextual connections with the story of Judah and Tamar.

43. Zwickel, "Fabrications, Functions, and Uses of Textiles," 197.
44. David Shepherd illustrates gendered violence in Ruth 2 with the vulnerability of the women in the fields. See David J. Shepherd, "Ruth in the Days of Judges: Women, Foreignness and Violence," *Biblical Interpretation* 26.4–5 (2018): 537–40.

Ruth's story opens with Ruth initiating a covenantal verbal pledge to Naomi after the men have died. She covenants with Naomi and to remain faithful, unlike Judah. Here, readers encounter a foreign woman who represents the faithful חסד (loving-kindness, covenant-faithfulness), which a patriarch could not fulfill. The subversive elements of carnival are in full dialogue with these two stories, where the marginalized are given platforms to speak and social conventions are inverted.[45] The marginalized exhibits חסד-type faithfulness. The patriarch, Judah, shirks his responsibility, not only by withholding his third son but also by sending Tamar back to her father's house (Gen. 38:11). Ruth, by her words, exceeds readerly expectations by fulfilling her promise to Naomi. Tamar, by her actions, fulfills the levir duty that Judah neglects to implement to completion with his final son, Shelah.

Covering and Uncovering: Provocative Redemption

Bethany Joy Wagstaff, in her work on the material-cultural approaches to clothing in the Hebrew Bible, demonstrates how ethnographic studies on clothing in other cultures contribute a more dynamic and performative use of clothing, "broadening the Western perceptions of clothing."[46] Wagstaff details the constructive power

45. Carnival is the medieval genre of folk humor which highlights the inversion of social roles. Rabelais uses powerful exaggerated mediums to convey a message of societal inversion of roles with body imagery, sexual activity, defecating, and feasting. Bakhtin's research with Rabelais demonstrates how this literary genre will "disunite those things that have been falsely brought together" in order to reveal "false connections that distort the authentic nature of things, false associations established and reinforced by tradition and sanctioned by religious and official ideology." With Ruth and Tamar, sexual activity and dress invert social roles. Irony is employed in the Hebrew Bible but not the type of laughter and humor commonly associated with this genre. See Bakhtin, *Dialogic Imagination: Four Essays*, trans. Caryl Emerson and Michael Holquist (Austin: University of Texas, 1981), 169.

46. Wagstaff, "Redressing Clothing in the Hebrew Bible," 69. Wagstaff gives a supportive list from ethnographic studies that include: Chloe Colchester, "Objects of Conversion: Concerning the Transfer of Sulu to Fiji," in *The Art of Clothing: A Pacific Experience*, ed. Graeme Were and Susanne Küchler (London: UCL Press, 2005), 33–46; Chloe Colchester, "Relative Imagery: Patterns of Response to the Revival of Archaic Chiefly Dress in Fiji," in *Clothing as Material Culture*, ed. Susanne Küchler and Daniel Miller (Oxford: Berg, 2005), 139–58; Elizabeth Cory-Pearce, "Surface Attraction: Clothing and the Mediation of Maori/European Relationships," in Were and Küchler, *The Art of Clothing*, 73–87; Amiria Henare, "Nga Aho Tipuna (Ancestral Threads): Maori Cloaks from New Zealand," in Küchler and Miller, *Clothing as Material Culture*, 121–38; Michael O'Hanlon, "Under Wraps: An Unpursued Avenue of Innovation," in Were and Küchler, *The Art of Clothing*, 61–9; Susanne Küchler and Graeme Were, "Introduction," in Were and Küchler, *The Art of Clothing*, xix–xxx; Mosko, "Fashion as Fetish: The

of clothing, which is often missed as a critical component in the construction of identity and desire:

> They have their own material properties and form, which can never be fully controlled or follow the expectations set by people. This effectively challenges the conventional anthropocentric expectation in biblical scholarship that an object's power and agency is always inevitably reliant on people. Nevertheless, clothes are also able to index personhood through their entanglement with other people. The boundaries between people and things are frequently blurred, since they can be seen to share in each other's power and agency, imprinting themselves onto the other. The intimate entanglement that exists between clothing and people, as well as acknowledging that clothes can restrict or enable people's power and movement through their own materiality, enables a fresh understanding of the conventional expression that "clothes maketh the man." Through my analyses in this chapter it can be recognised that people construct clothing and clothes construct people.[47]

Ruth's clothing constructs her identity. Through her material and social self, she asserts the ultimate concern for an inheritance, informed by her spiritual self. This scene uncovers a body and uncovers a plan.

> 3:1 Then Naomi, her mother-in-law, said to her, "My daughter, shall I seek for you a resting place, that will be good for you?"[48]

> 3:2 And now, is not Boaz our kinsman, with whose young women you have been. Behold! He is scattering barley on the threshing floor this night,"

> 3:3 Now wash, anoint and set a mantle upon yourself and go down to the threshing floor. Do not let yourself be made known to the man until he has finished eating and drinking."

> 3:4 And it will be when he lies down, know the place which he will lay down and come in and uncover his feet and lie down. He himself will declare to you that which you are to do."

> 3:5 Then she said to her, "All that you have said to me, I will do."

> 3:6 Then she went down to the threshing floor and she did all that her mother-in-law commanded.

Agency of Modern Clothing and Traditional Body Decoration among North Mekeo of Papua New Guinea," *Contemporary Pacific* 19.1 (2007), 39–83; Hermkens, "Clothing as Embodied Experience of Belief," in *Religion and Material Culture: The Matter of Belief*, ed. David Morgan, 1st ed. (London: Routledge, 2010), 231; Pia Tohveri, *Weaving with the Maya: Innovation and Tradition in Guatelama* (CreateSpace Independent Publishing Platform, 2012).

47. Wagstaff, "Redressing Clothing in the Hebrew Bible," 71.

48. Biblical translations are those of the author, unless otherwise noted.

Naomi has instructed Ruth to remove her widow garments and then to רחץ (wash), סוך (anoint), and set שמלה (clothes) upon herself. Ruth is prompted by Naomi to change from her widow's garments to different שמלה (clothing). The use of this term occurs twenty-nine times, is wide and varied, and carries a generic sense of "clothing."[49] In connection with the perfume Ruth is instructed to use, the time at night, and a plan of redemption, Ruth's "clothing" becomes significant as she changes from her widow's garments to different items of dress for a redemption request.

The mantle—שמלה (clothing)—was a garment that had multiple uses for men and women. Zwickel notes that "it must be identified as a long garment … made by two rectangular pieces of textile sewn along the sides" (with openings for the arms and the head) because its function was as a covering for the body (Gen. 9:23; Exod. 3:22) and it was used to transport goods (Exod. 12:34) and "as a mat for presenting items (Judges 8:25)."[50] The same three verbs in succession in Ruth 3:3 are also in 2 Sam. 12:20. Here, David will רחץ (wash), סוך (anoint) and change his שמלה (clothing) after the mourning period following the death of his son. This succession of verbs signifies a specific moment of transition in both stories, from mourning and fasting then back to normal life rhythms.

To anoint (סוך) is the use of oil to perfume oneself. In 2 Sam. 14:2, Joab instructs the wise woman of Tekoa to anoint herself with oil so that she will not represent a widow in mourning. It is worth noting that perfume and the sprinkling of myrrh and spices on a bed is connected with seduction and sexual activity in Prov. 7:17, Song of Songs 4:14, and possibly Prov. 27:9. Though different words are used, the use of perfume in Ruth 3:3 and the startling of Boaz in the night could indicate that he was startled by her fragrance. Boaz woke up trembling and twisting (Ruth 3:8).[51] If the oils she used were similar to oils connected to smells of seduction, this could have added to his fright in the middle of the night. The manner of Boaz being awakened, along with the aroma of seduction, could indicate a legitimate fear connected to ancient Near Eastern superstitious beliefs in night demons. Grossman comments that the night demon Lilith was considered to be "a dangerous seductress who believed to attack men at night."[52] The scent of anointing

---

49. שלמה (clothing) is used as a literary motif in the Joseph story (37:34; 41:14; 44:13; 45:22).

50. Zwickel, "Fabrications, Functions, and Uses of Textiles," 209.

51. The verb חרד (to tremble) is often connected to the idea of an unanticipated situation, not merely a night chill. The verb לפת (to turn) is in two other places: Judg. 16:29 and Job 6:18. Grossman notes that some have then suggested this indicates that touch that woke Boaz up. I suggest that the aroma of perfume in connection with touch and nighttime imaginative possibilities (as Grossman illustrates), such as the night demon Lilith, could explain such a startling arousal. Jonathan Grossman, *Ruth: Bridges and Boundaries* (Bern, Switzerland: Peter Lang, 2015), 215–16.

52. Ibid., 215–16, n. 49.

oils could lead the way in this startling first moment and the surprise (and relief!) of Boaz when he realizes it was the woman Ruth lying at his feet.

The manipulation of clothing is significant and intentional. Having changed out of her widow's clothing, Ruth is instructed by Naomi to lay down next to Boaz and uncover his feet. This movement of clothing is intentional. Naomi coaches Ruth to allow Boaz to tell her what to do after his feet are uncovered. This very ambiguous moment during midnight puts Ruth at risk. The potential for violence in the fields is noted in chapter 2. Boaz has proved protective as he instructs his workers not to lay a hand on Ruth (Ruth 2:9). Readers are left to wonder if he will continue in this protective role, at this time of night after festivities, when inhibitions are less guarded.

The time and manner of Ruth's approach toward Boaz indicates a desire to remain unrecognized. The text does not reveal Ruth "veiling" herself for secrecy with dress, but her approach at midnight creates the veil of night, allowing a stealthy approach. "Then Boaz ate and drank and his heart was glad, and he came in to lie down at the end of the grain heap. She came in secretly and she uncovered his feet and lay down. (3:7)."

Ruth לט (secretly) comes to the threshing floor at midnight, seeking an encounter with Boaz. Her movement in her clothing is performative. Out of the nine occurrences, לט is often used adverbially and translated as "quietly" or "secretly" with the preposition ב (Gen. 37:25, 43:11; Exod. 7:22, 8:3, 8:14; Judg. 4:21; Ruth 3:7, 1 Sam. 18:22, 24:5). The only other use in connection with a woman is that of Jael in Judg. 4:21 when she "secretly" went into the tent and drove a tent peg through the temple of Sisera. With very different intentions, Ruth and Jael both moved secretly to execute a plan. Though Ruth 3:7 is the only use of לט that has been debated, seen in light of its use with Jael, I contend that "secretly" is the intentional use, rather than "softly." The use of "softly" has been suggested because it could potentially be related to the root of the adverb, לט.[53] "If *lāt* derives from *'t* (gentleness), then 'softly, quietly' is a more appropriate translation … but if *lāt* is related to *lwt* (wrap, cover), then 'secretly' or 'stealthily' may be a more suitable rendering."[54] Another use of לט (secretly, stealthily) is in 1 Sam. 24:5 when David secretly enters the cave to cut off the extremity כנף (wings, extremity) of Saul's robe.[55]

The interpretation of this adverb by previous scholars has been part of Ruth's identification and characterization as a demure and gentle figure. The danger and

53. Francis Brown, S. R. Driver, and Charles A. Briggs, *The New Brown, Driver, and Briggs Hebrew and English Lexicon of the Old Testament* (Lafayette: Associated Publishers and Authors, 1981), 4836.

54. See Andrew E. Hill and Malcolm J. A. Horsnell in #4319 "לט" in *New International Dictionary of Old Testament Theology and Exegesis* (vol. 2), ed. Willem A. Van Gemeran (Michigan: Grand Rapids, 1997), 794–5.

55. Jennifer Matheny, "Judges 19-21 and Ruth: Canon as a Voice of Answerability," PhD dissertation, University of Kent, Canterbury, 2018.

secrecy of entering at night, along with the undebated other uses within the canon, reveal that Ruth moved secretly similar to David and Jael (i.e., not out of gentleness but out of stealth). With the covering of night, Ruth is beginning to execute Naomi's plan and uncover her own. The irony of identity along with the performative use of dress (clothing and perfume) will continue to thread through this scene as Ruth creates a possible loophole for herself through her request. Ruth's request departs from her mother-in-law's instructions. Not only will Ruth request redemption for the property but she will also request Boaz to act as a redeeming one, to fulfill a role that will enact a levirate marriage.

Ending with Life

The term מרגלות (place of the feet) is controversial in this chapter of Ruth. It is derived from the noun רגל (foot). The meaning of this term and the understanding of what body part/s are exposed has ranged from Ruth uncovering the foot of Boaz to uncovering his genitalia. Euphemisms are common in the Hebrew Bible. "Feet," "hand," and "flesh" can be associated with genitals. Examples of these euphemistic uses are also found in ancient texts outside the Bible.[56]

Ruth may have uncovered herself, revealing a ploy of seduction. The term used for the place of the of מרגלות (place of the feet) is found five times in Ruth and in only one other place in the Hebrew Bible, with the terrifying vision in Dan. 10:6. Sasson remarks that this term "foot" is "contrasted with arms so is rendered legs," and it is derived from the noun רגל (foot). רגל in the Hebrew Bible is normally associated with sexual organs (male: Exod. 4:25; Judg. 3:24; 1 Sam. 24:3, 4; and female: Deut. 28:57; Ezek. 16:25).[57] What is interesting is that the use of גלה (to uncover) in the piel is seen twice with foot, and both occurrences indicate an act of uncovering the body. In Isa. 47:2, the exposure of the leg of the woman, Babylon, is an indication of her shame. The use of גלה (uncover) in the piel in Hos. 2:12 is associated with the idea of nakedness and shame.

The intertextual connections with nakedness and shame with the use of גלה and מרגלות indicate that the ambiguity may be intentional as to *what* body part is exposed along with *whose* genitalia may have been exposed. Naomi's plan was targeted at Boaz, a wealthy landowner, and could have "centered around sexual

---

56. Flesh for genitalia is found in impurity texts. "Seminal and abnormal discharge from a man's 'flesh' and menstrual or other discharge from a woman's 'flesh' makes them 'unclean' or ritually impure, unable to participate in the community's religious ceremonies." Hand used as a euphemism for an erect phallus is found in a Ugaritic text (second millennium BCE). There is also an example in a community rule text from the Dead Sea Scrolls, where an exposed phallus warrants punishment for thirty days. See Michael Coogan, *Sex and God* (New York: Twelve, 2010), 14.

57. Jacques Sasson, *Ruth: A New Translation with a Philological Commentary and a Formalist-Folklorist Interpretation* (Baltimore, MD: John Hopkins University Press, 1979), 69.

entrapment using Ruth as bait."[58] The question that seems most appropriate in this discussion is to ponder whether or not the text artisan intended the use of "foot" to be intentionally ambiguous. Nielsen remarks that because it is not implicit in the text, the reader "must draw conclusions."[59] This appears to be one of the ironic comedic ploys throughout the text of Ruth, and the elusiveness is intentional ambiguity. Tikva Frymer-Kensky writes that "there are only two possibilities: she is uncovering him, or herself, and the narrator may be playing with the reader by not making the scene absolutely clear."[60] The use of the term "foot," alongside the intertextual connections (Gen. 19, 38), reveals that the secrecy, crisis of lineage, and sexual connotations guide the reader to view this as intentional ambiguity. It is probable that this term מרגלות, in connection with the piel form of גלה, could reveal that Ruth uncovered her own body. This intentional rhetorical device of ambiguity is an invitation for readerly imagination and becomes even more provocative when read with the ambiguity surrounding Tamar's veiling.[61] Nudity, prostitution, seduction, foreignness, and inheritance negotiation create a powerful dynamic of intertextual dialogue drawing the reader closer into the story. A surprising twist awaits, where these women, previously characterized by immorality and otherness, will become archetypal models of righteousness within Israel.

Ruth's agency stands out in her double request of Boaz (Ruth 3). Naomi directs Ruth to request redemption. Ruth requests redemption *and* a levirate marriage. Barbara Green regards this scene in 3:9 as a key to understanding the whole:

> This verse is a most crucial one for my understanding of the story. It will be my contention that Ruth and Naomi and the storyteller are carefully distinguishing between requests for marriage and redemption, and yet are deliberately associating them here in order to both maintain suspense and keep us from guessing how the story will turn out.[62]

The request for Boaz to fulfill two different but related roles is acknowledged by several scholars (e.g., Campbell, Nielsen, Hubbard, Green). Naomi has indicated to Ruth in 2:20 that Boaz is a גאל (redeeming one). Noting that he is not *the* גאל but *a* גאל, it is clear that Naomi and Ruth specifically desire Boaz to fulfill the role.

58. Charles Halton, "An Indecent Proposal: The Theological Core of the Book of Ruth," *Scandinavian Journal of the Old Testament* 26.1, 30 43 (Taylor & Francis, 2012), 32.

59. Kirsten Nielsen, *OTL Library: Ruth* (Louisville, KY: Westminster John Knox, 1997), 68–9.

60. Frymer-Kensky, *Reading the Women of the Bible*, 248.

61. The intentional ambiguity is noted by several scholars such as Edward F. Campbell Jr., *The Book of Ruth* (Grand Rapids, MI: William B. Eerdmans, 1988), 121.

62. Barbara Green, "A Study of Field and Seed Symbolism in the Biblical Story of Ruth," dissertation, Graduate Theological Union, Berkeley, CA, 1980, 28, n. 1.

They have chosen him. Coupled with the time Ruth approaches Boaz, midnight, and how she secretly enters the threshing floor, it is clear that Ruth and Naomi want Boaz alone to hear the request. The legal material in the Hebrew Bible (Lev. 25:24-34, 47-55; Num. 35:19ff; Deut. 19:6, 12; Josh. 20:3ff; 1 Kgs 21:3; Jer. 32:7ff; Job 19:26; Isa. 43:1), in reference to this role to act the redeemer, does not assume a marriage. In fact, the role indicates that the one redeeming will purchase back property or persons connected to what has been forfeited or sold. Nielsen observes that the "redeemer does not appear to be duty bound to marry a childless widow unless he is at the same time the woman's brother-in-law."[63] As witnessed in Genesis 38, the role to redeem was given to the brothers of the deceased individual.

What is unusual with Boaz is that he is a relative but not one of the brothers. In fact, his reply indicates that he is not the first one in line to act in this role. Naomi must have been aware of this as is evident in 2:20 when she mentions that Boaz is "one of our redeemers." The boldness of the plan is clearer when one realizes that Boaz was chosen by these women as the one *they* desired to act in the role of redeemer. Sending Ruth at night, secretly, indicates that they only wanted Boaz to know of their request.

Ruth now diverges from the plan birthed by Naomi and requests not only redemption but also marriage as she also requests for Boaz to spread כנף (wings) over her nakedness, indicating betrothal imagery (Ruth 3:9). Various interpretations have suggested that "wings" harken back to Ezekiel's betrothal imagery (Ezek. 16:8). The wing has been suggested to be the edge or the corner of the garment. Some translations suggest this was a request to spread the "corner" of the garment over another person. Near Eastern iconography reveals that the more common uses indicate sewn fringe. "Traditional translation with 'corner' appears to be wrong. Instead, it is a question of a sewn fringe as it is shown in Near Eastern pictures."[64] The function of כנף (wings) in intertextual use suggests a sense of protection (Ruth 2:12) and also marriage (Ezek. 16:8). Here, the image of God spreading wings over Jerusalem and her nakedness, after she had grown up and matured, opens the way for the marriage metaphor to once again call the beloved, Jerusalem, back to her lover, God.

Naomi, in the beginning of the chapter, told Ruth to uncover Boaz and wait for *him* to tell her what to do. Ruth fulfills Naomi's request in the uncovering, and in an ironic twist, *she* tells Boaz what she would like him to do. In the following chapter, Boaz will marry Ruth, and it will become clear that he fulfills both requests after his initial hunt for the closer גאל (redeeming one).

The intriguing aspect to this marriage is the query as to whether this particular marriage to Ruth would fall under the category of an actual levirate marriage (Deut. 25:5-10). What perplexes scholars is the nature of Boaz's relationship with Naomi, perhaps as one being too far removed from the normative brother-in-law

---

63. Nielsen, *Ruth*, 75.
64. Zwickel, "Fabrication, Functions, and Uses of Textiles in the Hebrew Bible," 212.

role. What is pertinent to the discussion here is that through dialogue, Ruth reiterated the words of Naomi and reinterpreted them into something new for herself and for Boaz. Koosed rightly observes that by using the term "wing," Ruth is "echoing his language from chapter 2 but substituting Boaz himself for God (3:9) … she is not waiting for God to provide but taking initiative, taking what she needs and calling on Boaz to provide."[65] The next scene is a foreshadow of how Boaz will fulfill Ruth's request, as he instructs her to hold out another article of clothing, her מטפחת (cloak), in 3:15. This is an interesting term as it has only one other occurrence in the Hebrew Bible, which is in Isa. 3:22. In Isaiah, it is in the context of judgment and the lord removing outer garments, among other items of apparel. The list in Isaiah is useful as it suggests, in the context of Ruth, that the מטפחת (cloak) is an extra item of clothing, for warmth and/or discretion for the nightly encounter. Boaz responds to Ruth in kindness, as his answerability reveals not condemnation, violence, or judgment but acceptance and provision. He fills the מטפחת (cloak) with grain, and Ruth returns to Naomi, still clothed in her שמלה (clothing).[66] שמלה is a "multi-functional garment used both by men and women (Exodus 3:22; Deut. 22:5, 17; Isa. 4:1; Ruth 3:3) as garment … and a cover at night."[67]

Boaz generously fills her מטפחת (cloak) with grain, and as the harvest foreshadows the lineage in this story, he will soon provide seed for an heir. Aschkenasy notes the humor in Boaz's quick decision to play the proper gentleman and to hastily give Ruth some of the harvest:

> The comedy of the body continues when Boaz, in a theatrical gesture, measures out a significant portion of barley and tells Ruth to hold up her apron so that he can fill it up (3:15). Boaz's commendable action is reduced to physical farce: one can only imagine the bawdy visual possibilities, the semiotic signification, of Ruth returning home with her apron bulging provocatively.[68]

Clothing and seed function narratologically as a comedic element within the Ruth story, highlighting the function of seed as sustenance and seed as progeny. Dress communicates the anticipated inheritance to come through the body of Ruth. The next item of dress removal will be between two men, two potential redeemers for Ruth and Naomi. Boaz will initiate a conversation at the city gate with the unnamed redeemer, one who is a closer relation to Naomi. Fortunately, the

---

65. Jennifer Koosed, *Gleaning Ruth: A Biblical Heroine and Her Afterlives* (Columbia: University of South Carolina, 2012), 91.

66. The amount of grain is stated in the text as six measures. The ranges of interpretations are quite extensive, but it is evident that it must have been an amount that one person could carry. Sasson lists a range from a *Homer* (1740 lbs) to an 'Omer (30 lbs). Sasson, *Ruth*, 96.

67. Zwickel, "Fabrications, Functions, and Uses of Textiles in the Hebrew Bible," 209.

68. Nehama Aschkenasy, "Reading Ruth through a Bakhtinian Lens: The Carnivalesque in a Biblical Tale," *JBL* 126.3 (2007), 451.

unnamed redeemer will refuse, and this exchange is made official by the removal of his sandal.

The use of a sandal to conduct a legal exchange is one of the intrigues of Ruth 4:7-8:

> 4:7 Now this was formerly the custom in Israel, to confirm all the words upon redemption and exchange, a man drew off his sandal and gave it to his companion, and this was the testimony in Israel.

> 4:8 And the redeeming one said to Boaz, "Buy it for yourself!" And he drew off his sandal.

Sandals were common articles of dress within the Hebrew Bible and throughout the ancient Near East. Krause notes that sandals were simply made, "usually consisting of no more than a sole made of leather and or sometimes wood, fastened to the foot by a thong."[69] The sandal removal adds a historical element to the story, along with a legal-symbolic transaction. It is a custom of "former days," and one of which nobody at that point could quite remember! There is an analogous example in a Nuzi text that testifies to a real-estate transfer with a sandal.[70] Hubbard demonstrates that in the Hebrew Bible, sandals often symbolize "power, possession, and domination" (Josh. 10:24; Exod. 3:5; 2 Sam. 15:30; Ezek. 24:17, 23).[71] The removal of a shoe in a legal real-estate transfer of ownership is evidenced in Nuzi texts and provides a corresponding analogy with Ruth 4:7. An intertextual example is found in Deut. 25:9, where the levirate marriage role is discussed. In this passage, if the brother of the deceased refuses his opportunity to marry the widow, she pulls off his sandal, spits in his face, and pronounces upon him that his house will be known in Israel as "the house of him who had his sandal pulled off" (Deut. 25:10).[72] This final transaction involving the removal of a shoe by the unnamed redeemer in Ruth 4:8 indicates the removal of his desire to take on the widow Ruth and the land of Naomi. Boaz would redeem the inheritance for the family, therefore raising the name of the dead. Ruth's bold actions, initiated through a change of dress, sought to begin the inheritance negotiation in Ruth 3. Ruth's request on the threshing floor is answered after the removal of the sandal in Ruth 4:8.

---

69. Joachim J. Krause, "Barefoot before God: Shoes and Sacred Space in the Hebrew Bible and Ancient Near East," in Berner et al., *Clothing and Nudity in the Hebrew Bible*, 316.

70. Ernest R. Lacheman, "Note on Ruth 4:7–8," *JBL* 56 (1937), 53–4.

71. Robert L. Hubbard, *The Book of Ruth* (Grand Rapids, MI: Eerdmans, 1998), 251.

72. Sandals were removed for sacred reasons. Before entering a place of worship, sandals would be removed. Krause finds examples of this within later Jewish sources and early Christian examples "from Mesopotamian and Levantine sources." Krause references these examples, "Stol, 'Schoh', 290; Dürr, 'Bedeutung,' 411(evidence from Mesopotamia); and Dalman, *Arbeit*, 296 (later Jewish practice)." See "Barefoot before God," 316, n. 17.

Conclusion

Tamar and Ruth are texts in dialogue. Dress is an intentional means of communicating identity and desire within these two stories related through intratextual lexical connections (Tamar in Ruth 4:12) and intertextual themes of foreignness and redemption. Intertextual connections of death, motifs of seed, clothing, and genealogy reveal that Ruth is in canonical dialogue with Genesis 38.

Bakhtin's category of recognition and nonrecognition highlights some of the irony found in each of these stories and how they relate in the canon. Ruth's story will interweave the agricultural motif of emptiness and fullness, as well as famine and harvest. The women in Ruth begin the story empty. The husbands have died and the place where they live—Moab—is in the midst of a famine. This famine extends to family as there is no heir to carry forth the name of the dead.

In one of the heights of irony in the story, Naomi proposes a rhetorical question to the women: "Then Naomi replied, 'Return my daughters for how will you go with me? Are there still sons in my womb who could be husbands for you?'" (Ruth 1:11). Intertextually, the rhetorical humor of Naomi coupled with Judah's empty promise of offering Tamar his youngest son heightens the ironic intertextuality. Naomi cannot fulfill her desires to provide an inheritance through more sons. Judah *has* a son and promises his youngest to Tamar but intentionally neglects to fulfill his duty. In the end, he will unknowingly fulfill his own promise. Through Ruth and Tamar's provocative acts of redemption, stories that begin with the death of two sons become reversal birth stories of redemption. These birth stories redeem a family and restore the inheritance by raising the name of the dead. Initially, the memory of these families would have been forgotten, but the risk taken by Ruth and Tamar continued a lineage that resulted in an ancestry of King David.

These two stories share the unique desire for a male relative to fulfill the specific duties of family redeemer. The closest familial redeemers in both stories will not perform in that role (Shelah in Genesis and the unnamed redeemer in Ruth). Women's agency and foreign identity provide a subversive link that connects these two women. Through material, social, and spiritual constituents of the unified self, Tamar and Ruth secure a future inheritance by covering and uncovering clothing on their bodies. Each woman moves the narrative forward within patriarchal systems, using their bodies in vulnerable and risky approaches. Judah and Boaz live out their answerability to these women by making life-affirming decisions. Ultimately, Tamar and Ruth succeed in inheritance negotiation and are remembered as "righteous" (Gen. 38:26) and more worthy than "seven sons" (Ruth 4:15).

Chapter 6

DRESSING BENJAMINITES, DEFINING KINGSHIP: DRESS AS A ROYAL PREROGATIVE FOR THE TRIBE OF BENJAMIN

Ellena Lyell

Genesis 27 narrates Jacob's deception of his father Isaac, with the help of his mother Rebekah. Rebekah took the בגדי עשׂו בנה הגדל החמדת אשׁר אתה בבית ותלבשׁ את־ יעקב בנה הקטן ("finest clothes of Esau, her eldest son, that were with her in the house, and she put them on Jacob, her youngest son," v. 15).[1] These clothes concealed Jacob's true identity, and as a consequence, Isaac transferred to Jacob his firstborn blessing reserved for Esau.[2] Jacob later married Rachel and they had two sons: Joseph and Benjamin (Gen. 30:23-24; 35:16-18). Jacob famously gifted his favorite son Joseph a כתנת פסים (a multicolored garment,[3] Gen. 37:3), drawing the

This chapter is indebted to Laura Quick, Cat Quine, and Joseph Scales for their insight and support. Also, to those in the Pacific Northwest Research Group on Dress for such helpful feedback on early drafts

1. This translation, and the ones that follow, are the author's own.

2. See Heather A. McKay's chapter in this volume. In Gen. 25:25, Esau is described as אדרת שׂער (a hairy cloak). In Gen. 27:16, Jacob wears the ערת גדיי העזים (skin of young goats) in order to disguise himself as Esau. When Rebekah took Esau's חמדה (finest) clothes (v. 15), which may have referred to animal fur, it reinforces Esau's love for hunting and for the outdoors.

3. I favor this translation, rather than a "long sleeved tunic," because of the cultural connotations behind פסים. Furthermore, the only two characters to wear כתנת פסים in the Hebrew Bible are Tamar (2 Sam. 13) and Joseph (Gen. 37). The LXX Gen. 37:3, 23, 31-33 renders the phrase χιτῶνα ποικίλον as "multicolored tunic" thus giving rise to the idea of Joseph and the "amazing technicolor dream coat" famous from the Andrew Lloyd Webber musical of the same name. However, the LXX[B] 2 Sam. 13:18-19 uses χιτών καρπωτος (garment reaching to the wrist) and the LXX[L] 2 Sam. 13:18-19 says χιτών αστραγαλωτος ("garment reaching to the ankle"), rather than "multicolored"; see Sara M. Koenig, "Tamar and Tamar: Clothing as Deception and Defiance," in *Dress and Clothing in the Hebrew Bible: "For All Her Household Are Clothed in Crimson,"* ed. Antonios Finitsis (London: T&T Clark, 2019), 87–108 (104); Manfred Görg, "Der gefärbte Rock Josefs," *BN* 102 (2000), 9–12;

theme of clothing into the Joseph narratives. A number of scholars have previously demonstrated the significance of dress as an important motif in the Joseph story.[4] Indeed, this garment motif in Joseph has prompted other studies of clothing elsewhere in the Hebrew Bible.[5] Given the significant role Benjamin played in the Joseph narratives and the close relationship between the brothers, it is surprising that the use of clothing in these narratives about Benjamin remains to be explored.[6] As such, this chapter traces the thread of Benjaminite dress from Benjamin himself to the time of the judges, the time of the monarchy, and into the postexilic period.

Previous scholarly interest in literary connections between Genesis and the Deuteronomistic history[7] and, more specifically, comparative textual links between Judges and the books of Samuel demonstrate the value of intertextual studies.[8] Ellen van Wolde's statement that "it is not the chronology of texts that should occupy the centre of attention, but the logical and analogical reasoning of the reader in

Heath Dewrell, "How Tamar's Veil Became Joseph's Coat: The Meaning of *kĕtōnet (hap) passim*," *Bib* 87 (2016), 161–74.

4. Victor Matthews, "The Anthropology of Clothing in the Joseph Narrative," *JSOT* 65 (1995), 25–36; John Huddlestun, "Divestiture, Deception, and Demotion: The Garment Motif in Genesis 37–39," *JSOT* 98 (2002), 47–62; Franziska Ede, "The Garment Motif in Gen. 37–39," in *Clothing and Nudity in the Hebrew Bible*, ed. Christopher Berner, Manuel Schäfer, Martin Schott, Sarah Schulz, and Martina Weingärtner (London: T&T Clark, 2019), 389–402.

5. On Joseph and the story of Judah and Tamar, see Huddlestun, "Divestiture," 47–62; Ede, "Garment Motif," 395–9; Koenig, "Tamar," 87–108. On Joseph, Esther, and Mordecai, see Laura Quick and Ellena Lyell, "Clothing, Conformity and Power: Garment Imagery in the Book of Esther," *VT* (forthcoming).

6. While there may be some historical continuity between Benjamin in Genesis, the Benjaminite line in Deuteronomistic history, and the geographical region of Benjamin in southern Judah, the argument of this chapter does not depend on such connections.

7. Joseph Blenkinsopp, *Treasures Old and New: Essays in the Theology of the Pentateuch* (Grand Rapids, MI: Eerdmans, 2004), 102–19; David Noel Freedman, "Dinah and Shechem, Tamar and Amnon," in *Divine Commitment and Human Obligation*, ed. John R. Huddlestun (Grand Rapids, MI: Eerdmans, 1997), 485–95; A. Graeme Auld, "Reading Genesis after Samuel," in *The Pentateuch: International Perspectives on Current Research*, ed. Thomas B. Dozeman, Konrad Schmid, and Baruch J. Schwartz (Tübingen: Mohr Siebeck, 2011), 471–88; Dominic Rudman, "The Patriarchal Narratives in the Books of Samuel," *VT* 54 (2004), 239–49; Keith Bodner, *David Observed: A King in the Eyes of His Court* (Sheffield: Sheffield Phoenix, 2005), 140–52; Keith Bodner and Ellen White, "Some Advantages of Recycling: The Jacob Cycle in a Later Environment," *BibInt* 22 (2014), 20–33.

8. Yairah Amit, *Hidden Polemics in the Biblical Narrative* (Leiden: Brill, 2000); Marc Brettler, "The Book of Judges: Literature as Politics," *JBL* 108 (1989), 395–418; Marvin A. Sweeney, "Davidic Polemics in the Book of Judges," *VT* 47 (1997), 517–29.

interaction of the text" is paramount for this study.[9] Intertextual conclusions about the sartorial customs of the characters associated with Benjamin are made possible by drawing on recent scholarly interest in the sociological, anthropological, and cultural approaches and implications of references to clothing, adornment, and the body in the Hebrew Bible.[10] Dress is the various clothing, items of adornment, and paraphernalia described in the Hebrew Bible;[11] dress communicates cultural values, notions of identity, and tradition.[12] In particular, dress is crucial in the construction and communication of power. Dress offers insights into the characteristics of the tribe of Benjamin and comments on the suitability of their prerogative to reign. I shall argue that the garment motif throughout Benjaminite history creates a rise-and-fall trajectory for the key men of Benjaminite heritage.[13] As such, clothing (or its absence) bears important narrative functions for Benjaminite characters, with implications for understanding their intentions, levels of social status and power, and, ultimately, their turbulent relationship to the throne. To demonstrate this, I will first explore the motif of dress associated with the character of Benjamin in Genesis; then I shall continue to study this theme through the books of Judges with Ehud and warrior Benjaminites in the narrative of the Levite's concubine, and Samuel with the Benjaminites Saul, Jonathan, Michal, and Mephibosheth. This

---

9. Ellen van Wolde, "Trendy Intertextuality?" in *Intertextuality in Biblical Writings: Essays in Honour of Bas van Iersel*, ed. S. Draisma (Kampen: J.H. Kok, 1989), 43–9 (43).

10. See Heather A. McKay, "Gendering the Discourse of Display in the Hebrew Bible," in *On Reading Prophetic Texts*, ed. Bob Becking and Meindert Dijkstra (Leiden: Brill, 1996), 169–200; Heather McKay, "Clothing, Adornment and Accoutrements as Cultural and Literary Signifiers in the 'Historical' Books," in *Samuel, Kings and Chronicles I*, ed. Athalya Brenner-Idan and Archie Lee (London: T&T Clark, 2018), 238–52; Heather A. McKay, "Gendering the Body: Clothes Maketh the (Wo)man," in *Theology and the Body*, ed. Robert Hannaford and J'annine Jobling (Herefordshire: Gracewing, 1999), 84–104; Laura Quick, *Dress, Adornment and the Body in the Hebrew Bible* (Oxford: Oxford University Press, 2021); Norman J. Cohen, *Masking and Unmasking Ourselves: Interpreting Biblical Texts on Clothing and Identity* (Woodstock: Jewish Lights, 2015); and the collected essays in Berner et al., *Clothing and Nudity* (London: T&T Clark, 2019), and Antonios Finitsis, ed., *Dress and Clothing in the Hebrew Bible: "For All Her Household Are Clothed in Crimson"* (London: T&T Clark, 2019); cf. Ora Horn Prouser, "Suited to the Throne: The Symbolic Use of Clothing in the David and Saul Narratives," *JSOT* 71 (1996), 27–37.

11. This idea goes hand in hand with material culture, such as jewelry or surviving pigments and fabrics, which should also be taken into account to understand contemporary Israel and Judah. This chapter, however, centers on the biblical textual descriptions to provide the logical thread of the Benjaminite line.

12. See the chapters by S. J. Parrott, Selena Billington, and Jennifer M. Matheny in this volume.

13. Only Michal, a Benjaminite woman, is associated with dress. Her garment motif conforms to the rise-and-fall trajectory but is not as strong as the men of the Benjaminite tribe and their relationship to the throne: they will rise and they, ultimately, will fall.

exploration of Benjaminites ends with a study of Mordecai's dress in the book of Esther.

Dressing Benjamin in Genesis

The theme of dress is significant in the Joseph story, and, as such, this section will show the theme is also parallel in the brief narratives about Benjamin in Genesis. Victor Matthews argued that clothing signaled changes in Joseph's status: enslavement and imprisonment surrounded by an *inclusio* of two investiture ceremonies (when Jacob gave Joseph the כתנת פסים [Gen. 37:3] and when Pharaoh adorned him in a fine Egyptian robe [Gen. 41:42]).[14] Benjamin has a similar garment motif; thus Benjamin becomes a reflection of Joseph himself. Since Jacob thought Joseph was dead, he favored Benjamin in Joseph's place as his favored son. Jacob did not send Benjamin to Egypt with his other brothers for he did not want any harm to come to him (Gen. 42:4). Joseph, however, was alive, disguised, and wanted to know how his brothers would act toward Benjamin if a crisis arose, which explains his demand that they bring Benjamin along. To test the brothers, Joseph deceived Benjamin, which resulted in his imprisonment, but, significantly, the brothers reacted in the way Joseph longed for. Thus Joseph revealed his true identity to them, and Benjamin was freed and rewarded by Joseph for the inconvenience.

Let us undress these events further and draw out the significance of clothing and adornment. Though Jacob did not give Benjamin physical clothing to show favor as he did with Joseph, Jacob's life is described as קשר (knitted, bound) to Benjamin's, so that if Benjamin were to die, so would Jacob (Gen. 44:30-31).[15] Their lives are inextricably bound together, like cords and fabrics knitted and woven together. If anything, Benjamin's relationship with Jacob surpasses Joseph's special bond with their father; קשר goes beyond the gift of a כתנת פסים.

The narrative states that Joseph arranged for a servant to put a silver cup in Benjamin's bag, and after the brothers departed, Joseph sent a steward after them to accuse them of stealing the cup and Benjamin was imprisoned (Gen. 44:2-12). Joseph was falsely accused of sexual advances toward Potiphar's wife when he left his cloak behind, which subsequently led to his imprisonment (Gen. 39:13-20). Benjamin was also wrongly accused and restrained. The silver cup corresponds to Joseph's garment; both are the instruments of false accusation. Furthermore, after the servant found the cup in Benjamin's bag, all of the brothers tore their שמלת (mantles, Gen. 44:13), recalling the mantle (שמלה) Jacob tore when he was told

---

14. Matthews, "Anthropology," 25–36.

15. The omission of names in these verses blurs the distinction between the two lives further; see Mark A. O'Brien, "The Contribution of Judah's Speech, Genesis 44:18-34, to the Characterization of Joseph," *CBQ* 59 (1997), 429–47 (443).

about Joseph's death (Gen. 37:34).[16] The brothers mourned the fact that not only might Benjamin die as a result of this, but because his life is knitted with their father's (Gen. 44:31), Jacob may also die.

Judah begged Joseph for permission to take Benjamin's place. His plea provides evidence of a character transformation; he was the brother who proposed selling Joseph into slavery (Gen. 37:26-27).[17] As such, Joseph revealed his identity to his brothers and bestowed gifts and garments upon them. He gave them שׂמלת חלפות (changes of garments). In Gen. 45:22 Joseph gave Benjamin extra silver, which incidentally was the material that marked him out for punishment in the first place, along with five sets of garments (וחמש חלפות שׂמלת). Just as Jacob gave Joseph a כתנת as a tangible marker for his favored son, Joseph mirrored this motif by giving Benjamin *five* sets of שׂמלת (cf. Gen. 43:34), showing a preference for Benjamin over his other brothers. Elsewhere in the Hebrew Bible, חליפה (a change) is used in relation to בגדים (a general term for "clothes"; see Judg. 14:12, 13; 2 Kgs. 5:5, 22, 23; cf. Judg. 14:19); only in the book of Genesis do we find חליפה and the verbal form חלף (to change) in relation to שׂמלת.[18] In Gen. 35:2, before the narrative describing Benjamin's birth, Jacob built an altar at Bethel and instructed his household to "change your clothes" (חליפו שׂמלתיכם); so they removed their earrings (v. 4) and followed Jacob. Later, in Gen. 41:14, when Pharaoh sent for Joseph, he shaved himself and "changed his clothes" (יחלף שׂמלתיו) implicitly suggesting a transformation from his prison outfit to Egyptian garments. Therefore, חלפות שׂמלת in Genesis 45 functionally replaces the brothers' ripped שׂמלת and, perhaps, also Jacob's torn שׂמלה, but in the case of Benjamin, it acts as a literary device to show his transition from prisoner to a man of status.

From the point of view of narrative structure, the garment motif underscores the parallel narrative arks for Joseph and Benjamin. Joseph was adorned in a colorful robe; he lost the robe and was enslaved; he was then wrongly accused of advances toward his master's wife because she held his garment. Joseph was imprisoned in prisoner's clothes, but then he successfully interpreted Pharaoh's dreams and so was adorned in fine Egyptian regalia. Joseph's status of favored son, to slave and prisoner, to a high Egyptian official is a rollercoaster conveyed by dress. But as we have seen, this garment motif also extends to Benjamin, who undergoes a similar transformation. He became the favored son, where his life

---

16. Reuben also tore his garments after he returned to the pit and saw Joseph was no longer there (Gen. 37:29-30). Interestingly, David ended his mourning period by washing, oiling himself, and changing into this exact same garment (שׂמלתו) in 2 Sam. 12:20.

17. The gradual movement within Judah's discourse through the shift in person from plural ("we," "your servants") to singular ("I," "your servant") correlates with a shift from their collective responsibility to his personal responsibility; see Meir Sternberg, *The Poetics of Biblical Narrative: Ideological Literature and the Drama of Reading* (Bloomington: Indiana University Press, 1985), 308; cf. Robert Alter, *The Art of Biblical Narrative* (London: Basic Books, 1981), 175.

18. Cf. 2 Sam. 12:20 and fn 16 above.

was tied together with the life of his father. This "knitting" goes beyond the gift of Joseph's garment from Jacob and focuses on the fabrics and cords that make up the garment. Later, Benjamin was imprisoned because he was wrongly accused of taking a cup, mirroring Joseph's own imprisonment in Egypt on false charges. But then Joseph revealed himself to his brothers and gifted Benjamin fine garments, ending the up-and-down trajectory on a high. For both brothers the progressive complications in their respective narratives are marked by garments. Furthermore, both narrative trajectories are marked by value-positive endings.

Dressing the Benjaminites in Judges

In this section, I shall explore key characteristics of the tribe of Benjamin and their relationship to dress in the book of Judges. I will demonstrate that the rollercoaster of status and power as portrayed by the garment motif attached to Benjamin in Genesis can be mapped onto the Benjaminite characters in Judges. Let us pick up from the last mention of Benjamin in Genesis. In Genesis 49, Jacob had blessed his sons on his deathbed, portraying Benjamin as a זאב יטרף (ravenous wolf, v. 27). It seems incongruous to liken Benjamin to a predatory animal because he comes across as quite a passive character and in need of protection (Gen. 42:4; 43:29; 44:20-23). Further, the imagery of a wolf elsewhere in the Hebrew Bible coincides with military themes,[19] often appearing hand in hand with descriptions of a lion as a symbol of power.[20] The implied message seems to be that Benjamin and his tribe will overcome their enemies militarily. The idea that a Benjaminite will overcome and surpass those from outside the tribe is a theme found in Judges.[21] The account of Ehud, a Benjaminite and one of Israel's first judges, offers a clear example.[22] Ehud defeated the Moabite king Eglon in Judges 3, and dress is central to Ehud's

19. For example, the horses of the Chaldean army are compared to wolves (Hab. 1:6, 8).

20. Isa. 11:1-10; Ezek. 22:23-31; Zeph. 3:1-4.

21. It is no surprise then that the territory of Benjamin was located in the southern Judean highlands; Benjamin lay between Judah (the preeminent southern tribe) and Ephraim (the preeminent northern tribe); its location was strategic. As such, there is a long-standing scholarly debate about the affiliation of the territory of Benjamin and its relations to the kingdoms of Israel and Judah, Oded Lipschits, "Benjamin in Retrospective: Stages in the Creation of the Territory of the Benjamin Tribe," in *Saul, Benjamin, and the Emergence of Monarchy in Israel: Biblical and Archaeological Perspectives*, ed. Joachim J. Krause, Omer Sergi, and Kristin Weingart (Atlanta, GA: SBL, 2020), 161–200; Benjamin D. Giffone, "'Special Forces': A Stereotype of Benjaminite Soldiers in the Deuteronomistic History and Chronicles," *SJOT* 30 (2016), 16–29. In the early stages, the tribe of Benjamin was identified as the sons of Benjamin with Abidan, son of Gideoni, as their leader (Num. 2:22; 7:60) and some 35,400 people (Num. 1:37; 2:23; 10:24) and later with a population of 45,600 (Num. 26:41).

22. Israel's first two judges, Othniel and Ehud in Judges 3, are highly significant for Judah-Benjamin-Joseph relations. See Benjamin D. Giffone, *"Sit at My Right Hand": The*

deception and saving of the Israelites from Moabite oppression.[23] The story recounts how Eglon conquered regions of Israel and demanded tribute from them for eighteen years. To save the Israelites, YHWH raised up Ehud the Benjaminite who is איש אטר יד־ימינו (a man restricted as to his right hand), and thus left-handed (Judg. 3:15).[24]

In verse 16 Ehud made a חרב (dagger), which had two edges, was a גמד (cubit) in length, and was חגר (girded) underneath his מד (armor) on his ירך ימינו (right thigh).[25] He was sent to pay tribute to Eglon but claimed to have a message for the Moabite king from YHWH (v. 20). As Eglon rose from his throne to hear this message, Ehud reached with his left hand, drew the dagger from his right thigh, and thrust it into Eglon's stomach (v. 22). Ehud was forced to use deception to expel the Moabite ruler.[26] The חרב and מד have multiple military connotations throughout the Hebrew Bible with a specific connection to the tribe of Benjamin.[27] Ehud the Benjaminite wore this particular weapon under a particular protective garment, which indicated his military and martial power. He was able to conceal his weapon on an unexpected side of the body,[28] taking advantage of his left-handedness and, thus, concealing his true intentions. The short length of the dagger also is a key description in that it allowed the sword to remain hidden when adorned upon Ehud's right side, but this secrecy comes full circle once it has been thrust into Eglon's belly: his חלב (fat) consumed the dagger, concealing it again.[29]

Chronicler's Portrait of the Tribe of Benjamin in the Social Context of Yehud (London: T&T Clark, 2016), 135–9.

23. Broadly on dress as deception, see Heather A. McKay in this volume.

24. Suzie Park, "Left-Handed Benjaminites and the Shadow of Saul," *JBL* 134 (2015), 701–20 (701–4). Interestingly, after Rachel's death in Genesis 35, Jacob renames Benjamin from בן־אוני (son of my sorrow) to בנימין (son[s] of the south or son[s] of the right hand, v. 18). בנימין as "son(s) of the right hand," that is, the left-handed Benjaminites, is an important characteristic of the tribe of Benjamin.

25. Stone argues this suggests a narrator to whom this weapon is new, as the description is "awkward"; Lawson G. Stone, "Eglon's Belly and Ehud's Blade: A Reconsideration," *JBL* 128 (2009), 649–63 (660–3).

26. Sweeney, "Davidic Polemics," 524.

27. See below for מד as Saul and Jonathan's armor and as the military clothes of the defeated Benjaminite (1 Sam. 4:12). It is a particular garment specific to martial dress and is crucial in stories about Benjaminites and their relation to royalty and power.

28. It is reasonable to assume Eglon's security only checked Ehud's left side, expecting any dangerous actions to be evoked with the right hand, the hand usually utilized by warriors. See Victor H. Matthews, *Judges and Ruth* (Cambridge: Cambridge University Press, 2004), 60; Park, "Left-Handed," 708; Susan Niditch, *War in the Hebrew Bible: A Study in the Ethics of Violence* (Oxford: Oxford University Press, 1993), 117.

29. See two different interpretations on this consumption: Stone, "Eglon's Belly," 650–4; Park, "Left-Handed," 708; cf. Athalya Brenner, "Who's Afraid of Feminist Criticism? Who's Afraid of Biblical Humour? The Case of the Obtuse Foreign Ruler in the Hebrew Bible," *JSOT* 63 (1994), 38–55; Lowell K. Handy, "Uneasy Laughter: Ehud and Eglon as Ethnic

Ehud's left-handedness became a source of power that allowed him to discreetly and cunningly hide his חרב via his מד, which single-handedly delivered his fellow Israelites from the rule of Eglon.

Furthermore, dress is central to the underlying sexual prowess embedded in this event. The relationship between dress and sexual euphemisms is another key connection associated with the tribe of Benjamin. In Judges 3, Ehud's dress and adornment suggest that his assassination of Eglon can be read figuratively as sexual shaming.[30] Primarily, the size and shape of the חרב would raise in the mind of the audience the image of an exaggerated phallus.[31] In fact, military weapons were commonly perceived euphemistically across the ancient Near East.[32] The

---

Humour," *SJOT* 6 (1992), 233–46; J. Clinton McCann, *Judges* (Louisville, KY: John Knox, 2002), 44–5; J. Alberto Soggin, *Judges: A Commentary* (Philadelphia, PA: Westminster, 1981). James Aitken argued, however, that Eglon's weight should be interpreted positively in the passage: he is a successful king, grown healthy and prosperous on other people's offerings; James K. Aitken, "Fat Eglon," in *Studies on the Text and Versions of the Hebrew Bible in Honour of Robert Gordon*, ed. Geoffery Khan and Diana Lipton (Leiden: Brill, 2011), 141–54. His successful fatness serves as a contrast to his eventual downfall. The name Eglon means "calf" and the "fatted calf" relates to sacrifice: thus Eglon's name presupposes him as a specimen for sacrificing. See Alter, *Art of Biblical Narrative*, 39; Aitken, "Fat Eglon," 146–7; Soggin, *Judges*, 49; Stone, "Eglon's Belly," 650–7; Jack M. Sasson, "Ethically Cultured Interpretations: The Case of Eglon's Murder (Judges 3)," in *Homeland and Exile: Biblical and Ancient Near Eastern Studies in Honour of Bustenay Oded*, ed. Gershon Galil, Mark Geller, and Alan Millard (Leiden: Brill, 2009), 571–96 (588); Marc Brettler, *The Book of Judges* (London: Routledge, 2001), 20–32.

30. This is reinforced by other sexual readings of the narrative: verse 15 states that Ehud was "bound" (אטר) in the right hand, a roundabout way of indicating that Ehud was left-handed. Right hands were a symbol of masculinity, which indirectly implied left hands were the opposite; cf. the folklore studies that argued this extensively. Robert Hertz, *Death and the Right Hand* (Aberdeen: University Press, 1960), 89–116. Left-handedness also signaled something crafty, secret, and violent; Sternberg, *Poetics*, 333; Park, "Left-Handed," 708. Understanding יד (hand) as "penis," a popular euphemism across the Hebrew Bible (cf. Isa. 57:8; Jer. 5:31, 50:15; Song 5:4), strengthens the sexual connotations attached to this narrative.

31. Geoffery P.Miller, "Verbal Feud in the Hebrew Bible: Judges 3:12-30 and 19-21," *JNES* 55 (1996), 105–17 (114); Marc Brettler, "Never the Twain Shall Meet? The Ehud Story as History and Literature," *HUCA* 62 (1991), 285–304 (295); Niditch, *War*, 117. In the ancient warrior culture of the Levant, weapons such as the bow and sword frequently had phallic implications. As we will see below, these are two weapons heavily associated with characters in the tribe of Benjamin.

32. Harry A. Hoffner, "Symbols of Masculinity and Feminity: Their Use in Ancient Near Eastern Sympathetic Magic Rituals," *JBL* 85 (1966), 326–34; Cynthia R. Chapman, *The Gendered Language of Warfare in the Israelite-Assyrian Encounter* (Winona Lake, IN: Eisenbrauns, 2004), 52–4.

detail where the חרב was גמד (a cubit) in length contributes further to the sexual connotations of this narrative. גמד has an Arabic cognate meaning, "to be hard," and the נצב (handle) of the חרב (v. 22) is only known to mean "handle" in a rare Arabic expression, otherwise the more usual range of connotation carries the sense of "erect."[33] The weapon was girded on his right thigh under his מד; the thigh or loins is the seat of male fertility (cf. Gen. 46:26; Exod. 1:5).[34] Ehud thrust his חרב into Eglon, made an escape, and locked the doors behind him.[35] As his servants came to check on Eglon, they concluded he was מסיך הוא את־רגליו (covering his feet, Judg. 3:24). The feet are well-known euphemisms throughout biblical literature,[36] and here, likely relates to urination or defecation.[37] In Josephus, this idiom suggests that either a person who stood to urinate dropped his clothes to the floor and covered his feet or that the squatter was shielding their feet with their robes (cf. Josephus, *War* 2.147–9). Dress is once again crucial in Ehud's escape and success. On the one hand, it exaggerates his sexual potency, and on the other, it leaves his opponent exposed and shamefully uncovered. Furthermore, in this case, Eglon's clothes around his feet formed a ruse for his servants and allowed Ehud to flee.

Given Benjamin is a זאב יטרף (ravenous wolf) in Genesis, it is interesting that the verb טרף (to tear, rend) is used by Jacob to describe the wolf-like Benjamin and to describe the fate of Joseph when his sons handed to Jacob Joseph's bloody robe. He recognized it and exclaimed a wild beast has devoured it, and thus "Joseph is surely torn to pieces" (טרף טרף יוסף, Gen. 37:33; cf. 44:28). The shared verb suggests

33. Philippe Guillaume, *Waiting for Josiah: The Judges* (London: T&T Clark International, 2004), 27 n. 59, 62; Deryn Guest, "Judges," in *The Queer Bible Commentary*, ed. Deryn Guest, Robert E. Shore-Goss, Mona West, and Thomas Bohache (London: SCM, 2006), 167–89 (171).

34. Niditch, *War*, 117; Miller, "Verbal Feud," 114. On girding of the loins and masculine power: Katherine Low, "Implications Surrounding Girding the Loins in Light of Gender, Body, and Power," *JSOT* 36 (2011), 3–30.

35. The emphasis upon the opening and closing of doors ("a set of words that are well anchored in metaphors of sexuality") and the expression where Ehud "approached" Eglon, interpreting the verb בוא (to come), warrant a euphemistic reading of the narrative. Ehud also had a "word" from God for him (here, דבר "word" can also mean "thing," slang for genitals). See Alter, *Art of Biblical Narrative*, 37–41; Miller, "Verbal Feud," 113–16; Niditch, *War*, 117–18; Brettler, "Never the Twain," 285–304; Park, "Left-Handed," 707–11. For בוא as a sexual euphemism, see, for example, Gen. 16:2; 29:21, 23; 30:4; 38:2; Judg. 16:1; 2 Sam. 11:4; 12:24; 16:21-22. Contra, Stone ("Eglon's Belly," 654 n.19), who questions the use of בוא as it "hardly demands a sexual nuance since this verb occurs over twenty-five hundred times in the Hebrew Bible. Is every 'entry' phallic?"

36. See, for example, Gen. 19:2; Deut. 28:57; Judg. 3:24; 19:21; 1 Sam. 24:3; 2 Sam. 11:8; 2 Kgs. 18:27; Isa. 7:20; Ezek. 16:25; Ruth 3:4.

37. This same idiom happens in the cave with Saul (1 Sam. 24:4); see Sasson, "Ethnically Cultured," 586. "Water of the feet" is also a euphemism for urine in 2 Kgs. 18:27 and the Qere of Isa. 36:12.

that Benjamin has overcome his brother's fate. Other references to dress and the Benjaminites in Judges center around the idea of "tearing." In chapters 19–21, the people of the Benjaminite town of Gibeah abused and killed a concubine. The Levite took her body back home, cut her into parts, and sent the parts throughout Israel to muster tribal allegiance against the Benjaminites (Judg. 19:29-30). The cutting of the woman recalls a significant cutting of a שלמה (mantle)[38] in 1 Kgs 11:30. Here, the prophet Ahijah cut his שלמה into twelve pieces and gave ten of the fabric fragments to Jeroboam; this represented the division of Solomon's kingdom.[39] Though the twelve tribes will never be united again in 1 Kings 11, the Levite tried to bring eleven tribes together to fight against the twelfth in Judges 19. Furthermore, just as Joseph's brothers tore Joseph apart and stripped him of his כתנת in Genesis, Judges describes the tribes coming together to tear apart the Benjaminites because of their treatment of the concubine. Judg. 20:15-16 describes the twenty-six thousand Benjaminites armed with a חרב to fight against the other tribes. Seven hundred Benjaminites from Gibeah were specifically singled out as אטר יד־ימינו (bound on the right hand) such that each could sling a stone at a hair with their left hand and not miss. After this battle, the Benjaminites were almost extinct, but following complex politics they were allowed to rejoin as part of the collective Israelite tribes (Judg. 21:15-24). Again, the clothing motif in the Joseph narratives serves as a paradigm for the way clothing is used to describe Benjamin and his descendants.

Through a web of cultural connotations—where being left-handed suggests one is inactive, secret, and passive compared to the openly aggressive and active nature associated with the right hand—the stories of left-handed Benjaminites insult future political abilities and delegitimize kingship.[40] Their skill in combat, military prowess, and warrior-like characteristics, however, point to their inherent abilities, qualities indicative of masculinity and so, fundamentally, their right to royal authority. Overall, these characteristics of the Benjaminites manifest through dress, where the garment motif initially sets out to single out the Benjaminites for royalty, but ultimately the motif fails because of their deviant sartorial behaviors.

Dressing the Royal Benjaminites

In the Books of Samuel

Judges 17–21 is positioned as a link between the stories of the "judges" and of the kings as leaders of Israel. The narratives serve as an example of the corruption of

---

38. Both שלמה here and שמלה above denote a "mantle" (BDB, 971; *HALOT* 3: 1331–2). The roots connect Ahijah and the twelve tribes, Jacob and his twelve sons, and the Levite and the parts of the concubine, through dress.

39. Cf. other texts that parallel bodies and clothing, for example, Gen. 49:11; Ps. 109:18-19; Quick, *Dress*, 47–83; and Carmen Joy Imes in this volume.

40. Park, "Left-Handed," 708; Miller, "Verbal-Feud," 114.

Israel without a proper government,[41] providing a rationale for monarchy. Thus Samuel is introduced. He restored order and prepared the way for Saul, the first king of Israel (1 Sam. 8-12). 1 Samuel 9 opens with ויהי־איש מבנ־ימין ושמו קיש ... בן־איש ימיני גבור חיל: ולו־היה בן ושמו שאול ("and there was a man of Benjamin, and his name was Kish ... son of a Benjaminite man, a mighty man of power. And he had a son, and his name was Saul"). Scholars argue that Saul is ubiquitously present in Judges, especially in chapters 19–21,[42] and the major towns of Benjamin described in these chapters were also associated with Saul throughout the books of Samuel.[43] The physique and prowess associated with the Benjaminites make it clear why Saul the Benjaminite was chosen as the first king of Israel. He was well built, impressive, and tall.[44] Given the significant role dress plays in the Benjamin narratives of Genesis and Judges, we should not be surprised to see dress featured in Saul's narratives as well.

In the books of Samuel, the cutting or tearing of clothing was a symbolic act that signaled the end of royal rule.[45] For example, when Saul ripped Samuel's מעיל (robe), it symbolized the transfer of his kingdom to David (1 Sam. 15:27). Alternatively, when David cut off the hem of Saul's מעיל (1 Sam. 24:4), this marked David's symbolic taking of the kingdom from Saul.[46] It is important to note that here a king tore a *priest's* מעיל, thus ending Saul's reign, but when a king cut a *king's* מעיל, that also ended Saul's reign. The מעיל has theological connotations and is used as a literary device to characterize Samuel as a priest and increase the legitimacy of Samuel over Saul.[47] In 1 Samuel 15, where Saul ripped Samuel's מעיל, the tearing

41. Marti Nissinen, *Homoeroticism in the Biblical World: A Historical Perspective* (Minneapolis, MN: Fortress, 1998), 51.

42. Amit, *Hidden Polemics*, 178–88; Brettler, "Book of Judges," 412–18; Sweeney, "Davidic Polemics," 517–29.

43. Gibeah, mentioned throughout Judges 19–21, particularly as the location of the concubine's rape (Judg. 19), is the birthplace and the main city associated with Saul (1 Sam. 10:26; 14:2; 22:6; 23:19; 26:1); Jabesh-Gilead is the only city that does not come to the assembly at Mizpah (Judg. 21:1-14) and is the city rescued by Saul at the beginning of his reign (1 Sam. 11:1-13); and Mizpah is the gathering place of the Israelite coalition army (Judg. 21:1) and also where Saul is publicly selected as king (1 Sam. 10:17-27). For further examples, see Park, "Left-Handed," 716–17.

44. P. S. Vermaak, "The Prowess of the Benjaminites," *JBQ* 22 (1994), 73–84 (81–2); cf. "good in form" as a marker of beauty; Michael Avioz, "The Motif of Beauty in the Books of Samuel and Kings," *VT* 59 (2009), 341–59.

45. Cf. the narrative of Athaliah in 2 Kgs. 11:14. See Quick, *Dress*, 36–9; Paul Kruger, "The Symbolic Significance of the Hem (כנף) in 1 Samuel 15.2," in *Text and Context: Old Testament and Semitic Studies for F.C. Fensham*, ed. W. Classen (Sheffield: JSOT, 1988), 105–16.

46. Prouser, "Suited," 29; cf. Mark Verman, "Royalty, Robes and the Art of Biblical Narrative," *SJOT* 30 (2016), 30–43.

47. The use of the מעיל קטן (little robe) in 1 Samuel 2 characterized Samuel as a legitimate priest in contrast to the wicked sons of Eli; see Ellena Lyell and Joseph Scales, "Uncovering

goes further than "symbolizing" the monarchy being torn away from Saul, but physically marked the beginning of it.[48]

Saul later disguised himself to travel to En-Dor to consult a medium, but after the medium conjured up a spirit, the medium proved her abilities by seeing through Saul's disguise and recognizing him.[49] Saul then identified the ghost of Samuel by his מעיל (1 Sam. 28:8-25), which hearkens back to when Saul tore Samuel's מעיל previously.[50] The מעיל served as a marker that predicted and began Saul's downfall, and in 1 Sam. 28:14, the מעיל creates an *inclusio* by predicting Saul's death. Indeed, Saul died shortly thereafter (1 Sam. 31). After Saul died, the Philistines stripped Saul of his כלי (armor, 1 Sam. 31:9),[51] but those from the Benjaminite city of Jabesh-Gilead came to bury him. The Philistines removed Saul's כלי to indicate loss of his masculine authority and so, his right to rule. It also finalized the transfer of power to David.

The power of Jonathan, Saul's firstborn son, is similarly associated with dress. In 1 Sam. 18:4, Jonathan gave his מעיל, מד, חרב, קשׁת (bow) and his חגור (belt) to David, symbolic of his claim to the throne and identity as the prince of Israel. He thus transferred the right of succession from himself to David.[52] The gift of his מעיל (an article of clothing associated with his father Saul), מד (armor that is elsewhere associated with Ehud and the tribe of Benjamin), and חרב (a Benjaminite dagger, which Ehud uses to kill Eglon) suggest the קשׁת and the חגור may also have Benjaminite associations and associate the Benjaminites with royalty.

One reason for this association is that in Gen. 48:22, Jacob owned both a חרב and קשׁת, and now Jonathan is giving two like items to David. The קשׁת is depicted primarily as a weapon of a hunter or warrior in the Hebrew Bible.[53] Jonathan's shooting abilities are described in 1 Sam. 20:20. Harold Dressler argues that the

---

the Dead, Dethroning the King: Divine Embodiment in 1 Samuel 28," *Hebrew Studies* 62 (2021), 97–115.

48. Prouser, "Suited," 29; Kruger, "Symbolic Significance," 106.

49. See Richard Coggins, "On Kings and Disguises," *JSOT* 50 (1991), 55–62.

50. On the significance of the מעיל (robe) in the Samuel narratives, see Lyell and Scales, "Uncovering," 110–14; Scott R. A. Starbuck, "Disrobing an Isaianic Metaphor מְעִיל צְדָקָה (*MEʾÎL SEDĀQÂ* 'Robe of Righteousness') as Power Transfer in Isaiah 61:10," in Finitsis, *Dress*, 143–60.

51. Sean E. Cook, "Is Saul Among the Philistines? A Portrayal of Israel's First and Flawed King," in Finitsis, *Dress*, 109–24 (123–4). On the treatment of Saul's body by the Philistines following his death, see Francesca Stavrakopoulou, "Curating King Saul: The Transformation of a Troublesome Corpse," in *To Gaul, to Greece and Into Noah's Ark: Essays in Honour of Kevin J. Cathcart on the Occasion of His Eightieth Birthday*, ed. Laura Quick, Ekaterina E. Kozlova, Sona Noll, and Philip Y. Yoo (Oxford: Oxford University Press, 2019), 19–35.

52. Prouser, "Suited," 32; Cook, "Is Saul Among," 116.

53. *HALOT* 2: 1155–6; see Gen. 27:3; 1 Sam. 2:4; 2 Sam. 22:35; Isa. 7:24; 21:17; Zech. 9:10; 10:4; Hos. 2:20; Ps. 18:35; Job 20:24.

removal of the bow signifies the removal of the man's "fighting spirit" so that the soldier becomes "weak and docile" like a woman.[54] The קשת has another level of meaning; however, like the חרב in the Eglon and Ehud story, there are underlying sexual connotations attached to the קשת. At Ugarit and elsewhere in the ancient Near East, the bow is a symbol of masculinity.[55] For example, the bow in the Aqhat epic can be understood as an "extra-somatic body part," namely, a symbol for the male genitalia.[56] Furthermore, Assyrian evidence for the sexual connotation of the bow is found in the use of the bow in potency incantations.[57] When one removes the bow from the body, it can signify castration or phallectomy thus feminizing the individual.[58] As Jonathan gave David a phallic symbol, David is hypermasculine. To corroborate the significance of the bow as a weapon and as a sexual symbol, in 2 Sam. 1:17, David lamented for the two Benjaminites, Saul and Jonathan. Scholars have particularly studied verse 26 in light of a sexual relationship between David and Jonathan.[59] Not only is this lament called "the bow" (קשת), but Jonathan's קשת and Saul's חרב are described in verse 22.

A second reason for associating the Benjaminites with royalty through Jonathan's dress is the חגור, a leather belt (2 Sam. 20:8), or sometimes a linen garment, akin to a loincloth (Prov. 31:24). Jonathan gave David another item that has sexual connotations: this time, the חגור is worn closely beside the intimate

---

54. Harold Dressler, "Is the Bow of Aqhat a Symbol of Virility," *UF* 7 (1975), 217–25 (219).

55. Quick, *Dress*, 90; Delbert Hillers, "The Bow of Aqhat: The Meaning of a Mythological Theme," in *Orient and Occident: Essays Presented to Cyrus H. Gordon on the Occasion of His Sixty-Fifth Birthday*, ed. Harry A. Hoffner (Neukirchen-Vluyn: Neukirchener Verlag, 1973), 71–80; cf. also Baruch Margalit, *The Ugaritic Poem of Aqhat: Text, Translation, Commentary* (Berlin: de Gruyter, 1989), 53, who suggests that the bow represents maturity and manhood.

56. Hoffner, "Symbols of Masculinity," 329–32; Mark Smith, *Poetic Heroes: Literary Commemorations of Warriors and Warrior Culture in the Early Biblical World* (Grand Rapids, MI: Eerdmans, 2014), 133. Cf. weapons as a classical Hittite sign of masculinity; Tarja Philip, "Gender Matters: Priestly Writing on Impurity," in *Embroidered Garments: Priests and Gender in Biblical Israel*, ed. Deborah W. Rooke (Sheffield: Sheffield Phoenix, 2009), 40–59 (48); Claudia Bergmann, "We Have Seen the Enemy, and He Is Only a 'She': The Portrayal of Warriors as Women," *CBQ* 69 (2007), 651–72 (665).

57. Hoffner, "Symbols of Masculinity," 331; Chapman, *Gendered Language*, 53; Bergmann, "We Have Seen," 666.

58. Chapman, *Gendered Language*, 53.

59. Many have argued for a sexual interpretation of David and Jonathan's relationship, and the gift of Jonathan's weapons as phallic symbols strengthens this idea. See, for example, Susan Ackerman, who compares David/Jonathan to Gilgamesh/Enkidu, hinting Jonathan takes the woman/wife role; Susan Ackerman, *When Heroes Love: The Ambiguity of Eros in the Stories of Gilgamesh and David* (New York: Columbia University Press, 2005), 165–99. Also see Nissinen, *Homoeroticism*, 53–6; Silvia Schroer and Thomas Staubli, "Saul, David and Jonathan—The Story of a Triangle? A Contribution to the Issue of Homosexuality in the First Testament," in *Samuel and Kings: A Feminist Companion to the Bible*, ed. Athalya

parts of his body. Laura Quick argues this gift goes beyond the mere transfer of succession and serves a protective function: Jonathan's clothing is an extension of his personhood—to harm a person wearing his garments would be to harm himself.[60] In fact, 1 Sam. 18:1 explicitly states Jonathan's life was קשׁר (knitted, bound) with David's life. The same idiom, as previously noted, describes the bond between Jacob and Benjamin (Gen. 44:30-31). Therefore, with the symbolic transfer of clothing, David and Jonathan's lives were bound together; if David (dressed in Jonathan's clothing) was to die, then so would Jonathan.[61]

In 1 Sam. 17:38-39, Saul dressed David in some of his מד (armor) on the battlefield, but it was too bulky and heavy, and so David rejected it. When David received Jonathan's מעיל and מד, it ironically fit like a glove.[62] David received clothing (1 Sam. 17:38-39; 18:4) and Saul lost it (1 Sam. 17:38-39; 24:4; 31:9), eventually appearing naked (1 Sam. 19:24).[63] A clear garment motif connects Saul and David. This garment motif becomes threefold as the narratives of Saul's daughter and David's wife, Michal the Benjaminite, also connect to dress. The clothing links between Michal, Jonathan, and Saul resemble that of Benjamin, Joseph, and Jacob, contributing to the typical Benjaminite clothing imagery theme where dress reflects the success and downfall of the character.

Saul's daughter Michal, like Jonathan, had a close connection with David; she became his wife. 1 Samuel 19 describes Saul's repeated attempts to kill David. He sent his servants to David's house to kill him, but Michal intervened (vv. 11–17). She deceived Saul by letting David escape through the window, placing תרפים (teraphim) on David's bed and covering it with בגדים (clothes) so that Saul could not kill him (vv. 11–13). From the use of תרפים in Genesis 31, one would expect the teraphim to be relatively small.[64] Yet, Michal used the idol to give the illusion of David. Most significantly, this illusion includes בגד, a type of clothing.[65] Many scholars have connected the teraphim Michal used and the one Rachel

Brenner (Sheffield: Sheffield Academic Press, 2000), 22–36; Ken Stone, "1 and 2 Samuel," in Guest, Shore-Goss, West, and Bohache, *The Queer Bible Commentary* 195–222 (207–208).

60. Quick, *Dress*, 35–6; cf. Cook, "Is Saul Among," 116.

61. Quick, *Dress*, 36.

62. On this irony, see J. P. Fokkelman, *Narrative Art and Poetry in the Books of Samuel. Vol. 2: The Crossing Fates* (Assen: Van Gorcum, 1986), 199; Cook, "Is Saul Among," 117; Quick, *Dress*, 34–6.

63. Prouser, "Suited," 27–37.

64. On the size of teraphim, see Karel van der Toorn, "The Nature of Biblical Teraphim in the Light of the Cuneiform Evidence," *CBQ* 52 (1990), 203–22; Edith Deen, "King Saul's Daughter—David's First Wife," in *Telling Queen Michal's Story: An Experiment in Comparative Interpretation*, ed. David J. A. Clines and Tamara C. Eskenazi (Sheffield: Sheffield Academic Press, 1991), 141–5 (142).

65. Contra van der Toorn ("Nature," 208) who argued Michal did not dress it up as a human, on the grounds the בגד was merely a covering to serve the purpose of deception, I disagree as בגד is the most common term for clothing in the Hebrew Bible.

used.[66] In fact, scholars have generally made links between the narratives of Laban, Jacob, and Rachel in Genesis and Saul, David, and Michal in 1 Samuel.[67] In this context, it is interesting to note that the theme of clothing also binds Rachel and Michal together. Not only was Michal a direct descendant from Rachel through Benjamin, but also the continuation of this motif of clothing through the Benjaminite line is significant. In Genesis, Benjamin was a vulnerable character in need of protection, and the use of adornment reflected his status; in Judges, the Benjaminites are presented as warrior-like, deceiving, and deviant, again through dress. Here, Michal protected David by covering the teraphim with בגד and successfully creating a deception. The downfall trajectory comes later, as a sexual-political statement is made through dress when her husband David wore inappropriately revealing clothing in 2 Samuel 6.[68] Michal consequently despised David, but David likely spurned her to end the line of Saul and ensure his rise.[69] At stake here is an ideology of kingly prerogative, and dress is a foundational element of this ideology.[70]

Dress also plays a significant role in the narratives of Mephibosheth, son of Jonathan and grandson of Saul, who behaved in a way that marked the end of the royal rule of the Benjaminites. In 2 Sam. 19:25 Mephibosheth came to meet David, but he had עשה רגליו ולא־עשה שפמו ואת־בגדיו לא כבס ("not cared for his feet, nor trimmed his beard, nor washed his clothes"). Previous studies have argued that Mephibosheth is disabled,[71] and his disheveled appearance suggests he is in a state of mourning.[72] Mephibosheth's dress gave him a sincere look, which worked in his

---

66. For example, Alter, *Art of Biblical Narrative*, 120; Bodner and White, "Some Advantages," 20–33. It is also noteworthy that teraphim are also used in the book of Judges; see Peter Bauck, "1 Samuel 19: David and the Teraphim and the Emplotted Narrative," *SJOT* 22 (2008), 212–36.

67. See also the essays in Clines and Eskenazi, *Telling Queen Michal's Story*; and John Dekker, "'May the Lord Make the Woman Like Rachel': Comparing Michal and Rachel," *TynBul* 64 (2013), 17–32.

68. Scholars argue it was not nakedness per se, but skimpy garments that alternately concealed and revealed the offended; see William H. C. Propp, *Exodus 19–40* (New York: Doubleday, 2006); 185; Deborah W. Rooke, "Breeches of the Covenant: Gender, Garments and the Priesthood," in Rooke, *Embroidered Garments*, 19–37 (24); Ian D. Wilson, "The Emperor and His Clothing: David Robed and Unrobed before the Ark and Michal," in Finitsis, *Dress*, 125–42.

69. Joel Baden, *The Historical David: The Real Life of an Invented Hero* (New York: HarperCollins, 2013), 190; cf. Wilson, "The Emperor," 136.

70. Wilson, "The Emperor," 141; cf. Bruce Rosenstock, "David's Play: Fertility Rituals and the Glory of God in 2 Samuel 6," *JSOT* 31 (2006), 63–80.

71. Jeremy Schipper, *Disability Studies and the Hebrew Bible: Figuring Mephibosheth in the David Story* (London: T&T Clark, 2006), 56; cf. A. Graeme Auld, *I & II Samuel: A Commentary* (Louisville, KY: Westminster John Knox, 2012), 552.

72. This event is similar to the wise woman of Tekoa who dressed up in the clothes of a mourner (בגדי אבל) when she asked David to judge her fictitious dispute with her family (2

favor when Ziba, Saul's servant, wrongly informed David that Mephibosheth had been disloyal.[73] On the contrary, P. Ackroyd compares Mephibosheth's appearance to that of the Gibeonites in Josh. 9:4–5 and thus questions his honesty.[74] Either way, the dress of Mephibosheth the Benjaminite confirms the end of the Saulide reign and switches the focus to David.

In the Book of Esther

While this narrative is a different genre and not part of Deuteronomistic history, Mordecai is a Benjaminite and dress functions symbolically in his story.[75] His genealogical line links back to Kish (Est. 2:5), which was the name of Saul's father (1 Sam. 9:1),[76] and like his ancestors before him, dress reflects Mordecai's up-and-down social status. He changed from his everyday clothes into sackcloth and tore his clothes to show his despair and distress over Ahasuerus's decree, petitioning and pleading for those around him to do the same (Est. 4:3). Esther sent him clothes to wear so that he could remove his sackcloth, but to no avail, so she took matters into her own hands and issued a plea to the king to save her people (Est. 4: 15–16). Mordecai's dress manifests his opposition to the decree; this is a dangerous protest expressed through sartorial choices.[77] Haman expressed his wish to be king through clothing preferences, wanting to be adorned in royal regalia featuring the signet ring. Instead, Mordecai received these adornments (Est. 8:15). The king bestowed on him two kinds of garments consisting of two

---

Sam. 14:2), and the Amalekite who lied to David about killing Saul appeared before David dressed as a mourner (2 Sam. 1:2).

73. Jeremy Schipper, "'Why Do You Still Speak of Your Affairs?' Polyphony in Mephibosheth's Exchanges with David in 2 Samuel," *VT* 54 (2004), 344–51.

74. P. Ackroyd, *The Second Book of Samuel* (Cambridge: Cambridge University Press, 1977), 181. Jeremy Schipper furthers the connection between Mephibosheth and the Gibeonites in terms of their characterization when Mephibosheth next appears in 2 Samuel 21; Schipper, "Why Do You Still Speak of Your Affairs," 345.

75. See Selena Billington in this volume; Quick and Lyell, "Clothing"; Jopie Siebert-Hommes, "'On the Third Day Esther Put on her Queen's Robes' (Esther 5:1): The Symbolic Function of Clothing in the Book of Esther," *LDiff* 1 (2002), 1–9; Joshua Joel Spoelstra, "Mordecai's Royal Vestments: Princely And/Or Priestly," *OTE* 32 (2019), 174–96.

76. Verman, "Royalty," 41–2; Yairah Amit, "The Saul Polemic in the Persian Period," in *Judah and the Judeans in the Persian Period*, ed. Oded Lipschits and Manfred Oeming (Winona Lake, IN: Eisenbrauns, 2006), 647–61 (653–6); Jon D. Levenson, *Esther: A Commentary* (Louisville, KY: Westminster John Knox, 1997), 56–7; Yitzhak Berger, "Esther and Benjaminite Royalty: A Study in Inner-Biblical Allusion," *JBL* 129 (2010), 625–44; Aaron J. Koller, "The Exile of Kish: Syntax and History in Esther 2.5-6," *JSOT* 37 (2012), 45–56.

77. According to Köhlmoos, the wearing of sackcloth is the most pervasive biblical ritual of mourning. Melanie Köhlmoos, "Tearing One's Clothes and Rites of Mourning," in Berner et al., *Clothing and Nudity*, 303–15.

different purple fabrics and two white-colored fabrics and a great golden crown. Understanding the cultural significance behind these colored fabrics and precious metals demonstrates just how valuable these robes were.[78]

Mordecai's bestowal of לבוש מלכות (royal apparel) was not just a reward but also marked the end of a long history of oppression from the Amalekites. In Judges 3, Eglon, the obese king of Moab, formed an alliance with the Ammonites and the Amalekites (vv. 13–14); Ehud the Benjaminite saved the Israelites from their enemies by hiding a חרב under his מד and killing Eglon.[79] In 1 Samuel 15, Saul the Benjaminite defeated the Amalekites but saved their king, Agag (vv. 8, 9, 20, 32, 33). Subsequently, Samuel rejected Saul as king, and Saul ripped Samuel's מעיל, which marked the beginning of Saul's downfall. Thus in the book of Esther, when Haman, the enemy of the Jews, is called an "Agagite," the narrative inevitably recalls the hostility between the Israelites and the Amalekites.[80] Therefore when Mordecai defeated Haman, which ends this long history of Amalekite oppression, he was appropriately rewarded with the finest of garments (Est. 8:15).[81]

Therefore, an *inclusio* is at play here. The prominent role of clothing in the Joseph narratives led me to an exploration of the association between dress and Benjamin. The garment motif attached to those with Benjaminite heritage ends in the book of Esther, where the dress of Mordecai the Benjaminite presupposes that of Joseph. Mordecai's clothing was similar to what Pharaoh gave Joseph (and perhaps what Joseph gave Benjamin)—but ultimately it surpasses them.[82] Mordecai underwent several changes of clothing in the course of the narrative, changing from his everyday clothes into sackcloth (Est. 4:1), and then into royal garments of purple and fine linen (Est. 8:15). This mirrors, but goes beyond, Joseph's change from prison clothes to fine linen (Gen. 41:42). Joseph is gifted with בגדי־שש (garments of fine linen) representing his introduction into the Egyptian court, adopting their royal robes and distinguishing his new authority in Egyptian eyes as a ruler. Mordecai's introduction to the Persian court goes further as he is adorned with בלבוש מלכות תכלת וחור (royal apparel of purple and white) *and* ותכריך בוץ וארגמן (a robe of fine linen and purple). As we have seen, garment imagery in

78. Multiple scholars have recognized that there are also affinities between Ahasuerus's palace (Est. 1:6) and Mordecai's clothing (Est. 8:15); Mordecai's status is thus somewhat analogous to that of King Ahasuerus. See Spoelstra, "Mordecai's Royal Vestments," 185; Levenson, *Esther*, 45; John Hartley, *The Semantics of Ancient Hebrew Colour Lexemes* (Louvain: Peeters, 2010), 85; Quick and Lyell, "Clothing"; Alison Salvesen, "כתר (Esther 1:11; 2:17; 6:8): Something to do with a Camel?" *JSS* 44 (1999), 35–46.

79. The Ammonites and Amalekites were introduced in the narrative to account for how the ineffectual Eglon could have successfully subjugated any Israelite territory; see Handy, "Uneasy Laughter," 235.

80. Berger, "Esther," 633–4; Amit, "Saul Polemic," 653–4; Joshua Joel Spoelstra, "Surviving the Agagites: A Postcolonial Reading of Esther 8–9," *OTE* 28 (2015), 168–81 (172).

81. Quick and Lyell, "Clothing"; cf. Selena Billington in this volume.

82. Quick and Lyell, "Clothing."

the stories about the Benjaminites relates to their right to rule. Dress, however, demonstrates that this ambition and potential is never fulfilled; not until Mordecai, who finally achieves the Benjaminite royal potential, symbolized by his final apparel.[83]

Redressing Kingship and the Benjaminite Line: Implications of Garment Imagery

Benjamin was the only child born to Jacob after he changed his name to "Israel" (Gen. 35:9-15), which anticipated Israel's origins as a nation in Benjaminite territory but also the Benjaminite identity of Israel's first king.[84] The Genesis narratives build up the tension between the vulnerable Benjamin and the predominant Judah, in which Judah demonstrated unexpected remorse toward Benjamin.[85] In Judges, the Benjaminites battled against the Judahites (and the rest of the tribes under the Israel umbrella) but were then reaccepted. Throughout the monarchic period, the tribes of Benjamin and Judah have a hostile relationship: King Saul, from the tribe of Benjamin, versus King David, from the tribe of Judah (1 Sam. 17:12).[86] Dress reflects these tensions. For example, Judah tore his שִׂמְלָה at the thought of losing Benjamin, signaling a transformation in his character compared to his treatment of Joseph. The Benjaminites used particular daggers (חֶרֶב) as part of their weaponry to try and defeat the Judahites and the other tribes after the concubine was cut into pieces. Finally, both Saul and Jonathan the Benjaminites lost or gave away their clothing, and David the Judahite, ultimately, gained it.

Through the manifestation of dress in descriptions of Benjamin, of the Benjaminite tribe and Ehud in Judges, the king would have inherent characteristics of left-handedness, passiveness, deviance, military superiority, in addition to sexual prowess communicated euphemistically. Many of the clothing items are specifically items of martial dress. David has a special group of Benjaminite archers who assisted him as security (1 Chr. 12:1-2). Benjaminites could use the sling left-handed and not miss a target by a breadth of hair (Judg. 20:16). Jonathan's shooting abilities were also well known (1 Sam. 20:20). The sons of Ulam, who all belonged to the descendants of Benjamin, were recognized for their military prowess (1 Chr. 8:40; 2 Chr. 14:8). P. S. Vermaak argues the physical prowess of the

---

83. Ibid.

84. Benjamin D. Giffone, " 'Israel's' Only Son? The Complexity of Benjaminite Identity between Judah and Joseph," *OTE* 32 (2019), 956–72 (964).

85. Hyun Chul Paul Kim, "Reading the Joseph Story (Genesis 37-50) as a Diaspora Narrative," *CBQ* 75 (2013), 219–38 (234).

86. On the Benjaminite-Judahite conflicts, see Amit, "Saul Polemic," 647–61; and Joseph Blenkinsopp, "Benjamin Traditions Read in the Early Persian Period," in Lipschits and Oeming, *Judah and the Judeans in the Persian Period*, 629–45.

Benjaminites was key in why a member of this tribe was chosen as the first king of Israel.[87] This is true to some extent, but the dress and adornment of armor, bows, and slingshots also allude to the continuation of Benjaminites in the emerging Israelite monarchy.

The specific martial accessories and weaponry that dressed a Benjaminite body (חגור, חרב, and קשת) have not only warrior associations but also sexual implications. For example, the חרב is the weapon the Benjaminite tribe armed themselves with against the other Israelite tribes in Judges, a consequence of sexually abusing the concubine. Ehud specifically made a חרב, placed it on his right thigh under his clothing, and stabbed Eglon with it, after perhaps misleading him with sexual advances. Furthermore, Jonathan took off his חרב, חגור, and קשת and gifted it to David. As they either lie on an intimate place on the body or are a phallic symbol, this gift is a transferal of virility that ultimately feminizes Jonathan and makes David a hypermasculine character.

Conclusions

The character of Benjamin in Genesis has a significant relationship to dress: Benjamin became the favored son whose life was knitted and sewn to his father Jacob; when he was wrongly imprisoned, his brothers tore their garments. However, ultimately, Joseph revealed his true identity and gifted Benjamin five sets of fine garments. This garment motif indicates a theme throughout the Benjaminite line: the up-and-down trajectory anticipates the fate of a Benjaminite. In Judges, Ehud used his devious military abilities and attached a knife to his right side, disguised under his clothing. He killed the ruler and was hunted; he successfully escaped via a ruse associated with the king's clothing ("he covered his feet") and thus saved Israel from its enemies. In Judges 19–21, the Benjaminites behaved in an aggressive, irrational, and violent manner toward the concubine and thus instigated civil war in Israel, requiring that they themselves put on items of martial dress. They fell to the other tribes and were eventually allowed back into the Israelite community. This trajectory also maps onto Saul: the Benjaminite was Israel's chosen king who tore the hem of Samuel's cloak marking the beginning of his downfall, which ends with his death in battle via his own dagger and the stripping off of his armor. The turning point in Benjamin's line is where Jonathan, well known for his armor and military prowess, *chose* to give his dress to David, and this choice consequently saw him fall. Michal went on to protect David using dress as deception, but David's skimpy outfit marked the end of their relationship and ensured his rise over any Saulide (i.e., any Benjaminite) descendants. Mephibosheth's mourning dress too reflects the downfall of the Benjaminite line. This long-standing preoccupation with dress raises questions about authorial intention: did each subsequent author pick up on the theme and carry it forward?

87. Vermaak, "Prowess," 84.

Or is the thread that unites these stories a coincidence? I favor the former as the substantial body of evidence points to intention rather than a mere quirk of redaction. Clothing is crucial in the construction and communication of power, and in the case of the Benjamin tribe, dress offers insights into the characteristics of an Israelite king and presages the success of their reign.

More specifically, the role of dress throughout the Benjaminite history reflects the rise-and-fall pattern of the key men of Benjamin heritage—through social status and levels of power. The ending of Judges calls for the rise of Saul, and the ending of Saul calls for the rise of David. The relationship of adornment between two of Saul's children (Jonathan and Michal) and David ensure this rise is successful, sustainable, and unlike Saul's. The cyclical up-and-down regime of the Benjaminites paves the way for the rise of the Benjaminite tribe again, arguably via Mordecai. Mordecai fulfills the hope manifested in the larger garment motif associated with the Benjaminite line, clad in fine garments surpassing those of his ancestors, and brings an end to the age-old enemy of the Saulide dynasty, the Amalekites.

Crucially, the warrior-like and deviant characteristics associated with the line of Benjamin are emphasized through their items of dress and adornment. A larger garment motif associated with Benjaminites links Benjamin in Genesis with the tribal line in Judges and royalty in Samuel and Esther. The genealogy of Benjamin contains multiple threads of dress imagery, to the extent that the construction of a stitch in a piece of fabric (weaving the thread up and down) mirrors the construction of a king who rises and falls. The garment motif indicates the royal potential of the Benjaminites, but this same motif highlights their failures and downfall.

Chapter 7

JUST CLOTHING? THE FUNCTION OF DRESS METAPHORS IN IMPRECATORY PSALMS

Carmen Joy Imes

While both Jewish and Christian communities of faith have long cherished the book of Psalms, the imprecatory psalms in particular have not fared well. Many readers share Artur Weiser's assessment that these psalms at least occasionally exhibit "undisguised gloating and the cruel vindictiveness of an intolerant religious fanaticism."[1] However, closer examination reveals that these psalms do not display unhinged violence or cruelty. Instead, they participate in a measured "social analogy" of legal petition through prayer. Like other ANE imprecatory texts, the psalmists consistently express a desire for justice constrained by the specific crimes of their enemies.

Imprecatory psalms are a subcategory of lament psalms. In a lament, the psalmist bemoans his or her circumstances, often in the form of complaint to God. Technically speaking, to imprecate is "to pray for or invoke (evil, a curse, etc.)."[2] An imprecatory psalm, therefore, is a psalm in which the supplicant petitions God to bring harm upon an enemy. By my count, at least 35 of the 150 canonical psalms (23 percent) include imprecatory language.[3] In nearly every case, the desired

---

I would like to thank my TAs, Abigail Bruggeman and Karen Hagens, who assisted with aspects of psalm analysis and commentary research early on in this project. I am also grateful for four years of stimulating interaction with everyone in our clothing research group, but especially for the in-depth feedback from my primary respondents, Jenny Matheny, Brady Alan Beard, and Scott Starbuck, and for the unflagging leadership of Tony Finitsis.

1. Quoted by Erich Zenger, *A God of Vengeance? Understanding the Psalms of Divine Wrath*, trans. Linda M. Maloney (Louisville, KY: Westminster John Knox, 1996), 15.

2. Michael Agnes, ed., *Webster's New World College Dictionary*, 4th ed. (Cleveland, OH: Wiley, 2008), 717.

3. Not including psalms that *describe* but do not *request* negative consequences, such as Psalm 137, where the psalmist indicates a desired outcome but stops short of requesting it. By my count, psalms that contain imprecatory language include Pss. 3, 5, 7, 9, 10, 12, 17, 28, 31, 35, 40, 54, 55, 56, 58, 59, 68, 69, 70, 71, 73, 74, 79, 83, 86, 94, 108, 109, 119, 129, 139, 140, 141, 143, and 144.

punishment fits the crime. In three cases, the desire seems lighter than merited.[4] Only once is the desired punishment greater than the offense, but in that psalm the victim is YHWH, not the psalmist, so the request is not motivated by personal vindication but rather a desire to restore the divine reputation.[5]

The Bible's imprecatory psalms do not advocate random violence but rather petition YHWH to issue a just decision in a human social context for which justice seems otherwise unlikely. Shalom E. Holtz notes the ubiquity of juridical language in the Psalms, suggesting that such language reflects "a fundamentally legal conception of prayer itself."[6] The psalmists call upon God "not to leave the guilty unpunished" (cf. Exod. 34:6-7), appealing to YHWH's own character. In that sense, imprecatory psalms align with the law of *lex talionis*, "an eye for an eye and a tooth for a tooth" (Exod. 21:23-25), by trusting that YHWH shares the concern for justice and will adjudicate in their favor using appropriate means of punishment. While these prayers may seem harsh or unforgiving to modern ears, imprecatory psalms are in fact expressions of deferred violence; rather than taking revenge on their enemies, the psalmists make their case in prayer and entrust a just verdict to God.[7]

I work here with a contextual definition of "justice" in the Hebrew Bible. Specifically, I have in mind the concepts signaled by the words *mišpaṭ* and *ṣədāqāh*. Vincent Bacote explains that these terms "emphasize God's role as lawgiver and just judge as well as the attribute of rectitude."[8] That is, justice is concerned with an appropriate response to human action expressed in "due regard and proper treatment" that results in "social, political, and relational practices [that] correspond to the righteous character of God."[9] The imprecatory psalms articulate the psalmists' quest for justice as a legal petition directed to the deity and designed for maximum rhetorical effectiveness. Two dimensions of this rhetoric we will consider are sound play and a creative use of metaphor to depict analogical punishments.[10]

---

4. Pss. 40, 70, and 86.

5. Ps. 79.

6. Shalom E. Holtz, *Praying Legally*, BJS (Providence, RI: Brown Judaic Studies, 2019), 5.

7. For a vindication of the ongoing relevance of the imprecatory psalms as Christian Scripture, see Kit Barker, *Imprecation as Divine Discourse: Speech Act Theory, Dual Authorship, and Theological Interpretation*, vol. 16 of *JTISup* (Winona Lake, IN: Eisenbrauns, 2016). For a contemporary Christian appropriation of the imprecatory psalms, see chapter 6 in Esau McCaulley, *Reading While Black: African American Biblical Interpretation as an Exercise in Hope* (Downers Grove, IL: IVP, 2020).

8. Vincent E. Bacote, "Justice," in *Dictionary for Theological Interpretation of the Bible*, ed. Kevin Vanhoozer (Grand Rapids, MI: Baker Academic, 2005), 415.

9. Ibid.

10. By "analogical punishments," I mean punishments that fit the crime, in that the punishment is similar in nature to the crime committed.

In the pages that follow, I will examine several imprecatory psalms from the Hebrew Bible that utilize clothing imagery to make their case. I will strive to show the reasons why clothing metaphors are especially fitting for expressing the psalmists' aim to persuade the deity to enact justice on their behalf. First, to give us a sense of context, it will be helpful to consider examples of ritual or social analogy in imprecation from cognate literature of the ANE.

Ritual Analogy in ANE Imprecation

Imprecatory psalms in the Hebrew Bible usually call upon God to respond to the psalmist's enemies who try to inflict physical harm or ruin the psalmist's reputation. Most ANE imprecatory prayers respond more narrowly to various forms of witchcraft. Of course, like biblical prayers, witchcraft may seek physical or reputational harm, but the means of inflicting that harm involves incantations or other magical rituals of some kind.[11] Both types of texts—biblical psalms and ANE incantations—employ analogy as a means of making sense of the world and bringing it into order.[12] That is, they call for a punishment that fits the crime.

For example, extant Akkadian literature dating between 1500 and 1000 BCE includes a prayer that seeks to turn sorcery back upon its source. In "III.41c To Gods of the Night: Against Witchcraft," the afflicted one prays:

> May she be the one to die, let me live!
> May her sorcery, spells, and black magic be dissolved …
> Her spell, that of the wicked sorceress,
> Her speech is turned back to her mouth, she is tongue-tied …
> May the three watches of the night dissolve her wicked spells!
> May her mouth be tallow, her tongue be salt,

---

11. The distinction between ritual and social analogy may not be significant. Starbuck and Gunkel both argue that a redactor edited ritual out of the Psalms in order to resituate them in a covenantal framework. Scott R. A. Starbuck, *Court Oracles in the Psalms: The So-Called Royal Psalms in Their Ancient Near Eastern Context*, SBL Dissertation (Atlanta, GA: Scholars, 1999), 98–100; Hermann Gunkel, *An Introduction to the Psalms*, Mercer Library of Biblical Studies, trans. James D. Nogalski (Macon, GA: Mercer University Press, 1998), 306–10. Holtz argues instead that the Psalms operate with an essentially legal conceptual framework for prayer. Holtz, *Praying Legally*. Given the legal nature of the covenant, perhaps all three authors are getting at the same thing from a different angle: Holtz arguing synchronically, while Gunkel and Starbuck argue diachronically. Yelle explains the similarities between ritual and social analogy by appealing to rhetoric. Both utilize sound play and analogical punishments for rhetorical persuasion. Robert A. Yelle, "Rhetorics of Law and Ritual: A Semiotic Comparison of the Law of Talion and Sympathetic Magic," *JAAR* 69.3 (2001), 627–47.

12. David P. Wright, "Ritual Analogy in Psalm 109," *JBL* 113.3 (1994): 402–4.

> May she who said the evil word against me melt like tallow,
> May she who worked sorcery be dissolved like salt,
> May her magic knots be untied, her contrivances be destroyed.[13]

Notice the connection between the maleficent behavior and the imprecation voiced by the supplicant—the "evil word" is turned back upon the sorceress and her mouth is unable to function, her "magic knots" are untied. Not only are her spells dissolved but she herself dissolves so that no more spells are possible.

Incantations, prayers, and rituals against witchcraft dating to the late Babylonian period (first millennium BCE) exhibit similarly analogical imprecations against those responsible for sorcery. In one text, the supplicant describes the devious behavior of his adversaries with a number of different metaphors:

> They worked and keep on working against me,
> To roll me up like a mat,
> To clamp down on me like a bird trap,
> To wreck me like an embankment,
> To close over me like a net,
> To cord me like cordage,
> To climb over me like a rampart,
> To fill a foundation ditch with me, as if (I were) dishwater,
> To pitch me out at the door like sweepings!

He invokes the power of Marduk and Asalluhi to respond in kind:

> Roll up my sorcerer and my sorceress like a mat,
> Clamp down on them like a bird trap,
> Wreck them like an embankment,
> Close over them like a net,
> Cord them like cordage,
> Climb over them like a rampart,
> Fill a foundation ditch with them, as if (they were) ditch water,
> Pitch them out at the door like sweepings.[14]

As with the other examples, this prayer does not exhibit unhinged violent tendencies but rather a desire for just retribution. Each imprecation corresponds directly to the harm done. The perception of the supplicant is that such a request will succeed in persuading the deities to act.

"The Lament of Nabu-shuma-ukin" from the first millennium BCE wrestles with unwarranted suffering, appealing to Marduk to enact justice on his behalf. Like

---

13. Benjamin R. Foster, *Before the Muses: An Anthology of Akkadian Literature*, 2nd ed. (Bethesda, MD: CDL, 1996), 666–7.

14. Ibid., IV.49c, 997, lines 1–8, 11–18.

the biblical lament psalms, Nabu-shuma-ukin recalls Marduk's past enactments of justice before making his own appeal:

> Marduk can undo the most artful snare
> So the wind can bring down the one who relied on his own artfulness.
> Marduk glowers at the shifty eye,
> He has Girra burn up lips that speak evil.[15]

Based on Marduk's past actions, the supplicant requests intervention in his case. As in biblical laments, the punishment fits the crime:

> [O Marduk], smash in the heads of those who glower at me!
> You know full well the one whose arts seek to harm me, strike him down!
> With conciliatory words on his lips, his heart freight[ted] with lies … [ ]
> Probe the one who worked up this conspiracy to harm me,
> [send him] down to hell!
> Surround the malefactor with the same cruel web
> with which he artfully surround[ded me]! …
> Single out for harm the one who stirred up harmful talk of me![16]

Unlike the other ANE texts cited, Nabu-shuma-ukin's lament concerns gossip and palace conspiracy rather than witchcraft, making it a closer match to biblical imprecation.

While the examples above use a variety of analogies other than clothing to articulate ritual desire, David P. Wright cites a Hittite example that involves dress:

> May [i]t (the evil) be a *kureššar*-hat (for her, i.e. the sorceress)!
> May she set it up on her head!
> … May it be a girdle for her!
> May she bind [them] (the evils) on herself!
> May it be a shoe for her!
> May she put it on![17]

According to this petition, the supplicant envisioned retributive justice as three articles of clothing: a hat, a girdle, and a shoe. These articles of clothing apprehend the sorceress in such a way that the supplicant imagines that justice is served. This text brings to the fore two aspects that I consider important. First, dress can function as a form of entrapment. The use of the verb "to bind" highlights this

---

15. Ibid., IV.9, 853, lines 7–10.

16. Ibid., IV.9, 854, lines 45–49, 53.

17. *KUB* 24.9 + I 16-19. Cited in Wright, "Ritual Analogy in Psalm 109," 399, n. 35. Wright claims that "clothing is common in ancient Near Eastern ritual analogy," but more exploration is needed to bolster this claim.

notion. The implication seems to be that dress binds and hence defines one's public identity the same way that evil actions do. Second, in order for "due regard and proper treatment" to take place, the intended evil must not only return but also affix to its source. Dress, in this sense, is an extension and part of one's public self. This may explain why the supplicant lists dress items that cover the sorceress from head to toe.

Two clear similarities with biblical imprecation emerge from this sampling of ANE imprecations. First, like biblical imprecations, supplicants request a punishment that fits the crime—that is, they call for reflexive action, so that the harm intended for them would return to the one sending it. Second, like biblical imprecations, supplicants utilize a variety of metaphors to make their request. However, unlike the Bible's imprecatory psalms, their primary concern is usually sorcery rather than concern over toxic social dynamics such as mockery or false accusations.

Social Analogy in Imprecatory Prayers of the Hebrew Bible

As with the ANE examples above, metaphorical language plays a key role in most imprecatory psalms in the Hebrew Bible. Following Landau, Robinson, and Meier,

> Metaphors are here defined as figures of speech in which relatively concrete, tangible concepts (referred to as *source concepts*) are used to represent more abstract concepts (referred to as *target concepts*). Such metaphors generally associate a concrete object, image, or event to a social category that typically (but not exclusively) occurs in the role of the target domain. Importantly, target and source concepts generally refer to categories of stimuli that have nothing to do with each other.[18]

The imprecatory psalms utilize a variety of source concepts to represent the objectionable behavior of the psalmists' enemies via conceptual metaphor.[19]

---

18. Mark J. Landau, Michael D. Robinson, and Brian P. Meier, *The Power of Metaphor: Examining Its Influence on Social Life* (Washington, DC: American Psychological Association, 2014), 155; original emphases.

19. Conceptual metaphor theory recognizes that metaphors configure the ways we think and act as they invite us "to understand one domain of experience in terms of another." George Lakoff and Mark Johnson, *Metaphors We Live By* (Chicago, IL: University of Chicago Press, 1980), 117. For a sophisticated but accessible introduction to conceptual metaphor theory, see Zoltán Kövecses, *Metaphor* (New York: Oxford University Press, 2010). The conventional way to express a conceptual metaphor is a complete statement in small capital letters. For a brief summary of Kövecses's approach and application of conceptual metaphor theory to biblical law, see Carmen Joy Imes, "Metaphor at Sinai: Cognitive Linguistics in the Decalogue and Covenant Code," *BBR* 29.3 (2019), 342–60.

The psalmists thereby articulate appropriately analogous punishments for these enemies. Consider the following examples (Table 7.1), in which the metaphors describing the desired consequences correspond closely to the metaphors describing the offense, drawing on imagery related to the same source concept to craft an analogous punishment. For example, in Psalm 35, the psalmist prays that God would cause the wicked to fall into the traps they have set for the psalmist. To portray his enemies as hunters strengthens the psalmist's own helplessness (he is the prey) and thereby the persuasive urgency of his appeal to God for intervention.

In each of these examples, the use of metaphor conveys the desperation of the psalmist. Drawing on a vivid source concept, the psalmist illustrates the devastation wrought by his enemies (the target concept), petitioning God for an analogous punishment. Because the petition uses imagery from the same source concept,

Table 7.1 Examples of analogous punishment in imprecatory prayers from Psalms

Imprecatory passage	Source concept	Target concept	Conceptual metaphor	Analogous punishment
"For without cause they hid for me their net; a pit without cause they dug for me. Let ruin come in unnoticed and his net that he hid—may it capture him. In ruin let him fall into it." (Ps. 35:7-8)	Hunting imagery	Those trying to kill the psalmist	ENEMIES ARE HUNTERS	Trap them in their own nets Let them fall in their own pit
"They put in my food bitter poison, and for my thirst they gave me vinegar to drink. May their table before them become a trap, and their prosperity a snare." (Ps. 69:22-23)	Meal imagery	Those who hate and seek to destroy the psalmist (vv. 4, 14)	ENEMIES ARE DUPLICITOUS HOSTS	Trap them at their own table
"Against my back those who plow plowed; they prolonged their furrows ... May they be like grass of the roof, which before it is pulled up, dries, which does not fill the palm of the one who reaps or the lap of one who binds sheaves." (Ps. 129:3, 6-7)	Farming imagery	Enemies of Israel and haters of Zion	OPPRESSORS ARE FARMERS; OPPRESSED ISRAEL IS THE FIELD	May their harvest be meager
"Save me, God, for waters come up to my neck! I am sinking in deep mud, and there is no foothold; I enter deep waters and a current sweeps me away ... May you pour out on them your indignation, and the anger of your nostrils overtake them." (Ps. 69:1-2, 25)	Perilous water imagery	Enemies trying to destroy the psalmist (v. 14)	ENEMIES ARE PERILOUS WATERS	Pour out indignation on them
"Venom is theirs, like the venom of a snake, like a deaf cobra he stops his ear, who does not listen to the voice whispering, a charmer [in the] company of the wise. God, knock out his teeth in his mouth; the jawbone of young lions demolish, *YHWH*." (Ps. 58:5-7 [ET 4-6])	Animal imagery	Rulers who devise injustice and spread lies (vv. 1-3)	UNJUST RULERS ARE POISONOUS SNAKES	Knock out their teeth so their lies will be silenced

the response seems fitting and proper. The psalmists' request is not random, and it does not exhibit violence out of proportion to the crime done against him. The judicious use of metaphor is therefore essential to the psalmists' purposes. As Sallie McFague explains, "Far from being an esoteric or ornamental rhetorical device superimposed *on* ordinary language, metaphor *is* ordinary language. It is the *way* we think."[20] In each case the viability of the petition depends on the metaphor. The social analogy invoked by each image is essential to its fulfillment.

Clothing is another source domain for the metaphorical language of imprecatory psalms. As I hope to demonstrate, dress and costume metaphors are particularly well suited to imprecation (pun intended).[21] They are neither arbitrary nor expendable but convey the petition for justice in precisely appropriate ways, given the nature of the crimes. The dress metaphors of the imprecatory psalms illustrate the truth of McFague's claim that "good metaphors shock, they bring unlikes together, they upset conventions, they involve tension, and they are implicitly revolutionary."[22] We will first consider the motivation for clothing metaphors, followed by a more detailed exposition of the passages in which they appear.

Motivation for Clothing Metaphors

Robert A. Yelle demonstrates how magic rituals and law codes both utilize sound play to express analogic punishments. This acoustic technique is not merely ornamental but functions in both settings by making the analogy less arbitrary and more persuasive, thus strengthening the relationship between punishment and crime, or ritual and result.[23] Yelle suggests "a punishment that bears an analogical

---

20. Sallie McFague, *Metaphorical Theology: Models of God in Religious Language* (Philadelphia, PA: Fortress, 1982), 16; original emphases.

21. Pravina Shukla, in *Costume: Performing Identities through Dress* (Indianapolis: Indiana University Press, 2015), defines "costume" as "special dress that enables the expression of extraordinary identity in exceptional circumstances." She explains,

> In wearing costume we do not become someone else; rather, we become in some context a deeper or heightened version of ourselves. Costume provides an outlet for the expression of certain identity markers that do not have an outlet in ordinary life. Like ritual, costumed events are distinct from daily existence, and therefore they allow for extreme forms of dress to aid in the formation of an alternative identity. (14–15)

22. McFague, *Metaphorical Theology*, 17.

23. Yelle, "Rhetorics of Law and Ritual." De Saussure shows that words are more-or-less arbitrary but are motivated by meaning associations as well as by phonemic similarities. Ferdinand de Saussure, *Course in General Linguistics*, ed. Charles Bally and Albert Sechehaye, trans. Wade Baskin (New York: McGraw-Hill, 1959), 122–34.

relation to its crime is impressive not only to the individual prospective criminal as a deterrent but also to society as a whole."[24]

Two main factors make metaphors for dress especially fitting for imprecatory prayer. Not surprisingly, the first is acoustic. Because of the phonemic similarity between לבשׁ (*lbš*; *qal*: to wear; *hithpael*: to clothe) and בשׁת (*bšt*: shame) or בושׁ (*bôš*: to be ashamed), clothing is an acoustically pleasing metaphorical vehicle to use on occasions of public shaming. Consider these examples of the phonological pairing of these two terms outside the book of Psalms:

Job 8:22

| שֹׂנְאֶיךָ יִלְבְּשׁוּ־בֹשֶׁת | Your enemies **will be clothed in shame** (*yilbəšû-bošet*), |
| ואהל רשעים איננו | And the tent of the wicked will be empty. |

Bildad assures Job of the justice of YHWH: God will punish the guilty. Evildoers will receive their just reward, namely, public shaming and removal from society. The sound play between "clothed" (*yilbəšû*) and "shame" (*bošet*) reinforces the logical connection between them.

The reverse of this image in Zechariah achieves the same effect. When God purifies Judah, prophets who have once given false prophecy will be ashamed and will cease to wear the garments designating them as prophets.

Zech. 13:4

והיה ביום ההוא	And on that day,
יֵבֹשׁוּ הנביאים איש מחזינו	Each of the prophets **will be ashamed** (*yebo:šû*)
בהנבאתו	of his prophetic vision
ולא יִלְבְּשׁוּ אדרת שער למען כחש:	And he **will** not **wear** (*yilbəšû*) the hairy robe to deceive.

The shame resulting here is not solely a psychological phenomenon but also denotes physical and social diminishment. In the same way that dress (i.e., the hairy robe) brought honor to the prophets it will become a visible marker of their shame. That is, the humiliation of false prophets will be publicly conspicuous.[25]

This leads to another factor encouraging the use of dress metaphors in these laments, namely, the communicative power of clothing common to every culture. While the particular message of dress varies from culture to culture, its potency is common to all, preceding and even exceeding the impact of speech in the creation of social identity.[26] Dress is more than a means of protection from the

24. Yelle, "Rhetorics of Law and Ritual," 641.

25. See Matthew J. Lynch, "Neglected Physical Dimensions of 'Shame' Terminology in the Hebrew Bible," *Bib* 91.4 (2010), 499–517.

26. Mary Ellen Roach-Higgins and Joanne B. Eicher, "Dress and Identity," *Clothing and Textiles Research Journal* 10 (1992), 5. See also Heather A. McKay's chapter in this volume.

elements. It functions as a "social skin." As Terence Turner explains in the *Journal of Ethnographic Theory*, "The surface of the body seems everywhere to be treated, not only as the boundary of the individual as a biological and psychological entity but as the frontier of the social self as well."[27] Social interactions begin at first sight. Dress negotiates the initial assessment of power dynamics and hierarchy as they relate to individual and collective identities. Humans in every culture send messages about their relationship to the society in which they participate by wearing or not wearing particular symbols. These become nonverbal indicators of status, profession, class, gender, and, in some cases, marital status. A person can be quite oblivious to these dynamics, but their social position is reinforced nonetheless, as either insider or outsider, regardless of whether their participation is deliberate. Dress also facilitates creation of likeminded subgroups by openly signaling commitments. Investiture or divestiture of clothing effectively signals a change of social status. Hartenstein notes that by dressing and undressing, clothing becomes a vehicle for dishonor.[28]

The wearing of clothes that fall outside the normal scope of daily dress is a particularly potent expression of some aspect of that person's identity. For example, new students on our campus participate in a full-day simulation of international travel. This year I walked around wearing my graduation robes to quiz groups as they completed particular challenges. Most students had never seen me in doctoral regalia. Together with my brusque arrogance, the costume communicated power and reinforced compliance with my unreasonable demands.

In his exploration of clothing metaphors in Greek literature, Douglas Cairns makes the following claim:

> Dress, even in its concrete, literal form, is laden with symbolism. It extends, prosthetically, the body's capacity to express thought and emotion. These physical expressions of emotion are then available as symbols for the emotional concepts that they express.[29]

---

27. Terence S. Turner, "The Social Skin," *HAU: Journal of Ethnographic Theory* 2.2 (2012), 486.

28. Friedhelm Hartenstein, "Clothing and Nudity in the Paradise Story (Gen. 2-3)," in *Clothing and Nudity in the Hebrew Bible*, ed. Christoph Berner, Manuel Schafer, Martin Schott, Sarah Schultz, and Martina Weingartner (New York: T&T Clark, 2019), 369.

29. Douglas L. Cairns, "Clothed in Shamelessness, Shrouded in Grief: The Role of 'Garment' Metaphors in Ancient Greek Concepts of Emotion," in *Spinning Fates and the Song of the Loom: The Use of Textiles, Clothing and Cloth Production as Metaphor, Symbol and Narrative Device in Greek and Latin Literature*, Ancient Textiles Series 24, ed. Giovanni Fanfani, Mary Harlow, and Marie-Louise Nosch (Oxford: Oxbow, 2016), 38. Cairns seems to focus primarily on the *emotion* of shame, rather than the act of shaming or the more concrete expression of loss, but he recognizes the communicative potential of clothing imagery.

The biblical text preserves evidence of this communicative power of dress in society. Of course, textual analysis of clothing in the Hebrew Bible differs from sociological study because we "see," "hear," "taste," and "smell" only what the author conveys in words. As such, the picture is not nearly as complete. Still, the social aspects of dress are textually encoded. This is especially true for dress metaphors in imprecatory prayers because they express the desired social effects of the clothing openly.

In ancient Israel, as in any culture, dress contributes to the social power dynamic described above. Changes of clothing rearticulate social identities, affecting how individuals are received and either signifying their exaltation or debasement by members of the community.[30] "Expectancy violations theory" (hereafter, EVT) offers one way to describe the effects of dress on social dynamics. When someone's dress or costume violates societal expectations, the added attention "instigates an appraisal and evaluation process that results in the violation being valenced as positive or negative."[31] For this reason, dress is a natural image to use for prescribing a desired status change with public ramifications, especially in cases where the supplicant has been misunderstood or poorly treated in the public arena.

Closely related to EVT is an approach we will call "social validation theory" (hereafter, SVT), which focuses on the wearer rather than the observer. Social scientist G. P. Stone elucidates the steps involved in the acquisition or public construal of identity. A person first announces their identity by dressing in a particular way (the "program"). Others assess the individual ("review"). If the perception of others matches the expectation of the individual, then "validation" has taken place.[32] However, Roach-Higgins and Eicher explain, "If, on the contrary, the meaning signaled by dress is different for presenter and reviewer, interaction may proceed with difficulty or be terminated."[33] In other words, a person's choice of clothing carries with it expectations for how others will perceive and respond to them. Wearing white garments ought to elicit praise and increase influence, while wearing a costume such as sackcloth in mourning elicits pity.[34] If dress does not elicit the expected validation, the relationship suffers from awkwardness or distance. As such, EVT and SVT approach the same moment of identity construal from different angles, EVT from the observer's perspective, and SVT from the wearer's perspective.

---

30. On the inversion of social expectations with dress, see Susanna Rees's chapter in this volume.

31. Judee K. Burgoon, Norah E. Dunbar, and Christ Segrin, "Nonverbal Influence," in *The Persuasion Handbook: Developments in Theory and Practice*, ed. James Price Dillard and Michael Pfau (Thousand Oaks, CA: Sage, 2002), 458.

32. Roach-Higgins and Eicher, "Dress and Identity," 5. Citing G. P. Stone, "Appearance and the Self," in *Human Behavior and the Social Processes: An Interactionist Approach*, ed. A. M. Rose (New York: Houghton Mifflin, 1962), 86–118, 93.

33. Roach-Higgins and Eicher, "Dress and Identity," 5.

34. See Jennifer Brown Jones's chapter on Zechariah in this volume.

What follows is my attempt to isolate the richest examples of metaphorical clothing and costume in imprecatory Psalms in order to elucidate these social dynamics. We will examine two main types of dress metaphors: (i) those deriving from conventional practices, and (ii) those that extend and creatively exploit dress in nonconventional ways. EVT and SVT offer a helpful framework for talking about the unintended effects of the psalmist's clothing on his reception as well as the desired outcome for his legal petition. Costume studies will prove to be a helpful resource as well.

Metaphors in Action

Two psalms serve as excellent case studies. Both are imprecatory, and both employ metaphors related to clothing. The first main example, Psalm 35, focuses on the conventional practice of wearing sackcloth as an expression of grief or intercession, exploiting this common practice in metaphorical ways. We will briefly explore Psalm 69 as another example of this type of dress metaphor.

The second main example, Psalm 109, employs an unconventional clothing metaphor—violent cursing as a garment—but ends with an analogical request for justice—that the enemies would be clothed with shame. This metaphor is unconventional in that we have no evidence of actual dress related to cursing, but it is not anomalous; Psalm 109 shares some similarities with Psalms 71 and 73 as well as the Hittite text considered above. In Psalm 109, the psalmist petitions God using a creative dress metaphor to make more vivid the enemy's full identification with this malevolent behavior.

Psalm 35

Clothing is not the primary metaphor in Psalm 35, but clothing imagery reinforces the central theme: a plea for vindication. The psalmist implores in verse 1:

ריבה יהוה את־יריבי	Contend, YHWH, with my contenders;
לחם את־לחמי׃	fight with those fighting me!

He further prays that God would pursue his enemies the way they have pursued him (vv. 4–6) and that his enemies would fall into the trap they themselves set for him (vv. 7–8). Because they have hated him "without cause" (v. 19) and devised deceit against a "quiet land" (v. 20), he cries out for deliverance and vindication. Their insolence is not only visually evident but also embodied: gnashing teeth (v. 16), winking eye (v. 19), mouth open wide (v. 21), seeing him (maliciously; v. 21), and desiring to "swallow" the psalmist (v. 25). Each of these nonverbal, bodily actions communicates public disrespect, provoking the psalmist's petition that those shaming him would be shamed.

The enemies are brokers of social control, carefully maintaining their public identities by collectively attacking the one they see as a threat. Notice their persistent power play: they contend, fight, pursue, devise harm, tyrannize, gather against, devise treacherous words, rejoice over (the psalmist's) distress, and exalt themselves over (him), showing greater strength and violence. In the face of this onslaught, the psalmist turns to the only possible source of deliverance—YHWH the warrior—calling upon God to meet the challengers with weapons unsheathed. The legal conceptual framework for Psalm 35 is evident in the presence of "witnesses" (v. 11), "false accusations" (v. 20), the call for YHWH to "rise to my defense" (v. 23), to "contend" (vv. 1, 23), and to "vindicate" the psalmist (vv. 24, 27).

Psalm 35 engages this toxic social dynamic by asking God to shame the shamers: "They have shamed me, so may they be shamed."[35] Their response

35. The astute reader will wonder whether this contributes to an honor-shame dynamic. The most recent scholarship on the subject downplays the pairing of honor and shame. Shame words are often not set against honor words and vice versa, especially in the Psalms. See especially Johanna Stiebert, *The Construction of Shame in the Hebrew Bible: The Prophetic Contribution*, JSOT 346 (New York: Sheffield Academic Press, 2002). Stiebert calls for extreme caution in the application of modern anthropological case studies to ancient texts. Not only is such application anachronistic, but the texts themselves may or may not reflect the realities of communities' daily interactions and values. She notes that shame language in the Bible is especially prominent in exilic and postexilic contexts. For that reason, anthropological insights from stable societies are less relevant. See ibid., 165. The Bible primarily attributes honor to God, and shame is experienced quite democratically. See ibid., 166.

Certainly, there are cases in the Psalms where the investiture of clothing denotes a bestowal of honor or where divestiture of clothing communicates shame. See, for example, Lyn M. Bechtel's article in which she says that "people's clothing formed a covering which protected their vital parts from the physical environment (rain, heat, cold, wind) and, most of all, psychologically from having the private areas of the body exposed to the gaze of others." Lyn M. Bechtel, "Shame as a Sanction of Social Control in Biblical Israel: Judicial, Political, and Social Shaming," *JSOT* 49 (1991), 67. Matthew Lynch contributes to this discussion, arguing not only that "shame" terms are not necessarily paired with honor terms in the HB, but that they often denote physical weakness or deprivation, rather than a primarily psychological-social sense of embarrassment. Lynch, "Neglected Physical Dimensions of 'Shame' Terminology."

In a number of cases, words for honor or shame appear near clothing words. Occasionally both occur in the same psalm. However, clothing imagery does not always contribute to this dynamic. Yael Avrahami makes the striking observation that honor words do not appear on the list of antonyms for בוש or its synonyms in the Psalms. She goes as far as to claim that honor words such as כבד, יקר, and חדר "do not appear in conjunction with בוש anywhere in the Hebrew Bible." Yael Avrahami, "BWSH in the Psalms—Shame or Disappointment?" *JSOT* 34.3 (2010), 303. Instead, בוש (*hiphil/hophal*) denotes "the experience of a disconnection between expectations and reality" (308). Cf. Lynch, "Neglected Physical Dimensions of 'Shame' Terminology," 517.

to the psalmist has been incongruent with his posture toward them. While he has mourned and prayed over them, wearing sackcloth as a symbol of his self-humiliation on their behalf, they have responded to his own distress with slander and mockery. In terms of EVT, the psalmist's deviation from normal dress garnered attention that was intended to show solidarity with the neighbor and therefore elicit a positive response. Instead, the neighbor repaid him with mockery, treating his distress as a source of shame.[36]

In terms of SVT, Psalm 35 exhibits a failed attempt at social validation. The sufferers do not receive the psalmist's overtures of friendship mediated by outward displays of grief—wearing sackcloth, fasting, praying, and remaining unkempt. Instead they mock and mistreat him, repaying evil for good.[37] Their behavior is reminiscent of David's debacle with the Ammonites in 2 Sam. 10:1-2. David sent envoys to comfort King Hanun regarding his father's death, but the messengers encountered suspicion and were treated shamefully. In her published dissertation, Xuan Huong Thi Pham explains, "The Ammonites consequently shame David's representatives by distorting a common rite of mourning," shaving half of their beards and removing the lower half of their garments, sending them home exposed.[38] Typically, mourners in ancient times tore their garments and tied sackcloth around their waists, leaving their chests or breasts (or at least arm and shoulder) bare.[39] The partial nakedness common to mourners bears enough similarity with shameful exposure that the Ammonites were able to invert the symbol to humiliate David's men.[40]

In Psalm 35, the psalmist responds to the lack of validation and positive evaluation from his enemies by petitioning that these opponents be "clothed with shame and insult" (v. 26) by dressing them in a costume that ensures their treachery would become publicly conspicuous:

36. To wear sackcloth publicly represents a significant risk. EVT suggests that not being well dressed usually makes someone less persuasive to their audience. Burgoon et al., "Nonverbal Influence," 461.

37. Whether their mockery directly related to his mourning is debatable. The word "repay" (v. 12) and the conceptual connection between "bowing down" (v. 14) and "stumbling" (v. 15) suggest to me that their mockery related to his mourning. At the very least, a disjuncture between the loyal friendship the psalmist expects and the mistreatment he receives points to the injustice of his situation.

38. Xuan Huong Thi Pham, *Mourning in the Ancient Near East and the Hebrew Bible*, vol. 302 of *JSOTSup* (Sheffield, England: Sheffield Academic, 1999), 34.

39. Edwin M. Yamauchi and Marvin R. Wilson, "Mourning and Weeping," *Dictionary of Daily Life: In Biblical & Post-Biblical Antiquity* (Peabody, MA: Hendrickson, 2017), 1232–45.

40. For more on the shame associated with nudity, see Hartenstein, "Clothing and Nudity in the Paradise Story (Gen. 2-3)."

יבשו ויחפרו יחדו	Let them be ashamed and disgraced together
שמחי רעתי	—those rejoicing over my distress.
ילבשו־בשת וכלמה	Let them be clothed with shame and insult
המגדילים עלי:	—those exalting themselves over me.

These ruffians have rejoiced over the psalmist's misfortune, but he prays that the celebration would transfer to those longing for his vindication. As such, the costume imagery he metaphorically invokes embodies the just retribution that is his main concern. Ironically, by wrapping them with shame as with a garment, the enemies will be seen for what they truly are. Their costume will expose them to the same public ridicule the psalmist has endured. Psalm 35 offers a good example of the legal conceptual framework that Holtz describes:

> The speaker, whom human justice has failed, turns to God with a plea. The enemies present their accusations, and the speaker has not found a forum in which to lodge a successful response, but for God. In the world of this psalm and its speaker, God is the ultimate arbiter, who hears the speaker's side of the story and who will administer justice on the speaker's behalf.[41]

Psalm 69 exhibits a similar social dynamic to Psalm 35 involving sackcloth. In Psalm 69, the psalmist wept, fasted, and put on sackcloth to signal that he was in mourning (vv. 11–12), ostensibly because the temple was defiled in some way ("zeal for your house devoured me," v. 10). It is possible that the temple's destruction, or at least its defilement, prompted his public display of grief.[42] His grief so altered his physical appearance that his family could no longer recognize him (vv. 9–10). However, as in Psalm 35, instead of prompting solidarity, his enemies met these signs of distress with mockery (v. 12). Again, in terms of EVT, the psalmist's expectancy signaling incurred a negative evaluation by his peers. Or in terms of SVT, his costume represents a failed attempt for validation.

In this example, the conventional image of sackcloth is bound to the enemies' response acoustically; "clothing" and "mocking song" share two identical consonants (ל and ש) and an additional voiced labial consonant (מ/ב).[43] "Sackcloth"

41. Holtz, *Praying Legally*, 31.
42. On this, see Gerald H. Wilson, *Psalms, Volume 1*, NIVAC (Grand Rapids, MI: Zondervan, 2002), 952.
43. Kline defines "paranomasia" as "the relationship that obtains between two or more words that sound similar, differ in meaning, occur in close proximity, and have been deliberately juxtaposed in order to draw the reader's attention." Jonathan G. Kline, *Allusive Soundplay in the Hebrew Bible*, Ancient Israel and Its Literature (Atlanta, GA: SBL, 2016), 8. He goes on to argue that only the first two items on this list are required, since allusive soundplay is possible at great distance and in some cases could be unintentional. Identical consonants are not necessary. He cites Greenstein's suggestion that for qualifying examples "at least half the consonants, usually two of the common root's three, are identical *or phonologically similar.*" Kline, *Allusive Soundplay*, 23 (emphasis added). Citing Edward

and "beer" share sibilants and velar consonants (שׂ/שׁ; ק/כ), linking them as well. Meanwhile, the third and fourth lines are doubly linked, not just consonantally but assonantly, creating a rhyme effect between "sitting" and "drinking" (*yōšbēy* and *šôtēy*) and between "gate" and "beer" (*šāʿar* and *šēkār*) that are bound to one another by sibilants.[44] These acoustic connections strengthen the thematic links. The result is a tightly constructed passage that connects the wearing of sackcloth to its unintended result—mockery:

Ps. 69:11-12

וָאֶתְּנָה לְבוּשִׁי שָׂק	When I put on as clothing (*lbûšy*) sackcloth (*śq*),
וָאֱהִי לָהֶם לְמָשָׁל:	I became for them a mocking song (*lmšl*).
יָשִׂיחוּ בִי יֹשְׁבֵי שָׁעַר	They obsess over me—those sitting (*yōšbēy*) at the gate (*šāʿar*),
וּנְגִינוֹת שׁוֹתֵי שֵׁכָר:	And the taunt-song of those drinking (*šôtēy*) beer (*šēkār*).

"Those sitting at the gate" may refer to community elders (cf. Ruth 4), while "those drinking beer" could be the lower echelon of society, forming a merism. If so, the effect is that the entire community disdains the psalmist for his show of grief over YHWH's house. He also reports that "scorn covered my face" (v. 8), using the verb כסה, which is often, though not exclusively, paired with clothing nouns (e.g., Gen. 24:65, 38:14; Exod. 28:42; Ps. 104:6), adding to his public humiliation via physical appearance, that is, the social negotiation of his identity as one shamed.[45]

In Psalm 69 the clothing imagery is not picked up again in the retributive part of the psalm. Instead, food, water, and body images are used without reference to dress (dark eyes, quivering hips; v. 24). These physical petitions echo the bodily shame he has experienced. Still, the use of the conventional sackcloth and its reversal by the enemies into an object of shame is a helpful analogue to Psalm 35, another example of expectancy violation signaled through dress (this time nonmetaphorical) with the resulting absence of social validation.

The expectancy violation of sackcloth in Psalm 69 augments its more developed use in Psalm 35. In both psalms, sackcloth is a costume that elicits undeserved public disgrace and highlights the ways in which social order is upset. In turn, it prompts a plea for a proper divine response, one that metes out an analogous

---

Greenstein, "Wordplay, Hebrew," *ABD* 6, 968–71. Cf. Thomas P. McCreesh, *Biblical Sound and Sense: Poetic Sound Patterns in Proverbs 10–29*, vol. 128 of *JSOTSup* (Sheffield, England: Sheffield Academic, 1991), 25. Ability to demonstrate the function of the soundplay is one factor that makes it more plausible.

44. Berlin includes gate/beer as an example of a Hebrew sound pair that is not also a word pair. Adele Berlin, *The Dynamics of Biblical Parallelism*, rev. and exp. ed. (Grand Rapids, MI: Eerdmans, 2008), 109.

45. Wilson suggests that this could refer to spittle of those mocking the psalmist. See Wilson, *Psalms, Volume 1*, 952.

punishment to the offender. The source concept of clothing provides a vivid way to link the punishment with the crime.

Psalm 109

Psalm 109 utilizes less conventional clothing imagery, drawing on clothing in clearly metaphorical ways. The following analysis presumes that verses 6–19 record the petition of the psalmist. While this opinion is not unanimous, it has strong reasons to commend it.[46] As in other imprecatory psalms, the psalmist cries out to God for a punishment that fits the crimes done to him. Specifically, he asks God not to be silent while others speak lying words (vv. 1–2). Hatred has been returned for love and evil for good (vv. 4–5). Now he asks for a wicked accuser to stand against his wicked accuser so that his lawsuit may be seen for what it is—"wicked" (vv. 4, 6–7).[47] Holtz demonstrates that in light of the juridical

---

46. Some translations and commentaries understand verses 6–19 as the violent words of the wicked rather than an imprecatory prayer by the psalmist. So NRSV, Hans-Joachim Kraus, *Psalms 60–150*, trans. Hilton C. Oswald, CC (Minneapolis, MN: Fortress, 1993), 335–42; John Goldingay, *Psalms 90–150*, BCOT (Grand Rapids, MI: Baker Academic, 2008), 276, for example. Perhaps the strongest support for seeing verses 6–15 as a quotation is the fact that the speech of the wicked in verses 2–3 and 20 forms "bookends" for the passage in question. However, these sections could just as easily be the motivation for the imprecatory prayer couched in the central passage. Typically, when the wicked are quoted in the Psalms they make short statements. A soliloquy of this length is unprecedented on the lips of the psalmist's enemies, calling for clear contextual introduction, which this psalm lacks. Therefore, the most natural reading is to understand it as the psalmist's plea for God to deal justly with his enemy (a collective singular). Change in number does not necessitate a change in speaker. Many psalms exhibit shifts in number without any change in speaker (e.g., Pss. 17:9-13; 35:3-26). See Wright, "Ritual Analogy in Psalm 109," 394, n. 22.

Another issue to address is the inherent ambiguity of Hebrew verbal aspect. Jussive forms are not always present where jussive meanings are intended. With sufficient contextual support, a simple imperfect verb form can carry jussive force. One clue in this passage is the use of אַל for negation in verse 12. Compared to לֹא, Waltke and O'Connor argue that אַל communicates urgency and is more likely to be jussive than otherwise. Bruce Waltke and M. O'Connor, *An Introduction to Biblical Hebrew Syntax* (Winona Lake, IN: Eisenbrauns, 1990), 34.2.1b and 34.3b. Joüon also cites examples of jussive force without jussive form in verses 7 and 10. Paul Joüon and T. Muraoka, *A Grammar of Biblical Hebrew* (Roma: Pontifical Biblical Institute, 2006), 114gN and 119k. The clothing metaphors in verses 17–18 in particular ought to be taken as jussives because verse 19 is jussive in form and verse 29 makes clear that the act of clothing the enemies has not yet occurred. Wright, "Ritual Analogy in Psalm 109," 397. Contra Goldingay, *Psalms 90–150*, 274.

47. Holtz argues that in verse 7 בהשפטו refers to litigation brought forward by the accuser, rather than judgment. He suggests the translation, "when he sues." Holtz, *Praying Legally*, 20.

framework of the psalm the word תפלה in verse 7 should be taken in its legal sense as a petition in court.[48] The psalmist also refers to his own legal petition (תפלה) in response to their accusations (v. 4). On the basis of the predatory behavior of the wicked toward the needy (v. 16), the psalmist petitions that they would experience public humiliation and the loss of legacy (vv. 8–15). The psalmist then employs ontological metaphor, conceiving of curses and blessing as physical entities (v. 17):[49]

ויאהב קללה ותבואהו	He loved cursing, so may it enter him—
ולא־חפץ בברכה ותרחק ממנו	and did not delight in blessing, so may it be far from him.

In verses 18–19 the ontological metaphor is given even more vivid specifications, using the source domain of dress or costume in unconventional ways to illustrate just retribution for one so bent on bringing harm to others:

וַיִּלְבַּשׁ קְלָלָה **כְּמַדּוֹ**	**He clothed himself** with cursing **as his garment**,
וַתָּבֹא כַמַּיִם בְּקִרְבּוֹ	So may it enter like water into his innards,
וְכַשֶּׁמֶן בְּעַצְמוֹתָיו	And like oil into his bones.[50]
תְּהִי־לוֹ **כְּבֶגֶד יַעְטֶה**	May it be for him **like clothing he wraps around himself**,
וּלְמֵזַח תָּמִיד יַחְגְּרֶהָ	**Or like a belt** continually **buckled**.[51]

Like the Hittite example considered earlier, the psalmist here imagines cursing as a costume for the wicked—a person so identified with vile and destructive words that

---

48. Ibid., 19, 29–31. He notes that Hittite word for prayer, *arkuwar*, also functions as a legal term to refer to the petition or defense of the accused. While it is not a cognate to the Hebrew word תפלה, it serves as a "conceptual and semantic parallel," providing support for the blending of the concepts of prayer and legal petition (28).

49. As I have defined elsewhere, an ontological metaphor "provides concreteness by which we may talk about abstract concepts such as emotions, ideas, or activities." Imes, "Metaphor at Sinai," 350. Cf. Kövecses, *Metaphor*, 40.

50. Or "so it entered like water." For a defense of the jussive reading above, see Wright, "Ritual Analogy in Psalm 109," 393–5.

51. I am avoiding the English word "girdle," which has connotations of a restrictive women's undergarment. In the Hebrew Bible, both men and women wear "girdles," and a number of different words refer to these (see *DCH* 3: 160). Given the flowing tunics and draped fabric of ancient costume, it makes sense that the ancients used various kinds of belts. As far as I can tell, none of these correspond to the English "girdle" but rather a belt of leather, bronze, or cloth. Sometimes these belts held weapons, seals, or other valuables. Douglas R. Edwards, "Dress and Ornamentation," in *The Anchor Bible Dictionary*, 1st ed., 6 vols., ed. David Noel Freedman (New York: Doubleday, 1992), 2: 233. To "gird the loins" is to tuck longer tunic skirts into the girdle or belt for ease of movement. See Mark F. Rooker, "חגר," in *New International Dictionary of Old Testament Theology and Exegesis*, ed. Willem VanGemeren (Grand Rapids, MI: Zondervan, 1997), 2: 22–24.

these destructive words are as publicly conspicuous as the clothing he wears: they define him. The psalmist then extends and develops that image in unconventional ways. Since the accuser is so wrapped up in cursing (pun intended), the psalmist imagines the garment becoming a liquid that can soak through his skin and seep into his bones, so that he cannot escape it. Then, lest the visual evidence of cursing be lost as it penetrates, the psalmist returns to the image of a cloth garment again, or a belt tied around his enemy's waist. Because the accuser has laced his speech with curses, the psalmist prays that God would make it so that the wicked cannot escape his own curses. In the supplicant's imagination, the costume has become a trap. His choice of dress and behavior are linked. The imagery is not only vivid but carries additional connotations exploited by the psalmist regarding the public nature of the crime and therefore the punishment that justice requires. The cumulative effect is more powerful than a straightforward request for God to punish. As William Brown expresses, "Living metaphors invariably create conceptual and emotional friction by which new meaning is created and the impossible becomes conceivable."[52] These metaphors use the powerful cultural symbolism of dress to accomplish these aims.

After calling upon God to save him, the psalmist expresses confidence that God will respond favorably to his request (vv. 28–29):

יְקַלְלוּ־הֵמָּה	They may curse,
וְאַתָּה תְבָרֵךְ	But you will bless.
קָמוּ וַיֵּבֹשׁוּ	They arise, **but will be shamed** (*wyybšû*),
וְעַבְדְּךָ יִשְׂמָח	And your servant will rejoice.
יִלְבְּשׁוּ שׂוֹטְנַי כְּלִמָּה	May my adversaries **be clothed** (*ylbšû*) with **insult** (*klmh*),
וְיַעֲטוּ כַמְעִיל בָּשְׁתָּם	And wrap themselves **like a robe** (*km'yl*) **with their shame** (*bštm*).[53]

The final two lines are bound together acoustically by double paranomasia. As with previous examples, two shared consonants link the act of "clothing" (*ylbšû*) and "shame" (*bštm*), a bond anticipated by the first appearance of "shame" in verse 28. A second sound pair connects "insult" (*klmh*) and "robe" (*km'yl*), which share three consonants, featuring metathesis.[54] Note that the sound pairs do not correspond to the word pairs in these lines; the two verbs for the act of clothing are not the two that sound alike. Each verb pairs with the other verb's object. The overall effect is an acoustic ABBA pattern that binds these lines in a way that mimics their description of wrapped clothing. As such, they exhibit an innovative link that Berlin calls "a one-time nexus between sound and sense."[55] The bond of sound makes the analogy less arbitrary and more persuasive.

52. William P. Brown, *Seeing the Psalms: A Theology of Metaphor* (Louisville, KY: Westminster John Knox, 2002), 71.

53. Or verse 29 could be an additional statement of confidence rather than another imprecation, "My adversaries will be clothed with insult."

54. Also noted by Berlin, *Parallelism*, 120.

55. Ibid., 111.

The psalmist is confident that in the end his adversaries will be called to account for their wickedness. Their shameful behavior will be as obvious to the public as the clothing they wear. Their hateful and condemning words turn against them, while the psalmist openly praises YHWH for his advocacy (vv. 30–31). So strong is this psalm's plea for justice that Zenger labels it a "justice psalm."[56] While innovative, perhaps Psalm 109's inspiration to imagine the wicked in this way and to pray so boldly is not unique.

Psalm 71 also contains imprecatory language, utilizing unconventional costume metaphors for its request. Though less fully developed, these metaphors are central thematically as well as spatially. The psalm begins with the psalmist's request that YHWH not allow him to be ashamed (v. 1) and ends with rejoicing that his enemies have been shamed (v. 24). That is, the attempt of the enemies to harm the psalmist in his old age has been unsuccessful. They tried to take advantage of him, assuming that God had abandoned him and would never rescue him (v. 11). Grey hair is associated with weakness (vv. 9, 18). Their claim of divine indifference prompts an urgent request in the center of the psalm for God to not only save the psalmist but to bring retribution. In verse 13 the psalmist prays that his attackers would "be ashamed" and "finished off," and that they would "wrap themselves with scorn and insult:"

יֵבֹשׁוּ	**Let them be ashamed** (*yēbošû*).
יִכְלוּ שֹׂטְנֵי נַפְשִׁי	Let those attacking me **be finished off** (*yiklû*),
יַעֲטוּ חֶרְפָּה וּכְלִמָּה	<u>May they wrap themselves</u> with scorn and **insult** (*ûklimah*)—
מְבַקְשֵׁי רָעָתִי	**those seeking** (*məbaqšê*) <u>my harm.</u>

Wordplay binds these central lines together. The request in line 2 that his enemies be "finished off" (*yiklû*) shares two consonants and a vowel letter with the "insult" (*ûklimah*) they deserve in line 3.[57] The familiar "let them be ashamed" in line 1 shares two of three core consonants (ב שׁ) with "those seeking" in line 4. Another connection could have been forged by using "clothed" (ישׁבו//לבשׁ) rather than "wrapped" (עטה; cf. Ps. 35:26). This would have linked shame with clothing phonologically. Instead of this conventional paranomasia, the poet achieved an innovative rhythmic effect by using יַעֲטוּ with רָעָתִי (in underlined above). The relatively rare consonant ט in יַעֲטוּ also appears in "those attacking me" and "wrap" in lines 2 and 3 and the ע appears in lines 3 and 4 in "wrap" and "harm."[58] The result is acoustically pleasing and rhetorically persuasive.

56. Frank Lothar Hossfeld and Erich Zenger, *Psalms 3*, Hermeneia (Minneapolis, MN: Fortress, 2011), 128, quoted by W. Dennis Tucker and Jamie A. Grant, *Psalms, Volume 2*, NIVAC (Grand Rapids, MI: Zondervan, 2018), 585.

57. It also comes very close to the word pair in Ps. 35:4, where the psalmist prays for the enemies to be "ashamed and humiliated" (יֵבֹשׁוּ וְיִכָּלְמוּ). If this is meant to echo Psalm 35, the effect is striking: humiliation does not go far enough this time; the psalmist wants his enemies brought to their bitter end.

58. John Goldingay, *Psalms 42–89*, BCOT (Grand Rapids, MI: Baker Academic, 2007), 372.

The psalmist draws on a lifetime of reliance on God, exuberant about his faithful and righteous acts. He trusts that God will respond again to enact justice. Although the costume imagery does not pervade the psalm, it is the source concept for the psalm's central request for analogous punishment.

Psalm 73 is not imprecatory, but it describes the metaphorical dress of the wicked using similar terms. They are fat and free from trouble, with no need to work and plenty of time to devote to evil imaginations (vv. 4–7). The psalmist reports in verse 6:

לָכֵן עֲנָקַתְמוֹ גַאֲוָה	**Therefore** pride adorns **him**.
יַעֲטָף־שִׁית חָמָס לָמוֹ	Violence wraps a garment **around him**.

Phonologically speaking, these lines mimic the wrapping of the garment with an ABBA pattern. The verse begins and ends with the same letter sounds (*la…mô/ lamô*), framing the subtle rhythm of the verbs גַאֲוָה יַעֲטָף (*ga'awāh ya'aṭāf*), forming a subtle link between lines.

The wicked boasts of his violence, hoping for validation (v. 3). He "wears it on his sleeve," so to speak, making no effort to conceal his despicable behavior, mocking others, extorting their wealth, and proclaiming God's impotence to stop him (vv. 8–11). Clothing is the ideal conceptual vehicle for such a public display of violence. The turning point of the psalm is when the psalmist enters God's sanctuary and discerns that the reign of terror of the boastful will not last forever. He expresses confidence that God will eventually bring calamity on them. Note that the justice of Psalm 73 is not in response to prayer but flows from God's own intentions; that is, it reflects divine character. Could this recognition of YHWH's justice in response to public flaunting of violence have motivated both the metaphorical vehicle of violent clothing in Psalm 109 and its bold cry for divine retribution? It offers precedent for the "due regard and proper treatment" that Bacote says exhibits YHWH's own righteous character.[59] Whereas Psalm 73 offers precedent, Psalm 71 showcases the centrality of clothing as a source concept for legal petition. Both psalms stand alongside Psalm 109 as examples of the power of dress metaphor in the cry for justice. When the target concept—here the violence of the wicked—is as publicly conspicuous as the clothes they wear, dress becomes the ideal source concept with which to describe both their egregious behavior and the punishment they deserve.

Conclusion

It should be clear by now that references to dress in these psalms are and are not *just* clothing. Dress is not incidental or ornamental in any of these examples; it is not *merely* clothing. In each of the psalms we have explored above, the use of

59. See n. 8 above.

clothing imagery reinforces and articulates the psalmist's prayer for justice framed in legal terms. Each petition expects a tangible result in terms consonant with the public nature of the offense and the negotiation of social identities and social expectations. As such, the psalmists participate in a social dynamic negotiated in part by costume but convey this dynamic through sophisticated and rhetorically persuasive poetry; the acoustic symmetry strengthens their legal petition. Attending to these clothing metaphors and their mode of literary expression illuminates the central concerns of each psalm. Given the public nature of the offenses described, retribution ought also to be publicly conspicuous, effecting a change in social power dynamics. That is, the resulting costume ought to be *just* clothing, revealing the true nature of the wicked and garnering public scorn. In the end, this study demonstrates that these imprecatory prayers do not exhibit excessive violence but rather participate in the conceptual world of legal petition, entrusting the psalmists' concern to a deity who is able to reverse injustice.

Note: All Bible translations are mine unless otherwise noted.

Chapter 8

"WOMEN RULE OVER THEM": DRESSING FOR AN INVERTED WORLD IN ISAIAH 3

Susannah Rees

Through dress, the power structures of a society are both inscribed on and reproduced by the body.[1] Dress is not only one of the mechanisms by which the body is regulated along gendered norms but also a site at which the complex interplay of gender and social stratification is realized. Indeed, in Deut. 22:5, items of dress are explicitly coded as feminine and masculine.[2] Within this paradigm, feminine items of clothing are forbidden not merely to men (איש) but explicitly to the strong warrior (גבר), which, as Vedeler points out, "distinguishes not simply between male and female but also between different qualities of men."[3] There is a

This chapter is indebted to Jonathan Stökl, Laura Quick, and the other contributors to this volume for their help and support.

1. In this chapter, I follow Eicher and Roach-Higgins's definition of dress as both body modifications and supplements to the body, including not only clothes but also items of jewelry and cosmetics. Joanne B. Eicher and Mary Ellen Roach-Higgins, "Dress and Identity," *CTRJ* 10 (1992), 1–8.

2. I follow McCracken's understanding of dress as a code and his rejection of the speaking about dress as a language. Dress is not read in a linear fashion; it replicates and reinforces established meanings. See Grant McCracken, "Clothing as Language: An Object Lesson in the Study of the Expressive Properties of Material Culture," in *Material Anthropology: Contemporary Approaches to Material Culture*, ed. Barrie Reynolds and Margaret A Stott (Lanham, MD: University Press of America, 1987), 103–28.

3. Harold Torger Vedeler, "Reconstructing Meaning in Deuteronomy 22:5: Gender, Society, and Transvestitism in Israel and the Ancient near East," *JBL* 127 (2008), 459–76, here 473. Deborah Rooke makes a similar distinction between types of masculinities, arguing that the breeches worn by priests contribute to a construction of masculinity in that only men were permitted to wear them but also they are used to construct and perform other elements of social stratification; distinguishing between priestly male and the non-priestly male; the priest from the high priest and the priest from the Levite while also performing a "wifely submission" and feminization of the priests in the presence of the masculinity of YHWH. See Deborah W. Rooke, "Breeches of the Covenant: Gender, Garments and the

growing recognition that dress does not simply mark or signify preexisting qualities but rather that it actively constructs identity and status through repeated performance.[4] In an ancient context, this is exemplified by the great deal of scholarly attention that has been devoted to the significance of warriors wearing female-coded items of adornment and its perceived weakening effect.[5] However, the question of what it might mean for a woman to wear male clothing and adornment has, by comparison, received very little attention.[6] If a man dressed in female garb is effeminized and weak, then, by implication, "a woman who wears a weapon does not dress like a man, but behaves like a warrior."[7] This chapter acts as

Priesthood," in *Embroidered Garments: Priests and Gender in Biblical Israel*, ed. Deborah W. Rooke (Sheffield, England: Sheffield Phoenix, 2009), 19–37.

4. Building on the work of Judith Butler (*Gender Trouble: Feminism and the Subversion of Identity*, Taylor & Francis [New York: Routledge, 2002]; *Bodies That Matter: On the Discursive Limits of "Sex"* [New York: Routledge, 1993]) and Maurice Merleau-Ponty (*Phenomenology of Perception*, ed. Donald A. Landes [London: Routledge, 2014]), the rejection of the information signaling model of dress and the concomitant emphasis on embodiment theories is reiterated in a number of different fields, including archeology (see overview in Rosemary A. Joyce, "Archaeology of the Body," *ARA* 34 [2005], 139–58) and sociology (see discussion in Joanne Entwistle, "Fashion and the Fleshy Body: Dress as Embodied Practice," *FT* 4.3 [2000], 323–47).

5. Claudia Bergmann, "We Have Seen the Enemy, and He Is Only a 'She': The Portrayal of Warriors as Women," *CBQ* 69 (2007), 651–72; Harry A Hoffner, "Symbols for Masculinity and Femininity: Their Use in Ancient near Eastern Sympathetic Magic Rituals," *JBL* 85 (1966), 326–34.

6. However, a number of studies have explored the ways in which female-coded dress can be used, paradoxically, to perform masculine roles. See Laura Quick, "'She Made Herself Up Provocatively for the Charming of the Eyes of Men' (Jdt. 10.4): Cosmetics and Body Adornment in the Stories of Judith and Susanna," *JSP* 28 (2019), 215–36; Caryn Tamber-Rosenau, *Women in Drag: Gender and Performance in the Hebrew Bible and Early Jewish Literature* (Piscataway, NJ: Georgia, 2018); Amy Kalmanofsky, *Gender-Play in the Hebrew Bible: The Ways the Bible Challenges Its Gender Norms* (New York: Routledge, 2017), 107–8; Deryn Guest, "Modelling the Transgender Gaze: Performances of Masculinities in 2 Kings 9–10," in *Transgender, Intersex and Biblical Interpretation*, ed. Teresa J. Hornby and Deryn Guest (Atlanta, GA: SBL, 2016), 45–80. Although not along gendered lines, Heather A. McKay also powerfully explores the significance of a discord and incongruity between dress and the identity of the wearer. See "Dress Deployed as an Agent of Deception in Hebrew Bible Narratives" in this volume (pp. 31–55).

7. Kalmanofsky, *Gender-Play in the Hebrew Bible*, 7. There is a growing recognition in biblical studies that gender does not exists within a binary, dichotomous framework and that there are many masculinities and femininities. See, for example, the work on the female masculinity of queens: Laura Quick, "My Lord the Queen: Gender Discord in Comparative Perspective," *HeBAI* 8 (2019), 448–63; Hilary Lipka, "Queen Jezebel's Masculinity," in *Hebrew Masculinities Anew*, ed. Ovidiu Creangă (Sheffield, England: Sheffield Phoenix, 2019), 125–50; Cat Quine, "Bereaved Mothers and Masculine Queens: The Political Use

a corrective to this oversight and explores its implications for the oracle against the Daughters of Zion.

In this chapter, I explore the significance of the male-coded items of dress and adornment worn by the Daughters of Zion specifically in Isa. 3:16-24. I begin with a brief overview of scholarly opinions concerning the compositional and redactional history of Isaiah 3. I will show that a tendency to take an atomized approach toward the chapter has caused the thematic coherence of the chapter to be overlooked. I will demonstrate that the chapter as a whole participates in the trope of inversion, which is common throughout prophetic texts in the Hebrew Bible and in ancient Near East more broadly. Then, I will focus on the way this inverted world order is expressed through the items of dress worn by the Daughters of Zion. Many of these items of dress are elsewhere reserved for priests, kings, and those in positions of authority, which are typically the preserve of men in ancient Israel and Judah.[8] This dress is not merely symbolic. Rather, it has a constitutive function: these vestments and insignia enable individuals to perform masculine-coded positions of political power and cultic and religious expertise.[9] I will argue that when the Daughters of Zion wear this mode of dress, they are depicted as assuming political power, performing masculine identities, and, in the minds of the biblical author(s) and redactor(s), plunging the world into chaos.

Composition and Redaction in Isaiah 3

A general consensus that Isaiah 2-4 exists as a single section of the final form of the book of Isaiah has emerged due to its cohesive structure and content, which is chiefly concerned with the fates of Judah and Jerusalem.[10] This passage

of Maternal Grief in 1-2 Kings," *Open Theology* 6 (2020), 407-22. See also the analysis of the "wifely submission" communicated by the priestly breeches; Rooke, "Breeches of the Covenant."

8. This was first observed by Elizabeth E. Platt, "Jewelry of Bible Times and the Catalog of Isa 3:18-23:1," *AUSS* 17 (1979), 71-84.

9. The constitutive function of dress has been explored in relation to royal and priestly garments. See Shawn W. Flynn, "YHWH'S Clothing, Kingship, and Power: Origins and Vestiges in Comparative Ancient Near Eastern Contexts," and Carmen Joy Imes, "Between Two Worlds: The Functional and Symbolic Significance of The High Priestly Regalia," in *Dress and Clothing in the Hebrew Bible: "For All Her Household Are Clothed in Crimson,"* ed. Antonios Finitsis (London: T&T Clark, 2019), 11-28, 29-62.

10. For a discussion of the reasons for considering Isaiah 2-4 as one unit, see Marvin A. Sweeney, *Isaiah 1-4 and the Post-Exilic Understanding of the Isaianic Tradition* (Berlin, NY: de Gruyter, 1987), 35-6; H. G. M. Williamson, *A Critical and Exegetical Commentary on Isaiah 1-27*, vol. 1, *Isaiah 1-5*, ICC (London: T&T Clark, 2006), 238-9. Andrew Bartelt's argument that Isa. 3:1-4:1 comprises a single unit of text is something of an anomaly. See Andrew H. Bartelt, *The Book around Immanuel: Style and Structure in Isaiah 2-12* (Winona Lake, IN: Eisenbrauns, 1996).

can be further subdivided into a number of different units that originally existed independently and have a diverse range of composition dates. However, what comprises these units and the boundaries where redactional joints lie is still a matter of great contention. As a result, a number of different theories of the editorial history of Isaiah 2–4 abound. This problem is particularly pronounced in Isaiah 3.[11] As a result, the thematic coherence of the chapter is often overlooked, and Isa. 3:1-15 is treated somewhat separately to the description of the dress, adornment, and ultimate fate of the Daughters of Zion in Isa. 3:16–4:1.

However, as Couey observes, Isa. 3:1-15 "consists of variations on the themes of failed leadership and social disorder, proceeding associatively from one section to the next and frequently circling back to develop earlier motifs."[12] The chapter opens with the assertion that "the staff and stay of Jerusalem and Judah" are about to be removed (3:1). These supports and structures of Judean society are then explicitly identified in 3:2-3 as military leaders, advisers, and judges as well as those with religious and cultic expertise. Jerusalem and Judah are to lose a whole class of professional, elite men, including the warrior (גבור), the man of war (איש מלחמה), the judge (שופט), the prophet (נביא), the diviner (קסם), the elder (זקן), the captain of fifty men (שר־חמשים), the man of repute (נשוא פנים), the counselor (יועץ), the wise magician (חכם חרשים), and the expert in charms (נבון לחש). These prominent individuals are evidently central to the smooth running of the state and its administrative structures. Their removal represents the disintegration of social institutions and hierarchies and, ultimately, the collapse of civil life into chaos.

This motif of decaying moral and social order as the result of the loss of these prominent individuals is repeated three further times in 3:4, 3:12, and 3:25–4:1. Because no men remain who are fit to rule, YHWH announces, "I will make boys their rulers and children rule over them" (3:4). After a brief interlude describing the resulting disorder, we are again told, "My people, infants are their oppressors and women rule over them" (3:12).[13] As a result of the removal of the ruling men,

---

11. For a table with a number of different commentators' opinions, see Sweeney, *Isaiah 1–4*, 147–8.

12. J. Blake Couey, "The Disabled Body Politic in Isaiah 3:1, 8," *JBL* 133 (2014), 95–109, here 98.

13. The urtext and translation of this verse are not uncontroversial. The vocalization of נשים as "women" is attested in Symmachus, the Vulgate, and the Peshitta and is followed by most major rabbinic commentators. However, there have been a number of proposals to repoint the text as נשים (creditors) drawing on the LXX οἱ ἀπαιτοῦντες (those who demand payment) and the Targum (like creditors do they rule over it). This arguably reflects a deep-seated discomfort with the prospect of women and children ruling, and these versions instead opt to read verse 12 in the light of the exploitation of the poor in verses 14–15. Modern commentators who follow this emendation include Joseph Blenkinsopp, *Isaiah 1–39: A New Translation with Introduction and Commentary* (New York: Doubleday, 2000), 197–8; Hans Wildberger, *Isaiah: A Continental Commentary* (Minneapolis, MN: Fortress, 1965); Williamson, *Commentary on Isaiah 1–5*, 262. In a similar vein, BHS suggests emending מעולל to עללו on the basis that the Vulgate reads *spoliaverunt* (robbed); the LXX

those who would ordinarily be excluded from normative administrative structures, women and children, assume the most powerful positions. This represents a complete inversion of the perceived natural world order. The theme of the removal of men is taken up again in 3:25–4:1 albeit in a slightly different iteration. Here, the impact of a greatly reduced male population on the marriage market is explored:

> Your men will fall by the sword and your warriors in battle and her gates shall lament and mourn and she will be cleaned out whilst you sit on the ground. And seven women shall seize upon a single man on that day and say: "We will eat our own bread and we will wear our own garments but let your name be pronounced over us, remove our shame!" (3:25–4:1)

Isaiah 3 paints a picture of the "total breakdown of social order and decency in face of the devastations of war. No matter how strong the walls, if over a period of time one loses this many soldiers and leaders, the city will fall from within."[14] The motif of inversion of the world order is a theme that is repeatedly returned to in Isaiah 3: those who would attract respect by way of their age or honor are instead disrespected (3:5); the poor are exploited (3:14-15); and the brother is elevated over his father, the natural head of the household (3:6).[15]

The inversion of normative world order is a popular trope that is used to depict a chaotic world both in the Hebrew Bible and in the prophetic literature of the ancient Near East and Mediterranean more widely.[16] The defining characteristic of this topos is that the conceived notion of "ordinariness is replaced by its direct

reads οἱ πράκτορες ὑμῶν καλαμῶνται ὑμᾶς ('Your bailiffs have stripped you') and the Targum reads "whose officers plunder it like the gleaners of a vineyard." However, this is also not without its grammatical difficulties. עלל seems to be a trivalent verb, perhaps explaining the Targum's addition of the word "vineyard." For a detailed discussion, see Williamson, *Commentary on Isaiah 1–5*, 261–4. While plausible, this arguably does not fit as well with the repeated emphasis of the removal of the ruling men of Judah and Jerusalem.

14. John D. W. Watts, "Jerusalem: An Example of War in a Walled City (Isaiah 3–4)," in *"Every City Shall Be Forsaken": Urbanism and Prophecy in Ancient Israel and the Near East*, ed. Robert D. Haak and Lester L. Grabbe, JSOT (Sheffield, England: Sheffield Academic, 2001), 213.

15. Kruger explores the inversion trope in relation to Isa. 3:1-7. See Paul Albertus Kruger, "A World Turned on Its Head in Ancient Near Eastern Prophetic Literature: A Powerful Strategy to Depict Chaotic Scenarios," *VT* 62 (2012), 58–76, here 72.

16. For detailed discussion, see Paul Albertus Kruger, "Disaster and the Topos of the World Upside down: Selected Cases from the Ancient Near Eastern World," in *Disaster and Relief Management* (Tübingen: Mohr Siebeck, 2012), 391–424; Paul Albertus Kruger, "Mundus Inversus in the Hebrew Bible: A Kaleidoscopic Ancient Near Eastern Topos," in *Israel Zwischen Den Mächten*, AOAT 364 (Münster: Ugarit-Verlag, 2009), 173–93; Raymond C. Van Leeuwen, "Proverbs 30:21-23 and the Biblical World Upside Down," *JBL* 105 (1986), 599–610.

inverse."[17] F. W. Dobbs-Allsopp has identified a number of different expressions of this motif, including the breakdown of the family, important tasks remaining unfulfilled, the failure of transportation systems, singing turning into weeping, and disturbances in the animal kingdom and natural world.[18] This is not merely a change from the quotidian state but rather represents an aberration of normative values and the resulting cultural chaos. Indeed in an anthropological context, Babcock argues that:

> Symbolic inversion may be broadly defined as any act of expressive behaviour which inverts, contradicts, abrogates, or in some fashion presents an alternative to commonly held cultural codes, values and norms, be they linguistic, literary or artistic, religious, or social and political.[19]

As such, these inversions reflect a fundamental breakdown of moral and social order.

Particularly apposite for our study of Isaiah 3 is the common trope of inverted social relationships and power dynamics. For example, in addition to a series of disturbances in the animal kingdom, the Deir ʕAlla inscription describes a reversal of social order with venerable individuals reduced to venerators and venerators elevated to venerable positions, while the fool sees visions.[20] Both Meindert Dijkstra and Jo Ann Hackett have pointed to similarities between the Deir ʕAlla inscription and Isaiah 3.[21] Similarly, Babylonian planetary omens describe inverted social relationships in which wives no longer respect their husbands: "If Ištar becomes visible at daylight: men's wives will not stay with their husbands. If Ištar does not rise at night but rises at daylight: men's wives will commit adultery and run after men" (K.229: reverse 2 [on E], 16–17).[22] They also describe a reversal in status between the slave and the master: "If Ištar shows (herself) at the beginning of the year and disappears: slaves will ascend to their masters' bed and marry the women who hired them" (K.229: reverse 1–2 fragmentary, 10).[23] The

---

17. Kruger, "A World Turned on Its Head," 59.

18. F. W.Dobbs-Allsopp, *Weep, O Daughter of Zion: A Study of the City-Lament Genre in the Hebrew Bible* (Roma: Editrice Pontificio Istituto Biblico, 1993), 41.

19. Barbara A. Babcock, *The Reversible World: Symbolic Inversion in Art and Society* (Ithaca, NY: Cornell University Press, 1978), 14.

20. See translation in Jo Ann Hackett, *The Balaam Text from Deir ʕAllā* (Leiden: Brill, 1984), 29.

21. Meindert Dijkstra points to similarities between the inscription and Isa. 3:4-7, 24 in "Is Balaam Also among the Prophets?" *JBL* 114 (1995), 43–64, here 54 n.27. Jo Ann Hackett points to similarities between the inscription and Isa. 3:4-5 in "Some Observations on the Balaam Tradition at Deir Alla," *BA* 49 (1986), 216–22, here 217.

22. Erica Reiner and David Pingree, *Babylonian Planetary Omens: Part Three*, Bibliotheca Mesopotamica (Malibu: Undena, 1975), 184.

23. Ibid., 183.

Marduk Prophecy draws on similar imagery.[24] In the Marduk Prophecy, brothers turn against one another, free citizens are reduced to begging from the poor while "the sceptre grew short," which seems to be a metaphor for diminished authority and recourse to justice (II:1–11).[25] At the close of the prophecy, when the natural order is restored, we are told that wives once again revere their husbands and the prince returns to ruling his land (Assur 13348 V:1–5).[26] This trope is also attested in Egypt, particularly, in *The Dialogue of Ipuwer and the Lord of All*.[27]

One of the most prominent ways the inversion of social relationships and power dynamics is communicated in these texts is through dress. For example, the Deir ʿAlla inscription describes how "the poor woman prepares myrrh" while the prince wears only "a tattered loincloth" (line 11–12).[28] In the Babylonian Theodicy, "the son of the needy and naked (now) puts on [fine clothes]" (1.182).[29] The use of dress to communicate an inversion is particularly prominent in *The Dialogue of Ipuwer*. Here, rich ladies' "limbs are saddened because of old clothes" (3.4); "the offspring of the council are in ol[d clothes]" (8.10); and "(people) are stripped of clothes and unanointed with oil" (6.3). Yet those who typically might have worn old clothes are resplendent in finery and bejeweled with expensive adornment: "O, yet gold, lapis lazuli, silver, turquoise, garment, amethyst, diorite, our [fines stones] have been hung on the neck(s) of maidservants" (3:2-3); while "he whose hair had fallen out, who had no oil, has become the owner of *ḥbbt*-jars of sweet myrrh" (8.4). In places, the comparison of the reversal of dress and adornment is made explicit: "Look, the owners of linen are in old clothes; (yet) he who could not

24. There is some debate about whether the moniker "prophetic" is appropriate for this and a number of similar texts such as the Šulgi Prophecy, the Uruk Prophecy, and the Dynastic Prophecy. Nevertheless they "bear some resemblances to the genre of prophecy" and "contain descriptions of political events cast in a predictive style," which warrants their inclusion for consideration here. See Matthijs J. de Jong, *Isaiah among the Ancient Near Eastern Prophets: A Comparative Study of the Earliest Stages of the Isaiah Tradition and the Neo-Assyrian Prophecies* (Leiden: Brill, 2007), 187.

25. See the translation in Matthew Neujahr, *Predicting the Past in the Ancient Near East: Mantic Historiography in Ancient Mesopotamia, Judah, and the Mediterranean World* (Providence: Brown Judaic Studies, 2012), 30.

26. Ibid., 33.

27. Roland Enmarch, *A World Upturned: Commentary on and Analysis of the Dialogue of Ipuwer and the Lord of All* (Oxford: British Academy, 2009).

28. Translation from Hackett, *The Balaam Text from Deir ʿAllā*, 29. For a detailed discussion of the function of clothing in the Deir ʿAlla inscription, see Laura Quick, "Clothed in Curses: Ritual, Curse and Story in the Deir 'Alla Plaster Inscription," in *To Gaul, to Greece and into Noah's Ark: Essays in Honour of Kevin J. Cathcart on the Occasion of His Eightieth Birthday*, ed. Laura Quick, Ekaterina E. Kozlova, Sona Noll, and Philip Y. Yoo (Oxford: Oxford University Press, 2019), 95–109.

29. Cited in Ronald J. Williams, "Theodicy in the Ancient Near East," in *Theodicy in the Old Testament*, ed. James L. Crenshaw (Philadelphia, PA: Fortress, 1983), 42–56, here 46.

weave for himself is the owner of fine linen" (7.11-12).[30] It is this dress reversal that is the key to understanding the thematic coherence of Isaiah 3.

The emerging scholarly consensus that Isa. 3:18-23 represents a secondary expansion has cemented the tendency to consider this elaborate description of the items of adornment along with its encircling verses (3:16-17, 24-26; 4:1) as a distinct unit of analysis, isolated for consideration from the context of the rest of the chapter and its depiction of an inverted world.[31] As a consequence, the passage that treats the adornment of the Daughters of Zion (Isa. 3:16-24) is often seen to connect, at best, only loosely to Isa. 3:1-15. For instance, Blenkinsopp argues that "it is not immediately obvious why Isaiah (if it is he) turns at this point on the Jerusalemite women."[32] Williamson asserts that there is "something of a break following 3:15."[33] Sweeney suggests that 3:1–4:1 is a "prophetic judgement speech against the people of Zion," which he subdivides into 3:1-15, which he sees as being directed "against the leaders (male)," and 3:16–4:1, which is "against the women."[34] Viewed as a judgment oracle, a number of commentators have noted the similarities between Isa. 3:16-24 and Amos 4:1.[35] The implication seems to be that the women of Israel contribute to "their husbands' oppression of the poor by their constant demand for more."[36] Thus, the extravagant dress of the Daughters of Zion is seen merely as the product of the exploitation of the poor exacted by a ruling, male elite.

Yet this is not borne out by Isa. 3:1-15 and 3:25–4:1 with their repeated assertions that it is women and children who are ruling (3:4, 12) and that the ruling class of men have been removed by YHWH (3:1-3; 3:25–4:1). This should not be confused with a wholesale denial of the value of redaction criticism or read as a rejection of the evident redactional development of this chapter. However, by reading Isa. 3:16-24 in the holistic context in which it

30. Enmarch, *A World Upturned*, 222–40.

31. For an overview of differing scholarly opinions on the composition and redaction history of Isaiah 3, see Otto Kaiser, *Isaiah 1-12: A Commentary* (London: SCM, 1983), 267–9. There are some notable exceptions who defend the authenticity of Isa. 3:18-23. See Sweeney, *Isaiah 1-4*, 156; J. B. Couey, *Reading the Poetry of First Isaiah: The Most Perfect Model of the Prophetic Poetry* (Oxford: Oxford University Press, 2015), 105–7.

32. Blenkinsopp, *Isaiah 1-39*, 201.

33. Williamson, *Commentary on Isaiah 1-5*, 286.

34. Sweeney, *Isaiah 1-4*, 36.

35. George Buchanan Gray, *A Critical and Exegetical Commentary on the Book of Isaiah 1-27* (Edinburgh: T&T Clark, 1912), 289; Alexander Zeron, "Das Wort Niqpä, Zum Sturz Der Zionstöchter (Is. III 24)," *VT* 31 (1981), 95–7, here 97 n. 9; Blenkinsopp, *Isaiah 1-39*, 201.

36. J. J. M. Roberts, "Bearers of the Polity: Isaiah of Jerusalem's View Of the Eighth-Century Judean Society," in *Constituting the Community: Studies on the Polity of Ancient Israel in Honor of S. Dean Mcbride, Jr*, ed. S. Dean McBride, John T. Strong, and Steven Shawn Tuell (Winona Lake, IN: Pennsylvania State University Press, 2005), 151.

is transmitted to us rather than focusing on smaller text-units, a somewhat different characterization of the Daughters of Zion emerges. Indeed, the use of dress and adornment to demonstrate inverted hierarchies in the texts discussed above is particularly illuminating. The trope of inversion that runs throughout Isaiah 3 is the hermeneutic key to understanding the significance of the items of dress worn by the Daughters of Zion.

The Finery of the Daughters of Zion (3:16–4:1)

The reader is told that the women attract condemnation "because the Daughters of Zion are haughty, walking about with outstretched necks and painted (ומשקרות) eyes, and go tottering as they walk and jingling with their feet" (Isa. 3:16).[37] As a result of their deportment, YHWH uncovers the heads of the Daughters of Zion and makes their foreheads bare (Isa. 3:17).[38] The Lord removes all the finery of the Daughters of Zion, leaving them instead with decay, rope, baldness, sackcloth, and a branding (Isa. 3:24).[39] In the words of Zeron, "Where the once adorned women strutted about, they now lie emaciated, half-naked, leprous and

---

37. The word ומשקרת is a hapax term that is either translated as "painted eyes" or as a type of look. See, for example, "glancing wantonly" (ESV, KJV, NRSV); "wanton eyes" (JPS); or "flirting with their eyes" (NIV). All of these translations claim support from the root סקר, which can mean "to look at" or "to observe," or alternatively "to colour red" in Midrashic Hebrew and Aramaic (HALOT III: 1350; Jastrow 1021; DJBA 829). A substantive, סקרא, is also attested, which means red-colored facial make-up (HALOT III: 1350). For further discussion, see Roland Gradwohl, *Die Farben Im Alten Testamen: eine terminologische Studie* (Berlin: A. Töpelmann, 1963), 22, 83–4. See also Lowth, who argues the text has been mispointed and should read שקר (to behave falsely, or break a contract) and so "falsify their eyes." William Lowth, *A Commentary upon the Prophet Isaiah* (London: W. Taylor, 1714), 41.

38. The meaning of the phrase פתהן יערה, understood here as "to make a forehead bear," is highly contentious. I follow Williamson contra the Talmud (b. Shab. 62b), which interprets it as YHWH "will afforest with hair their pubic regions." The practice of using depilatories to remove female pubic hair (b. Naz 59a), may have drawn upon this understanding of pubic hair as a punishment inflicted on women by YHWH. For further discussion of the reception of Isa. 3:17 and its implication for contemporary cosmetic practices, see Noah Bickart, "He Found a Hair and It Bothered Him: Female Pubic Hair Removal in the Talmud," *Nashim* 35 (2019), 128–52. For an overview of the text-critical difficulties surrounding verse 17 and a compelling solution, see Williamson, *Commentary on Isaiah 1–5*, 276–7.

39. Again, the translation of "branding instead of beauty" (כי־תחת יפי) is deeply controversial. For discussion of a number of possibilities, see Williamson, *Commentary on Isaiah 1–5*, 284–6.

terminally-ill."[40] Strikingly, Isa. 3:16-24 contains no explicit discussion of seduction, the desire to attract the male gaze, or illicit lovers.[41] Indeed, the only discussion of marriage prospects and the male gaze occurs in Isa. 4:1, after they have been stripped of their finery, and even here the encounter is better termed pleading rather than seduction.

Nevertheless, contained within this oracle is one of the richest and yet most enigmatic sources of cosmetic and clothing terminology in the Hebrew Bible (Isa. 3:16-24).[42] The passage is densely populated with hapax legomena and unusual lexemes with uncertain referents.[43] In his commentary, H. G. M. Williamson outlines a number of methodological approaches to determining the meaning of these items: (i) considering the context of the term; (ii) using comparative philology; and (iii) applying the evidence of ancient versions and Post-Biblical Hebrew.[44] All of these approaches call for measured caution but particularly the use of ancient versions of Isa. 3:16-24. These demonstrate a tendency to draw on their own cultural milieu to lend meaning to some of the obscure Hebrew terms, a phenomenon that Arie van der Kooij terms "acculturation, that is, adaption to the culture of the time."[45] For example, there are a number of instances in the LXX translation where no direct equivalents of the Hebrew are identifiable. Joseph Ziegler claims that "we cannot really call his work translation here."[46] Instead, Ziegler convincingly argues that the LXX translator seems to be following the fixed sequence used to enumerate items of jewelry in wills, the inventory of

40. Translated from the original German, Alexander Zeron, "Das Wort Niqpä, Zum Sturz Der Zionstöchter (Is. III 24)," 97. This violent act bares some similarity to Jer. 4:30-31; 13:22, 26; Ezek. 16:39-49; Hos. 2:11-12.

41. Compare this to the overtly sexual nature of passages such as Ezek. 16:15-17; 23:40; Jer. 4:30 where the purpose of adornment is explicitly to attract lovers. For a detailed discussion of the function of dress in Ezekiel 16, see S. J. Parrott, " 'Because of My הדר I Set upon You': Transformation through Dress in Ezekiel 16:1-14," in this volume (pp. 187-207).

42. Edward Ullendorff, "Is Biblical Hebrew a Language?," *BSOAS* 34 (1971), 241-55, here 241.

43. First Isaiah often ranks highly in statistical analyses of the distribution of hapax legomena in the Hebrew Bible, but this passage is particularly dense, possibly because it treats the topic of dress so exhaustively, see Frederick E. Greenspahn, "The Number and Distribution of Hapax Legomena in Biblical Hebrew," *VT* 30 (1980), 8-19, here 12 n.17. For an overview of these terms, see Table 8.1.

44. Williamson, *Commentary on Isaiah 1-5*, 277.

45. Arie van der Kooij, "Interpretation of the Book of Isaiah in the Septuagint and in Other Ancient Variations," in *"As Those Who Are Taught": The Interpretation of Isaiah from the LXX to the SBL*, ed. Claire Mathews McGinnis and Patricia K. Tull (Atlanta, GA: Society of Biblical Literature, 2006), 49-68, here 49.

46. Joseph Ziegler, *Untersuchungen zur Septuaginta des Buches Isaias*, Alttestamentliche Abhandlungen 12:3 (Münster: Aschendorffschen Verlagsbuchhandlung, 1934), 208.

temples, and other texts from contemporary Alexandria.[47] This phenomenon is by no means confined to ancient translations. For example, "The Holy Scriptures" as translated by Miles Coverdale in 1535 talks about spanges, cheynes, partlettes, hooves, brushes, glasses, smocks, bonettes, and taches; while the Geneva Bible of 1560 talks about slopes, tablets, flaunes, and stomachers; and the JPS of 1973 includes lace gowns, linen vests, and an apron.[48] Although, these translations have often departed from the intent and significance of the original Hebrew, the resulting text can be highly informative for the history of dress in the translator's own period and gives us significant insight into contemporary attitudes to dress and in particular to female ornamentation.

In the following, therefore, I focus primarily on the evidence of comparative philology, and I use a concordance to contextualize the use of the non-hapax terms in the Hebrew Bible. I explore the patterns of meaning that emerge with reference to extant archeological evidence. The context of Isa. 3:18-23 (Table 8.1) necessitates that we understand the terms as items of dress, although often the referent remains elusive:

On that day, the Lord will remove the finery of the anklets (העכסים) and the sun discs (השביסים) and the lunate jewelry (השהרנים), the earrings (הנטיפות), the bracelets (השירות), and the veils (הרעלות), and the headdresses (הפארים) and the armlets (הצעדות) and the sashes (הקשרים) and the amulets (בתי הנפש) and the charms (הלחשים), the signet rings (הטבעות) and the nose rings (נזמי האף), the white garments (המחלצות) and the cloaks (המעטפות) and the shawls (המטפחות) and the wraps (החריטים), and the coats (הגלינים), and linen tunics (הסדינים) and the turbans (הצניפות) and the veils (הרדידים). (Isa. 3:18-23)[49]

Indeed, it seems unlikely that women might wear all of these items at once, as Oswalt suggests: "The piling up of the details only adds weight to the figure ... expressing the depth of the prophet's anger."[50] The purpose of this passage is perhaps intended to create a vibrant visual image rather than serve as a historically accurate reconstruction of female dress. The meaning of this passage has variously

47. Ibid., 211. This finding is echoed by van der Kooij who compares Isa. 3:18-23 with the Elephantine papyri. See van der Kooij, "Interpretation of the Book of Isaiah in the Septuagint and in Other Ancient Variations," 53.

48. For further examples of acculturation in English translations, see Elizabeth E. Platt, "Jewelry of Bible Times and the Catalog of Isa 3:18-23: II," *AUSS* 17 (1979), 189-201.

49. For an overview of these terms and how they are used elsewhere in the Hebrew Bible, please refer to Table 8.1.

50. John Oswalt, *The Book of Isaiah, Chapters 1-39* (Grand Rapids, MI: Eerdmans, 1986), 151. Williamson makes a similar point arguing that the list "is merely a heaping up of every relevant term that the compiler could think of in order to convey the impression of comprehensiveness." Williamson, *Isaiah 1-5*, 291.

been interpreted as a condemnation of human pride,[51] a warning against affluence and the corrupting nature of extravagance,[52] and even as an example of self-worship as idolatry.[53] However, perhaps more pertinent given the context of women ruling in Isa. 3:1-15, Platt convincingly argues that a number of the items worn by the Daughters of Zion in this passage are reserved only for men elsewhere in the Hebrew Bible.[54] Indeed, Bertil Wiklander goes so far as to argue that "the list as a whole may be taken as referring to insignia of high office associated with the rulers in Judah and Jerusalem who derive their authority from a foreign sovereign."[55]

For example, the headdresses (פארים) worn by the Daughters of Zion (3:20) are elsewhere worn by the high priest (Exod. 39:28); by Levitical priests (Ezek. 44:18); and by bridegrooms (Isa. 61:3, 10).[56] Indeed, instead of mourning the death of his wife the prophet is told to put on his headdress (Ezek. 24:17). The only explicit reference to a woman wearing a פאר is here in Isaiah 3. Another term that features in the list of dress and adornment that may be imbued with priestly connotations is שירות, which is traditionally translated as "bracelets" based on the cognate Akkadian term *šawiru*, which can designate a ring or a bracelet.[57] However, Platt notes the similarity between this term and the term used to describe the "two chains of pure gold, twisted together like cords," that are attached to the High Priest's ephod שרשרות (Exod. 28:14, 22; 39:15), which is explicitly an item of male dress, although this is too limited to draw a firm conclusion.[58]

Similarly, the only other attestation of wraps (חריטים) occurs in 2 Kgs. 5:23 where Naaman, a military commander and powerful official, gifts two talents of silver wrapped in it to Gehazi the servant of Elisha. We are explicitly told that

---

51. Wildberger, *Isaiah*, 148.

52. Watts, "Jerusalem," 213.

53. Wildberger, *Isaiah*, 152.

54. Platt, "Jewelry of Bible Times and the Catalog of Isa 3:18-23: I"; see also Bertil Wiklander, *Prophecy as Literature: A Text-Linguistic and Rhetorical Approach to Isaiah 2–4* (Lund: C.W.K. Gleerup, 1984).

55. Wiklander, *Prophecy as Literature*, 79.

56. For a detailed discussion of the significance of the פאר in the Hebrew Bible as well as its possible referents as attested in the extant material culture and iconographic evidence, see Brady Beard, "What to Look For in a Headdress: פאר and תפארה in Material Culture and Iconography Significance and Signification," in this volume (pp. 15–29).

57. Paul V. Mankowski, *Akkadian Loanwords in Biblical Hebrew* (Winona Lake, IN: Eisenbrauns, 2000), 146. The use of Akkadian loanwords in this passage arguably coheres with Hays's conclusion that First Isaiah reflects a knowledge of Akkadian. Christopher B. Hays, *Death in the Iron Age II and in First Isaiah* (Tübingen: Mohr Siebeck, 2011), 25. Platt argues that the שירות are necklace cords based on reading of the items that precede it in the list. However, I am inclined to agree with Williamson that this perhaps overemphasizes the place of necklaces in an otherwise very diverse list of jewelry. See Platt, "Jewelry of Bible Times and the Catalog of Isa 3:18-23: I," 74; Williamson, *Isaiah 1–5*, 280.

58. Platt, "Jewelry of Bible Times and the Catalog of Isa 3:18-23: I," 74.

Table 8.1 Survey of dress items in Isa. 3:18-23

Term	Wearer	Proposed translation	Coding of dress
עכסים	Not used elsewhere as an item of dress. Possible corrupt attestation Prov. 7:22.	Anklets	Possibly female
שביסים	Hapax	Sun discs	Possibly associated with the male cultic officials removed from Jerusalem and Judah
שהרנים	Camels and Kings of Midian (Judg. 8:21, 26)	Lunate jewelry	Male, possibly with royal connotations
נטיפות	Kings of Midian (Judg. 8:26)	Earrings	Male, possibly with royal connotations
שירות	Hapax	Bracelets	Possibly male with priestly connotations
רעלות	Hapax	Veils	Indeterminate
פארים	High Priest (Exod. 39:28); bridegroom (Isa. 61:3, 10); prophet (Ezek. 24:17); House of Israel (Ezek. 24:23); Levitical priests (Ezek. 44:18)	Headdresses	Male, associated with status
צעדות	Hapax in this form, אצעדה appears in a list of plunder (Num. 31:50); Saul (2 Sam. 1:10)	Armlets	Possibly male, associated with power
קשרים	Bride (Jer. 2:32)	Sashes	Female
בתי נפש	Hapax phrase	Amulets	Possibly associated with the male cultic officials removed from Jerusalem and Judah
לחשים	Not used elsewhere as an item of dress (Isa. 3:3; 26:16; Jer. 8:17; Eccl. 10:11; Sir. 12:18)	Charms	Possibly associated with the male cultic officials removed from Jerusalem and Judah
טבעות	Pharaoh (Gen. 41:42); Joseph (Gen. 41:42); Num. 31:50; Ahasuerus (Est. 3:10; 8:2); Haman (Est. 3:10); Mordechai (Est. 8:2, 8, 10)	Signet rings	Male, associated with political power
נזמי אף	Rebekah (Gen. 24:22, 30, 47); Jacob's family (Gen. 35:4); wives, sons, and daughters of Israelites (Exod. 32:2-3; 35:22); Ishmaelites (Judg. 8:24-26); YHWH's wife (Ezek. 16:12); Prophet's wife (Hos. 2:15); Job (Job 42:11); snout of a pig (Prov. 11:22)	Nose rings	Associated with women, children, and dependents
מחלצות	Joshua (Zech. 3:4)	White garments	Male, with priestly connotations
מעטפות	Hapax	Cloaks	Indeterminate
מטפחות	Ruth (Ruth 3:15)	Shawls	Female

Table 8.1 (continued)

Term	Wearer	Proposed translation	Coding of dress
חריטים	Naaman (2 Kgs. 5:23)	Wraps	Male, possibly with status
גלינים	Not used elsewhere as an item of dress. Only other attestation Isa. 8:1	Coats	Indeterminate
סדינים	Samson (Judg. 14:12-13); woven by the wife (Prov. 31:24)	Linen tunics	Associated with female practice of weaving
צניפות	Joshua (Zech. 3:5); Job (Job 29:14); kings (Isa. 62:3; Sir. 11:5; 40:4; 47:6)	Turbans	Male
רדידים	Female lover (Songs 5:7)	Veils	Female

Naaman is a "commander of the army of the king of Syria" and "a great man with his master and in high favor" (2 Kgs. 5:1). The rather gendered translation of חריטים in Isa. 3:22 as "handbags" (ESV; NRSV) or "purses" (NIV; NET) is somewhat difficult to reconcile with the portrayal of Naaman in 2 Kgs 5.

Similarly, the only other attestation of white garments (מחלצות) outside of Isa. 3:22 occurs in Zech. 3:4 as part of the description of Joshua's clothing in his investiture as high priest. There is some debate as to whether מחלצות should be translated as "festive robes," "white garments," or "loincloths," or some item of military uniform. This discord largely rests on a divergence of opinions as to how the root חלץ should be understood. The contention that מחלצות are some sort of festive robes derives from an interpretation of חלץ as "to draw off or out," the implication of which is that these robes are "taken off in ordinary life."[59] Alternatively, Dale Winton Thomas argues from the basis of comparative philology that *ḥalaṣa* means "be pure, white" in Arabic and so advocates for "white garments."[60] By contrast, Platt points out that a secondary meaning of חלץ is "to equip for war" (*DCH* III: 239). Consequently, Platt suggests that a plausible interpretation of the מחלצות is some item of military uniform, such as a loincloth used to gird the loins for battle.[61] Whether the מחלצות are ascribed to the

59. *DCH* V: 219; BDB, 322. Since the seminal work by James Barr, there has been a growing recognition of the importance of context and usage for locating the meaning of a lexeme as opposed to its derivation. See, for instance, James Barr, *The Semantics of Biblical Language* (London: Oxford University Press, 1961), 107. This caution against the overreliance on etymology has been reiterated more recently, particularly in the work of James K. Aitken; see "Context of Situation in Biblical Lexica," in *Foundations for Syriac Lexicography III*, ed. Janet Dyk, Wido van Peursen, Dirk Bakker, P. van Keulen, and C. Sikkel (Piscataway, NJ: Gorgias, 2009), 181–202. While context should be privileged in lexicographic work, in the case of hapax legomenon and exceedingly rare terms, etymology can be used to guide plausible interpretations in the face of a paucity of other evidence.

60. D. Winton Thomas, "A Note on Zechariah III 4," *JTS* 33 (1932), 279–80.

61. Platt, "Jewelry of Bible Times and the Catalog of Isa. 3:18-23: I," 79.

category of priestly purity or warfare, it seems likely that it operates in a distinctly male sphere.[62]

The term used for Joshua's turban (צָנִיף) in Zech. 3:5 also appears among the list of items worn by the Daughters Zion (Isa. 3:23).[63] Elsewhere, צניפות are worn by kings (Isa. 62:3; Sir. 11:5; 40:4; 47:6), while Job is described as wearing justice like a turban (Job 29:14).[64] Again this item of dress appears to be associated not only with men but also highly elite or elect men. Isa. 3:23 is the only instance of the eight attestations of צניף where a woman is described as the wearer.[65]

Several other items in the list also appear to have royal or courtly associations. For instance, in the only other attestation of earrings (נטיפות) outside of Isa. 3:19, they are worn by the kings of Midian (Judg. 8:26).[66] Similarly, the term for armlets,

---

62. Contra Martin Hallaschka, who argues that "the meaning of מחלצות must be derived from Isa. 3:22 … The term מחלצות is thus part of the description of women's fine and rich clothing which has to be kept in mind for the rendering of the term." Martin Hallaschka, "Clean Garments for Joshua: The Purification of the High Priest in Zech. 3," in *Clothing and Nudity in the Hebrew Bible*, ed. Christoph Berner, Manuel Schäfer, Martin Schott, Sarah Schulz, and Martina Weingärtner (London: T&T Clark, 2019), 525–40, here 529. At the heart of this question is which text to privilege when attempting to unpick the gendered dynamics of the מחלצות. However, given the high number of dress terms in Isa. 3:16-24 that elsewhere in the Hebrew Bible occur only with reference to men as well as the priestly connotations of Zechariah 3, the balance of probability seems to suggest that מחלצות are likely a male-coded item of dress. Nevertheless, this need not undermine Hallaschka's insightful conclusion that

> the vision report on the reclothing of Joshua the high priest alludes to Isa. 3:16–4:6 because it seeks to show that the judgement of the inhabitants of Jerusalem (3:1–4:1) is over, that the time of salvation has begun, and that Joshua is cleansed, as announced in Isa. 4:2–6 … It should be noted that Zech. 3 alludes to Isa. 3:1–4:6 in reverse order … Whereas the Lord (אדני) will take away the finery of the Jerusalemite women as a sign of judgement, the angel of Yahweh declares that he will take away the filthy clothes as a sign of salvation. (533)

63. Platt notes that an etymologically related term for turban, מצנפת, is also used repeatedly of the headwear worn by the high priest (Exod. 28:4, 37, 39; 29:6; 39:28, 31; Lev. 8:9; 16:4). See Platt, "Jewelry of Bible Times and the Catalog of Isa 3:18-23: I," 79.

64. For a discussion of the use of clothing to symbolize physiological states and physical health and illnesses in the book of Job, see Laura Quick, "'Like a Garment Eaten by Moths' (Job 13:28): Clothing, Nudity and Illness in the Book of Job," *BibInt* Advanced Articles (2020), 3–4.

65. *DCH* VII: 136.

66. The term מטיפות derives from the root נטף, meaning "to drip" (*DCH* V: 678). There is some uncertainty as to whether this term means earrings or some kind of drop pendant. I, again, follow Williamson in opting for earrings in order to convey the comprehensiveness of the list, but this is by no means a certain translation. Williamson, *Commentary on Isaiah*

צעדות, is attested, albeit with a prothetic aleph (אצעדה), in Num. 31:50, among a list of items plundered from the Midianites. However, it is impossible to discern from the list of loot whether the original wearers were men or women.[67] Moreover, the exact referent of the term צעדות (Isa. 3:19) is the subject of some debate. Although the form as it occurs in Isa. 3:19 is hapax, the related noun צעדה, meaning "marching" (2 Sam. 5:24; 1 Chr. 14:15), seems to be derived from the root צעד, meaning "to step, march."[68] On the basis of this, the צעדות worn by the Daughters of Zion may be some form of anklet.[69] Alternatively, Platt suggests that the term instead relates to אצעדה, which stands in parallel to צמיד in Num. 31:50 and is a well-attested term meaning "bracelet."[70] אצעדה is also explicitly described as an item of jewelry worn on the arm in 2 Sam. 1:10. If Platt is right to associate the hapax term צעדות with אצעדה, then this is another reference to a symbol of male authority.[71] In 2 Sam. 1:10, an Amalekite warrior kills Saul and takes David his crown and his אצעדה as proof of Saul's death.[72] This armlet is, at a minimum, sufficiently distinctive that David would be able to identify it as Saul's. It is likely, however, that it is also an insignia of kingship as it is taken along with Saul's crown (2 Sam. 1:10). It is possible that these two items of dress were brought to David not only to confirm Saul's death but also to enable David to appropriate them when he is anointed king over Judah (2 Sam. 2:4). The importance of clothing and its role in conferring power and status are highlighted elsewhere in the narrative when Jonathan and David switch their clothing as part of Jonathan's renunciation of his rights as crown prince and the transferal of the royal succession to David (1 Sam.

1–5, 279. For an alternative suggestion that this refers to phallic-shaped drop pendants, see Laura Quick, *Dress, Adornment, and the Body in the Hebrew Bible* (Oxford: Oxford University Press, 2021), 126–9. In light of the male clothing adduced above, this is an interesting argument. Indeed, phallic-shaped apotropaic amulets that are commonly worn by young boys in Rome. See Nina Crummy, "Bears and Coins: The Iconography of Protection in Late Roman Infant Burials," *Britannia* 41 (2010), 37–93, here 51.

67. See the discussion in Williamson, *Isaiah 1–5*, 280.

68. *DCH* VII: 139.

69. BDB, 857; *DCH* VII: 139.

70. For references to צמיד , see Gen. 24:22, 30, 47; Ezek. 16:11; 23:42. Platt, "Jewelry of Bible Times and the Catalog of Isa 3:18-23: I," 76.

71. Williamson has suggested that the prosthetic aleph may be an anomalous plural form or a means of distinguishing between a male and female item of adornment. Given the context of numerous items of male adornment being worn by the Daughters of Zion, I am more inclined to follow the former explanation. Williamson, *Commentary on Isaiah 1–5*, 280.

72. For a detailed discussion of the treatment of Saul's corpse, including the removal of his armor and clothing, see Francesca Stavrakopoulou, "Curating King Saul: The Transformation of a Troublesome Corpse," in Quick et al., *To Gaul, to Greece, and into Noah's Ark*, 19–35.

18:4).[73] In the words of Laura Quick, this demonstrates that "the clothing items of the king are understood as an extension of the king himself."[74] It is particularly striking, therefore, that the Daughters of Zion wear an armlet that appears to be linked to kingship in Isa. 3:19.

Moreover, the signet rings (הטבעות) worn by the Daughters of Zion (Isa. 3:21) are elsewhere used by royal figures to convey honor onto courtiers and advisors and confer legal authority to act in the name of the king. We are told that the ring was taken from the hand of the king (Est. 3:10), which indicates that this term is perhaps best understood as referring to a finger ring.[75] In Gen. 41:42, Pharaoh gives his טבעת to Joseph. This represents a transfer of power to Joseph who is placed "over all the land of Egypt" (41:43) in order to oversee the prosperous administration of Egypt's harvests in accordance with his interpretation of Pharaoh's dream. Similarly, the term is used in Esther when the king's טבעת is given first to Haman in order to enable Haman to pursue his genocidal policy and then to Mordechai to confer favored status. The ring is used to seal edicts from the king (Est. 3:12; 8:8, 10) suggesting not only its practical administrative function but also the way in which this item of royal insignia served as a physical means of manifesting the king's power.[76] The ring is not only a symbol of authority but is constitutive of that role.[77] Perhaps unsurprisingly given the use of the טבעת to confer authority and political power, Isa. 3:21 represents the only instance where a woman is described as the wearer.

It is striking to find women associated with an item of dress so closely related to the exercise of political power. Indeed, for all of the examples discussed above, the oracle against the Daughters of Zion represents the only instance where a woman is explicitly attested wearing these items. Moreover, all of the items of dress and adornment discussed above are typically associated with warriors and military

---

73. For further discussion of the significance of clothing in this succession narrative, see Ellena Lyell, "Dressing Benjaminites, Defining Kingship: Dress as a Royal Prerogative for the Tribe of Benjamin," in this volume (pp. 123–42).

74. Quick, "Clothed in Curses," 103. Quick also discusses an Akkadian parallel (RS 17.159) in which an abdication is symbolized by the removal of the former king's clothing when he leaves the throne (n.26).

75. For a discussion of the importance of dress as a narrative device in the book of Esther, see Selena Billington, "Social Standing, Agency, and the Motif of Cloth and Clothing in Esther," in this volume (pp. 229–55).

76. For a detailed discussion of the function and significance of kingly signet rings, see Quick, *Dress, Adornment, and the Body in the Hebrew Bible*, 41–6; Carmen Joy Imes, "Belonging to YHWH: Real and Imagined Inscribed Seals in Biblical Tradition," in *Write That They May Read: Studies in Literacy and Textualization in the Ancient Near East and in the Hebrew Scriptures: Essays in Honour of Professor Alan R. Millard*, ed. D. I. Block, David C. Deuel, Paul J. N. Lawrence, and C. John Collins (Pickwick, 2020), 349–65.

77. For a discussion of dress and adornment as constitutive of power and authority, see Imes, "Between Two Worlds"; and Shawn W Flynn, "YHWH'S Clothing, Kingship, and

men, judges, prophets, elders, individuals of repute, and royal counselors. Indeed, a notable overlap exists between the groups of men who have been removed from Judah and Jerusalem (Isa. 3:2-3) and those who might wear these items of adornment.

A number of the other items of dress and adornment in the list seem to have religious or cultic connotations. For instance, Wildberger argues that שביסים is a diminutive form of "sun," noting the similarity of the phrase with the Ugaritic term for sun, *špš*,[78] and positing an interchange of מ in the Hebrew שמש for a ב.[79] Although somewhat speculative, it is possible that שביסים therefore refers to some sort of sun-disc or solar motif on an item of jewelry. Indeed, sun pendants seem to have been popular in the Levant and are attested both in the archeological record and in iconographic representations of Syro-Canaanites.[80] This argument is all the more compelling when it is read alongside the following noun, שהרנים, the etymology of which seems to necessitate some form of lunate jewelry.[81] Jewelry designed with a lunate motif was popular and is well attested in the Levant in both the Bronze and the Iron Age.[82] This crescent-shaped jewelry is sometimes connected to the worship of moon deities.[83] As a result, Wildberger argues that the Daughters of Zion attract condemnation for wearing items connected to the

Power: Origins and Vestiges in Comparative Ancient Near Eastern Contexts," in Finitsis, *Dress and Clothing in the Hebrew Bible*, 11–28, 29–62.

78. Gregorio del Olmo Lete, Joaquín Sanmartín, and W. G. E. Watson, *A Dictionary of the Ugaritic Language in the Alphabetic Tradition*, 2 vols., 3rd revised ed. (Leiden: Brill, 2015), 824–5.

79. Wildberger, *Isaiah*, 152. Alternatively, the term is sometimes understood as a type of ornamental headband drawing on the meaning of the verb שבץ (to plait, weave) in Post-Biblical Hebrew and the apparent LXX translation as ἐμπλόκια (braiding). However, as discussed above, the LXX is not a secure basis on which to build an argument and the Vulgate omits the phrase altogether while the Targum simply borrows from the Hebrew. For further discussion, see Williamson, *Commentary on Isaiah 1-5*, 278–9.

80. Amir Golani, "Revealed by Their Jewelry: Ethnic Identity of Israelites during the Iron Age in the Southern Levant," *PAM* 23 (2014), 269–96, here 271.

81. Williamson, *Commentary on Isaiah 1-5*, 279.

82. David Ilan, "The Crescent-Lunate Motif in the Jewelery of the Bronze and Iron Ages," in *Proceedings of the 9th International Congress on the Archaeology of the Ancient Near East*, ed. Rolf A. Stucky, Oskar Kaelin, and Hans-Peter Mathys (Wies: Harrassowitz Verlag, 2016), 137–50; K. R. Maxwell-Hyslop, *Western Asiatic Jewellery c.3000–612B.C.* (London: Methuen, 1971), 138.

83. Most recently, see Tallay Ornan, "Labor Pangs: The Revadim Plaque Type," in *Images as Sources. Studies on Ancient Near Eastern Artefacts and the Bible Inspired by the Work of Othmar Keel*, ed. Susanne Bickel (Fribourg: Academic Press, 2007), 215–35; Ilan, "The Crescent-Lunate Motif in the Jewelery of the Bronze and Iron Ages"; Irit Ziffer, "Moon,

idolatrous worship of gods other than YHWH.[84] Indeed a number of other items on the list seem to be connected to apotropaic charms or talismans.[85] For instance, the inclusion of amulets (בתי הנפש), which literally translate as "houses of life" or "houses of breath."[86] It has been suggested that this refers to some form of protective amulet or talisman, or possibly even a receptacle in which the soul was kept externally.[87] This interpretation is bolstered when read alongside the term that immediately follows it, לחשים, which is related to a verb used for charms and incantations against snakebites (Jer. 8:17; Ps. 58:6; Qoh. 10:11).[88] While not necessarily an insignia of male office, it is notable that the Daughters of Zion are wearing amulets, charms, and lunate and sun motif jewelry, given the removal of the diviner, the wise magician, and the expert in charms (Isa. 3:2-3). Indeed, the term used to describe the expert in charms, נבון לחש, derives from the same root as the charms (לחשים) that the Daughters of Zion are wearing in Isa. 3:20. This suggests that the Daughters of Zion may have assumed items of dress that are connected to the roles of these male cultic experts.

These items of male dress worn by the Daughters of Zion are juxtaposed by articles of dress and adornment coded as female, such as the sashes (קשרים), which are elsewhere worn by a bride on her wedding day (Jer. 2:32); the shawls (מטפחות) used by women for gleaning (Ruth 3:15); the linen tunics (סדינים) woven by women in domestic settings (Prov. 31:24); and the veil (רדיד) worn by the young lover (Song 5:7). These sumptuary items occur alongside items of jewelry such as nose rings (נזמי אף) and anklets (עכסים). It has been argued that both of these items of adornment are used as markers to constrict the female body and

Rain, Womb, Mercy the Imagery of the Shrine Model from Tell El-Far'ah North—Biblical Tirzah For Othmar Keel," *Religions* 10 (2019), 1–24, here 12.

84. Wildberger, *Isaiah*, 152.

85. For a detailed and incisive discussion of the role of the jewelry in Isaiah 3 as it relates to personal religion and the Temple Cult, see Quick, *Dress, Adornment, and the Body in the Hebrew Bible*, 121–50.

86. The exact meaning of the phrase בתי הנפש is contentious. The Vulgate appears to translate it as *olfactoriola* and a possible Akkadian cognate, *nipšu*, has been posited the meaning "scent." Hence, the translation "box of perfumes" (*DCH* V: 734; ESV; NIV; NRSV). Prov. 27:9 is sometimes cited in defense of this, although it is itself a very uncertain passage. Gray argues that this bag of perfume may have hung from the sashes (קשרים), which precedes the phrase in Isa. 3:20 and points to Songs 1:13 as evidence. However, as Williamson points out, נפש is a well-attested term, and it seems unlikely that it has a previously unrecognized and otherwise unattested homonym. For further discussion, see Williamson, *Commentary on Isaiah 1–5*, 281; Gray, *A Critical and Exegetical Commentary on the Book of Isaiah 1–27*, 73.

87. Blenkinsopp, *Isaiah 1–39*, 9; H Saggs, "'External Souls' in the Old Testament," *JSS* 19 (1974), 1–12, here 11–12.

88. The root לחש is possibly a reflex of the Akkadian verb *laḫāšu*, which occurs frequently in Mesopotamian incantation texts. A similar root in Ugaritic, *lḫš*, forms the basis of the

184 *Dress Hermeneutics and the Hebrew Bible*

inscribe social values, including female subservience onto it. In his study of anklets in the early Iron Age cemetery in Tell es-Saʔidiyeh, J. D. M. Green argues that "the greater the level of patriarchy and control of women in reproduction, marriage, and domesticity by men, the greater the contrast in 'restriction' between male and female adornment."[89] For Green, the physical attributes of the anklets worn by women, such as their weight and their physically restrictive properties, reflect how "concepts of ownership, obligation, objectification, and commoditisation may all be intertwined with physically and symbolically restrictive ornamentation."[90]

Laura Quick has advanced similar arguments in relation to the role of the נזם. She highlights the significance of piercing as an act of permanent body modification in several contexts, including the piercing of a slave's ear (Exod. 21:2-6; Deut. 15:12-16) as a mark of property acquisition and the transferal of property.[91] She then turns to the account of Rebekah's betrothal in Gen. 24:22, 47 in which Rebekah accepts the נזם from the servant of Isaac. Quick argues that "with the gift of the nose-ring, the servant of Isaac gifts along with it gender and status roles: the jewelry makes explicit Rebekah's new role as an Israelite wife. A pierced nose therefore indicates and controls gender roles, intentions and aspirations."[92] Nor can the site of the body, the nose, be insignificant. Elsewhere, נזמים are associated with controlling domesticated animals (Prov. 11:22).[93] Thus, the nose ring, like the anklets, draws on a complex web of interconnected ideas, including the commodification of women: the social control of women and socially constructed notions of permissible agency and submissiveness in gendered interactions and relations between men and women.[94]

When the dress and adornment of the Daughters of Zion is read together as an assemblage, these items of female-coded dress and adornment arguably serve as a reminder of the fitting and socially acceptable roles women might be expected

---

words *mlḫš*, meaning "exorcist," and *lḫšt*, meaning "whisper, murmur." See discussion in Hays, *Death in the Iron Age II and in First Isaiah*, 327 n. 565.

89. J. D. M Green, "Anklets and the Social Construction of Gender and Age in the Late Bronze and Early Iron Age Southern Levant," in *Archaeology and Women: Ancient and Modern Issues*, ed. Sue Hamilton, Ruth Whitehouse, and Katherine I. Wright (Walnut Creek, CA: Left Coast Press, 2007), 283–309, here 296.

90. Ibid.

91. Quick, *Dress, Adornment, and the Body in the Hebrew Bible*, 136; See also Sandra Jacobs, *The Body as Property: Physical Disfigurement in Biblical Law* (London: Bloomsbury, 2014), 190–220, on whose work Quick draws.

92. Quick, *Dress, Adornment, and the Body in the Hebrew Bible*, 138.

93. The use of nose rings to control domesticated animals is also attested in the archeological record; see M. A. Littauer and J. H. Crouwel, *Wheeled Vehicles and Ridden Animals in the Ancient Near East* (Leiden: Brill, 1979), 30–1.

94. For a further, detailed discussion of the significance of the נזם in the Hebrew Bible, see Susannah Rees, "The נזם and Navigating Power Structures," *BibInt* (published online ahead of print 2021).

to adopt, at least in the minds of the biblical author(s) and redactor(s). Several of the items are associated with brides and wives and the expected deference and tractability associated with those roles. Others allude to work that was typically consigned to the realms of female labor, such as weaving and gleaning.[95] These items of dress reflect the social constraints that were typically placed on women in the society in which these texts were produced and transmitted. This makes the appearance of the aforementioned items of dress and adornment associated with male power as part of this assemblage all the more shocking.

Platt argues that the point of describing the Daughters of Zion in both male and female adornment that reflects public office and authority "is that the *leaders* of the society, *both men and women* who wear the symbols of their offices, have corrupted that society by misuse of leadership at the expense of the poor."[96] However, this does not fully appreciate the gendered language used elsewhere in the chapter. This is not a cryptic way of criticizing men in positions of authority; rather it seeks to challenge the women who assume their power and the symbols of their authority in their absence. We are repeatedly told earlier in Isaiah that women and children are ruling (3:4, 12) and that the men of repute have been removed (3:2-3, 25-26; 4:1). Moreover, items of clothing and adornment are used to confer authority and reflect the power to rule.[97] This is clearly also a concern elsewhere in Isaiah 3 given that the presence of a cloak in the house of the man in Isa. 3:6-7 is seen as something that might equip him to rule. The passage concerning the dress of the Daughters of Zion fits into a broader pattern in Isaiah 3, which is concerned with women taking power, subverting social structures, and filling the power vacuum left after the removal of the male ruling class from Judah and Jerusalem. This is perhaps why, unlike the other sexual and marital metaphor texts, the Daughters of Zion are not criticized for whoring or taking lovers. Illicit seduction is not what is in view here.

Items of dress that are socially coded as female and are elsewhere associated with subservience, commodification, and female labor are, therefore, ironically inverted by their inclusion in an assemblage of dress alongside royal insignia and other items of dress coded with an elite, male status and constitutive of political power, dominance, and leadership. The image evoked is thus one of total confusion

---

95. Carol Meyers, *Rediscovering Eve: Ancient Israelite Women in Context* (Oxford: Oxford University Press, 2013), 125–39.

96. Platt, "Jewelry of Bible Times and the Catalog of Isa 3:18-23: II," 193. The emphasis is Platt's. This is followed by Wiklander who extends the argument to suggest that the lists of items of adornment are not only symbols of authority but also reflect a vassal relationship with a foreign sovereign. This, he argues, supports his broader view of Isaiah 2–4 as an attempt to dissuade the audience from forming a vassal relationship with a foreign power and to instead return to the covenant of YHWH. See Wiklander, *Prophecy as Literature*, 79–81.

97. Hatshepsut provides us with historically documented use of male-coded dress to legitimate a female ruler. See Uroš Matić, "(De)Queering Hatshepsut: Binary Bind in Archaeology of Egypt and Kingship Beyond the Corporeal," *JAMT* 23 (2016), 810–31.

and chaos. By literally assuming the mantle of male leadership, the Daughters of Zion represent another element of the inverted natural order in Isaiah 3 and the moral and social collapse it reflects. The honorable are dishonored (3:5); the brother is elevated over his father (3:6); and the Daughters of Zion are not only dressed as ruling elite men but are in fact ruling in their stead. Thus, the description of the dress and adornment of the Daughters of Zion should be read as another of the vignettes of political chaos in Isaiah 3 connected through their redaction and transmitted to us in their present context.

Conclusions

The description of the stripping of the Daughters of Zion of their finery in Isaiah 3 is not intended as a condemnation of female vanity or frivolous lifestyles and frippery, as some commentators have suggested. Rather, when read in the context of Isaiah 3 as it has been transmitted to us, the oracle against the Daughters of Zion reflects a complete inversion of the natural order in which women have assumed male positions of authority in the absence of male rulers and leaders.

The particular genius of this passage is that it draws on motifs and tropes that are commonplace elsewhere in the prophetic literature of the Hebrew Bible and the ancient Near East but reuses them in a unique and innovative way. It draws on elements of the sexual and marital metaphors (Jer. 13:22, 26; Ezek. 16:39-49; Jer. 4:30-31; Hos. 2:11-12) but disregards the concern with the male gaze and seduction that is found in these passages. Like texts such as *The Dialogue of Ipuwer* and the Deir ʿAlla Inscription, Isa. 3:16-24 communicates the inversion of the natural world order through dress and adornment. However, rather than describing an inverted social order in which the rich are elevated over the poor, Isaiah 3 opts to present this reversal along gendered lines in which women have been elevated to the status of rulers, leaders, and cultic experts over men. This concern with the appropriate gender dynamic is a prominent one elsewhere, for instance, in the *Marduk Prophecy*'s discussion about wives revering their husbands.

Dress is not merely a system of signs but rather actively constructs identity and status. Thus, from the perspective of the biblical author(s) and redactor(s), items of adornment that, when worn by men, can signify and confer elect status, power, and wealth represent a deeply troubled world order when worn by the Daughters of Zion.

Chapter 9

"BECAUSE OF MY הדר I SET UPON YOU": TRANSFORMATION THROUGH DRESS IN EZEKIEL 16:1-14

S. J. Parrott

Introduction

Dress is at once a necessity of life and a form of communication. Indeed, its universal necessity has not hindered its particular expression, both in time and space. Given the myriad of types, forms, meanings, and functions of clothing, research on the topic has burgeoned in the past thirty years.[1] A thread that runs through the majority of this research is the recognition that dress communicates identity. The essays collected in the volume *Dress and Identity* demonstrate this point.[2] Mary Roach-Higgins, an editor of the volume and a researcher of dress, writes that dress has two basic functions: as a means of communication and as an "alterant" to body processes.[3] Coming from the perspective of symbolic interaction theory, she writes that identities are acquired through social interaction in various settings, such as social, physical, religious, or biological. Given this, dress is a communicator of identity as it "announces social positions of wearer to both wearer and observers within a particular interaction situation."[4]

---

1. For example, see Mary Ellen Roach-Higgins, Joanne B.Eicher, and Kim K. P. Johnson, eds, *Dress and Identity* (New York: Fairchild, 1995); or R. A. Schwarz and J. M. Cordwell, eds, *The Fabrics of Culture: The Anthropology of Clothing and Adornment* (The Hague: Mouton, 1979); for a historical and global perspective on clothing, see Robert Ross, *Clothing: A Global History* (Cambridge: Polity, 2008).

2. Roach-Higgins et al., *Dress and Identity*.

3. What Roach-Higgins means by "alterant" is that the relationship between the body and clothing is intimate, and that clothing can be used (i) to modify a body, as by a tattoo or cosmetic surgery, or (ii) to supplement a body, as by a parka in cold weather to keep warm or by pockets that increase the body's capabilities. See ibid., 1–3, 10–11.

4. Mary Ellen Roach-Higgins, "Dress and Identity," in Roach-Higgins et al., *Dress and Identity*, 12.

While the relationship between dress and identity has only recently been researched, it is not a modern notion. Cynthia S. Colburn and Maura K. Heyn edited a volume of articles on bodily adornment and identity in ancient contexts.[5] The volume focuses on personal adornment as a dynamic means of communication within a society. They define "adornment" as an "active process used to shape embodied identities" and as a result "the body can often convey meaning more powerfully and convincingly than verbal communication."[6]

With this in mind, I am primarily interested in how YHWH's investiture of dress on Jerusalem in Ezekiel 16 forms her identity. This chapter of Ezekiel contains a graphic oracle describing the chaotic behavior of Jerusalem and her violent demise. While the graphic nature of the chapter is often the focus of scholars, the investiture of dress in verses 1–14 is overlooked.[7] Many commentaries contain but a few sentences describing the *six* verses consisting of YHWH's act of investiture.[8] Some state that the chapter as a whole refers to the history of Israel, with the investiture referring to the Solomonic dynasty;[9] others believe it to have no historical referent but rather see it as a pauper-to-princess fairy-tale taken from adopted material that derived elsewhere.[10] Still others believe it simply to be the generous giving of gifts, which Jerusalem later squanders, displaying no sense of gratitude. While the rhetorical nature of verses 1–14 in the context of the chapter cannot be overstated,[11] limiting ourselves to rhetoric can blind us to potential literary and theological implications.

5. Cynthia S. Colburn and Maura K. Heyn, eds, *Reading a Dynamic Canvas: Adornment in the Ancient Mediterranean World* (Newcastle: Cambridge Scholars, 2008).

6. Cynthia S. Colburn and Maura K. Heyn, "Bodily Adornment and Identity," in Colburn and Heyn, *Reading a Dynamic Canvas*, 1.

7. A recent article by Anja Klein ("Clothing, Nudity, and Shame in the Book of Ezekiel and Prophetic Oracles of Judgment," in *Clothing and Nudity in the Hebrew Bible*, ed. Christoph Berner, Manuel Schäfer, Martin Schott, Sarah Schulz, and Martina Weingärtner (New York: T&T Clark, 2019), 499–524) examines clothing and nudity in a general sense in Ezekiel 16 among other prophetic texts. She argues that it is "a means of depicting judgment on the unfaithful wife" (501). She does not give a detailed analysis of the dress itself or its symbolic or rhetorical function but instead focuses more primarily on dress as a foil for judgment and on nakedness denoting sexual violence.

8. See Walther Zimmerli, *Ezekiel: A Commentary on the Book of the Prophet Ezekiel*, vol. 1, ed. Frank Moore Cross and Klaus Baltzer (Philadelphia, PA: Fortress, 1979), 339.

9. This view has largely been rejected. For an example, see R. Bach and Moshe Greenberg's critique in *Ezekiel 1–20: A New Translation and Commentary*, The Anchor Bible, vol. 22 (New York: Doubleday, 1983), 300.

10. This was Gunkel's argument. For a critique, see Daniel Block, *The Book of Ezekiel: Chapters 1–24* (Grand Rapids, MI: Eerdmans, 1997), 301–2; or Greenberg, *Ezekiel 1–20*, 471.

11. See Thomas Renz, who states that the graphic imagery and language of Ezekiel is meant to force the exilic audience to stake a stance: either side with YHWH or with Jerusalem. Thomas Renz, *The Rhetorical Function of the Book of Ezekiel* (Leiden: Brill, 1999), 76–7.

This aim of this chapter is to offer a more robust account of the discourse of adornment in Ezekiel 16. I will demonstrate that dress is not incidental to the passage but crucial to it. YHWH's investiture of dress on Jerusalem constitutes her new identity as his royal and holy representative, a queenly identity with priestly allusions, the purpose of which is to make her an ambassador of YHWH among the nations. Without that dress, Jerusalem has no such identity and her relationship to YHWH remains unclear.

The Context

A brief and initial overview of the first eight verses of the chapter provides the context of the passage and the beginning point of Jerusalem's identity transformation in verses 1–14. Verses 1–3 open the chapter by stating its purpose, addressor, and addressee. Verses 3–5 launch the metaphorical narrative by describing the pagan origins of the infant Jerusalem and the complete neglect of any sort of attention or care. Jerusalem's Canaanite origin is meant to convey "all that is antithetical to Israel and to Yahwism"[12] and to "represent human depravity at its worst"; it is from these pagan people that Jerusalem has its spiritual roots.[13] The rhetorical function of these origins is polemical, so as to create a strong distaste in the mouth of the audience. It is a shocking statement: personified Jerusalem as the ideal figure or the holy city in which YHWH dwells has not descended from Israelite ancestors, Abraham and Sarah, but from pagan parents who have ultimately deserted her.

In verse 4, in a series of negated *hophal* and *pual* verbs Ezekiel rewrites Jerusalem's ancestry; these verbs describe the absence of any initiation rites or affirmation of personhood for Jerusalem.[14] The foundling is thrown to the field, an unowned area outside the legal borders of the community, resulting in an abdication of parental rights. With no initiation rites and no parental care, Jerusalem lacks an identity. She occupies liminal space, a nobody belonging to no one.[15]

YHWH then passes by the foundling in her naked and bloody state. YHWH's formulaic imperatives "in your blood, 'live!' "[16] have parallels in four sources from

---

12. Block, *Ezekiel 1–24*, 474.

13. Ibid., 475.

14. For more details on these rites, see Zimmerli, *Ezekiel 1*, 338–9.

15. See Maier Malul, "Adoption of Foundlings in the Bible and Mesopotamian Documents: A Study of Some Legal Metaphors in Ezekiel 16:1-7," *JSOT* 46 (1990), 104.

16. There is a variant on the second "live" command. Five MSS attest the original text without the dittography. Zimmerli states that the MT repeated it in error (*Ezekiel 1*, 323). Greenberg notes that a "genuine" repetition would have only involved "in your blood live" (*Ezekiel*, 276). The situation is parallel to Ps. 130:6c, which is also not repeated in the LXX. English translations are divided on whether the dittography is included: the NET, NASB, KJV, and ESV include it, whereas the RSV, NLT, NIV, and TLB do not. Block states that double pronouncement of "live!" is a reversal of the double negative in verse 5 that states that

the Old Babylonian period in the first half of the second millennium BCE[17] and can be interpreted as a formal declaration of adoption of the foundling.[18] Whether or not adoption is implied,[19] the scene depicts no tender care on YHWH's part.[20] Interestingly, as first compared by Jason Gile, a comparison of Deut. 32:10 with Ezek. 16:6-7 reveals a removal of vocabulary of care and compassion in the latter, which is present in the former.[21] Verse 7 ends with a disjunctive *waw* that interrupts the narrative to state that although YHWH has interacted Jerusalem and she has matured, she still remains naked and bare.[22]

Verse 8 describes the oath and covenant between YHWH and Jerusalem, involving the symbolic act of YHWH spreading his hem over her, an act that exercises the authority of YHWH over Jerusalem through which he acquires her; the result of this act is the new familial situation of Jerusalem.[23] Indeed, now that a covenant as marriage has been ratified between Jerusalem and YHWH the

no eye had pity and no one had compassion. Daniel I. Block, *By the River Chebar: Historical, Literary, and Theological Studies in the Book of Ezekiel* (Eugene, OR: Cascade, 2013), 53.

17. Two are legal documents, one is a letter, and the fourth is section 185 of the Code of Hammurabi. Malul, "Adoption," 106.

18. Ibid., 111.

19. Aaron Koller, for example, argues that Jerusalem is never adopted. See Aaron Koller, "Pornography or Theology? The Legal Background, Psychological Realism, and Theological Import of Ezekiel 16," *CBQ* 79 (2017), 406, 409–11.

20. See Mary E. Shields, "Multiple Exposures: Body Rhetoric and Gender Characterization in Ezekiel 16," *JFSR* 14 (1998), 8. Cf. Johanna Stiebert states: "There is nothing tender or nurturing in what may be YHWH's adoption of Jerusalem." Johanna Stiebert, *Fathers and Daughters in the Hebrew Bible* (Oxford: Oxford University Press, 2013), 197.

21. Jason Gile, "Ezekiel 16 and the Song of Moses: A Prophetic Transformation?" *JBL* 130 (2011), 87–108.

22. While negligence, child abuse, or emotional neglect could be claimed of YHWH's lack of intervention at the end of verse 7, this would, as Stiebert states, "impose modern psychology anachronistically and inappropriately on an ancient metaphor." Stiebert, *Fathers and Daughters in the Hebrew Bible*, 198.

23. It is debated as to what the spreading of the hem means and what it involves. The latter question is with respect to if the gesture involves sexual intercourse or not (Ruth 3:9 is often cited to support this). The verb בוא leaves room for ambiguity or double entendre as to what it involves. The question is whether sexual behavior can be attributed to YHWH in the Hebrew bible. For a discussion of views, see Sharon Moughtin-Mumby, *Sexual and Marital Metaphors in Hosea, Jeremiah, Isaiah, and Ezekiel* (Oxford: Oxford University Press, 2008), 172 n. 72. Also see Gile's comparison of the spreading of a hem/wing in Deuteronomy 32 with Ezekiel 16. For the former question, see Åke Viberg, "Covering a Woman with the Mantle," in *Symbols of Law: A Contextual Analysis of Legal Symbolic Acts in the Old Testament* (Sweden: Almqvist & Wiksell International, 1992); Karel van der Toorn, "The Significance of the Veil in the Ancient Near East," in *Pomegranates and Golden Bells: Studies in Biblical, Jewish, and Near Eastern Ritual, Law, and Literature in Honor of Jacob Milgrom*, ed. David P Wright, David Noel Freedom, and Avi Hurvitz (Winona Lake, IN: Eisenbrauns, 1995),

provision of garments is now his responsibility.[24] Tied to his name and as one under his authority, how YHWH dresses Jerusalem speaks volumes regarding what he is saying about himself in addition to the formation of Jerusalem's identity.

Only after verse 8 does immediate action occur in the form of cleansing, anointing, and the investiture of dress. In a series of actions over four verses (vv. 9–12) using nine *qal* and one *hiphil* rapid-fire verbs, YHWH does for Jerusalem that which was never done for her previously. There is an obvious sense of reversal and parallelism between verses 4–5 and 9–13. These verses describe Jerusalem's investiture: she is clothed, wrapped, and covered with three costly fabrics, furnished with fine leather sandals, adorned with copious amounts of jewelry, crowned, and bestowed with הדר, *hādār*, "splendor."

Several questions arise: What is the significance of the materials from which Jerusalem's dress items are made? Why are these materials used and not more common clothing-specific words? Is it significant that Jerusalem is adorned with a wide variety of jewelry? What does her crown signify? Given that Jerusalem flourishes to royalty in verse 13, does this mean she is dressed as a queen? What is the meaning and significance of הדר? What is the significance of YHWH's הדר *perfecting* Jerusalem's beauty? How does dress contribute to Jerusalem's new identity? And what is that identity? In short, what is the meaning and significance of Jerusalem's dress? And what does that mean about their relationship?

It should be stated that in considering Jerusalem's *investiture* we should always keep in mind her *divestiture* in verses 35–43. While the latter cannot be analyzed in this study due to space constraints, this tension should be held in the reader's mind as the study proceeds. Although Jerusalem is invested by YHWH with dress, she is later violently divested by YHWH, returning her to a state of nakedness. The purpose of divestiture is that YHWH would be known (v. 62) and Jerusalem would be shamed (v. 63).[25]

327–39. For a discussion of marriage as covenant, see Ka Leung Wong, *The Idea of Retribution in the Book of Ezekiel* (Leiden: Brill, 2001).

24. In Old Babylonian deeds of marriage, the acts of clothing the body and covering the head was the responsibility of the man. Van der Toorn writes: "It devolved upon the husband to provide his wife with such garments. By clothing and hatting her he was both fulfilling a matrimonial duty and exercising a husband's prerogative" ("Veil," 335).

25. The violence and divestiture of dress in Ezek. 16:15ff has been subject to numerous studies, the enormity of which cannot be focused on in the present study (my forthcoming work does address this imagery). Jerusalem's investiture itself is not without problem for some scholars. The following list is by no means exhaustive, but, for example, see: Moughtin-Mumby, *Marital Metaphors*; S. T. Kamionkowski, *Gender Reversal and Cosmic Chaos: A Study on the Book of Ezekiel*, JSOTSup 368 (Sheffield, England: Sheffield Academic Press, 2003); Julie Galambush, *Jerusalem in the Book of Ezekiel: The City as Yahweh's Wife*, SBL Dissertation Series, no. 130 (Atlanta, GA: Scholars, 1992); L. Day, "Rhetoric and Domestic Violence in Ezekiel 16," *BibInt* 8 (2000), 205–30; Shields, "Multiple Exposures;" K. P. Darr, "Ezekiel's Justification of God: Teaching Troubling Texts," *JSOT* 55 (1992), 97–117; J. C. Exum, "Prophetic Pornography," in *Plotted, Shot and Painted: Cultural Representations of Biblical*

Dressing Jerusalem: The Materials

Clothing

How and with what Jerusalem is clothed is not entirely clear. Jerusalem is not dressed in the typical terms such as בגד, *beged*, "garment," or שמלה, *simlāh*, "dress, mantle." Instead, Jerusalem is invested with either obscure materials or generic materials. The verbs used to describe her investiture are: לבש, *lābaš*, "to wear clothes;" נעל, *nāʿal*, "to sandal/furnish with shoes;" חבש, *ḥābaš*, "to wrap, bind;" and כסה, *kāsah*, "to cover, conceal." The first two verbs are by and large specific to dress, whereas the latter two are wider in their range of use. The more obscure materials used in conjunction with these verbs do not illuminate their use in

---

Women, JSOTSup 215, GCT 3 (Sheffield, England: Sheffield Academic Press, 1996), 101–28. The present study's focus on dress in verses 1–14 limits a developed discussion of these views. However, what I hope to show is that far from an exclusive need to control and possess Jerusalem, YHWH's investiture of dress differentiates her for a purpose among the nations. For a sample of studies that discuss divestiture of dress, which is by no means exhaustive, see: Shields, "Multiple Exposures;" Holly Morse, " 'Judgement Was Executed Upon Her, and She Became a Byword among Women' (Ezek. 23:10): Divine Revenge Porn, Slut-Shaming, Ethnicity, and Exile in Ezekiel 16 and 23," in *Women and Exilic Identity in the Hebrew Bible*, ed. Katherine E. Southwood and Martien A. Halvorson-Taylor (London: Bloomsbury, 2017), 129–54; Moughtin-Mumby, *Marital Metaphors*; Regina Weems, *Battered Love: Marriage, Sex, and Violence in the Hebrew Prophets* (Minneapolis, MA: Fortress, 1995); G.Corrington Streete, *The Strange Woman: Power and Sex in the Bible* (Louisville, KY: Westminster John Knox, 1997), 91–3; Carol J. Dempsey, "The 'Whore' of Ezekiel 16: The Impact and Ramifications of Gender-Specific Metaphors in Light of Biblical Law and Divine Judgment," in *Gender and Law in the Bible and the Ancient Near East*, ed. Victor Matthews, Bernard Levinson, and Tikva Frymer-Kensky (Sheffield, England: Sheffield Academic Press, 1998), 57–78; Daniel L. Smith-Christopher, "Ezekiel in Abu Ghraib: Rereading Ezekiel 16:37-39 in the Context of Imperial Conquest," in *Ezekiel's Hierarchical World: Wrestling with a Tiered Reality*, ed. Stephen L. Cook and Corrine L. Patton (Atlanta, GA: Society of Biblical Literature, 2004), 144–8; Peggy L. Day, "Adulterous Jerusalem's Imagined Demise: Death of a Metaphor in Ezekiel XVI," VT 50 (2000), 285–309; T. M. Lemos, "Physical Violence and the Boundaries of Personhood in the Hebrew Bible," *Hebrew Bible and Ancient Israel* 2 (2013), 500–31; Athalya Brenner, *The Intercourse of Knowledge: On Gendering Desire and "Sexuality" in the Hebrew Bible* (Leiden: Brill, 1997); Athalya Brenner, "On 'Jeremiah' and the Poetics of (Prophetic?) Pornography," in *On Gendering Texts: Female and Male Voices in the Hebrew Bible*, ed., Athalya Brenner and Fokkelien van Dijk-Hemmes (Leiden: Brill, 1993), 177–93; Fokkelien van Dijk-Hemmes, "The Metaphorization of Woman in Prophetic Speech: An Analysis of Ezekiel 23," in Brenner and van Dijk-Hemmes, *On Gendering Texts*, 167–76. Cf. the discussion of the stripping of corpses in 1 Sam. 31:8-10; Saul M. Olyan, "The Instrumental Dimensions of Ritual Violence against Corpses in Biblical Texts," in *Ritual Violence in the Hebrew Bible: New Perspectives*, ed. Saul M. Olyan (New York: Oxford University Press, 2015), 126–8.

significant ways. Comparative use of the terms in other passages in the Hebrew Bible will be the most helpful way to gain understanding of what the materials were, how they were used, and in what sorts of contexts.

As regards the first item of dress with which Jerusalem is clothed, רקמה, *riqmah*, is commonly translated as embroidered fabric or fabric of a variety of colors.[26] Based on Menahem Haran's work on the temple and temple service in which the term רקמה is included, a more fitting translation would be a fine mixed fabric without designs on it.[27] It is used eleven times in the Hebrew Bible as רקמה,[28] eight of which appear in Ezekiel. Three of these are in a lament for Tyre in chapter 27. There it is indicated that the fine mixed fabric is valuable and comes from Egypt (v. 7) and/or through exchange with Edom (v. 16). רקמה is also used in Ps. 45:15 of the princess' dress and in Judg. 5:30 as the booty desired by royal women.[29]

תחש, *tahaš*, is an obscure material used to sandal Jerusalem's feet. Understood as some sort of animal hide or leather, it is translated in a variety of ways: badger skins (KJV), sealskin (ASV), goatskin (RSV), porpoise skin (NASB and NEB), or sea cow hides (NIV). The last translation of sea cows is close to porpoise and is influenced by a potential connection to Arabic that has a similar word referring to a type of dolphin hide that was used to make sandals.[30] Another option that the NRSV uses is "fine leather," influenced by the Egyptian understanding of *ths*.[31]

Comparison of how תחש is used in the Hebrew Bible does not bring further clarity to Ezekiel 16. There are fourteen occurrences of תחש in the Hebrew Bible. Seven occur in Num. 4:6, 8, 10–12, 14, 25, all in reference to a covering made of תחש to spread over the ark of the covenant, the table of presence, the lampstand and its utensils, the gold altar, the utensils of service, and the tent of meeting. As for the purpose of תחש, it was to be used as a covering for the tent of the tabernacle, along with ram skins dyed red, as noted in Exod. 26:14, 36:19, and 39:34.

An article by Stephanie Dalley may bring insight into the meaning of תחש.[32] She traces the history of translation and conducts a cognate analysis of the word תחש in Akkadian, Sumerian, and Hurrian and shows that the common spelling of the equivalent for תחש in Akkadian was a late spelling in Babylonian, resulting from reductions of a weak root letter in the final syllable.[33] The change in spelling

---

26. Though Judg. 5:30 uses it in reference to mosaic stones. William L. Holladay, *A Concise Hebrew and Aramaic Lexicon of the Old Testament* (Grand Rapids, MI: Eerdmans, 1971), 347.

27. Haran's work was found in Carmen Joy Imes, *Bearing YHWH's Name at Sinai: A Reexamination of the Name Command of the Decalogue* (Pennsylvania, PA: Eisenbrauns, 2017), 155.

28. Ezek. 16:10, 13, 18; 17:3; 26:16; 27:7, 16, 24; Ps. 45:14; Judg. 5:30; 1 Chron. 29:2.

29. Zimmerli, *Ezekiel 1*, 340.

30. Ibid., 341.

31. Cf. תחש as dyed leather; see N. Kiuchi, "תַּחַשׁ," in *NIDOTTE* 4: 287.

32. Stephanie Dalley, "Hebrew *tahaš*, Akkadian *duhšu*, Faience and Beadwork," *Journal of Semitic Studies* 45 (2000), 1–19.

33. Ibid., 5.

identified the word as a Sumerian loanword in Akkadian from the Old Babylonian period, *duhšu*, and is originally Hurrian in origin.[34]

This provides new avenues of meaning. *Duhšu* was an unusual word and was often preceded by the sign for stone, leather, wool, or linen.[35] It denotes patterned beading and the attachment of pendants, inlaying of stones, metal, faience, and glass usually blue in color—not red as typically thought. It is usually done on leather but can also be done on wool, linen, or as a cloisonné in precious metals or wood. Dalley found from the various uses of *duhšu* in cuneiform texts along with excavated objects that it was used in a range of contexts.[36] One of these uses is of particular interest for this study. In the tomb of Tutankhamun leather beaded sandals were discovered and were "embellished with an intricate design of gold bosses and beadwork in carnelian, turquoise and possibly lapis lazuli."[37] The Amarna letter *EA 22* states that the Mittanian king requested "one pair of *duhšu*—shoes, studded with ornaments of gold," which Dalley interprets as this sort of beadwork. The letter would not only match the archeological evidence from Tutankhamun's tomb but also other beaded objects found in other excavations. Queen Puabi's tomb at Ur is one of these excavations. Her leather-based headdress was covered in lapis lazuli beads, which was contrasted with gold adornments.[38] There is further evidence of *duhšu* being used with carpets of multicolored patterns, with the color of the background of the beads traditionally being blue or turquoise.

Dalley concludes that the color and the surface effect of the patterned beading is accounted for in the LXX translation of the Hebrew as *huakinthinos*.[39] Furthermore, the covering of the tabernacle is said to be red-dyed skin or leather, which would set off blue or turquoise *duhšu* beading on the leather. The adornment of תחש sandals on Jerusalem finds parallels with the archeological evidence presented by Dalley from the tomb of Tutankhamun, along with the earlier analysis of the tombs of queens and the overabundance of beads found.[40]

---

34. A full account of Dalley's argument for the spelling changes can be found in ibid., 8–9.

35. Ibid., 6.

36. For example, it was used on the covering of royal boats, ceremonial necklaces and headdresses, luxury sandals, military items, and royal headrests (ibid., 12–16).

37. Ibid., 12.

38. Ibid.

39. With respect to the Greek translation of *huakinthos* and *huakinthinos* for תחש, a flower of this Greek name is said to have grown "from the blood of Ajax or the youth of Hyacinth." This is because the bulb of the flower is red. However, the flowers of the bulb are not red but are variable in color. Furthermore, Dalley notes that Theocritus says that the petals of these flowers are "inscribed," meaning "they were not plain but patterned." The patterned surface of the hyacinth flower, rather than its color, resembles a beaded surface. This relates to how *huakinthinos* is used in other texts to describe the fringes, selvedges, and coats of mail, showing a similar range of contexts as the Akkadian *duhšu*. Ibid., 12.

40. Ibid., 17.

However, an article by Benjamin J. Noonan questions Dalley's argument.[41] He disagrees with Dalley on account of her failure to adequately account for: the final û of the Akkadian *duhšû* and why Hebrew speakers would borrow an unusual dialect from Mari rather than a more common form found elsewhere. He further argues that she never adequately demonstrates that *duhšû* means "faience beadwork," stating that artifacts rarely come with self-identification, so the connection between the items excavated and terminology is tentative at best.[42] Noonan goes on to argue that the more likely etymology for תַחַשׁ is the Egyptian *ṯḥs*, a verb with reference to leather that Dalley "quickly" discounts. He goes on to compare the etymology of תַחַשׁ and the Egyptian *ṯḥs*, concluding that there are many associations made in the wilderness wandering texts that would support תַחַשׁ being "fine leather."

It remains inconclusive whether Dalley's suggestion of a Hurrian origin and Akkadian form of *duhšû* or Noonan's argument for an Egyptian origin can be certain. One thing to consider, though, is Jerusalem's Hittite and Amorite origins in Ezekiel 16 and whether this would influence how the term should be understood, perhaps answering Noonan's question from a literary standpoint as to why a more unusual dialect may be chosen.[43] Nevertheless, what can be concluded is that based on this evidence, תַחַשׁ in Ezekiel 16 is best rendered as luxury fine leather sandals, potentially with decorative beading. Such luxurious sandals are a privileged good of royalty and nobility. In the context of Ezekiel 16 and the statement in verse 13b that Jerusalem flourishes to become royalty, the archeological evidence presented by Dalley is appropriate to be considered in the context of Jerusalem's sandals.[44] These are shoes worn by those who do not have to do manual labor, work, or walk great distances.[45] They are a marker of distinction.

The next verb and the material listed in Ezekiel 16 are more peculiar in what they together signify: wrapping with שֵׁשׁ, *šēš*. שֵׁשׁ appears thirty-seven times in the Hebrew Bible, thirty of which are in Exodus in the priestly vestments and tabernacle descriptions. The tunic, turban, ephod, breast piece, and sash all use שֵׁשׁ in their construction. Various tabernacle and sanctuary curtains use שֵׁשׁ as well. Est. 1:6 uses it in the description of the grandeur of the king's palace and in Gen. 41:42 when Pharaoh clothes Joseph in fine linen. In Ezekiel 16, some state that wrapping with שֵׁשׁ refers to a head covering, as this is one way שֵׁשׁ is used in the priestly vestments.[46] However, שֵׁשׁ is also used of the priests' ephod

41. Benjamin J. Noonan, "Hide or Hue? Defining Hebrew תַחַשׁ," *Bib* 93 (2012), 580–9.

42. Ibid., 585.

43. Conversely, if the Pentateuch, whether in part or whole, is thought to have a historical basis, then an Egyptian origin must be weighed carefully.

44. I say consider since the evidence does not necessarily have to be conclusive. If תַחַשׁ is of Egyptian origins, it does not mean that sandals could not be decorated for royalty, whether by beading or other means.

45. Cf. Joachim J. Krause, "Barefoot before God: Shoes and Sacred Space in the Hebrew Bible and Ancient Near East," in Berner et al., 315–22.

46. For example, see Greenberg, *Ezekiel: 1-20*, 278.

and tunic. It may be redundant to treat the wrapping of שׁשׁ as a headpiece, since a crown is mentioned in verse 12. Another possibility is that it may be linen wrapped around the body—which is suggested by the summary statement in verse 13a that states Jerusalem's *clothing* was made of three materials, including fine linen.

While the wrapping of newborns was a common practice, as well as the wrapping of the dead, wrapping of the living is a question to be explored. Archeologist Janet Johnstone describes New Kingdom wrap dresses.[47] She observed a change in the style of dress during the reigns of Tuthmosis IV and Amenhotep II as the Egyptian empire expanded, reflecting the sociopolitical and religious changes.[48] Her research notes that the finest Egyptian linen was intricately wrapped, folded, and pleated on the women, serving as a canvas for the other adornments. Johnstone's research involved creating reconstructions of the wrap dress. In her dressing the models who wore them, she states that the dress alone, even though of the finest linen available, had "little visual impact." It was only when the women were fully dressed—including jewelry, accessories, and sandals—that the full effect was realized.[49] Put simply, the sum was greater than the parts.

It appears that both שׁשׁ and רקמה are fabrics of high quality and luxurious nature and were used in clothing construction. Though costly and opulent, both materials would serve as blank canvases for Jerusalem's jewelry.[50]

The final article in verse 10 is מֶשִׁי, *mešî*, and is traditionally translated as silk. While silk and imported products were often used to signal wealth and status by the rich and elite,[51] the only two occurrences of this word in the Hebrew Bible are in Ezek. 16:10 and 13. It is doubtful whether silk would have been known in Western Asia in the sixth century BCE.[52] It is difficult to reach conclusions about the nature of the material מֶשִׁי or in what way it is being used to cover Jerusalem. In the context of the investiture it is usually understood as a "costly material." The cumulative effect of the fabrics for Jerusalem seem to create a feel of refinement and luxury.

---

47. Janet M. Johnstone, "Wrapping and Tying Ancient Egyptian New Kingdom Dresses," in *Wrapping and Unwrapping Material Culture: Archaeological and Anthropological Perspectives*, ed. Susanna Harris and Laurence Douny (Walnut Creek, CA: Left Coast, 2014), 59–82.

48. Ibid., 59.

49. Ibid., 79.

50. The adornment of clothing can be seen in 2 Sam. 1:24. In David's poetic lament over Saul and Jonathan he says that Saul gave clothing and jewelry to the daughters of Israel and put gold jewelry on their clothes.

51. John Pilch and Bruce Malina, *Handbook of Biblical Social Values* (Peabody, MA: Hendrickson, 1993), 20.

52. See Greenberg, *Ezekiel: 1–20*, 278–9; or Block, *Ezekiel: 1–24*, 484.

Jewelry

The adornment of jewelry in Ezekiel 16 includes bracelets, a necklace, nose rings, and earrings. Taking all Jerusalem's jewelry together, her adornment is extensive, with virtually all her surfaces covered in gold and silver (v. 13a).[53] The mention of *all* of these jewelry items displays the extraordinary lengths taken to bedazzle Jerusalem. No generalities can do justice to Ezekiel's purpose in creating an image of Jerusalem that would bring astonishment.[54]

Jerusalem's bedazzlement peaks in verse 12, where a beautiful crown, תפארת עטרת, *'ăṭeret̲ tip̲'eret̲*, is placed on her head. The most honorable part of the body was the head, which must be honored by wearing appropriate gear.[55] It should go without saying that crowns can indicate royal status[56] and both men and women of high status wore crowns.[57] In the Hebrew Bible, עטרת occurs twenty-three times. The majority of these occurrences are in poetic and prophetic literature; other occurrences are one time each in 1 Chronicles, Esther, and 2 Samuel. עטרת is largely used metaphorically, being related to honor, beauty, or the prestige of people of royalty or noble status. The context determines if these attributes are gained by the crown being set on someone or lost by its removal.

Considering all the dress items together, nothing is spared in luxury or cost in dressing Jerusalem: from the top of her head to the bottoms of her feet she is adorned in dress of highest quality. She is clothed, wrapped, and covered in a fine mixed fabric, fine linen, and a costly fabric. Her feet are furnished with luxury leather sandals that are potentially beaded in a style similar to ancient kings and queens. These high-quality fabrics may be intricately wrapped and folded around her. They serve as a blank canvas for the copious adornment of jewelry

---

53. For a discussion of gold and silver relating to the sun and moon (or deities), see Brady Beard's chapter, "What to Look For in a Headdress: פאר and תפארה in Material Culture and Iconography Significance and Signification," in this volume.

54. Cf. the function of ornamentation/jewelry in Proverbs: Stefan Fischer, "Women's Dress Codes in the Book of Proverbs," in Berner et al., 543–56.

55. Pilch and Malina, *Biblical Values*, 21. Cf. Brady Beard's chapter on פאר in this volume. Also see Job 19:9, which uses a crown as a metaphor for his honor.

56. Archeological evidence from: the late Assyrian period in the palace of Assurnasirpal II (883–859 BCE) in Nimrud, a painting of King Tiglath Pileser III in the palace at Til Barsip (745–705 BCE), a depiction of Khorsabad of Sargon II (721–705 BCE), and reliefs of Sennacherib's grandson, Assurbanipal, in Neneveh (668–631 BCE) *all* depict their respective kings in elaborate, decorated, and beautiful crowns. See Guralnick, "Fabric Patterns as Symbols of Status in the Near East and Early Greece," in Colburn and Heyn, *Reading a Dynamic Canvas*, 84–114.

57. A discovery at Ur in Mesopotamia of the grave of a queen dating from around 3500 BCE was found wearing an elaborate royal tiara. It was a broad golden circlet and was placed on the head like a garland. Three wreaths surrounded it: of gold rings, beech leaves, and willow leaves. See R. Broby-Johansen, *Body and Clothes: An Illustrated History of Costume*, trans. Erik I. Friss and Karen Rush (New York: Reinhold Book, 1968), 41.

that follows. Her clothes and jewelry set her apart as someone to be noticed. The nature of the dress items listed in verses 9–13 seem to indicate that Jerusalem is dressed as royalty, transforming her during her liminal status into a queen, with her royal status stated explicitly as the outcome in verse 13b.

That Jerusalem's dress is of queenly nature finds support in further archeological remains. A recent article by Amy Gansell presents the findings from a newly discovered section of the harem quarters of the Northwest Palace at Nimrud, dating to around the eighth century BCE,[58] what has been termed the "Queens' Tombs," as the women have been confirmed as Neo-Assyrian queens. The tombs contained an abundance of golden items, namely vessels and elaborate headdresses, earrings, necklaces, bracelets, rings, and anklets.[59] Based on her observations of the material remains, Gansell argues that the dress supports the identification of distinctly "queen dress" items that functioned to "transform the canvas of the body 'into a picture,' … that visually and conceptually fuses flesh and dress into a new entity."[60] That is, the fusion of body and dress created the identity of "queen." Gansell adds that dress empowered the queens' imperial agency by being both aesthetic and also a sociopolitical construct, thereby securing the status and identity of Neo-Assyrian queens.[61]

The two queens from Tomb II were richly adorned, having hundreds of earrings, numerous necklaces, gold collars and torques, rings, and bracelets. There were two gold headdresses found, one with a three-tiered circle of gold rosettes, the other a diadem woven from gold wire. Fabric remnants were also found, including embroidered dresses, shawls, sheets, and shrouds. The tomb contained over two thousand gold appliques and various ornaments such as rosettes, enough to cover two garments with roughly eight hundred appliques per garment.

Gansell surmises that the scope of the items from the tombs suggests a 360-degree adornment from head to foot, with some incorporated moveable parts that would have reflected light or jingled when the living wearer moved. The typically queenly burial ensemble includes: a headdress, earrings, at least one necklace/torque/collar, beads, bracelets, rings, anklets, fibulas, seals with chains, and a highly ornamented garment. Gansell notes that the effect of the whole—all the lavish elements of queenly regalia—conveys the queen's identity.

As to the effect of the royal dress, Gansell states that it transformed the living *and* the dead into "ideal queens by activating, maintaining, and expressing attributes of feminine beauty, including sexuality, fertility, and purity, that undergirded and were reinforced by their divinely sanctioned power."[62] Dress not only displayed

---

58. Amy R. Gansell, "Dressing the Neo-Assyrian Queen in Identity and Ideology: Elements and Ensembles from the Royal Tombs at Nimrud," *American Journal of Archaeology* 122 (2018), 65–100.

59. Ibid., 66.

60. Ibid., 68.

61. Ibid., 68–9.

62. Ibid., 86.

identity but also construed, activated, and maintained it. This identity-forming power of dress was carried over to the "stratified domain of the netherworld" to serve as *the* vehicle for the continued maintenance of the queen's identity in eternity.[63] The raid of tombs and theft of jewels of royalty was thus "stealing the deceased's courtly, queenly, and personal identity."[64]

Furthermore, Colburn and Heyn make several points about royal dress based on archeological findings. First, dress was a means of social differentiation, especially with the ruling king, and was regulated by law.[65] Yet within this material stratification overlapping of identities is evident: motifs that appeared on the king's garments that communicated his elevated status *also appeared* on his children and the queen's garments, which shows the complexity of identity construction.[66] While Ezekiel 16 does not state that YHWH wears garments,[67] the idea that Jerusalem's dress could represent YHWH's own (higher) authority should be considered since YHWH *invested dress* upon Jerusalem.

Gansell's findings of the typical queenly ensemble are similar to Jerusalem's investiture: the nature and composition of the various costly fabrics, the large assortment of jewelry, and the crown; the only items missing from the list in Ezekiel 16 are fibulas, rings, anklets, and a seal. However, the mention of fine leather shoes can be considered alongside anklets as a lavish adornment of the foot.

The Function of Dress

As stated in the findings above, royal dress best achieved its function to reflect the wealth, status, aesthetic, and honor of royalty when all the pieces were in place: the total effect of the queen's regalia would be a sparkling, mesmerizing, inspiring, and beatific vision of one in power and with privilege. Royal dress was the vehicle to *maintain* this identity and the substance of the beatific vision. The queen was only the queen when wearing her queenly regalia.[68] In view of Ezekiel 16, the same is true. Viewed separately, none of the items of Jerusalem's adornment are forcibly convincing. Viewed together, Jerusalem's appearance is transformed from head to

---

63. Ibid., 87.

64. Ibid., 91.

65. Colburn and Heyn, *Dynamic Canvas*, 4, 6.

66. Ibid., 6.

67. The Hebrew Bible is sparse in descriptions of YHWH's garments, a peculiarity for the ANE. For a discussion of why this may be, see Ehud Ben Zvi, "Were YHWH's Clothes Worth Remembering in LPEH Yehud?" in *Dress and Clothing in the Hebrew Bible: "For All Her Household Is Clothed in Crimson,"* ed. Antonios Finitsis (New York: T&T Clark, 2019), 161–81.

68. Cf. Selena Billington's chapter, "Social Standing, Agency, and the Motif of Cloth and Clothing in Esther," on the cloth motif in Esther, including queenly dress, in this volume.

toe. When it is later removed, she will return to a liminal state in which her status will be drastically reduced.

Colburn and Heyn's observation that the identity created, maintained, and empowered by the dress of a king was also reflected in the dress of those associated with him, such as the queen or his children, is demonstrative of part of the *role* and a *function* of queens: to represent the king—his power, wealth, honor as a splendorous display of beauty and elite status.[69] Herein lies an important point for Ezekiel 16. Prior to YHWH's passing by in verses 6f, Jerusalem is naked and exposed, on the verge of death—the opposite to any sort of elite or royal status. Heather A. McKay has suggested that an important function of dress is to *enhance*.[70] It can enhance something that is good and declare it to be more—excellent or notable. It can also cover up something that is inferior or unpleasant or make a perceived deficiency 'good."[71] According to McKay, dress not only functions symbolically to convey goodness or excellence but also effectively or literally can transform something that is deficient into something that is good. There are questions, however, of the permanency of the goodness or excellence achieved by dress. Does its transformation of a human body into something good remain as such if the dress is removed? Or is it that so long as the dress is adorned the human person becomes more than what they are? Keeping these questions in mind, McKay's point is important for Ezekiel 16, as the origins and early life of foundling Jerusalem are, to the ancient Israelite, most unpleasant and undesirable. YHWH's act of investiture of dress should thus be considered as a means to make a perceived deficiency "good." Furthermore, the dress invested upon her can function as a determinative of the good actions that *should* come forth from Jerusalem. This means that actions are derivative from the identity, role, and function constituted in dress, rather than from gratitude.

69. Gansell describes that part of the role of the Neo-Assyrian *sēgallu*—queen—was to hold the office of the ceremonial partner of the king. She also notes this role even in death. Neo-Assyrian burial sites often typically buried men and women together or near one another, signifying the importance of the queens remaining "physically" on-site near their residence, "as representatives of the imperial household." See Gansell, "Neo-Assyrian Queen," 75. Also, this idea is seen in Esther when Queen Vashti is summoned by the king to wear her royal high turban and display her beauty, which, in the context of the chapter, was ultimately a display of the "riches of *his* royal glory and the splendour of *his* majestic greatness." See Est. 1:4, 10–12.

70. Cf. McKay's chapter, "Dress Deployed as an Agent of Deception in Hebrew Bible Narratives," in this volume, which examines both the various functions of dress in the Hebrew Bible and how the distortion of one of those functions renders dress a constituent of deception.

71. One's function as a good person or a bad person can be influenced by dress. That is, good or bad actions can flow from and be determined by dress that has made one good or enhanced one's goodness. McKay, "Gendering the Discourse," in *On Reading Prophetic Texts*, ed. BobBecking and Meindert Dijkstra (Leiden: Brill, 1996), 169.

McKay also highlights the relationship between decency, nakedness, shame, and dress in the Hebrew Bible. In a society where nakedness has largely negative connotations,[72] dress becomes a driving force "among the wise and godly."[73] The removal of dress would expose nakedness and cause shame. The removal of dress was therefore often used as a tool of punishment and of social and behavioral control, particularly of women.[74] McKay identifies many narratives in the Hebrew Bible where a lack of decency leads to shame. This often happens in the context of love, lust, sex, and sexuality in relation to dress or lack thereof. The resulting disruption of the social order is often blamed "on the stimulating beauty, and practised charms, of the one desired—usually a female. And the best way to prevent the disruption is for the female to be invisible."[75] Beauty is enhanced by dress, perfume, and hairstyle; it is also considered a precursor to desire or lust. Consequently, women were covered up: garments and veils created physical barriers to any beauty that could stimulate desire or lust in the eyes of the beholder. McKay writes, "Here dress has a mainly *interposing* function; it is a barrier to gaze and a barrier to [sexual] action."[76]

The concealment of female beauty as a means of protection against lust and sex is crucial to Ezekiel 16 and yet is peculiar in two respects. First, YHWH's act of investiture *makes* Jerusalem *extremely beautiful*. He does not conceal her with dress as a prohibitive function. Instead, he adorns her in an extravagant manner, making her notably beautiful. Second, the text speaks of the lust and desire *of Jerusalem*, not her perceivers. Jerusalem trusts in her own beauty and then plays the harlot with her idols and foreign nations, never satisfying her own desires. Furthermore, YHWH's act of divestiture results in the exposure of Jerusalem's nakedness (vv. 35–43), an act that is in response to Jerusalem's conduct; later it is stated that, as a result of YHWH's act, Jerusalem finally experiences shame.

Crucial to consider is that Jerusalem's investiture of dress transforms her from a destitute, despised pagan outcast to a beautiful queen only after YHWH initiates a covenant with her in verse 8. YHWH's actions can in one sense appear delayed until their appearance in verse 8. Nevertheless, they highlight the emerging relationship. It is only when YHWH is her husband is she adorned and flourishes to a royal status. Daniel Block states that Jerusalem attains the status of a monarch through YHWH's lavish investiture of the "treasures and culinary fare" of royalty on her.[77] Presumably then, if dressed by her husband as royalty,

---

72. See Jürgen van Oorschot, "Nudity and Clothing in the Hebrew Bible: Theological and Anthropological Aspects," in Berner et al., 240–1. Van Oorschot states that nakedness in Ezekiel 16 is both vulnerability and degradation (242).

73. McKay, "Gendering the Discourse," 190.

74. Ibid., 191.

75. Ibid., 193. For various examples, see Abram and Sarai, David and Bathsheba.

76. Ibid.; original emphasis.

77. Block, *Chebar*, 12, n. 7.

Jerusalem is queen. Consequently, YHWH is king,[78] and therefore, part of her role is to represent YHWH.

A Holy Veneer

The idea of Jerusalem's royal regalia signifying her representative role is further supported by way of comparison with the priestly regalia.[79] It cannot be coincidental that many of the materials—the fine mixed fabric, fine linen, fine leather, and gold and silver—used to clothe Jerusalem are also used in the tabernacle, curtains, and priestly vestment descriptions.[80] These allusions are not necessarily unusual for Ezekiel and his well-known priestly concerns seen throughout his book. The priestly vestments and tabernacle curtains served as a source of mediation between YHWH and the people. They were to represent and reflect the name, glory, and beauty of YHWH to the people in the outer areas of the temple complex. The curtains and the priests' dress not only signified their status to the people but also what constituted the priests ability to fulfill their role—purity and forgiveness was at stake and any violation of the building and construction of these items, or improper investiture or conduct in them, would result in death.[81] There were similar observations made about royal dress: that it was the royal dress that made bodies royal—that is, dress constituted and maintained an identity as "royal" and had an empowering function.[82]

However, the priestly vestments' purpose was to enable the priest to fulfill his role as mediator between the human and divine. In this sense the priestly vestments are dissimilar to royal dress. The commonality is the idea of representation. In a similar way, though not in a mediatory function, the queen represents the power, beauty, and glory of royalty, namely the king, in her lavish dress in the sight of others.

I suggest that the luxurious royal dress of Jerusalem is overlaid with a priestly veneer, the connecting points of which are the materials and the idea of

---

78. Ibid. Block notes that, overall, Ezekiel suppresses the memory of Israel's monarchy. However, when royal language occurs in the book, YHWH is the king. Such is the case in Ezek. 16:10-14, which is directly referenced by Block.

79. Also see Carmen Imes's chapter, "Between Two Worlds: The Functional and Symbolic Significance of the High Priestly Regalia," in Finitsis, *Dress and Clothing*, 29–62.

80. Exod. 25:5; 26:14, 36; 27:16; 28:39; 35:7, 23, 35; 36:37; 38:18; 39:29. See Block, *Ezekiel 1–24*, 485-6.

81. See Exod. 20:26 and 28:42. The latter passage states that the priest will die if his nakedness is exposed while serving as priest.

82. Cf. Ellena Lyell's chapter, "Dressing Benjaminites, Defining Kingship: Dress as a Royal Prerogative for the Tribe of Benjamin," in this volume on the garment motif used to trace Benjamite heritage, including its function in the ascension to the right to royal authority as well as its downfall.

representation. The overlapping images of royalty and queenly status, costly fabrics and jewelry, priest and tabernacle are important to view together—apart, they are interesting but not necessarily convincing. Rather, it is only after the *full* investiture of dress that verses 13b–14 speak of beauty, fame, and splendor before the watching nations. It is only when the individual pieces are viewed *together* that Jerusalem is perceived as the extreme opposite of her beginnings. Indeed, only after five and half verses of adornment does Jerusalem's transformation reach its culmination. Transformation through dress is in service of representation, an idea that is captured in YHWH's bestowal of his הדר.

The Bestowal of הדר

The culmination of Jerusalem's identity transformation is most clearly signified in her extreme beauty, which is the result of YHWH's bestowal of his הדר. הדר appears thirty-one times in the Hebrew Bible.[83] The expression הוד והדר, "majesty and splendor," appears six times in the Hebrew Bible:

1. 1 Chron. 16:27—1 Chronicles contains a psalm of exaltation and praise and says that הוד והדר emanates (לפניו) from YHWH, creating a sense of a visual encounter with YHWH's הוד והדר.
2. Ps. 96:6—The psalmist praises YHWH and tells the nations of his greatness. After stating that YHWH is worthy of praise, verse 6 creates the same visual appeal as 1 Chronicles 16 by using the same phrase הוד והדר לפניו, "majesty and splendor emanate from him [YHWH]."
3. Ps. 104:1—The opening line of the psalm first states the greatness of YHWH. Then, instead of הוד והדר *emanating* from YHWH, he is instead *clothed* (לבשת) with it.
4. Ps. 111:3—The psalmist uses the expression in reference to the works of YHWH, saying הוד והדר פעלו, "His work [is] majestic and splendorous."
5. Ps. 21:6—Verses 1–5 speak of the various gifts given to the king by YHWH. The first half of verse 6 states that YHWH's deliverance gives great honor to the king, followed by הוד והדר תשוה עליו, "majesty and splendor you [YHWH] place upon him [king]."
6. Job 40:10—In YHWH's second speech to Job he challenges him saying that if he is like YHWH then Job is to *adorn himself* with majesty and excellence, and to הוד והדר תלבש, "*clothe himself* with majesty and splendor."

These examples demonstrate that הדר concentrates around physical manifestations of splendor:[84] it emanates from YHWH, he is clothed in it, he sets it upon the king,

---

83. G. Warmuth, "הדר *hādhār*," in *TDOT* 3: 336.

84. This observation was first highlighted by Daniel Wu in *Honor, Shame, and Guilt: Social-Scientific Approaches to the Book of Ezekiel* (Winona Lake, IN: Eisenbrauns, 2016), 91–2.

and he challenges Job to clothe himself in it. The physical manifestations of הדר are also seen in the following:

1. Psalm 8—The psalmist marvels over YHWH's creation and gives praise to him for it, climaxing in verse 6, which expresses astonishment that YHWH notices humankind and that וכבוד והדר תעטרהו, "with glory and splendor you crowned [them]."
2. Ps. 45:5—The psalmist states a warrior *appears* in הדר.
3. Ps. 145:5—הדר, הוד, and כבוד are some of the objects of the psalmist's meditation.
4. Prov. 31:25—Personified wisdom is said to be *clothed* in הדר.
5. Isa. 35:1-2—In a description of a time of transformation, the desert wilderness is given the כבוד of Lebanon and the הדר of Carmel and Sharon, with the result that יראו כבוד יהוה הדר אלהינו, "they will *see* the glory of YHWH, the splendor of our God."
6. Isa. 53:2—The suffering servant is described as having *no* stately form, no הדר that would be looked at, and no special appearance.
7. Lam. 1:6—The הדר of Daughter Zion is said to have departed from her: הדרה ויצא מן בת ציון כל.
8. Ezek. 27:10—The men of Persia, Lud, and Put are drafted into Tyre's army, who then hang on Tyre a shield and helmet followed by נתנו הדרך, "they gave [you] your splendor."[85]

To summarize, הדר is used in relation to YHWH as a sign of royal dignity or as the dress he puts on. Furthermore, the works of creation attest to YHWH's הדר: they give reason to praise him and summon the nations to give YHWH honor and worship. It is also used for YHWH's mighty deeds in the history of Israel. When describing earthly kings, הדר is a divine gift placed upon him. In relation to humankind, הדר is a gift, often from YHWH, that enhances human appearance and is removable. For the purposes of this study it should be highlighted that הדר is often used in metaphorical constructions that express הדר as being placed on or clothing someone and results in an enhanced appearance. Moreover, it not only elevates the one adorned but is also related to and expresses the splendor of the one represented, most often YHWH.

---

85. There are further similarities between Ezekiel 27 and Ezekiel 16. Ezekiel 27, a lament for Tyre, is a nautical-themed metaphorical description of the downfall, or sinking, of Tyre. It opens with Tyre saying about herself (v. 3), אני כלילת יפי, "I am perfectly beautiful." Verses 4–11 describe the building of Tyre as a ship, with numerous war and nautical metaphors for how and of what material she is constructed. Verse 11 repeats the statement of verse 3 but this time states that "they," meaning Tyre's builders, have perfected her beauty. "Perfected beauty" is the same phrase used in Ezekiel 16, yet with the key difference that YHWH has perfected Jerusalem's beauty by setting *his* הדר on her.

Turning to YHWH's act of investiture in Ezekiel 16, it is clear that the climax and explanation for Jerusalem's beauty, royalty, and name is the הדר of YHWH. He has set his splendor upon her; in so doing he has enhanced her to the status and fame that she now holds. The splendorous effect of YHWH's הדר has several elements that contribute to Jerusalem's new status and should be discussed in order to better understand the effect of YHWH's הדר.

It should first be recalled that a result of YHWH's act of investiture is expressed in verse 13b. Jerusalem became *extremely* (במאד מאד) beautiful, attaining royal status. The extreme beauty and royalty of Jerusalem stands in stark contrast to the account of her birth and origins where she was despised and not treated with the compassion expected for an infant. YHWH's investiture has transformed her from bloody and abandoned to beautiful and admired.

Jerusalem's extreme beauty in verse 13b is expanded and explained by verse 14—Jerusalem's beauty is so extreme that it causes her name to go out among the nations and can only be attributed to the הדר of YHWH, which is said to "perfect" (כליל) her beauty. This is an important point intertextually that reveals more about who Jerusalem is and the role she has in relation to YHWH's הדר. The reputation of Jerusalem's perfect beauty and her wearing of YHWH's splendor among Israel and the nations is not unique to Ezekiel but appears elsewhere in the Hebrew Bible[86] and suggests that Jerusalem was, or came to be, widely known as a place of splendor and elevated or *perfected* beauty. Jerusalem's splendor and beauty are arguably part of her role and function in relation to YHWH: she was meant to be visually glorious as the dwelling place of YHWH and his name, glory, and honor.

It is worth returning to the sequence of Jerusalem's investiture at this point. YHWH's actions toward the foundling begin in verse 6, with the formation of a covenant in verse 8. It was noted earlier that it was only after the covenant was ratified that Jerusalem's investiture began. The difference and directionality between covenant to investiture, splendor, and fame can be compared to Deut. 26:19.

Jerusalem's name/fame (v. 14) has been mentioned as a result of the investiture but has not yet been addressed explicitly. In considering the conditionality and representative nature of Jerusalem's investiture, a question to be explored is whether this is Jerusalem's name or in fact is YHWH's. Carmen Imes's book proves helpful in exploring this.[87]

In the final chapter of her book Imes explores Israel's role among the nations. Deuteronomy develops this more fully, calling Israel special, treasured, and holy among the nations.[88] Imes's discussion of Deut. 26:18-19 is of particular interest. It is worth quoting in full her comments on these verses:

---

86. See Cant. 6:4; Pss. 27:4, 48:1-4, 50:1-2, 68:28-29, 102:16-17; Lam. 1:1, 4, 6-8; 2:14-15; Isa. 52:1, 60, 62:1-3.

87. Imes, *Bearing YHWH*.

88. Deut. 10:15; Imes, *Bearing YHWH*, 177.

> In this declarative speech act, YHWH appointed a new generation as his treasured vassal <u>so that the nations would see Israel and honor YHWH</u> (Cf. Deut. 4:6-8; 28:1). The performative or perlocutionary dimension of YHWH's statement, signalled by the *hiphil* form of אמר, enacted the appointment of a new generation of Israelites as his vassal. Deuteronomy described these intentions for Israel using three vivid words: "And he will set you high over all the nations that he has made, for *praise*, for a *name*, and for *splendor*" [לתהלה ולשם ולתפארת; v. 19]. Like the high priestly garments, designed "for glory and splendour" (לכבוד ולתפארת; Exod. 28:2, 40), so <u>Israel's obedience would be like a splendid garment, inspiring the admiration of all the nations</u>. The echoes of these lexemes from the instructions regarding the high priest underscore Israel's role as a kingdom of priests, bearing YHWH's name among the nations just as the high priest bore YHWH's name among his people. To honor him by keeping covenant would paradoxically result in their own fame as well.[89]

Imes's detailed analysis bears similarities to Ezekiel 16. While lexically there is only one word that overlaps directly with verses 13b–14, שֵׁם, the themes are similar between the two passages.[90] The similarities between the passages come forth not in the individual parts but in the final outcome of each passage. According to Imes, Israel itself was to be a "splendid garment" creating a name for itself by representing YHWH through their obedience in the sight of the nations, in a manner similar to the priestly vestments. In Ezekiel 16 YHWH's investiture of dress has resulted in a transformation of identity and appearance. The total effect of YHWH's act of investiture is a physical splendor that has enhanced Jerusalem such that she is the object of admiration causing *her* name to go out among the nations. Moreover, the sequence of covenant formation then glorification is similar between the passages as well.

   In light of the foregoing analysis of הדר, in Ezekiel 16 YHWH's הדר is arguably the final thing YHWH invests, or bestows, upon Jerusalem: it both enhances her appearance, thereby causing her *perfect* beauty, and also reflects YHWH, as it is *his* הדר, which is conditioned by relationship between Jerusalem and YHWH. Not only is Jerusalem dressed in a manner that she could never have achieved on her own. Furthermore YHWH's dressing actions keep enhancing her status leading to the coronation. YHWH's הדר transforms her so that her appearance is splendorous and her name gains fame. Queen Jerusalem is meant to be the holy representative of YHWH, as her perfect beauty and physical splendor are seen by the nations.

---

89. Ibid., 178; underline mine, italics original.

90. It is worth noting that תפארת appears in Deut. 26:19, Ezek. 16:12, and Exod. 28:2, 40, with the passages in Ezekiel and Exodus both referring to the appearance of dress items.

Conclusion

Taken as a whole, verses 13b–14 reveal Jerusalem's role: He has adorned her in the most lavish of ways to make her a sight worth looking at, as the "object of admiring gazes."[91] Viewed together, Jerusalem's extravagant dress and status displays her extreme beauty and royalty: she is dressed like a queen and would be admired as such. Yet, *associations* with the priestly vestments and tabernacle materials evoke a "holy" allusion, creating *expectations* incumbent upon Jerusalem in terms of her role, function, and behavior—the dress has a limiting effect as much as an empowering one. Just as the luxurious, beautiful, and abundant *dress* of ancient royalty *constitutes* the identity of the queen as queen, *empowers* her for her queenly roles, and *conveys* this to her onlookers, so, too, the dress of Jerusalem functions like the royal dress of queens. She is to be *noticed* and *empowered* by her dress; this is confirmed in verse 14. Yet, while her queenly dress constitutes her royal identity, the allusion to priestly garments ties her in a more particular way to YHWH as his holy representative. Dress has thus served as a differentiating choice with an intended result: she represents his glory and beauty as his holy and splendorous ambassador.[92]

---

91. Galambush, *Jerusalem*, 105.

92. A question to be asked is whether YHWH's investiture of dress upon Jerusalem bears resemblance to the royal (not divine) statuary of Mesopotamia. Irene J. Winter describes the sculptural images of rulers that were "subject to complex rituals of consecration, installation, and maintenance" as to be "living manifestations, empowered to act and speak on a ruler's behalf." Irene J. Winter, "'Idols of the King': Royal Images as Recipients of Ritual Action in Ancient Mesopotamia," *Journal of Ritual Studies* 6 (1992), 21–4; on 13. They were placed in a particular place, often temple sanctuaries or in funerary chapels, were inscribed with the name of the deity they belonged to, and were fed and adorned. These actions bear similarity to those that YHWH does for Jerusalem. The difference lies in that YHWH, a deity, is the one adorning and feeding a human that now belongs to him through a relationship for a royal and representative function. It is interesting to note that in the ritual of making/consecration, there is an incantation that was to be recited in the ritual that went as follows: "Sacred/pure image [alam.ku] *perfected* by a great ritual," which Winters states emphasizes the completion of the image in the ritual. While not overtly similar, the overlap with Ezekiel 16 and Jerusalem's perfect beauty is interesting.

Chapter 10

CODED CRITIQUE, VALIDATING VESTMENTS: JOSHUA'S GARMENTS IN ZECHARIAH 3

Jennifer Brown Jones

The night visions of Zechariah 1–6 include a dense web of intertextual references to other biblical texts, a point that is particularly relevant for the vision of the high priest Joshua's purification in Zechariah 3. Here, the Hebrew tradent evokes the rituals of Exodus and Leviticus but then draws on Isaianic language to describe Joshua's clothing. This lexical choice has contributed to various interpretations of the fourth night vision and of the wider Zecharian material, interpretations that the current discussion seeks to evaluate.

When Zechariah 3 opens, the high priest Joshua is standing in the divine council before a messenger of the Lord and an accuser.[1] Following YHWH's rebuke of the accuser, the messenger instructs other members of the divine council to remove Joshua's "filthy" clothing, stating that his sin has been removed and that the messenger will clothe the high priest with new garments. Next, Zechariah states that a turban should be placed on the high priest's head. Joshua is then dressed in the turban and garments and warned by the messenger.[2] He is also told that his human associates are a sign, that God will send his "Branch" or "Sprout" (צמח, ṣmḥ), and that YHWH will remove the land's iniquity in one day. While this basic outline glosses over many of the interpretive questions that arise in reading the vision, it lays a foundation for the topic at hand, which is how Joshua's dress influences the interpretation of the passage.

To address the significance of the priestly garments, the discussion below opens with a detailed examination of the lexical descriptions of Joshua's new garments,

I am deeply indebted to the Pacific Northwest Regional AAR/SBL's Research Group on Clothing in the Hebrew Bible for their feedback and suggestions for developing this research, particularly to Brady Beard, Antonios Finitsis, Carmen Joy Imes, and Scott Starbuck. Any shortcomings are, of course, my own.

1. The presence of the definite article makes it unlikely that this accuser is the New Testament "Satan." Cf. Paul Joüon and T. Muraoka, *A Grammar of Biblical Hebrew* (Roma: Pontificio Istituto Biblico, 2006), §137b.

2. See the discussion below about whether the messenger warns or assures Joshua.

their key intertextual references, and the differing interpretations. Having outlined the interpretive issues, the analysis then situates the scholarly debate within dress theory and communication theory,[3] concluding that the high priest Joshua's garments are best understood as a coded critique rather than as validating vestments.

Joshua and the High-Priestly Garments

To evaluate the interpretation of Joshua's dress in Zechariah 3 two issues must first be addressed: the priestly rituals and the intertextual references. First, the change of dress in Zechariah 3 evokes the rituals related to the high-priestly regalia and identity in Exodus and Leviticus,[4] more specifically the priestly investiture and Day of Atonement rituals.[5] Ronald Grimes suggests that rituals include seven elements: ritual actions, ritual actors, ritual places, ritual times, ritual objects, ritual languages, and ritual groups.[6] The vision in Zechariah 3 notably includes at least six of these elements (Table 10.1).[7]

Priestly clothing rituals are found on two occasions in the Torah: upon a priest's investiture, which is described in Exodus 29, 36, and Leviticus 8, and on the Day of Atonement, which is described in Leviticus 16.[8] These rituals (Exod. 29, Lev. 8, 16)

---

3. Dress can be defined as "an assemblage of modifications of the body and/or supplements to the body," including such things as hairstyle, coloring of skin, piercings, "scented breath … garments, jewelry, [and] accessories." Mary Ellen Roach-Higgins and Joanne B. Eicher, "Dress and Identity," *Clothing and Textiles Research Journal* 10.4 (1992), 1.

4. Boda notes the multiplicity of life settings represented in Zechariah 3, specifically identifying the legal court, the divine council, the priestly setting, and prophetic visions. Mark J. Boda, *The Book of Zechariah*, NICOT (Grand Rapids, MI: Eerdmans, 2016), 218–22.

5. See John W. Bailey, "The Usage in the Post Restoration Period of Terms Descriptive of the Priest and High Priest," *JBL* 70 (1951), 222–4; Boda, *The Book of Zechariah*, 231; Carol L. Meyers and Eric M. Meyers, *Haggai, Zechariah 1–8*, AB 25B (Garden City, NY: Doubleday, 1987), 180; David L. Petersen, *Haggai and Zechariah 1–8: A Commentary*, OTL (Louisville, KY: Westminster John Knox, 1984), 189; Janet E. Tollington, *Tradition and Innovation in Haggai and Zechariah 1–8*, JSOTSup 150 (Sheffield, England: Sheffield Academic, 1993), 126–31.

6. Ronald L. Grimes, *The Craft of Ritual Studies* (Oxford: Oxford University Press, 2014), 237–42. Ritual studies is a complex area of research. The point here is to establish the likelihood that Zechariah 3 would have evoked priestly rituals.

7. YHWH's comment that the land's guilt will be removed "in a single day" in Zech. 3:9 (NRSV) may well refer to a future Day of Atonement, reinforcing the ritual connotations of the chapter through reference to a "ritual time." If so, all of Grimes's elements would be found in Zechariah 3.

8. Lena-Sofia Tiemeyer, *Priestly Rites and Prophetic Rage: Post-Exilic Prophetic Critique of the Priesthood*, FAT 2.19 (Tübingen: Mohr Siebeck, 2006), 249.

Table 10.1 Ritual elements in Zechariah 3

Zechariah 3	Ritual element
Divine council (3:1-2)*	Ritual place
Joshua (3:1)	Ritual actor
Priesthood (Joshua as high priest; 3:1)	Ritual group
Messenger of the Lord (3:1)	Ritual actor
Stripping (3:4)	Ritual action
Declaration of removal of sin (3:4)	Ritual language
Dressing (3:5)	Ritual action
Turban (3:5)	Ritual object
Garment (3:4-5)	Ritual object

* The location is not explicitly named in the text but rather inferred by the participants identified in Zech. 3:1-2, including YHWH, the accuser, and a messenger of YHWH. See fn. 5.

are lexically tied to the detailed descriptions of the garments (Exod. 28, 39). The garments activate two different identities. First, Selena Billington observes that the high-priestly garments "affirm and project [Aaron's] social identity and social position."[9] However, they identified Aaron not only as a priest but also "as a royal figure," with the account in Exodus portraying him as "the equivalent of a priest *and* a monarch."[10] Carmen Imes agrees, acknowledging the royal connotations, but focusing on the priestly aspects of the dress and the differing attire for the investiture and the Day of Atonement. Imes notes that the ordination attire, which would have been worn during regular cultic service, represented YHWH's glory to the people; the simpler garments of the Day of Atonement represented corporate Israel before YHWH in the Most Holy Place.[11] Ultimately, both Imes and Billington point to two sets of identity connotations associated with the garments based on their materials, colors, manufacture, and embellishment.[12] In Zechariah 3, by activating the priestly

9. Selena Billington, "Glorious Adornment: The Social Function of Cloth and Clothing in Israel's Tabernacle," unpublished PhD dissertation, University of Denver, 2014, 26. Billington here is building on the anthropological work of Weiner and Schneider described below to address Aaron's garments.

10. Selena Billington, personal correspondence. March 24, 2018.

11. Carmen Joy Imes, "Between Two Worlds: The Functional and Symbolic Significance of the High Priestly Regalia," in *Dress and Clothing in the Hebrew Bible: "For All Her Household Is Clothed in Crimson,"* ed. Antonios Finitsis (New York: T&T Clark, 2019), 23. For further exploration of the priestly functions and the associated garments, see ibid., 19–25.

12. Note that Billington believes that the royal aspects of the high-priestly garments described in Exodus suggest that the book was written in the postexilic period; the priestly garb would then support the idea that a king was not necessary and that the high priest could fulfill royal functions (personal correspondence, March 24, 2018). It might be asked, though, how the portrayal of Moses in Exodus fits with this suggestion. For further discussion on this issue, see Danny Mathews, *Royal Motifs in the Pentateuchal Portrayal of Moses*, LHBOTS 571 (London: T&T Clark, 2012).

Table 10.2 Intertextual references about clothing in Zechariah 3 and Isaiah 3

Lexeme	Zecharian reference	Isaianic reference	Technical term(s) in Exodus/Leviticus
מחלצות (*mḥlṣwt*; pure/festal garments)	3:4	3:22	מעיל (*mʿyl*; robe)*
			כתנת (*ktnt*; tunic)†
צניף (*ṣnyp*; turban)	3:5	3:23	מצנפת (*mṣnpt*; turban)‡

* See Exod. 28:4, 31, 34; 29:5; 39:22-26; Lev. 8:7.

† See Exod. 28:4, 39-40; 29:5, 8; 39:27; Lev. 8:7, 13; 16:4.

‡ See Exod. 28:4, 37, 39; 29:6; 39:28, 31; Lev. 8:9; 16:4.

rituals through the use of Joshua's title and the acts of stripping and dressing, the Zecharian tradent evokes at least some aspects of the associated priestly identity. He also evokes the idea of restoration or perhaps blessing in that the priest has been clothed by a messenger of YHWH and can now function ritually.

Second, in addition to evoking the rituals of Exodus and Leviticus, Zechariah 3 also evokes the text of Isaiah 3 based on the intertextual links between the robes and headgear in the two texts (Table 10.2).

In Zech. 3:4 Joshua's new robe is described with the Hebrew מחלצות; the only other instance of this particular Hebrew lexeme is in Isa. 3:22, where it describes clothing that God will remove from the daughters of Zion as part of his judgment for their pride and associated actions (Isa. 3:16–4:1).[13] This term has been variously translated as denoting clean, pure, or festal garments,[14] with various scholars emphasizing different aspects. J. J. M. Roberts indicates that in Isaiah the robes "appear to be clean, white, or festive attire,"[15] while Hans Wildberger describes

13. These actions may include assuming masculine identities and roles as argued by Susannah Rees in her chapter, "'Women Rule over Them': Dressing for an Inverted World in Isaiah 3," in this volume. A question worth further consideration is whether the Zecharian tradent is alluding to women's garments based on the intertextual link to Isaiah 3. Here, Elizabeth Platt argues that the Isaianic oracle includes garments of both men and women, in part based on the reference to an ingredient of the priestly anointing oil in Isa. 3:24. However, this observation should be considered in light of Deborah Rooke's suggestion that the priests stood in a position of "wifely submission" in the presence of "an all-powerful heavenly male," positing that the priestly garments themselves pointed to a different construction of masculinity. Deborah Rooke, "Breeches of the Covenant: Gender, Garments and the Priesthood," in *Embroidered Garments: Priests and Gender in Biblical Israel*, Hebrew Bible Monographs, ed. Deborah W. Rooke (Sheffield, England: Sheffield Phoenix, 2009), 35.

14. For "pure" or "clean" garments, see D. Winton Thomas, "A Note on Zechariah iii 4," *JTS* 33.3 (1932), 279–80; for state robes as associated with the root חלץ, see *Enhanced Brown-Driver-Briggs Hebrew English Lexicon*, electronic ed. (Oxford: Clarendon, 1977), 323.

15. J. J. M. Roberts, *First Isaiah: A Commentary*, Hermeneia (Minneapolis, MN: Fortress, 2015), 64.

them as "clean, white clothing;"[16] both Roberts and Wildberger draw on the
Akkadian (*ḫalāṣu/ḫalṣu* denoting cleanliness) and Arabic (*ḫalaṣa* denoting clean
or white) cognate evidence.[17] Among Zecharian scholars, Carol and Eric Meyers
focus on the garment's cleanliness or purity, primarily based on the cognate
evidence and the immediate context that contrasts these new garments with the
filthy ones (הבגדים הצאים, *hbgdym hṣ'ym*) that have been removed (Zech. 3:3-4).[18]
On the other hand, David Petersen, Janet Tollington, and Mark Boda tend to focus
on the "festal" or "stately" aspect, based on the mentioned intertextual ties to Isa.
3:22 or the linguistic ties to the root חלץ (*ḥlṣ*), meaning "to draw off," thus denoting
what would not ordinarily be worn,[19] although such a sense does not exclude the
idea of cleanliness. Whichever sense is adopted, though, this garment is clearly not
described with the technical terms used in both Exodus and Leviticus for the high-
priestly garments (כתנת or מעיל).

Just as Joshua's robe ties intertextually to Isaiah 3 rather than to Exodus or
Leviticus, so too does his headgear. In Zech. 3:5 the term צניף describes Joshua's
new turban, a term that is also used to describe the turbans removed from the
women in Isa. 3:23. Citing the use of צניף in Zech. 3:5, some scholars argue that
the priestly role was being expanded to include royal prerogatives,[20] primarily
based on the royal associations found in Isa. 62:3 where it is used in construct
with מלוכה (*mlwkh*; kingdom; royal); however, not all scholars agree since צניף is
also used in contexts with nonroyal connotations (Job 29:14; Isa. 3:23).[21] While it

16. Hans Wildberger, *Isaiah 1–12: A Commentary*, Continental, trans. Thomas H. Trapp
(Minneapolis, MN: Fortress, 1991), 154.

17. This cognate evidence is the basis of Thomas's discussion noted above in fn. 19.

18. Meyers and Meyers, *Haggai, Zechariah 1–8*, 187, 190.

19. Petersen sees the opposition as being between dirty and ordinary robes and "stately
robes" but does not see a concern for the technical sense of priestly cleanliness (Petersen,
Haggai and Zechariah 1-8, 196); Tollington suggests the robes represent "all that is the very
best," in line with her view that the turban represents divine blessing (Tollington, *Tradition
and Innovation*, 157); Boda adopts the term "festal clothes" in line with the intertextual
reference to costly garb in Isa. 3:23 (*The Book of Zechariah*, 237–8; "Perspectives on Priests in
Haggai-Malachi," in *Prayer and Poetry in the Dead Sea Scrolls and Related Literature: Essays
in Honor of Eileen Schuller on the Occasion of Her 65th Birthday*, STDJ 98, ed. Jeremy Penner,
Ken M. Penner, and Cecilia Wassen [Leiden: Brill, 2012], 26).

20. Petersen suggests "royal overtones" (*Haggai and Zechariah 1-8*, 198); Meyers and
Meyers see a change in the priestly role (*Haggai, Zechariah 1–8*, 192) as does Eugene H.
Merrill, *Haggai, Zechariah, Malachi: An Exegetical Commentary* (Chicago: Moody, 1994),
122. These arguments can involve other parts of Zechariah and of this vision, but the
present focus is on the clothing.

21. Boda, "Perspectives of Priests," 27; Tollington, *Tradition and Innovation*, 157. Boda
also notes that the turban is described as clean rather than holy and that the description
does not include reference to the medallion (Exod. 29:6; 39:30; Lev 8:9) or the crown/
diadem (Exod. 39:30).

might be argued that the Zecharian tradent's use of the Isaianic terminology is coincidental, both the practice of utilizing sustained allusions in proto-Zechariah and further references to the Isaianic passage suggest otherwise.[22] To the latter point, Boda lists four additional parallel references between Zechariah 2–3 and Isa. 3:13–4:6, including Daughter Zion (Zech. 2:14[10]) and the daughters of Zion (Isa. 3:16; 4:1), the Branch or *Zemah* (Zech. 3:8; Isa. 4:2), filth (צֹאִי [ṣʾy], Zech. 3:3/צֹאָה [ṣʾh], Isa. 4:4), and divine protection by fire (Zech. 2:5-9 (1-5)/Isa. 4:5-6).[23]

In addition to the explicit mention of Joshua's new robe and turban in Zech. 3:4-5, the oracle in the latter part of the chapter mentions a stone on which YHWH will engrave an inscription (3:9). God's subsequent statement that he will "remove the guilt of this land in a single day" (NRSV) combined with the mention of Joshua's garments in verses 4–5 has led a number of scholars to associate this stone with the medallion (צִיץ, ṣyṣ) in Exod. 28:36-38. This medallion is attached to the high priest's turban (מִצְנֶפֶת) and absorbs or "bears" (נָשָׂא, nśʾ) any guilt related to the sacrifice.[24] If this interpretation of the stone is adopted,[25] the key point that should be noted here is that, again, the description does not draw on the Pentateuchal language.[26]

Returning to the robe and turban, the Zecharian tradent's use of the Isaianic terminology, particularly the headgear, has led scholars to generally interpret the vision in one of two ways: either as validating the postexilic priesthood, in some cases expanding its role to incorporate royal privileges, or as subtly critiquing it.[27] Petersen, and Meyers and Meyers, respectively, consider the dress in Zechariah 3 to be evidence that the high-priestly role in the postexilic period involved royal

---

22. See Michael R. Stead, *The Intertextuality of Zechariah 1–8*, LHBOTS 506 (New York: T&T Clark, 2009).

23. Boda, "Perspectives of Priests," 26–31.

24. Boda, *The Book of Zechariah*, 259–61; Petersen, *Haggai and Zechariah 1–8*, 211–12; Stead, *Intertextuality*, 169–70. VanderKam, while also interpreting the stone as relating to Joshua's garments, ties it to the breastplate and ephod ("Joshua the High Priest and the Interpretation of Zechariah 3," *CBQ* 53.4 [1991]: 567–9). For a discussion of this medallion, see Imes, "Between Two Worlds," 57–8.

25. Other scholars associate this stone with the foundation of the temple. See Meyers and Meyers, *Haggai, Zechariah 1–8*, 204–11; Martin Hallaschka, "Clean Garments for Joshua: The Purification of the High Priest in Zech. 3," in *Clothing and Nudity in the Hebrew Bible*, ed. Christoph Berner, Manuel Schäfer, Martin Schott, Sarah Schulz, and Martina Weingärtner (London: T&T Clark, 2019), 532.

26. VanderKam, "Joshua," 553–70, offers a helpful overview of the differing interpretations.

27. For a more comprehensive overview of the various interpretations than the one offered herein, see Lena-Sofia Tiemeyer, *Zechariah and His Visions: An Exegetical Study of Zechariah's Vision Report*, LHBOTS 605 (London: Bloomsbury T&T Clark, 2015), 130–3.

prerogatives.[28] Tollington also sees some level of validation, although she suggests that the turban points to "divine favour and blessings" rather than to royal privileges since in its use in each of its contexts outside of Zechariah the term צָנִיף relates to splendor.[29] In contrast, Boda believes the intertextual ties between the Zecharian attire and the catalog of clothing removed from the daughters of Zion in Isa. 3:18-23 suggest reservations and concerns about priestly behavior.[30] In some way, each of these scholars is dealing with the question of what Joshua's attire communicates about his role. These varying perspectives on the Hebrew tradition of Zechariah 3 indicate that the vision can thus be interpreted in a variety of ways: supporting royal privileges, indicating blessing, or subtly critiquing.

A dress studies approach clarifies the current state of research around Joshua's clothing. Primarily, the issues in Zechariah 3 focus on the "sociofacts" related to the social institution of the priesthood; contextually, the scholarship addresses the literary and historical settings, as well as the social circumstances and relationships of those who have returned from the exile. Drawing these pieces together, scholars draw conclusions about societal norms and "mentifacts," including beliefs and values.[31] But the question of how best to integrate the information remains open. Put differently, the interpretation of dress in Zechariah 3 raises questions about both the sociofacts and mentifacts of the postexilic community. Specifically, are the people to accept an expanded role for the high priest or are members of the priesthood to be careful that their behavior conforms to YHWH's expectations, perhaps with their fellow returnees holding them accountable? Here, the social

---

28. Petersen, *Haggai and Zechariah 1-8*, 198; Meyers and Meyers, *Haggai, Zechariah 1-8*, 192.

29. Tollington, *Tradition and Innovation*, 157, drawing on the evidence in Isa. 3:23; 62:3; Job 29:14.

30. See Boda, "Perspectives of Priests," 22-31. Boda addresses the priestly role in Zechariah 1-8, not just the clothing in Zechariah 3. Tiemeyer appears to agree, suggesting the vision includes a "subtle critique" and "ambiguous characterization" of Joshua (*Zechariah and His Visions*, 133).

Whether or not Joshua is believed to have royal privileges, verse seven affirms that his role and status are in view, addressing such issues as Joshua's governance of the temple, his charge of the courts, and his access to God via either prophets or the divine council. The first two of these issues have been interpreted as both the protasis and apodosis of a conditional statement. For the present discussion, the grammatical dilemma is not relevant since either interpretation indicates that the vision is addressing Joshua's responsibilities, whether they are a condition or an outcome. See Michael Segal, "The Responsibilities and Rewards of Joshua the High Priest according to Zechariah 3:7," *JBL* 126.4 (2007), 717-34; Boda, *The Book of Zechariah*, 242-7; Meyers and Meyers, *Haggai, Zechariah 1-8*, 194; Petersen, *Haggai and Zechariah 1-8*, 203-7, for further discussion.

31. See the introduction to this volume by Antonios Finitsis.

role of dress and the communicative role of nonverbal influences offer assistance in evaluating the varying conclusions.

Dress, Communication, and Ritual Efficacy

As has been seen in the discussion above, recent scholarship on Zechariah interprets Joshua's role and postexilic sociohistorical and political developments in various ways in large measure based on the high-priestly dress in Zechariah 3.[32] Whether explicitly stated or not, these conclusions all draw on anthropological conclusions that dress can be used to express identity and social position, with social scientists highlighting the ways that dress can both shape and reflect individuals and their identities.[33] Here, Terence Turner has described dress as a "social skin" that mediates "the social boundary between" individuals and those whom they encounter, with the "surface of the body" functioning "as the boundary of the individual as a biological and psychological entity … [and] as the frontier of the social self."[34] He further comments that dress not only negotiates identity between given individuals and their communities but also defines "categories or classes of individuals."[35] Mary Ellen Roach-Higgins and Joanne Eicher agree, noting that identity can be "communicated by dress as it announces social positions of [the] wearer to both wearer and observers within a particular interaction situation."[36] Such observations about dress fit with scholarly conversations about the role of dress in biblical texts. Chŏng-hun Kim notes that human clothing in the Hebrew Bible can symbolize "social status and role … inner or outer characteristics … [or] a wearer's allegiance,"[37] while D. R. Edwards highlights the role of priestly

32. The research frequently discusses the crowns in Zechariah 6, as well.

33. See Roach-Higgins and Eicher, "Dress and Identity"; Terence S. Turner, "The Social Skin," in *Not Work Alone: A Cross-Cultural View of Activities Superfluous to Survival*, ed. Jeremy Cherfas and Roger Lewin (London: Temple Smith, 1980), 112–40, reprint *HAU: Journal of Ethnographic Theory* 2.2 (2012), 486–504.

34. Turner, "The Social Skin," 503, 486.

35. Ibid., 503.

36. Roach-Higgins and Eicher, "Dress and Identity," 5. This concept is discussed within the context of studies on dress or appearance as early as Gregory Stone's work describing the contribution of "appearance" to identity formation and perception, including a discussion of the way in which a person's appearance is appraised by his or her audience. See Gregory P. Stone, "Appearance and the Self," in *Human Behavior and Social Processes: An Interactionist Approach*, ed. Arnold M. Rose (Boston, MA: Houghton Mifflin, 1962), 86–118. With respect to the current discussion, then, this observation suggests that not only might the clothing communicate something about Joshua and his role to the audience, but it may also communicate to Joshua himself, which would fit with the warning that will be discussed below.

37. Chŏng-hun Kim, *The Significance of Clothing Imagery in the Pauline Corpus*, JSNTSup 268 (London: T&T Clark, 2004), 11.

clothing in particular in expressing "power, prestige, and identity … [and] the priest's intercessory role."[38] Here we see the role that clothing can play in individual identity, expressing characteristics or allegiance, and in designating classes, particularly relating to priests and their roles.

Jane Schneider and Annette Weiner further contribute to our understanding of the way that cloth itself has been historically used "to consolidate social relations and mobilize political power," focusing on four "domains of meaning" that each have relevance for the high-priestly garments of the Hebrew Bible.[39] First, Schneider and Weiner consider the actual manufacture of cloth in which the laborers "harness the … blessings of … divinities to inspire or animate the product."[40] In Exodus, this idea is seen in God's instructions for and the people's construction of the priestly garments (Exod. 28, 39), as well as in the clothing's ability to communicate holiness (Exod. 28:3; cf. Ezek. 44:19). Second, they consider the "bestowal and exchange" of cloth, which can tie together "kinship groups" and multiple generations, at times "generat[ing] political power."[41] Third, the ceremonial use of cloth functions to "transmit the authority of earlier possessors or the sanctity of past traditions," legitimizing individuals in the present by tying them to the past.[42] This ceremonial use and the bestowal and exchange are both attested in Num. 20:23-28, which includes the passing of the high-priestly garments from Aaron to his son Eleazar immediately before the former's death. Here, the passing of the priestly regalia from Aaron to Eleazar creates continuity and legitimates Eleazar's ability to function as the high priest.[43] It also ultimately commits Eleazar to the same loyalty to YHWH and to the high-priestly obligations held by his father. The ceremonial domain thus appears to be tied to the second domain of bestowal, which according to Schneider and Weiner was not only about the generation of "political power" but also about "committing the recipients to loyalty and obligation in the future."[44] In the ceremonial domain, though, the focus is on legitimation. Finally, Schneider and Weiner note the way that cloth used in

---

38. D. R. Edwards, "Dress and Ornamentation," *ABD*, 233.

39. Jane Schneider and Annette B. Weiner, "Introduction," in *Cloth and Human Experience*, Smithsonian Series in Ethnographic Inquiry, ed. Annette B. Weiner and Jane Schneider (Washington, DC: Smithsonian Institution, 1989), 3.

40. Ibid. Note, here, that Weiner and Schneider describe these blessings as "imagined," which relates to a modern Western perspective rather than the ancient one attested in the biblical texts that are considered in the present analysis. See below for a discussion of "animation" related to material objects.

41. Ibid.

42. Ibid.

43. While Moses strips the garments from Aaron and clothes Eleazar, echoing Aaron's investiture ceremony in Leviticus 8, the description of this investiture does not include details beyond the stripping and dressing.

44. Ibid.

clothing has the ability "to reveal or conceal identities and values."[45] With respect to the biblical account, the high-priestly garments reveal the wearer's identity as one who represents God to the people and the people to God, a point noted above.

One further issue may be worth considering with respect to the high-priestly garments: their inherent efficacy. Building on archeological and anthropological research, Lars Fogelin and Michael Brian Schiffer investigate the intersection of material objects and ritual, particularly rites of passage. They explore the ways in which a given material object's "life history" interacts with rituals, with rites of passage in particular pointing to "shifting contexts and social meanings" for the objects.[46] In some cases, these material objects are perceived as having "causal effects," which ultimately relates to the idea that they have some form of agency, albeit different than notions of human agency.[47] Here, while Fogelin and Schiffer describe Bruno Latour's notion of object agency that focuses on the way that material objects interact with their environment,[48] they focus on the concept of "secondary agency" elucidated by Alfred Gell in which "the agency of the people who created or modified objects is ascribed to the object itself."[49] This interest in object agency is further developed into the concept of object animism, wherein "some people 'accord a spiritual, living nature to some artifacts, features, and the landscape.'"[50] Such animism appears to be attested in at least some ancient Near Eastern cultures, as seen in their use of divine images that require physical care.[51] While the ancient Israelite religion described within the Torah is notably

45. Ibid.

46. Lars Fogelin and Michael Brian Schiffer, "Rites of Passage and Other Rituals in the Life Histories of Objects," *CAJ* 25.4 (2015), 823.

47. Ibid., 822.

48. Ibid.; Bruno Latour, *Pandora's Hope: Essays on the Reality of Science Studies* (Cambridge, MA: Harvard University Press, 1999).

49. Fogelin and Schiffer, "Rites of Passage," 822. See Alfred Gell, *Art and Agency: An Anthropological Theory* (Oxford: Oxford University Press, 1998). Addressing clothing in the Hebrew Bible, Wagstaff objects to Gell's view that excludes the idea that objects in and of themselves have agency that can be seen in their ability to influence the world around them, "evad[ing] human control or expectations" since they force people to certain actions. Bethany Joy Wagstaff, "Redressing Clothing in the Hebrew Bible: Material-Cultural Approaches," PhD dissertation, University of Exeter, 2017, 50.

50. Fogelin and Schiffer, "Rites of Passage," 822, citing Christine S. VanPool and Elizabeth Newsome, "The Spirit in the Material: A Case Study of Animism in the American Southwest," *American Antiquity* 77.2 (2012), 243.

51. Fogelin and Schiffer discuss the work of Richard Davis, which focuses on Hindu images. Richard Davis, *Lives of Indian Images* (Princeton, NJ: Princeton University Press, 1999). The rituals described appear similar to those attested within the ancient Near Eastern context, particularly those relating to what John Walton has described as "the Great Symbiosis" wherein humanity met the ongoing needs of their deities for such things as food, drink, and housing. John Walton, "The Temple in Context," in *Behind the Scenes of*

aniconic, and indeed appears to reject such a notion of animism in Isa. 44:9-20, some level of agency may still be attested in the biblical corpus, notably in the idea that some objects, including dress items, possess a level of ritual efficacy.[52] Such a perspective moves the role of clothing beyond mere symbolism, instead suggesting that clothing can actually contribute to a person's identity and ability to perform certain (ritual) tasks.[53]

Is it possible, though, that the high-priestly garments were perceived as more than simply symbolic but actually in some way ritually effective? Both the biblical text and secondary literature appear to suggest so. First, the idea that the garments consecrate Aaron for service (Exod. 28:3) and that priests must not wear the holy garments among the people so that they do "not communicate holiness to the people with their vestments" (Ezek. 44:19, NRSV) suggest that some kind of ritual efficacy is attributable to the garments themselves: they are able to make people holy (Piel קדשׁ, qdš). Further, Aaron is deemed to bear the people's guilt related to their offerings by means of the ציץ (diadem, rosette; Exod. 28:36-38).[54] Finally, Imes remarks that the high-priestly garments were "constitutive" of the high-priestly role, enabling the performance of his duties.[55] Thus, it appears reasonable to consider the possibility that the high-priestly garments were not merely symbolic but in actuality deemed to be ritually effective.

Turning back to the priestly clothing in Zechariah 3, Joshua is explicitly identified as the high priest (3:1), and his sin is explicitly taken away (3:4);

---

the Old Testament: Cultural, Social, and Historical Contexts, ed. Jonathan S. Greer, John W. Hilber, and John H. Walton (Grand Rapids, MI: Baker Academic, 2018), 350–1.

52. See Wagstaff, "Redressing Clothing," where she argues for the agency of clothing in the Hebrew Bible, including the concept of ritual efficacy, particularly with respect to Joseph's *ketonet passim* in Genesis and Elijah's *adderet* in 1-2 Kings. Christian Frevel also suggests that the binding of the frontlet in Deut. 6:8 may have included "an apotropaic function." Christian Frevel, "On Instant Scripture and Proximal Texts: Some Insights into the Sensual Materiality of Texts and Their Rituality in the Hebrew Bible and Beyond," *Postscripts* 8.1–2 (2012), 62.

53. Wagstaff, "Redressing Clothing," 401–2.

54. Baruch Schwarz notes that the expression to "bear sin" in the priestly writings relates to ritual, with the diadem (ציץ) enabling Aaron to bear the sin in order to remove it. Baruch Schwarz, "The Bearing of Sin in Priestly Literature," in *Pomegranates and Golden Bells: Studies in Biblical, Jewish, and Near Eastern Ritual, Law, and Literature in Honor of Jacob Milgrom*, ed. David Pearson Wright, David Noel Freedman, and Avi Hurvitz (Winona Lake, IN: Eisenbrauns, 1995), 16. Note, however, that Menahem Haran focuses instead on the symbolic aspect of the diadem rather than on the concept of ritual efficacy. Menahem Haran, *Temples and Temple-Service in Ancient Israel: An Inquiry into the Character of Cult Phenomena and the Historical Setting of the Priestly School* (Oxford: Clarendon, 1978), 214–15.

55. Imes, "Between Two Worlds," 23.

however, he is not clothed in the ritually efficacious garb found in Exodus and Leviticus. The discussion above suggests at a minimum that the focus of the Zecharian account may not be on Joshua's ability to function ritually, returning the discussion to the implications of his dress. Having described the lexical terminology used in Zechariah 3, identified the intertextual references to Isaiah 3, and considered the relevance of the garments through the lens of anthropological and sociological research, it is now time to evaluate the varying scholarly interpretations.

Joshua's Priestly Garments and Expectancy Violations

Judee Burgoon et al.'s discussion of "expectancy signaling and ... violations" provides a helpful tool to assess the opposing Zecharian interpretations.[56] These scholars note that communicators possess expectations about the "background, attitudes, beliefs, and ... communication behavior" of those with whom they communicate,[57] including expectations about nonverbal factors, such as dress. Violations of those expectations "elicit corresponding positive or negative outcomes, including attitude and behavioral change or resistance."[58] That is, when an audience's expectations are violated, their response is influenced, either negatively or positively. Within "expectancy violations theory (EVT), deviations from expectations create an "orientation response ... in which the violation galvanizes attention to itself and its source, deepens information processing, and instigates an appraisal and evaluation process that results in the violation being valenced as positive or negative."[59] For our purposes, Burgoon et al. further note that violations related to an individual's appearance are nearly always valenced negatively, with the exception to this appraisal taking place when one's appearance creates "negative expectations that are positively violated by the verbal message."[60]

Through the lens of EVT, then, the issue becomes what the communicator or audience would have believed to be the expected norm or appearance,

---

56. Judee K. Burgoon, Norah E. Dunbar, and Chris Segrin, "Nonverbal Influence," in *The Persuasion Handbook: Developments in Theory and Practice*, ed. James Price Dillard and Michael Pfau (London: Sage, 2002), 457. It must be acknowledged that their discussion relates to contemporary communication theory and not to the ancient world. However, given the noted communicative role of the priestly clothing, it offers a framework that may at least be suggestive for the present discussion.

57. Burgoon et al., "Nonverbal Influence," 457.

58. Ibid. Stone also discusses appearance, expectations, and evaluation. See Stone, "Appearance and the Self," 88–93.

59. Burgoon et al., "Nonverbal Influence," 458. The discussion of Joshua's role reflects just this type of orientation response among contemporary scholars.

60. Ibid., 461.

whether this norm had been violated, and, if so, how it should be valenced.[61] In Zechariah 3, the dressing ritual and priestly identity have evoked the high-priestly garments described in Exodus and Leviticus along with their royal, sacral, and ritualistically efficacious aspects. In order to determine whether an audience might have expected the Pentateuchal terminology to be used, though, several points should be noted. First, Meyers and Meyers describe the conservative nature of the priestly regalia, which resulted in minimal change to ritual attire over time.[62] This conservatism suggests that it would have been appropriate for the tradent to use the available technical language if it suited his rhetorical purpose.[63] Second, although Lena-Sofia Tiemeyer has appropriately observed that the Zecharian tradent may not have been familiar with the technical language for the clothing in Exodus and Leviticus,[64] the references to the tabernacle accounts in Exodus 25, 37, and Numbers 8 found in the lampstand vision of Zechariah 4 strongly suggest that the tradent would have been familiar with at least the Exodus material.[65] These two points suggest that the tradent was likely both to be familiar with the technical language and to be willing to use intertextual references to craft his message. That is, even if the terminology had changed over time for specific types of dress, the tradent's use of other language specifically tied to the tabernacle suggests that he could have used the technical dress language if he had so desired. His familiarity with the traditions and willingness to use them also support the suggestion by Meyers

61. A concern for such valencing is attested in the scholarly analyses of the Hebrew tradition described above, although their valencing is based on the intertextual references. The present approach addresses this valencing incorporating communication theory with the intertextual links.

62. Meyers and Meyers, *Haggai, Zechariah 1–8*, 192. They explicitly note that the form of the priestly regalia would not have changed "appreciably" and that "the elaborate nature of the priestly garb is a condition that would have existed from earliest times." This observation suggests that Zechariah's use of different language to describe the garments was unlikely to be an effort to evoke priestly dress that differs from the tabernacle traditions. Further, Roach-Higgins and Eicher also comment that "religious dress in many societies resists fashion change." Roach-Higgins and Eicher, "Dress and Identity," 3.

63. Note that if Billington's conclusion about Exodus originating in the Persian period is correct, then an association between the Zecharian and Pentateuchal material might be even stronger and more likely to be expected.

64. Tiemeyer, *Zechariah and His Visions*, 133. The focus on the Pentateuchal literature is due to its foundational nature for understanding the priestly garments. It should also be noted that while Boda highlights the sustained allusion to Isaiah, he believes the Day of Atonement ritual of Leviticus 16 was in view as well based on God's "removal of 'guilt'" (עָוֹן, 'wn) in one day. Boda, *The Book of Zechariah*, 261.

65. Stead, *Intertextuality*, 173–5. See the wider volume for his extended discussion of sustained allusions in proto-Zechariah. Further, Stead suggests that the reference to the

and Meyers, which Tollington echoes, that the lexical selection around Joshua's attire may well have been "intentional and significant."[66]

The next issue is what the book's audience would have expected. Would the audience have been aware of the use of Isaianic vocabulary for the garments? While any answer to this question must remain to some extent tentative, the very effectiveness of the previously noted sustained allusions requires knowledge of the texts or traditions behind them. As such, although it cannot be definitively stated that the audience would have known the language, the persistent use of allusion in the Zecharian material suggests that the intended audience would have been familiar with the background texts and traditions, and that it may well have possessed knowledge of the technical Pentateuchal language. A second issue related to the audience is what they would have expected based on their historical context and the Zecharian material. The dating of the book's final form varies by scholar, but the text of proto-Zechariah offers some assistance, including three date formulae (1:1, 7; 7:1), ranging from October or November of 520 to December 7, 518 BCE.[67] The final redaction of the first part of the book likely took place within a short time frame after the final date in 518 given the lack of reference to the temple's completion. According to Ezra 6:15 the project was finished on March 12, 515 BCE,[68] thus dating proto-Zechariah to the late sixth century. This dating and the content of the material fit well with Boda's observation that Zechariah seeks to confront his audience's limited view of restoration, which is focused on the rebuilding of the temple and the renewal of its services. Instead, Zechariah presents a multifaceted restoration that involves not only a rebuilt temple and city but also spiritual renewal, material prosperity, and a future impact on the nations.[69] Key for this discussion are the audience's already existing expectations for the restoration of the temple and its service. In this service the priests would have worn specific garments (Exod. 35:19), about which the audience I have described would have likely been aware.[70] Thus, the audience's expectations were likely to have been violated.[71]

silver and gold for manufacturing the crown in Zech. 6:9-15 echoes the gold and silver referenced for the construction of the tabernacle in Exod. 25:3 (153).

66. Meyers and Meyers, *Haggai, Zechariah 1–8*, 191; Tollington, *Tradition and Innovation*, 157.

67. Meyers and Meyers, *Haggai, Zechariah 1–8*, xlvi.

68. Boda, *The Book of Zechariah*, 33.

69. Ibid., 33, 43.

70. Note that Zechariah was the initial audience of the vision. His personal insertion into the vision, noting the need for a turban, may indicate that he was aware that something was off.

71. The Old Greek (OG) translation of the passage may also support this understanding of the audience's expectations. Lexically, OG Zechariah 3 explicitly ties Joshua's garments to Aaron's investiture garments in Exodus, with some manuscript evidence even reversing the order in which Joshua is dressed to agree with the ordering in the Exodus passage. Patricia Ahearne-Kroll, "LXX/OG Zechariah 1–6 and the Portrayal of Joshua Centuries after the

Returning to EVT, then, the question is whether this expectancy violation would have been perceived positively or negatively. Again, Burgoon et al. have suggested that expectancy violations for appearance are generally negatively valenced unless that appearance lowers the audience's expectations and those expectations are subsequently exceeded. Here, giving us a point of reference for the discussion, they cite an example of a hippie-type speaker advocating tax reform.[72] In such a case, the speaker's appearance would lower the expectations of a fiscally conservative audience, expectations that would then be violated—dare-I-say pleasantly—and thus positively valenced.

Addressing the valencing of Joshua's attire, the first question is whether the description of the clothing in Zechariah using Isaianic language raised or lowered the audience's expectations. If, as has been suggested, the audience expected the Pentateuchal language for the priestly attire, this clothing would have evoked notions of ritual efficacy in the sacral realm as well as royal connotations. That is, the expectations evoked by the Pentateuchal terminology were quite high and actually could have included the concept of royal prerogatives argued to be part of the actual Zecharian terminology by Petersen, Meyers, and Meyers; the Pentateuchal term may also have included the sense of blessing understood by Tollington due to the garments' ritual efficacy that allowed for the removal of the land's guilt.[73]

While the identity and role expectations related to the Pentateuchal terminology are quite high, the same does not appear to be the case for the Zecharian terminology based on the sustained allusion to Isa. 3:16–4:6. While the clothing terminology from Exodus and Leviticus evoke the concepts of royal prerogatives and ritually effective sacral capacity, the clothing terminology in Isaiah recalls the failures of the daughters of Zion as well as the consequences.

Restoration of the Temple," in *Septuagint Research: Issues and Challenges in the Study of the Greek Jewish Scriptures*, , SCS 53, ed. Wolfgang Kraus and R. Glenn Wooden (Atlanta, GA: Society of Biblical Literature, 2006), 179–92. Here, then, we have a hint, albeit several centuries later, as to what an audience might have expected of the Zecharian passage—a tie to the Pentateuchal material. While the difference in intertextual ties may indicate either a lack of awareness of the Isaianic link or a desire to validate the priesthood at the time of translation, the importance of the Exodus material as it relates to Joshua is clear.

While it is possible that historically speaking the priestly garments would not have been worn without a functioning temple (or tabernacle), the literary portrayal of Joshua in YHWH's presence and the ritual of undressing and dressing a temple functionary suggests that using the priestly garments would be appropriate. Even if the priestly garments would not have been deemed acceptable, though, the Zecharian tradent did not have to adopt the rare terminology from the Isaianic passage.

72. Burgoon et al., "Nonverbal Influence," 461.

73. Ultimately, though, while the Pentateuchal terminology evokes these concepts, it may well be that they could have been eclipsed by the sacral nuances given the ritual aspect of Zechariah 3 that evoked them.

However, when considering the wider intertextuality of Zechariah 2–3 and Isaiah 3–4, this clothing may also evoke the restoration described in Isa. 4:2–6:

> On that day the branch of the LORD shall be beautiful and glorious, and the fruit of the land shall be the pride and glory of the survivors of Israel. Whoever is left in Zion and remains in Jerusalem will be called holy, everyone who has been recorded for life in Jerusalem, once the Lord has washed away the filth of the daughters of Zion and cleansed the bloodstains of Jerusalem from its midst by a spirit of judgment and by a spirit of burning. Then the LORD will create over the whole site of Mount Zion and over its places of assembly a cloud by day and smoke and the shining of a flaming fire by night. Indeed over all the glory there will be a canopy. It will serve as a pavilion, a shade by day from the heat, and a refuge and a shelter from the storm and rain. (NRSV)

Here in this restoration we see the idea of cleansing and a reference to the "branch" that echo the language of Zechariah 3. While the sense of "branch" in Isa. 4:2 is debated, with some scholars adopting a messianic interpretation and others focusing on agricultural abundance,[74] the focus here is not on a precise overlap in meaning but rather on the lexical ties that suggest that not only does the Zecharian tradent have the punishment in view but also restoration.[75] However, the idea that reversal is in view does not preclude the use of the Isaianic clothing as a warning. Present restoration does not mean that the danger of falling short does not exist. While Zechariah 3 does involve reversal, this same reversal could also have been achieved by using the priestly regalia, perhaps even more effectively since it would have focused on Joshua's ability to carry out his ritual responsibilities. As the text stands, the clothing not only points to restoration but it also recalls the guilt and punishment of the daughters of Zion. This focus on punishment and restoration more broadly conceived rather than on royal prerogatives and ritual efficacy suggests that the Zecharian description of the clothing may indeed have lowered its audience's expectations.

While the expectancy violation described above does lower expectations, the question remains whether Joshua is deemed to exceed these expectations, thus leading to a positive valencing of his appearance. In assessing Joshua's performance it

74. Roberts, *First Isaiah*, 68.

75. Just such a reading is adopted by Hallaschka, who believes that the removal of Joshua's filthy clothing offers "a sign of salvation" and a reversal of the Isaianic judgment, specifically commenting that "the allusions to Isa. 3:1–4:6 do not imply negative overtones." Hallaschka, "Clean Garments," 533. Hallaschka also comments that "the customary cleansing rites cannot fulfill the task of cleansing and restoring the high priest, but only atonement in the divine sphere. The earthly mediator needs the mediation of the angel of the Lord" (535). Here Hallaschka sees the angel's mediatorial role as strengthening Joshua's position. However, given that Hallaschka believes the divine intervention was *necessary*, it is questionable whether that same necessary intervention should be deemed to strengthen the priestly role, particularly since he describes verses 6–10 as a commissioning without dealing with the condition in Zech. 3:7 that will be discussed below (534).

must be noted that the text of Zechariah 3 itself does not attest to Joshua's actual performance, although it might be argued that the reference in verse 9 to the stone and YHWH's removal of guilt allude to his ritual efficacy. This position proves problematic. First, the stone is not explicitly associated with Joshua's garments in the literary envelope emphasizing Joshua's receipt of the turban itself (Zech. 3:4-5).[76] Second, the stone is neither made of the same material as the golden medallion of the Pentateuchal traditions nor is it attached to the front of the turban (Exod. 28:37; ‏אֶל־‎ ‏מוּל פְּנֵי־הַמִּצְנָפֶת‎; '*l-mwl pny'-hmṣnpt*); rather, it is placed before Joshua (Zech. 3:9; ‏הָאֶבֶן‎ ‏אֲשֶׁר נָתַתִּי לִפְנֵי יְהוֹשֻׁעַ‎; *h'bn 'šr ntty lpny yhwš'*). That is, Joshua is not *wearing* the stone as part of some ritually effective garb; as such, it does not relate to Joshua's ritual efficacy. Finally, the stone does not yet bear the inscription; YHWH himself still needs to engrave it. While this stone may ultimately relate to God's future cleansing of the land, the Zecharian tradent does not tie it to Joshua's ritual garb, supporting his ritual efficacy. Rather, the engraved stone is associated with the future work of YHWH.

In addition to considering the possible role of the stone in evaluating Joshua's performance one has to also examine the ambiguity of the verb in this verse. Specifically, whether or not the verb used could contribute to the so-called halo effect, in which the characteristics of an attractive source "may be interpreted more charitably and judged as more desirable than those of unattractive sources,"[77] must be addressed. Perhaps due to a high priest's stature and role in the community, Zechariah's audience may have interpreted Joshua's dress or actions charitably, especially if the audience does perceive him as possessing the royal prerogatives discussed by some scholars. Here, the oracle in Zech. 3:6-10 proves relevant, including two further points that suggest that any expectations about Joshua's performance were in danger of not being met. First is the choice of the Hiphil verb ‏עוּד‎ ('*wd*) with the preposition ‏בּ‎ (*b*) in 3:6. Both *HALOT* and *DCH* note that this collocation implies a warning or an admonition.[78] While *DCH* mentions that it *may* denote an assurance, Zech. 3:6 is listed as the only case of this sense. Based on this information, the verse could be translated in two different ways:

The messenger of YHWH **warned** Joshua, saying:

or

The messenger of YHWH **assured** Joshua, saying:

76. I am indebted to Scott Starbuck for pointing out this issue. Meyers and Meyers discuss the literary envelope (*Haggai, Zechariah 1–8*, 190).

77. Burgoon et al., "Nonverbal Influence," 459. Lennon et al. comment that people form impressions by "integrating various bits of information about another person to form an overall impression." Sharron J. Lennon, Kim P. Johnson, and Nancy A. Rudd, *Social Psychology of Dress* (New York: Fairchild, 2017), 98. The analysis of the halo effect recognizes that not only would Joshua's clothing have influenced an audience's perception but that his dress would have been integrated with his identity and other clues in the Zecharian text to form an overall impression.

78. *DCH* 6: 288; *HALOT* 795.

However, given that every other use of the collocation in the Hebrew Bible bears a negative connotation, Zech. 3:6 should be similarly translated (warned) unless we possess strong evidence supporting a positive nuance.

Examining the content of this warning or assurance cautions us from too quickly adopting a positive connotation. Herein lies the second piece of evidence to address the potential "halo effect," with verse seven including YHWH's conditional statement that addresses such issues as Joshua's obedience, his governance of the temple, his charge of the courts, and his access to God via either prophets or the divine council.[79] Joshua is admonished to walk in God's ways (ב־דרכי תלך, *b-drky tlk*) and to meet his priestly obligations (את־משמרתי תשמר, '*t-mšmrty tšmr*). Meyers and Meyers note that the notion of walking in God's ways contains juridical connotations, referring to "a premonarchic system of civil justice,"[80] with Petersen highlighting the prevalence of the expression in the Deuteronomic literature.[81] Tollington draws on this literature to note the juridical role of the Levitical priesthood (Deut. 17:8–11),[82] ultimately concluding that such a role for the priesthood should be interpreted as a return to an earlier form of administration rather than "an enhancement of Joshua's status."[83] Key here is the observation that judicial responsibilities do not necessarily fall within the civil or royal purview but rather can fall within Levitical responsibilities. The next two points of the conditional statement have been interpreted as both the protasis and the apodosis of the condition due to the ambiguity of the syntax; however, for this discussion, the key is not whether they are part of the condition or the outcome, but their content. Here, as with the two conditions already noted, the parallel content points to a judicial concern ("judge in my house;" תדין את־ביתי, *tdyn 't-byty*) and a priestly one (NRSV: "have charge of my courts;" תשמר את־חצרי, *tšmr 't-ḥṣry*). In these two cases the judgment specifically relates to the temple, a place that Michael Stead notes the monarchy had *not* had juridical authority.[84] Thus, the content of the oracle following the dressing ritual (i) relates to responsibilities already possessed by the priesthood according to the Pentateuchal material, which Stead's sustained allusions and the research of Meyers and Meyers indicate was available in some form during this period, and (ii) includes the implicit possibility that Joshua would not adequately carry out these preexisting responsibilities based on the grammatical form—a condition. Returning, then, to the question of whether this oracle includes a warning or an assurance, the content does not

---

79. Finitsis highlights the "conditionality of Joshua's rule" (*Visions and Eschatology: A Socio-historical Analysis of Zechariah 1–6*, LSTS 79 (London: T&T Clark, 2011), 130), commenting "that the priests have certain standards to meet in order to maintain their privileges" (152).

80. Meyers and Meyers, *Haggai, Zechariah 1–8*, 194.

81. Petersen, *Haggai and Zechariah 1–8*, 204.

82. The Meyers' acknowledge this point (*Haggai, Zechariah 1–8*, 194). See also their discussion in ibid., 77–9.

83. Tollington, *Tradition and Innovation*.

84. Stead, *Intertextuality*, 163.

require interpreting the collocation positively, suggesting that its typical negative connotation should be adopted. YHWH is warning Joshua.[85]

Thus, the content of this oracle relates to acknowledged priestly duties, warning Joshua that they must be kept. Neither the content nor the nature of expression—a warning—suggest that expectations for the high priest are expected to be exceeded or perhaps even met. Instead, the oracle ties Joshua to previously existing Levitical duties and expresses at least some doubt about whether or not he will effectively carry them out. It seems reasonable to suggest, then, that the Zecharian tradent may have adopted the Isaianic terminology for two reasons. On the one hand, drawing on Isaiah in Zechariah 3 evokes the general connotations of restoration; on the other hand, it would lower the audience's expectations and *avoid* the additional connotations of royal prerogatives and perhaps even ritual efficacy,[86] although the latter may have been of less concern give the likely reference to the Day of Atonement in Zech. 3:9. This avoidance, then, combined with the warning oracle, suggests that Boda's interpretation is preferable, namely, that when situated within the wider Haggai-Malachi corpus the garments represent a "creatively allusive undermining" that expresses reservations about the priesthood.[87]

Conclusion

In conclusion, if the combination of EVT with an intertextual analysis holds as a viable framework for evaluating Zechariah 3, then the use of Isaianic language to describe the high-priestly garments would most likely not be valenced positively. Notions of royal prerogative and blessing were already embedded in the garments of the Exodus and Leviticus traditions. The adopted Isaianic language avoids these connotations, although it may allude to blessing in the sense of the hoped-for restoration. However, the warning in verses 6–8 further tempers the likelihood of

---

85. A point of note here, the previously described "halo effect" may actually be influencing modern translations of the עוד ב־ collocation.

86. Considering the royal interpretation adopted by some scholars, if the attire denotes expanded responsibilities rather than a return to previously held ones, the subsequent communication would actually then lower expectations for this role since such responsibilities are not addressed. That is, while political or royal concepts may be alluded to in the passage by reference to the *Zemah*, a royal role for Joshua himself would be *diminished*. As such, it seems unlikely that even if a royal interpretation is adopted for the garments, they should be interpreted as a validation of Joshua in Zechariah 3.

87. Note, Boda reads the crowns in Zechariah 6:9-15 as a prophetic sign-act that points to the *Zemah* and the temple-building project (Boda, *The Book of Zechariah*, 380–6); he also notes that both the crowns and the thrones could be used by "lesser figures within royal courts ... most likely related to receiving counsel" (Boda, "Perspectives of Priests," 25, 24–5). Thus, the idea that Zechariah 3 includes a subtle critique or undermining is not contradicted by the wider context of proto-Zechariah.

any expanded expectations for the high priest given its explicit focus on priestly duties. Thus, the reference to Joshua's dress should be seen as a coded critique, warning Joshua and the book's audience to closely follow the ways of YHWH, rather than as validating vestments.

Chapter 11

SOCIAL STANDING, AGENCY, AND THE MOTIF OF CLOTH AND CLOTHING IN ESTHER

Selena Billington

The book of Esther is full of extravagant exaggerations and extremes, laden with irony and brimming with farcical elements.[1] Some obvious elements recur throughout the book—notably motifs such as feasting/banquets and fasting. Another prominent motif within Esther is that of cloth and clothing. The manner in which the motif of cloth and clothing works throughout the book of Esther— its use as a literary device that provides narrative structure, identifies social standing, and illuminates the relationship between characters—is the focus of this chapter.[2]

The text of Esther includes a rich and varied vocabulary associated with cloth and clothing. In keeping with the character of the book as full of exaggerations and extremes, cloth and clothing are presented in Esther in an extreme manner—with sackcloth and ashes on the one hand, and literally the finest imaginable fabrics on the other. Twelve passages from Esther refer to either cloth or clothing (or dress, more generally, including the king's signet ring and scepter), from the opening

---

1. The genesis of this chapter was a paper for a class on "Ruth and Esther," taught by Mark K. George, who later served as my dissertation advisor. I am grateful for Mark's guidance throughout my graduate studies. I am grateful to all the members of the SBL Pacific Northwest Region's Research Group on Dress for their feedback on earlier drafts of this essay, and am especially grateful to Shannon Parrott and Jen Jones, whose lot it was to carefully review the 2019 and 2020 drafts, respectively, and to Tony Finitsis, for his consistently insightful suggestions.

2. There are three extant versions of the book of Esther: the Hebrew Masoretic Text (MT Esther) and two Greek texts—LXX Esther and AT Esther. Unless otherwise noted, the book of Esther referred to in this chapter is MT Esther. For a nice summary of the history of the understanding of the relationship between MT Esther, LXX Esther, and AT Esther, see Meredith J. Stone, *Empire and Gender in LXX Esther* (Atlanta, GA: SLB, 2018).

scene in Ahasuerus's palace to Mordecai's triumphant ceremonial "going-out" before the people of the city of Susa.[3] These passages are:

1:6	Ahasuerus's palace
1:11	Vashti's headdress
2:17	Esther's headdress
3:12	Ahasuerus's ring to Haman
4:1-4	Mordecai's ritually torn clothes, and sackcloth (and ashes)
4:11	Ahasuerus's scepter
5:1	Esther's royal robes
5:2	Ahasuerus's scepter
6:6-11	Mordecai in the king's robes/the horse's headdress
8:2	Ahasuerus's ring to Mordecai
8:4	Ahasuerus's scepter
8:15	Mordecai's prestigious clothing

Demonstrably, the motif of clothing in Esther offers significant opportunities for investigation from different perspectives. One truly fine example is Adele Berlin's 2000 SBL presidential address, in which she noted conventional literary motifs associated with Persia by Greek writers of the late fifth and fourth centuries BCE, discussed how these motifs have lent verisimilitude to Esther and therefore muddied the water about its historicity, and demonstrated how motifs can also play a role in exegesis. "Motifs have connotations; they can function like semiotic signals or codes. Knowledge of a motif's connotation can take us a long way toward decoding the meaning of a passage or episode."[4] She illustrates this with an exegesis of 6:6-11—the ceremony of honor that Haman designed and Mordecai received—drawing on motifs about clothing from the biblical corpus[5] and on

3. Ahasuerus's gold scepter is not discussed in this chapter. Ahasuerus uses it to signal clemency to those in general who approach him in the inner court without having been summoned (Est. 4:11), including Esther in particular (Est. 5:2, 8:4).

4. Adele Berlin, "The Book of Esther and Ancient Storytelling," *JBL* 120 (2001), 3–14, 11.

5. A number of scholars have explored motifs from various other biblical books that show up in Esther as well. An early example is the study by Sandra Beth Berg, drawing on parallels between the book of Esther and the Joseph story. Sandra Beth Berg, *The Book of Esther: Motifs, Themes, and Structure* (Missoula, MT: Scholars, 1979). More recently, Matthew Michael explores the motifs shared between the books of Esther and Daniel, among which are: a conspiracy by royal officials to kill the main character (referring to Mordecai, not Esther); excessive banqueting; and bowing down to a statue or person. Michael also reviews previous studies on shared motifs between Esther and the books of Genesis, Exodus, Samuel, and Kings. The conclusion of his study is that while Esther and Daniel use the same motifs and same narrative milieu of postexilic discourse, "it seems Daniel seeks to undermine or challenge the ideology in the book of Esther." Matthew Michael, "Daniel at the Beauty Pageant and Esther in the Lion's Den: Literary Intertextuality and Shared Motifs between the Books of Daniel and Esther," *OTE* 29 (2016), 116–32, 127.

motifs about Persian use of royal clothing from Greek sources such as Plutarch's *Artaxerxes* and Xenophon's *Cyropaedia*.

Approaching the motif of clothing in Esther from a different perspective, David J. A. Clines applies semantic analysis (structuralism) to the book of Esther to investigate the "code of clothing" therein. Clines notes that clothing in Esther becomes conspicuous ultimately in 8:15 when it proclaims Mordecai's identity as a Persian—"as Persian as it is possible for a Jew to be."[6]

In addition, three recent studies have addressed the motif of clothing in Esther. Two of those studies are intertextual biblical analyses. In one, Ayelet Seidler considers sackcloth (4:1-4) among the motifs shared between the books of Esther and Jonah, in order to draw out hints of theological implications in MT Esther.[7] In the other, Joshua Joel Spoelstra carefully examines the motif of clothing throughout Esther as background for an analysis of Mordecai's prestige clothing in 8:15 vis-à-vis Exodus 28 and 39 and Zechariah 6. Spoelstra asks whether those garments are princely and/or priestly, and what implications there would have been for the contemporary reader.[8] Finally, in a very recent study, Laura Quick and Ellena Lyell explore the imagery of clothing in Esther, focusing on how differences in clothing develop distinctions between the power and status of the various characters. They conclude that a variety of intertexts relating to clothing and kingship magnify Mordecai as the fulfillment of the Benjaminite royal line.[9]

Clothing is associated with each of the five main characters in Esther, whether that clothing is explicitly worn (Vashti, Esther, and Mordecai), loaned (Ahasuerus), or aspired to (Haman). Most of the explicit description of clothing is associated with Mordecai, and so I have chosen to parse the author's use of

---

6. The semantic analysis is one of a number of modern literary interpretive tools that Clines employs in his insightful and satisfying study. The methods he experiments with for the book of Esther are: formalism, structuralism (actanial and semantic analyses), feminism, materialism, and deconstruction. David J. A. Clines, "Reading Esther from Left to Right: Contemporary Strategies for Reading a Biblical Text," in *The Bible in Three Dimensions: Essays in Celebration of Forty Years of Biblical Studies in the University of Sheffield*, JSOTSup, ed. David J. A. Clines, Stephen E. Fowl, and Stanley E. Porter (Sheffield, England: JSOT, 1990), 31–52, 39.

7. Ayelet Seidler, "'Fasting,' 'Sackcloth,' and 'Ashes'—From Nineveh to Shushan," *VT* 69 (2019), 117–34.

8. Joshua Joel Spoelstra, "Mordecai's Royal Vestments: Princely and/or Priestly?," *OTE* 32 (2019), 174–96.

9. Laura Quick and Ellena Lyell, "Clothing, Conformity and Power: Garment Imagery in the Book of Esther," *VT* (forthcoming). This article came to my attention prior to its publication, and shortly before the publication deadline for this volume, so unfortunately I have not been able to engage with it in the remainder of this chapter. For more on the clothing of the Benjaminite Mordecai as part of the biblical narrative about the relationship of dress to the fortunes of the Benjaminites, see Ellena Lyell, "Dressing Benjaminites, Defining Kingship: Dress as a Royal Prerogative for the Tribe of Benjamin," in this volume.

the clothing motif generally into two main narrative threads, one focusing on Mordecai's clothing and the other involving Vashti's and Esther's (and the horse's) dress. Of course, intersections and overlaps occur between these two narrative threads, and additionally there are the relationships expressed via the particular assemblage of clothing coveted by Haman, loaned by Ahasuerus, and worn by Mordecai. Accordingly, the outline of this chapter comprises: (i) setting the scene— Ahasuerus's palace; (ii) Mordecai's clothing; (iii) Vashti's and Esther's clothing; and (iv) intersections and loose ends.

Setting the Scene—Court of the Garden of Ahasuerus's Palace

The first of the six passages in which the motif of cloth and clothing occurs in Esther is the marvelous description of the court of the garden of Ahasuerus's[10] palace, as follows:

> There were white [חוּר; *ḥûr*] cotton [כַּרְפַּס; *karpas*] curtains and blue [תְּכֵלֶת; *təkēlet*] hangings tied with cords of fine linen [בּוּץ; *bûṣ*] and purple [אַרְגָּמָן; *'argāmān*] to silver rings and marble pillars. There were couches of gold and silver on a mosaic pavement of porphyry, marble [בַּהַט־וָשֵׁשׁ; *bahaṭ* and *šēš*], mother-of-pearl [דַּר; *dar*], and colored stones [סֹחָרֶת; *sōḥāret*]. (Est. 1:6; NRSV)[11]

This is an extraordinary verse. Commentators consistently point out how strikingly different it is from the rest of Esther and, indeed, from other biblical literature. Timothy Beal comments, "In a narrative that is otherwise quite sparse with regard to descriptive details, [verses 6–8] are remarkable."[12] David Lees singles out Est. 1:6 as "peculiar in Esther and in the biblical corpus," and following Arndt Meinhold,

---

10. Ahasuerus is the Hebrew name for Xerxes I, who ruled Persia from 485 to 465 BCE. Timothy K. Beal, *Esther*, in *Ruth and Esther*, authors Tod Linafelt and Timothy K. Beal, respectively; Berit Olam (Collegeville, MN: Liturgical Press, 1999), xv. The latest possible date for the composition of MT Esther is mid-second century BCE (Maccabean period). Some argue for a composition in the late Persian or the early Hellenistic period (fourth century). For example, Adele Berlin, *Esther: The Traditional Hebrew Text with the New JPS Translation/Commentary by Adele Berlin* (Philadelphia, PA: Jewish Publication Society, 2001), xli–xlii; W. Lee Humphreys and Sidnie White Crawford, "Introduction and Annotations to Esther," in *The HarperCollins Study Bible, Fully Revised and Updated*, New Revised Standard Version, ed. Harold W. Attridge, Wayne A. Meeks, Jouette M. Bassler, Werner E. Lemke, Susan Niditch, and Eileen M. Schuller (New York: HarperOne, 2006), 680–91, 680. Others more generally offer fourth through third centuries as the possible compositional period. For example, Jon D. Levenson, *Esther: A Commentary*, OTL, ed. James L. Mays, Carol A. Newsom, and David L. Petersen (Louisville, KY: Westminster John Knox, 1997), 26.

11. All translations used in this chapter are from the NRSV.

12. Beal, *Esther*, 7.

attributes its uniqueness to both the contents of the verse and the abrupt change in writing style.[13] Jonathan Grossman comments on the "clumsy style" of 1:6.[14] Spoelstra, following Frederik William Bush, suggests that 1:6 may have been a later editorial insertion.[15]

The uniqueness of 1:6, coupled with the commonly held view articulated by Max Rogland that "the verse is purely descriptive in nature and as such is not particularly significant for the book's plot,"[16] raises the question of why it is included at this point in the narrative. Commentators frequently offer some explanation along the lines that the intent is "to enhance the sense of extreme opulence,"[17] or to convey an overwhelming impression of "spectacular lavishness."[18] Lees argues convincingly that this explanation is inadequate. He quotes Robert Gordis, "Whatever is not germane to [the author of Esther's] purpose is rigorously excluded … Nothing in the book is superfluous; everything bears upon the central theme … The author, a superb storyteller, wastes no words on unessential details."[19] I agree with Lees that the explanation of conveying opulence is inadequate or at least that it is incomplete—I claim that the description of the court of the garden serves at least one other purpose, namely that of introducing the motif of cloth and clothing in the book of Esther as an important narrative device.[20]

---

13. David Lees, "*Hapax Legomena* in Esther 1.6: Translation Difficulties and Comedy in the Book of Esther," *BT* 68 (2017), 88–108, 89. Lees cites Arndt Meinhold, *Das Buch Esther*, 13 (Zurich: Theologisher Verlag, 1983).

14. Jonathan Grossman, *Esther: The Outer Narrative and the Hidden Reading* (Winona Lake, IN: Pennsylvania State University Press, 2011), 43. Grossman cites Timothy S. Laniak for pointing out that there is no predicate to 1:6; "There were" has been added in the NRSV. Timothy S. Laniak, *Shame and Honor in the Book of Esther*, 165 (Atlanta, GA: Scholars, 1998), 47. Grossman also quotes G. R. Driver as saying that the opening words of the verse "hang in the air." G. R. Driver, "Problems and Solutions," *VT* 4 (1954), 225–45, 235.

15. Spoelstra, "Mordecai's Vestments," 184. Spoelstra cites Frederic William Bush, *Ruth/Esther*, 9 (Dallas, TX: Word Books, 1996), 343.

16. Max Rogland, "The Cult of Esther: Temple and Priestly Imagery in the Book of Esther," *JSOT* 44 (2019), 99–114. For additional grammatical and lexical discussion of 1:6, Rogland cites Robert D. Holmstedt and John Screnock, *Esther: A Handbook on the Hebrew Text* (Waco, TX: Baylor University Press, 2015), 44–7.

17. Levenson, *Esther*, 43.

18. Beal, *Esther*, 7.

19. Lees, "*Hapax Legomena* Esther 1:6," 90. Lees quotes Robert Gordis, *Megillat Esther: The Masoretic Hebrew Text, with Introduction, New Translation, and Commentary*, Megillat Esther (New York: Rabbinical Assembly, 1974), 14, 21.

20. Lees's assertion is that naming a few stones at the end of the description of the court of Ahasuerus's palace does not constitute "an over-the-top exclamation of luxury." His answer to the question of why the author would include a unique description of a physical environment here is that the author is continuing to mock Ahasuerus. See fn. 23 below. Rogland's answer to question is that the terminology of 1:6 is a subset of "verbal cues in

One contributing factor to the uniqueness of Est. 1:6 has to do with the extraordinary vocabulary contained within it. In this one verse, there are four *hapax legomena* (*karpas, bahaṭ, dar, sōḥāret*), a term (*ḥûr*) that is unique to Esther, another term (*bûṣ*) that occurs only in late biblical Hebrew, and two terms (*təkēlet, 'argāmān*) that allude to the sumptuous textiles of the tabernacle.²¹ Of these eight terms, at least five (*ḥûr, karpas, təkēlet, bûṣ,* and *'argāmān*) are related to cloth.²² In addition, an interesting case has been made that the other three *hapax legomena* (*bahaṭ, dar, sōḥāret*), usually translated as stone components of the palace's (mosaic pavement) floor, are actually words that refer to cloth—to textiles which together make up the palace flooring, that is, carpets.²³

Esther that evoke the Temple's furnishings, functionaries, structure and rituals" and that "the author's employment of cultic imagery to compare the Persian court to the Temple—and by extension, the Persian king to God—is a literary tool that would allow him to subversively critique the Persian Empire while maintaining enough subtlety to avoid getting into trouble." Rogland, "Cult of Esther," 99 and 106.

21. Frederick Greenspahn refers to Est. 1:6 as one of the twenty-eight verses that contain more than one *hapax legomenon* apiece. Of them, "fourteen include lists which by their very nature treat a particular topic more exhaustively than would normally be the case, whether it is the species of forbidden animals or the kinds of decoration installed in a royal palace." Frederick E. Greenspahn, "The Number and Distribution of Hapax Legomena in Biblical Hebrew," *VT* 30 (1980), 8–19, 12.

22. There are two other *hapox legomena* in Esther related to clothing: Vashti's and Esther's headdress, and Mordecai's mantle. Of the five *hapax legomena* in 1:6 that are unambiguously related to cloth (and clothing), the terms *ḥûr, təkēlet, bûṣ,* and *'argāmān* are discussed in the body of this essay. The remaining term *karpas* refers to cotton, which was relatively novel and a luxury item. Cotton was domesticated in India and thence introduced into the ANE. It was an exotic novelty at the time of Sennacherib of Assyria (reigned 705–681 BCE), whose impressive garden boasted "wool-bearing trees" that were "sheared" and whose "wool" was woven into garments, according to Sennacherib's annals. Daniel David Luckenbill, *The Annals of Sennacherib*, OIP 2 (Chicago, IL: University of Chicago Press, 1924), col. VIII, line 64; col. VI, line 56. See also Stephanie Dalley, *The Mystery of the Hanging Garden of Babylon: An Elusive World Wonder Traced* (Oxford: Oxford University Press, 2013). By the sixth century BCE, cotton was available for embellishing luxury textiles in Egypt; Herodotus reports the gift of a breastplate, of 360-ply (!) linen and embroidered with gold and cotton, by Pharaoh Amasis (Ahmose II; reigned 570–526 BCE), dedicated to Athena in Lindus. Herodotus, *Hist.* 3.47; Peter A. Clayton, *Chronicle of the Pharaohs: The Reign-by-Reign Record of the Rulers and Dynasties of Ancient Egypt* (London: Thames and Hudson, 1994).

23. The terms *bahaṭ, dar,* and *sōḥāret* are *hapax legomena*. Together with the word *šēš* (here meaning linen or marble), they have something to do with the flooring of Ahasuerus's palace. Most commonly they are translated as stones, as in "a mosaic pavement of porphyry, marble (*šēš*), mother-of-pearl, and colored stones" (NRSV). Less commonly the terms are translated as colors of stones, as in "a pavement of green, and white, and shell, and onyx marble" (JPS) or "a pavement of red and blue and white and black marble." Stephanie Dalley, "Ancient Assyrian Textiles and the Origins of Carpet Design," *Iran* 29 (1991), 117–35, 139.

Four of the terms in 1:6 that are unquestionably cloth terms—*təkēlet, ḥûr, bûṣ,* and *'argāmān*—are reprised in 8:15, where they are used as part of the description of Mordecai's clothing near the end of the story. In light of this, the four terms are briefly explicated here.[24]

Təkēlet and 'argāmān

These two terms refer to (cloths made of) purplish-blue and reddish-purple wools, respectively, almost certainly imported from the vicinity of Sidon. The dyes involved are animal based. Hundreds of plants have been used to create dyes but very few animal species; according to Dominique Cardon, only about twenty-five animal species altogether have been used for dye production, including fifteen species of molluscs (all of which produce purples such as *təkēlet* and *'argāmān*). Animal-based dyes create brighter colors than plant-based dyes, are color-fast, and labor intensive. Thus, "animal dyes represent extreme examples of the role of coloured textiles as status symbols."[25]

David Lees presents an interesting alternative, making a case for interpreting the three *hapax legomena* as textiles that form a cloth carpet. He relates *bahaṭ* to the rare Akkadian word *beḥaṭ*—some type of fabric or garment that was included among a list, in the Tell el-Amarna tablets, of luxurious and expensive gifts given by Tušratta to Amenhotep IV. Lees, "Hapax legomena Esther 1:6," 99. Lees also makes (less convincing) cases for *dar* as decorated with gold and *sōḥāret* as referring to miscellaneous colored adornments, so that the concluding phrase of 1:6 could be read as "a flooring of regal carpets with golden thread and other brightly coloured adornments" (103). Lees argues that the interpretation of the flooring as textiles is more satisfying than the interpretation as mosaic pavement stones, for two reasons. First, the stones generally proposed do not accord with known Persian palatial flooring stones, and second that by outing Ahasuerus for having soft floors, Esther's author introduces another comedic element to the Esther story, getting a dig in along the lines of Xenophon's lament that the Achaemenid rulers had lost their way since Cyrus's day:

> I should like to explain their effeminacy more in detail. In the first place, they are not satisfied with only having their couches upholstered with down, but they actually set the posts of their beds upon carpets, so that the floor may offer no resistance. (*Cyropaedia* VIII.VIII.16)

Lees sees the purpose of 1:6 as not so much to convey lavishness and opulence, but rather as "a Hebrew joke to show the weakness of Ahasuerus in the midst of a setting of supposed great state and military leaders" (Lees, "Hapax Legomena Esther 1:6," 102).

24. The discussion of the terms *təkēlet, 'argāmān,* and *karpas* comes from my PhD dissertation: Selena Billington, "Glorious Adornment: The Social Function of Cloth and Clothing in Israel's Tabernacle," PhD dissertation, Iliff School of Theology and the University of Denver, 2014.

25. Dominique Cardon, *Natural Dyes: Sources, Tradition, Technology and Science* (London: Archetype, 2007), 551.

Təkēlet and *'argāmān* are the two most prestigious colors/dyes/textiles in the Hebrew Bible. Of the two, *təkēlet* was valued even more highly than *'argāmān*, although *'argāmān* would achieve greater status later among Romans as the imperial purple. The two terms necessarily evoke the sumptuous cloths of the tabernacle, which consisted of *təkēlet*, *'argāmān*, and *tôla'at šānî* (the latter referring to wool—probably crimson—dyed using dye probably imported from Ararat).[26]

Ḥûr

The word translated as white in 1:6 and 8:15 occurs nowhere else in the Bible. There seems to be no question that *ḥûr* means "white stuff" of some kind—either linen or cotton.[27]

Bûṣ

Seven terms for linen, linen garments, or flax are used in the Hebrew Bible,[28] of which *šēš* and *bûṣ* are synonymous and refer to the finest quality of linen, such as that used in the construction of the tabernacle (Exod. 26, 36) and the high-priestly vestments. Both terms are generally translated as "fine linen," and both are rendered in the LXX as βύσσος.[29] The term *šēš* occurs most commonly of all the linen

---

26. Robert Alter mistakenly translates *təkēlet* as "indigo," which is a plant-based dye, and mistakenly translates *'argāmān* as "crimson"/"scarlet." Given the very high value placed by the biblical writers on both *təkēlet* and *'argāmān* I disagree with his comment that "it makes no sense to put two colors in a list of sumptuous fabrics, so both terms should be instances of hendiadys, two words joined by 'and' that refer to a single concept." Robert Alter, *The Hebrew Bible: A Translation with Commentary; Vol. 3: The Writings* (New York: W.W. Norton, 2019), 718.

27. BDB, 301.

28. In alphabetical order: אֵטוּן (*'ēṭûn*); בַּד (*bad*); בּוּץ (*bûṣ*); פֵּשֶׁת (*pēšet*); פִּשְׁתָּה (*pištâ*); סָדִין (*sādîn*); שֵׁשׁ (*šēš*). Linen was a primary export of Egypt, so it is not surprising that some of the seven terms are loan words from Egyptian, specifically *šēš*, *'ēṭûn*, and possibly *bûṣ*.

29. From the Greek βύσσος comes the English word "byssus," meaning:

an exceedingly fine and valuable textile fibre and fabric known to the ancients; apparently the word was used, or misused, of various substances, linen, cotton, and silk, but it denoted properly (as shown by recent microscopic examination of mummy-cloths, which according to Herodotus were made of βύσσος) a kind of flax, and hence is appropriately translated in the English Bible "fine linen." OED Online

As explained by Felicitas Maeder among others, the meaning of the word "byssus" unfortunately became seriously muddled by a sixteenth-century mistranslation of Aristotle's description of the fan shell *Pinna nobilis L.*, which is the largest shellfish of the Mediterranean, where it is endemic. It is rooted in sandy places or in weeds near

terms.[30] The term *bûṣ* is synonymous with *šēš* but occurs only in late biblical writings (Chronicles, Ezekiel, and Esther).[31]

As noted above, the four terms just reviewed—*təkēlet*, *ḥûr*, *bûṣ*, and *'argāmān*—are reprised in 8:15, where they are used as part of the description of Mordecai's clothing near the end of the story. Furthermore, the phrase "fine linen and purple" in 1:6 is exactly replicated in 8:15. Thus, not only does 1:6 introduce the motif of cloth and clothing in general but it also sets the scene for the narrative thread concerning Mordecai's clothing by providing specific vocabulary important to that thread.

Mordecai's Status Revealed by His Clothing

Clothing is mentioned for four named characters in Esther: Vashti, Esther, Mordecai, and Ahasuerus.[32] However, the only mention of Ahasuerus's clothing

the coast with a beard of very fine, strong protein filaments or fibers, generated by a gland in the foot of the mussel. These fibers are "the raw material for sea silk, known since antiquity: a silk like textile material famous and highly appreciated for its natural iridescent brown-golden colour." Felicitas Maeder, "Byssus and Sea Silk: A Linguistic Problem with Consequences," in *Treasures from the Sea: Sea Silk and Shellfish Purple Dye in Antiquity*, ed. Hedvig Landenius Enegren and Francesco Meo (Havertown, PA: Oxbow, 2017), 13–42, 14. Ever since the mistranslation, the *Pinna nobilis L.* fibers, and the textiles made from them, are known as byssus. Therefore, sea silk is now synonymous with byssus but would not have been prior to the sixteenth century CE. For a complete etymology of "byssus," see Maeder, "Byssus and Sea Silk." See also Daniel McKinley, "Pinna and Her Silken Beard: A Foray into Historical Misappropriations," *Ars Textrina* 29 (1998), 9–223; and Elena Soriga and Alfredo Carannante, "Tangled Threads. Byssus and Sea Silk in the Bronze Age: An Interdisciplinary Approach," in Enegren and Meo, *Treasures from the Sea*, 51–85.

30. The term *šēš* actually has three meanings: six, linen, or marble; it is generally understood as used with the latter meaning in 1:6, although Lees reads it as "linen" (see fn. 23 above) and LXX Est. 1:6 ends with a reference to a cloth spread.

31. For example, in Exodus, the divider between the Holy and the Holy of Holies in the tabernacle was made of *təkēlet*, *'argāmān*, and *tôla'at šānî*, and *šēš mošzār*, whereas in Chronicles, the equivalent divider in Solomon's temple was made of *təkēlet*, *'argāmān*, *karmîl*, and *bûṣ* (Exod. 26:31-33; 36:35; 2 Chr. 3:14). Note that the temple *karmîl* is synonymous with the tabernacle *tôla'at šānî*, as the temple *bûṣ* is synonymous with the tabernacle *šēš*. See Avi Hurvitz, "The Usage of שש and בוץ in the Bible and Its Implications for the Date of P," *HTR* 60 (1967), 117–21.

32. Haman's clothing is not explicitly mentioned. However, in 6:12 he is described as "mourning, and with his head covered," and in 7:8, when Ahasuerus accuses Haman of assaulting Esther, "as the words left the mouth of the king, they covered Haman's face."

is in the context of its being worn by Mordecai (and his signet ring only in the context of being entrusted to others). Most of the explicit description of clothing, by far, is associated with Mordecai, and the fact that Mordecai wears different clothing in different parts of the story invites further exploration.

Social scientists are clear about the importance of clothing in human cultures.[33] In particular, those who study the anthropology of clothing concur that whatever other functions clothing serves in any particular human society, such as providing protection from the environment and/or from supernatural forces, the "principle function of clothing is to differentiate members of society into age, sex and class or caste."[34] Terence S. Turner comments that dress and bodily adornment constitute a cultural "medium through which we communicate our social status, attitudes, desires, beliefs and ideals (in short, our identities) to others."[35] Joanne Entwistle posits that it is the "universal human propensity to communicate with symbols" that forms the basis for this role of clothing.[36] Simply put, clothing affirms and projects social identity and social position. It is this understanding of the social function of clothing that predominates in current anthropological and sociological studies of clothing, dress, and/or adornment, in general, and in many recent studies of clothing in the Bible, in particular.[37]

33. Among pertinent disciplines are: psychology of clothing, sociology of clothing, linguistics of clothing, anthropology of clothing (and anthropology of cloth).

34. Ronald A. Schwarz, "Uncovering the Secret Vice: Toward an Anthropology of Clothing and Adornment," in *The Fabrics of Culture: The Anthropology of Clothing and Adornment*, ed. Justine M. Cordwell and Ronald A. Schwarz (The Hague: Mouton, 1979), 23–45, 27.

35. Terence S. Turner, "The Social Skin," *HAU: Journal of Ethnographic Theory* 2 (2012), 486–504, 487. Turner also speaks of bodily adornment (including clothing) as being the language through which the drama of socialization is expressed (486). For more on "the language of clothes" applied to biblical studies, see Claudia Bender, *Die Sprache des Textilen: Untersuchungen zu Kleidung und Textilien im Alten Testament*, BWANT 177 (Stuttgart: Kohlhammer, 2008).

36. Joanne Entwistle, *The Fashioned Body: Fashion, Dress and Modern Social Theory* (Cambridge: Polity, 2000), 58.

37. My own PhD dissertation is one such example. Another example is an essay by Deborah Rooke about the high priest's linen underwear. In rejecting the explanation, proposed by numerous commentators, that the purpose of the underwear is modesty, Rooke notes that clothing "is an extremely important indicator of both gender and social status, serving to differentiate male from female and to enforce as well as create social hierarchies." Deborah W. Rooke, "Breeches of the Covenant: Gender, Garments and the Priesthood," in *Embroidered Garments: Priests and Gender in Biblical Israel*, ed. Deborah W. Rooke, Hebrew Bible Monographs (Sheffield, England: Sheffield Phoenix Press, 2009), 19–37, 20. For more general overviews of dress/adornment in the Hebrew Bible, see Heather A. McKay, "Gendering the Discourse of Display in the Hebrew Bible," in *On Reading Prophetic Texts: Gender-Specific and Related Studies in Memory of Fokkelien van Dijk-Hemmes*, ed. Bob Becking and Meindert Dijkstra; Biblical Interpretation Series

With the notion in mind that clothing affirms and projects social identity and social position and differentiates members of society into age, sex, and class or caste, it is now appropriate to examine Mordecai's various clothing. The first specification of Mordecai's clothing occurs in 4:1-4, following the first edict (which called for the massacre of the Jews some months hence), at the nadir of Mordecai's fortunes:

> When Mordecai learned all that had been done, Mordecai tore his clothes and put on sackcloth and ashes, and went through the city, wailing with a loud and bitter cry; he went up to the entrance of the king's gate, for no one might enter the king's gate clothed with sackcloth. In every province, wherever the king's command and his decree came, there was great mourning among the Jews, with fasting and weeping and lamenting, and most of them lay in sackcloth and ashes. When Esther's maids and her eunuchs came and told her, the queen was deeply distressed; she sent garments to clothe Mordecai, so that he might take off his sackcloth; but he would not accept them. (Est. 4:1-4)

Three distinct actions related to clothing are expressed here: Mordecai tears his clothes, he puts on sackcloth and ashes, and Esther sends non-sackcloth garments to Mordecai, who refuses them. Esther's action of sending garments to Mordecai, and his refusal of them, is one of the topics discussed in the section titled "Intersections and Loose Ends."

Our understanding of the rite of tearing one's clothes in public has been significantly furthered by a recent study by Melanie Köhlmoos, in which she analyzed the dozens of biblical examples of persons tearing their clothes.[38] Her analysis reveals three important points about this rite. First,

> tearing one's garment can be performed by any class or gender, publicly or privately, by individuals and groups, on one's own accord, on somebody's

---

(Leiden: E.J. Brill, 1996), 169–99; Heather A. McKay, "Gendering the Body: Clothes Maketh the (Wo)man," in *Theology and the Body: Gender, Text and Ideology*, ed. Robert Hannaford and J'annine Jobling (Herefordshire: Gracewing, 1999), 84–104; and Laura Quick, *Dress, Adornment, and the Body in the Hebrew Bible* (Oxford: Oxford University Press, 2021). Most of the essays about dress/undress in the Hebrew Bible in this current collection and in two other recent collections are underpinned by the understanding of clothing as affirming and projecting social identity and social position: Antonios Finitsis, ed., *Dress and Clothing in the Hebrew Bible: "For All Her Household Are Clothed in Crimson"* (London: T&T Clark, 2019); Christoph Berner, Manuel Schäfer, Martin Schott, Sarah Schulz, and Martina Weingärtner, eds, *Clothing and Nudity in the Hebrew Bible* (London: T&T Clark, 2019).

38. Melanie Köhlmoos, "Tearing One's Clothes and Rites of Mourning," in *Clothing and Nudity in the Hebrew Bible*, ed. Christoph Berner, Manuel Schäfer, Martin Schott, Sarah Schulz, and Martina Weingärtner (London: T&T Clark, 2019), 304–13.

orders, and even vicariously. Hence, tearing the garment is a very common rite, presumably with a well-understood meaning.[39]

Second, there were many possible occasions for tearing one's garments, such as sickness, rape, defeat, treason, blasphemy, or the death of a family member, a close friend, or a national celebrity. Third, not every occasion of death or impending death calls for the rite of tearing one's clothes; for example, it is not required when death is not completely unexpected, like a woman dying in childbirth or a father dying of old age.[40] Köhlmoos's contribution is to identify the criterion that renders situations appropriate for the special rite of tearing one's clothes.[41] Specifically, Köhlmoos posits that "tearing one's garment is required (or at least socially appropriate) in cases of unexpected catastrophe"—situations that are shocking, inexplicable, or improbable, as in experiences of "unexpected violence and/or inexplicable, terrifying mysteries."[42] Her conclusion is that the "point of the rite appears to be a way of channeling shock and terror in the face of catastrophe by way of a socially acceptable act of destruction."[43]

The specific example of Mordecai tearing his clothes is not addressed by Köhlmoos. Nonetheless, her analysis is apt; the edict calling for the state-sanctioned slaughter of all Jews is the epitome of an "unexpected catastrophe" and must be entirely shocking to Mordecai. His response is entirely suitable to the occasion.[44]

The wearing of sackcloth (שַׂק; *śaq*) is an important component of ritual mourning in the Bible, and examples are numerous.[45] Examples of the wearing of

39. Ibid., 305.

40. Thus, according to Köhlmoos, tearing of one's clothes is *not* the central rite associated with mourning, contra other scholars with whom Köhlmoos engages. In her view, the primary rite associated with mourning is the wearing of sackcloth.

41. Traditionally, scholars have understood the tearing of one's clothes to be part of mourning rites—a form of expressing grief. In addition, scholars have also proposed that another cause for the tearing of one's clothes is the expression of humiliation or self-diminution.

42. Ibid., 306, 307.

43. Ibid., 312.

44. One further note on the tearing of one's clothes: Tearing one's garments could symbolize, among other things, a change in status. Seidler ("Fasting, Sackcloth, and Ashes," 129) cites Nathan Klaus for this observation. Nathan Klaus, "The Tearing of Garments as the Main Symbol of Mourning in the Bible," *Beit Mikra* 56 (2011), 71–99. A particularly striking example is Tamar's public tearing of her robe after her status changed from virgin to nonvirgin upon being raped (2 Sam. 13). Sara Koenig points out that the tearing marked "the destruction of [Tamar's] royalty, her modesty, and her virginity." Sara Koenig, "Tamar and Tamar: Clothing as Deception and Defiance," in *Dress and Clothing in the Hebrew Bible: "For All Her Household Are Clothed in Crimson,"* ed. Antonios Finitsis (London: T&T Clark, 2019), 87–108, 108. See also McKay, "Gendering Discourse of Display," 195.

45. As per fn. 40 above, according to Köhlmoos, the primary rite associated with mourning is the wearing of sackcloth. But cf. Klaus, "Tearing of Garments."

sackcloth and ashes (שַׂק וָאֵפֶר; *śaq* and *'ēper*) occur less frequently. The term *śaq* refers to the coarsest possible clothing, of a dark-colored fabric of goat's or camel's hair.[46] The phrase "in sackcloth and ashes" means being clothed in sackcloth and having ashes sprinkled on one's head as a sign of lamentation or abject penitence. This signifies either mourning or a humbling of oneself as part of supplication before the deity associated with fasting.[47] Notice that the term *śaq* occurs *four* times in these four verses; the repetition has the effect of emphasizing the direness of the situation and the depths of Mordecai's despair.

The next scene in which Mordecai's clothing plays a role is that in which Haman's advice to the king about how to honor himself (Haman) goes badly awry:

> So Haman came in, and the king said to him, "What shall be done for the man whom the king wishes to honor?" Haman said to himself, "Whom would the king wish to honor more than me?" So Haman said to the king, "For the man whom the king wishes to honor, let royal robes be brought, which the king has worn, and a horse that the king has ridden, with a royal crown on its head. Let the robes and the horse be handed over to one of the king's most noble officials; let him robe the man whom the king wishes to honor, and let him conduct the man on horseback through the open square of the city, proclaiming before him: 'Thus shall it be done for the man whom the king wishes to honor.'" Then the king said to Haman, "Quickly, take the robes and the horse, as you have said, and do so to the Jew Mordecai who sits at the king's gate. Leave out nothing that you have mentioned." So Haman took the robes and the horse and robed Mordecai and led him riding through the open square of the city, proclaiming, "Thus shall it be done for the man whom the king wishes to honor." (Est. 6:6-11)

An abundance of information is relayed in this passage about the relationships between Haman, the king, and Mordecai, and about their characterizations, and these will be discussed in the section titled "Intersections and Loose Ends." Here I focus specifically on the clothing worn by Mordecai during this episode.

The verb לָבַשׁ (*lābaš*) is used three times in 6:8-11, as Mordecai *is dressed* in the royal robes in which the king *had been dressed.* The noun translated as "robe" or

---

46. "Modern" sackcloth, in contrast, is some coarse fabric used for sacking grain or bird seed, for example. OED Online (accessed March 31, 2019).

47. Mourning: Jer. 6:26, Ezek. 27:30-31, Jon. 3:6. Self-humbling: Isa. 58:5, Dan. 9:3. Seidler ("Fasting, Sackcloth, and Ashes," 118) classifies the mourning in both Esther and Jonah as petitionary mourning and sees the motifs shared between Esther and Jonah—of fasting, sackcloth, and ashes—as evidence that the author of Esther intentionally alluded to Jonah to "hint" at some theological implications that are lacking explicitly in MT Esther. In this, she is in accord with Grossman, whose approach to Esther is to uncover the concealed meanings hidden behind the revealed themes. He says, "All biblical narratives conceal messages beneath the surface, but Esther seems to epitomize this phenomenon" (Grossman, *Esther*, 4).

"robes" (לְבוּשׁ; ləbûš) is a generic term for clothing related to the verb *lābaš*. No particular type of garment is implied—what matters are not the actual garments involved but the fact that they had been worn by the king. On the other hand, the royal headdress (*keter*) that the horse wears is quite special and will be discussed in the section on Vashti's and Esther's clothing.

The contrast between this scene and the preceding clothing scene is extreme. Robert Alter correctly notes, concerning Haman's motivation, that wearing garments and riding a horse "that are not merely regal but that the king has actually used" puts the would-be kingly clothed rider "in metonymic contact with the body of the king—in a way, becoming the king."[48] Thus, Mordecai goes from being clothed in sackcloth to being clothed so nearly like the king as to almost *be* the king. (In another reversal, he also goes from taking an active role—in tearing clothes, putting on sackcloth, going through the city, wailing, going up to the king's gate, refusing to accept more seemly clothes from Esther—to being entirely passive—being robed and being led, but that is a topic for the section "Intersections and Loose Ends.")

At this point in the story, Mordecai is being honored by the king, and for this short period of time he is fortunate, but immediately following the ritual honoring, "then Mordecai returned to the king's gate" (6:12), presumably to resume his sackcloth and ashes, given that the first edict is still in effect and there is still a death sentence pending over all Jews. So we see an alternation in Mordecai's clothing associated with an alternation in his fortunes, from sackcloth and ashes to royal robes and then back to sackcloth and ashes. From a spatial point of view, he seems to be moving—from low to high, then back to low—a down-up-down pattern.

The final scene in which Mordecai's clothing is specified occurs after he had been set over the house of his deceased enemy Haman, had been given the king's signet, and had written on the king's behalf the second edict, which effectively neutralized the first one.

> Then Mordecai went out from the presence of the king, wearing royal robes [לְבוּשׁ מַלְכוּת; *ləbûš malkût*] of blue and white [תְּכֵלֶת וָחוּר; *təkēlet* and *ḥûr*], with a great golden crown [עֲטֶרֶת זָהָב גְּדוֹלָה; *'ăṭeret zāhāb gədôlâ*] and a mantle [תַכְרִיךְ; *takərîk*] of fine linen and purple [בּוּץ וְאַרְגָּמָן; *bûṣ* and *'argāmān*], while the city of Susa shouted and rejoiced. (8:15)

In the same sense that the "densest" verse with regard to cloth and clothing vocabulary in Esther is 1:6, the next densest one is 8:15. Much of the specific vocabulary used for the cloths of the palace in 1:6 is reprised in 8:15: *təkēlet*, *ḥûr*, *bûṣ*, and *'argāmān*. The phrase "fine linen and purple" from 1:6 is exactly replicated. The phrase "royal robes" is exactly replicated from 6:8. Two new clothing vocabulary words are introduced in 8:15: *'ăṭeret* and *takərîk*. The term

---

48. Alter, *3: Writings*, 732.

ʿăṭeret is the common Hebrew word for a royal crown, occurring twenty-three times in the Hebrew Bible. The term *takərîk* is a *hapax legomenon*, translated into English variously as "cloak,"[49] "garment,"[50] "mantle,"[51] "robe,"[52] or "wrap."[53]

In this scene, perhaps even more than in 6:8 (!), Mordecai is portrayed royally. This time he wears a crown—the same kind as worn by David[54]—which is moreover great and golden. He is again in "royal robes," but now the robes are described as "blue and white," reflecting the "white cotton curtains and blue hangings" of Ahasuerus's palace as described in 1:6, in which the cloth and clothing motif was introduced. In addition, Mordecai wears a mantle "of fine linen and purple;" the same phrase is used to describe the cords in 1:6.[55] Recall that the blue and purple stuff here and in 1:6 are wools dyed with the two most prestigious dyes in the world and that the fine linen is the finest possible linen. Those three fabrics are among the precious materials that made up the tabernacle, which clearly is being evoked here.[56] The white of Mordecai's blue-and-white robes also recollects the white of the exotic and sumptuous cotton curtains of the palace. Moreover, there is an indication that blue and white were colors associated with Persian royalty.[57] Taken *ensemble*, Mordecai's clothing in this scene is over-the-top royal.

The implication is that Mordecai paraded through the city in these prestigious clothes while the city rejoiced, in explicit contrast with 4:1, in which Mordecai "went out through the city" in sackcloth and ashes while the

49. NJB.
50. NASB.
51. NRSV.
52. NIV.
53. Alter, *3: Writings*.
54. 2 Sam. 12:30; 1 Chr. 20:2.
55. Referring to Esther, Athalya Brenner explicitly equates "the formula חוּר + תְּכֵלֶת + בּוּץ + אַרְגָּמָן" as "expensive ... cloth symbolizing royal splendor, power, and authority." Athalya Brenner, *Colour Terms in the Old Testament*, JSOTSup 21 (Sheffield, England: JSOT, 1982), 149.
56. Spoelstra not only associates the cloth and clothing of Est. 1:6 and 8:15 with the cloth of the tabernacle (Exod. 26, 36) but also (reasonably) with the liturgical clothing of the high priest (Exod. 28, 39). In addition, among the many instances of *ʿăṭeret* crowns in the Hebrew Bible, an *ʿăṭeret* of silver and gold shows up in a political oracle of the postexilic prophet Zechariah (Zech. 6:11-13). It is to be set on the head of the high priest Joshua, son of Jehozadak, who will stand at the side of the throne of the governor ("the Branch"), "with peaceful understanding between the two of them" (Zech. 6:13). Spoelstra (less reasonably) connects Est. 8:15, Exodus 28, 39, and Zechariah 6 to conclude that "therefore ... perhaps Mordecai is literarily portrayed, and henceforth viewed, as a princely-priestly amalgam to the tenor of Joshua and the Branch in Zech 1-6 [sic]—a figurehead of hope for the post-exilic community" (Spoelstra, "Mordecai's Vestments," 192).
57. See the discussion below in "Vashti's and Esther's Statuses Revealed by Their Clothing" for Curtius Rufius's description of the Persian king's *keter*.

city was in confusion (3:15). The commonalities in both instances are that: (1) Mordecai and his garments are very much in public view; and (2) Mordecai's dress seems to reflect public sentiment. The former is also the case in 6:11, when Mordecai was led on horseback in royal robes "through the open square of the city." (The text does not mention the public's reaction in 6:8 but instead focuses on Haman's.)

It is possible that at one time Esther concluded with chapter 8, at 8:17.[58] If so, the triumphal parade in 8:15 would have not only been Mordecai's final appearance in the book but also constituted the triumphal conclusion to the book. It is therefore particularly meaningful that so much of the vocabulary of Mordecai's clothing in 8:15 corresponds to the vocabulary of 1:6, which both demonstrated the opulence of the interior of the palace and introduced the motif of cloth and clothing.[59] Verses 1:6 and 8:15 become "up" bookends around the down-up-down alternation in Mordecai's fortune in the central part of the story. Mordecai ends up being dressed in extravagantly opulent clothes similar to the cloth that furnishes the interior of the palace; he becomes a palace insider.[60]

Returning to the notion with which this section began, that clothing affirms and projects social identity and social position and differentiates members of society into age, sex, and class or caste, it is clear that in the book of Esther, the motif of cloth and clothing precisely does that affirmation and projection for the character of Mordecai. Mordecai's clothing varies dramatically from one scene to another over the course of this story, and his age, sex, ethnicity, religion, family relationships, and so on do not. What does change is his place in the social hierarchy, from the lowest of lows to the highest of highs, twice over no less. And

---

58. Following Beal's commentary, the style and vocabulary of chapters 9 and 10 are so different from the narrative material in the previous chapters that many scholars consider all or parts of chapters 9 and 10 to be later additions by another author. On the other hand, scholars are far from consensus that there is a disjuncture in the *content* between chapters 1–8 and 9–10. Beal nuances the complicated situation admirably:

> Whether or not one believes that an earlier ("original"?) version of the story ended at 8:17, we can at least acknowledge that chapters 9 and 10 involve a strikingly different—even incongruous—mode of narration. Perhaps a different author or different authors were involved here; perhaps a new secretary was hired at this point; perhaps the same writer or writers wrote this part some time after, or before, writing the material chapters 1–8; perhaps chapters 9 and 10 were heavily edited by later editors. More than likely, still other factors were involved which we cannot imagine. (*Esther*, 108)

59. See fn. 15. If 1:6 is a later insertion, this suggests that the purpose of the insertion was at least in part to provide an opening to Esther to match the closing.

60. Clines says, "As Persian as it is possible for a Jew to be." Clines, "Esther Left to Right," 39.

this is perhaps appropriate for a story that can be read as "a literary farce," playing "on broad improbabilities and exaggerations."[61]

Vashti's and Esther's Statuses Revealed by Their Clothing

Aside from Mordecai, the other characters whose clothing is noted are Vashti, Esther, and Ahasuerus—but, of course, Ahasuerus's clothing is never otherwise mentioned except as being worn by Mordecai (6:8-11). Three passages constitute the motif of cloth and clothing as it relates to Vashti and Esther.[62] First, at the end of the seven-day-long banquet with which the book opens, the wine-affected King Ahasuerus commanded his attendants "to bring Queen Vashti before the king, wearing the royal crown (כֶּתֶר; *keter*), in order to show the peoples and the officials her beauty" (1:11). For some reason we are not told, she refused to come at the king's command, so he deposed her.[63] Second, Esther "won his favor and devotion, so that he set the royal crown (כֶּתֶר; *keter*) on her head and made her queen instead of Vashti" (2:17). Last, when Queen Esther needed an audience with the king to try to save the lives of all the Jews, "Esther put on her royal robes and stood in the inner court of the king's palace" (5:1) within eyesight of Ahasuerus's throne, without having been called by him—an act that was punishable by death, except that in this case she again "won his favor."

61. Timothy K. Beal, *The Book of Hiding: Gender, Ethnicity, Annihilation, and Esther*, ed. Danna Nolan Fewell, David M. Gunn, Amy-Jill Levine, and Gary A. Phillips (London: Routledge, 1997), ix.

62. Perhaps the oil of myrrh and perfumes and cosmetics of Esther's beauty treatment (1:12) could be considered as part of her adornment, but they are neither cloth nor clothing per se. For a treatment of the use of cosmetics in Esther (and Ruth) as "akin to a speech act, able to communicate the social status and sexual intentions of the wearer to those around them," see Laura Quick, "Decorated Women: A Sociological Approach to the Function of Cosmetics in the Books of Esther and Ruth," *BibInt* 27 (2019), 354–71, 354.

63. Linda Day ("Vashti Interpreted: Nineteenth and Twentieth Century Literary Representations of the Book of Esther," in *Proceedings, Eastern Great Lakes & Midwest Biblical Societies* [vol. 23 of 2003], 1–14) points out that commentators commonly offer speculations for why Vashti refuses.

> Perhaps she finds the task degrading, to parade herself in front of drunken spectators. Perhaps it flies against the custom in ancient Persian society for women to dine with men. Perhaps she feels a great responsibility of hospitality, to take care of her own party guests. Or perhaps, like the king, she herself is too drunk after all the partying to make clear decisions. (2)

Goldman cites *Midrash Rabbah* as suggesting that Vashti was commanded to appear before the men wearing no clothing *except* the *keter*. Stan Goldman, "Narrative and Ethical Ironies in Esther," *JSOT* 15 (1990), 15–31.

The motif of clothing inextricably ties Vashti and Esther together. Most obviously, they are bound together via the *keter*. This is perhaps the most enigmatic single item of cloth or clothing in the book of Esther. The nature of the headdress is the topic of an excellent article by Alison Salvesen,[64] from which the following is taken. The term *keter* occurs biblically only in Esther, and only as part of the expression "*keter maləkût*"—the royal *keter*.[65] It is generally accepted that *keter* "is related in some way to the Greek word κίδαρις/κίταρις, used by classical authors to describe the distinctive headgear of the Persian kings in the Achaemenid period and which Alexander also assumed. But the underlying etymology of both Greek and Hebrew words is uncertain."[66] Salvesen works through the possible etymologies and the varying (and sometimes conflicting) classical sources. Two possible forms of headdress emerge. First, the *keter* might be a high or domed hat resembling a camel's hump, as in the pointed fabric cap (*tiara*[67]) worn by many figures in Persian art with the top flopping forward, but by the king (only!) with the crown of the hat upright. Understanding *keter* in this way gives rise to the translation of *keter* as "crown" in many English translations.[68] Second, the *keter* might be a "διάδημα, i.e. a cloth fillet bound around (διαδέω) the head and tied in a knot at the back: the *diadema* was the ultimate symbol of Hellenistic rulership and the word was used in a metaphorical sense then as now."[69] "Assyrian, Achaemenid, and Parthian art depicts all sorts of people wearing fabric headbands, from greatest to least."[70]

It is likely that a Persian king would have worn both a *diadema* and an upright *tiara*, with the *diadema* around the upright *tiara*, as in Xenophon's description of Cyrus the Great and as in a few confirmatory pieces of art. Salvesen concludes that "כתר in Esther is best explained as referring to a head-band worn widely in the Persian Empire and beyond, but with a version specific to royalty in its fabric or colour, כתר מלכות."[71] As to that color, among the Greek sources used by Salvesen,

<hr>

64. Alison Salvesen, "כֶּתֶר (Esther 1:11; 2:17; 6:8): 'Something to do with a Camel?,'" *JSS* 44 (1999), 35–46.

65. Siebert-Hommes translates it as "crown of the kingship." Jopie Siebert-Hommes, "'On the third day Esther put on her queen's robes' (Esther 5:1): The Symbolic Function of Clothing in the Book of Esther," *LDiff* (2002).

66. Salvesen, "Camel?" 35–6.

67. This technical term is not to be confused with the jeweled, crested, and semicircular form of modern tiaras.

68. However, if there is any historical verisimilitude in Esther, the fact that the *only* person to wear the upright tiara of headdress was the king argues against this understanding of *keter*. To put on the upright tiara was to declare oneself king. Neither Vashti nor Esther would have worn it (ibid., 37–8).

69. Ibid., 39.

70. Ibid., 42.

71. Ibid., 45. Again following Salvesen, this identification of *keter* has the added advantage of making sense of the horse's wearing the *keter* in 6:8; reliefs at Ninevah and Persepolis portray horses with ornate trappings hanging down from their heads, or with the top of their manes tied with a ribbon.

Curtius Rufius, writing in the mid-first century CE, describes the headdress of the Persian kings as including a blue-and-white diadem, or possibly instead as "a blue turban/diadem with white spots, which went around the head."[72] Either way, it is useful to note the presence of blue and white colors, as in the curtains and hangings of Ahasuerus's palace (1:6) and Mordecai's royal robes (8:15).

Returning now from Salvesen's explication of the *keter* headdress to the topic of Vashti's and Esther's clothing, certainly the royal *keter* links Vashti and Esther. It is less immediately obvious, but nevertheless true, that Vashti and Esther are also connected via the garments that Esther put on before seeking an audience with Ahasuerus. The phrase in 5:1 is וַתִּלְבַּשׁ אֶסְתֵּר מַלְכוּת (*wattilbaš 'estēr malkût*), that is, Esther dressed royally or in a royal manner.[73] The garments in which she dressed herself are not "her" garments but rather those she wears in her capacity as queen. That is to say, they are equivalent to the clothing in which Vashti must have dressed for royal occasions when she was queen, before she was deposed, in exactly the same way as Esther's headdress is equivalent to Vashti's (whether or not it was the same material item). Nothing in Esther's clothing distinguishes her from Vashti, and the only garment of hers mentioned explicitly (the royal *keter*), in contrast, serves to equate her to Vashti.

Recall that a fundamental premise of anthropology is that clothing affirms and projects social identity and social position—it differentiates people as to age, sex, class, and other social categories. This function of clothing is clear for Vashti and Esther in the narrative of the book of Esther. The royal *keter* identifies its wearer as queen. At the beginning of the story Vashti is always referred to as "Queen Vashti." In the political crisis that ensued after her refusal to wear the *keter* in front of the king and his guests at the banquet, she stops being "Queen Vashti" and becomes merely "Vashti" instead.[74] The time when Esther stops being merely "Esther" and becomes the queen instead of Vashti is identified in the text as the moment when Ahasuerus "set the royal *keter* on her head" (2:17). However, because the text names Esther as "Queen Esther" only when she is in interaction with the king, it happens that twelve of the next thirteen times she is named in the text, it is simply as "Esther."[75] The switch to more frequent use of her title occurs in 5:1— she is "Esther" before she dresses royally and is "Queen Esther" when so dressed

---

72. Ibid., 40–1.

73. Bea Wyler comments that "no translation captures the precise meaning of the Hebrew" and renders it as "dressed in 'royalty.'" Bea Wyler, "Esther: The Incomplete Emancipation of a Queen," in *A Feminist Companion to Esther, Judith and Susanna*, Feminist Companion to the Bible, ed. Athalya Brenner (Sheffield, England: Sheffield Academic Press, 1995), 111–35, 128. Levenson says the phrase is literally "Esther donned royalty." Levenson, *Esther*, 89. Jopie Siebert-Hommes renders the phrase as "she put on the kingship." Siebert-Hommes, "Symbolic Function".

74. "Queen Vashti": Est. 1:9, 11, 12, 15, 16, 17. "Vashti": Est. 1:19, 2:1, 4, 17.

75. The one exception is 2:22, when she tells the king in Mordecai's name of a plot to assassinate the king.

and seeking her audience with the king.[76] The effect is that *this* is the time in the story when Esther finally *really* becomes the queen—and it only happens with her donning particular clothing. (Or perhaps it is appropriate to identify *two* times in the text when Esther makes the transition from simply Esther to Esther the Queen. The motif of clothing underlies each and occurs nowhere else with regard to Esther.)

Thus, assuredly Vashti and Esther are inextricably bound together. No matter that Vashti departs the narrative early, she remains part of Esther's story. When the one is up, the other is down, and when the one is down, the other is up. One actively refuses to wear the *keter*, the other passively accepts it. One refuses to go to the king when bidden, the other does so voluntarily and unbidden.[77] Beal puts the connection between the two of them another way: Vashti is the erasured character whose traces remain in the one who replaces her.[78] And, to my mind, what is significant is that all of the connectors that bind Vashti and Esther together are communicated, like their royal status, through the medium of clothing.

Intersections and Loose Ends

Royal Robes that the King Has Worn, and a Horse that the King Has Ridden

The clothing passage in Esther that reveals the most about the relationships between the main male characters concerns the particular assemblage of clothing aspired to by Haman, loaned by Ahasuerus, and worn by Mordecai (6:6-11). Here Ahasuerus asks Haman's advice about how to honor someone, and Haman, assuming the honoree is to be himself, advises based on his own aspirations/ambitions. At this stage, the relationship between the king and Haman is such that the king follows Haman's advice precisely, but ironically the honoree is Haman's rival and enemy, Mordecai. To make matters worse from Haman's perspective, he is the one charged with performing all the actions that honor Mordecai. This includes the mortification of personally and publically having to lead the king's horse upon which Mordecai, dressed in the king's royal robes, is riding, and having to personally and publically proclaim that the king is honoring Mordecai. Stan Goldman describes this as "the bitterest irony imaginable for Haman."[79]

---

76. Zefira Gitay explores the reception history of Esther, whose crown has decorative value only, versus Queen Esther, who is a fully fledged queen. Zefira Gitay, "Esther and the Queen's Throne," in *A Feminist Companion to Esther, Judith and Susanna*, Feminist Companion to the Bible, ed. Athalya Brenner (Sheffield, England: Sheffield Academic Press, 1995), 136–48.

77. Athalya Brenner, "Looking at Esther through the Looking Glass," in Brenner, *A Feminist Companion to Esther, Judith and Susanna*, 71–80.

78. Timothy K. Beal, "Tracing Esther's Beginnings," in Brenner, *A Feminist Companion to Esther, Judith and Susanna*, 87–110.

79. Goldman, "Ironies in Esther," 18.

The passage is most telling about Haman's ambitions. As mentioned above, Alter notes that by wanting clothing, horse, and headdress "that are not merely regal but that the king has actually used," Haman would have put himself "in metonymic contact with the body of the king—in a way, becoming the king."[80] Similar conclusions are drawn by others.[81] What Berlin points out is that the implication of Haman's request can be seen independently by recourse to narrative motifs.[82] An illustrative example would be when Solomon, the king-to-be, rides on the mule of the old king (David) on his way to and from the ceremony where he is anointed king.[83] Among the pertinent biblical motifs are numerous examples in which transferring a garment from one person to another signals the transferal of office.[84] From motifs in Greek sources we learn that ceremonies for the initiation of a new Persian king involved his laying aside his personal robe and putting on the robe of Cyrus the Elder, and that it was forbidden for anyone else to wear the king's robe.[85] Taken altogether, everything about Haman's designed ceremony shouts of his ambition to be king himself.

As a final note on this passage, and on the role of the *keter* in particular, Jopie Siebert-Hommes opines that not only does Haman wish to become the king for one day but the "fact that Haman wishes the *queen's crown* on the head of the horse on which he will ride creates the impression that Haman in his fantasy is not so much thinking of a royal horse from the court-stables, but rather of having the *queen* for one night....!"[86] And as is well known and Berlin points out, another motif from the Bible and from Greek sources is that of a usurper taking the king's wife or concubine.[87]

Who Dresses, and Who Is Dressed? Agency and Implications

One of the notable features of the scene in which Mordecai wears the king's robes and rides the king's horse is that Mordecai is a passive figure. "So Haman took the

---

80. Alter, *3: Writings*, 732.

81. Following Berlin note 21, see Levenson, *Esther*, 97; Michael V. Fox, *Character and Ideology in the Book of Esther*, 2nd ed. (Grand Rapids, MI: Eerdmans, 2001), 77; Laniak, *Shame*, 101. See also Spoelstra, "Mordecai's Vestments," 180.

82. Berlin, "Esther and Storytelling," 11–13.

83. 1 Kgs 1:32-49. Levenson points this out as well. Levenson, *Esther*, 97.

84. Aaron's son Eleazar donning the priestly garments of his father (Num. 20:25-28); Elisha receiving Elijah's cloak (2 Kgs 2:13-15); David cutting off a corner of Saul's cloak (1 Sam. 24:4).

85. Berlin cites Plutarch's *Artaxerxes* 3, and *Artaxerxes* 5. She also provides other examples. See her article for more. Berlin, "Esther and Storytelling," 12.

86. Siebert-Hommes, "Symbolic Function," 21–2; emphases in the original.

87. 2 Sam. 3:7; 16:21-22; 1 Kgs 2:15-17, 22. For a Greek source, Berlin cites Plutarch, *Artaxerxes* 26.2.

robes and the horse and robed Mordecai and led him riding through the open square of the city" (6:11). This is in sharp contrast to the previous scene involving Mordecai and clothing (4:1-4), in which he took an active role: tearing clothes, putting on sackcloth, going through the city, wailing, going up to the king's gate, refusing to accept more seemly clothes from Esther. This highlights the fact that one aspect of the motif of cloth and clothing in Esther is the distinction between putting on clothing, on the one hand, and having clothing put on one, on the other. As Spoelstra puts it, "The act of robing and disrobing is often just as significant as the clothing itself."[88]

Thus, we note that Vashti is the only one of the main characters whose every interaction with clothing is active, not passive—she actively refuses to wear the *keter*. Each of the other characters is passive at least some of the time: the *keter* is put on Esther (2:17), the royal robes are put on Mordecai (6:6), the king follows Haman's advice verbatim in issuing the order as part of the honoring ceremony (6:10), and Haman has to accept the order of the king to robe Mordecai and lead him and the horse around the square (6:11).

At places in the story, both Esther and Mordecai *become* active with respect to clothing. As discussed above with regard to Esther's clothing, her transformation from passive to active occurred when she dressed herself royally to seek an audience with the king (5:1), cementing her transition from "Esther" to "Queen Esther." From this point onward in the story, Esther consistently takes the initiative and becomes an active character.

Along similar lines, as noted several times already in this chapter, Mordecai is passive in the account of the honoring ceremony devised by Haman, in which Mordecai wears the king's royal robes (6:8-11). He was dressed and led by Haman. Contrasting that scene and the final clothing scene in the book is interesting. This time Mordecai takes an active role; he "went out from the presence of the king, wearing royal robes" (8:15). This time the royal clothing is described in detail, and this time the implication is that the garments are his own.

Another aspect of the motif of clothing in Esther is the movement of clothing— its dynamics—between characters. Clothes are transferred a number of times during the story. It is implicitly understood that Vashti's headdress is taken away from her. The king transfers it to Esther. Esther attempts to give Mordecai non-sackcloth clothes. The king's royal robes are temporarily loaned to Mordecai. The king entrusts his signet ring to Haman's keeping (3:12), takes it back, and then entrusts it to Mordecai (8:2).[89] It is generally the case that the one who does the giving, taking, or loaning is the one in higher social standing than the recipient.[90] This raises the interesting point that when Esther gives Mordecai clothing in 4:1, she

---

88. Spoelstra, "Mordecai's Vestments," 178.

89. For more on Ahasuerus's signet ring, see Susannah Rees, "'Women Rule over Them': Dressing for an Inverted World in Isaiah 3," in this volume.

90. Spoelstra makes a similar observation with respect to the actions of one person dressing another. Spoelstra, "Mordecai's Vestments," 182.

is referred to as "the queen," not as either "Esther" or as "Queen Esther." Mordecai's refusal to accept the new garments from the queen has more significance than if it had been simply his ex-ward Esther doing the giving.

Rhetorical Irony and the Motif of Cloth and Clothing in Esther

The book of Esther is laden with irony. Throughout my observations about Mordecai's, Vashti's, and Esther's clothing, I have noted in passing a number of places in which ironic reversals have occurred, such as: the overturning of Haman's expectations with regard to wearing Ahasuerus's royal garments; the repeated alternations of Mordecai's social status (outsider/insider, down/up/down/up), as revealed by his clothing; and the reversal of Vashti's and Esther's fortunes, symbolized by the royal *keter*. In his influential analysis of irony in Esther, Goldman cogently states:

> Ironic reversal is a central theme of Esther. In fact, the entire story is a development of these words: "the very day on which the enemies of the Jews had expected to get them in their power, the opposite happened; and the Jews got their enemies in their power" (9.1) ... Such an overt statement of irony suggests that Esther is not a work written using irony here and there as a literary device but a literary work whose narrative hangs on ironic reversals.[91]

Goldman's analysis of irony in Esther goes well beyond rhetorical irony, but it is rhetorical irony in general, and two types of rhetorical irony in particular, that seem especially relevant to the motif of cloth and clothing in the book of Esther.[92]

The first of those types of rhetorical irony is *irony of incident or plot*. The reversals/alternations I noted are examples of irony in the plot of Esther. Goldman provides another example in relation to Vashti's and Esther's royal *keter*: ironically, by deposing Vashti for disobeying his command to wear the *keter*, Ahasuerus gets a new queen who will be disobedient twice—each time by approaching him on his throne unbidden—and who moreover is rewarded for it.[93]

91. Goldman, "Ironies in Esther," 21. Here Goldman cites Berg, *Motifs, Themes, Structure*, 103–12. Fox also considers reversal to be the primary theme in Esther. Fox, *Character and Ideology*, 158–63.

92. Goldman, "Ironies in Esther," 15. Goldman categories irony as: (i) rhetorical irony (an autonomous literary device or trope); (ii) generative irony (by which the reader may develop a new response to ethical issues raised in the text); and (iii) intuitive irony (the author's narrative strategy). Five variations of rhetorical irony are: irony of incident or plot, irony of narrative perspective or point of view, irony of characterization, irony of language, and irony of theme. Goldman says that "rhetorical irony is an extremely subversive idiom because it says or shows the opposite of what is meant" (16).

93. Est. 5:1, 8:3. Esther dresses royally in 5:1; no mention is made of her clothing in 8:3.

The second relevant type of rhetorical irony is *irony of language*, which "can be seen in the extraordinary amount of hyperbole or exaggeration in the story."[94] Ironical language is evidenced in the remarkable description of the court of Ahasuerus's palace in 1:6, with its extravagantly luxurious textile furnishings. It is apparent that the author of Esther has made good use of the motif of cloth and clothing in his irony.

Debating the Identity of the Main Character

One topic that has engaged scholars is the identity of the main character in the book of Esther: is it Esther or Mordecai or both? My impression is that those who argue for Esther alone as the main character are in the minority among contemporary scholars. Seibert-Hommes is one of those arguing for Esther alone, asserting that "Esther is the most important character in the book that bears her name. She is the only one in the story who is 'dressed with the kingship'. And she knows how to make use of it."[95] Anthony J. Tomasino is another such scholar. He offers a new macrochiasm model for the structure of the book of Esther as an alternative to previously proposed chiastic structures.[96] The hinge of Tomasino's chiasm is 5:1-8 (Esther invites the king to a feast). For Tomasino, the significance of his proposed chiasm is that it identifies Esther as the central character. Again, my impression is that Tomasino is mistaken in his claim that "most scholars ... believe that it is Esther, not Mordecai who is the main character of this story. She is certainly the most fully developed character of the narrative."[97]

Several contemporary scholars acknowledge the case for Esther as the main character, but also see an equal case for Mordecai. In this view, articulated by Seidler, "the two characters share the role of leader, whether in turn, in parallel or jointly."[98] Clines belongs in this camp, although his evaluation of the shared role of main character is less positive:

---

94. Goldman, "Ironies in Esther," 21.

95. Siebert-Hommes, "Symbolic Function."

96. Anthony J. Tomasino, "Interpreting Esther from the Inside Out: Hermeneutical Implications of the Chiastic Structure of the Book of Esther," *JBL* 138 (2019), 101–20. Tomasino engages with previously proposed structures by Fox, Berg, and Levenson: Fox, *Character and Ideology*, 153–8; Berg, *Motifs, Themes, Structure*, 103–13; Levenson, *Esther*, 8.

97. Tomasino, "Interpreting Esther," 116. Tomasino gives no direct evidence for his claim that most scholars consider Esther to be the main character. Instead he merely observes that "so remarkable is [Esther's] development through the course of events that her character has been the subject of several monographs, as well as numerous shorter studies." Ironically, the works he cites for Esther's character development include those whose authors argue for Mordecai as the main character. For example, Fox, *Character and Ideology*.

98. Seidler, "Fasting, Sackcloth, and Ashes," 123.

The book as a whole purports to portray a triumph for a woman. For its name is Esther's, and it is the story of her success as a woman over her upbringing as a traditional woman and over the expectations of her as a woman at the Persian court. Even so, the ending of the book raises some doubts about how thorough a success hers is. For some sexual-political struggle between the figures of Esther and Mordecai seems to be going on in ch. 9 ... And then finally Esther is lost sight of altogether and the book itself peters out with wishy-washy generalities about *Mordecai* (10.1-3), for all the world as if the story had really been about him all the time.[99]

To my mind, the best argument for the identity of the main character as shared between Esther and Mordecai comes from Jonathan Grossman, who carefully compares the cases for Mordecai and Esther. He notes that until 8:1,

at no point do both characters, Mordecai and Esther, behave as protagonists simultaneously. In the first part of the narrative [prior to 8:1], Mordecai plays the protagonist; in the second part, it is Esther who plays the hero. In each half, the nonheroic character is presented as secondary to the hero: in the first half, Esther is nothing more than Mordecai's proxy inside the palace, whereas in the second half, Mordecai obeys Esther's instructions. However, we cannot conclude this discussion without noticing how the narrative ends; from the moment that Esther presents Mordecai to the king [8:1], the two characters become joint protagonists of the story.[100]

Grossman arrives at the "complex conclusion" that "in the first part of the narrative, Mordecai and Esther alternate as protagonists, while in the concluding chapters, they become joint protagonists."[101]

The most compelling case for Mordecai alone as the main character is argued by Michael V. Fox:

Mordecai is the dominant figure in the book. He is introduced first (2:5) and praised last (10:2-3), and his glorification lies at the book's turning point and presages the Jews' victory. His initiative begins the rescue effort, his edict is the mechanism of deliverance, and his epistle guides the people in the establishment of the new holiday. His unalloyed success, personal and public, for himself and for his people, shows that his behavior is to be taken as exemplary.[102]

99. Clines, "Esther Left to Right," 44.
100. Grossman, *Esther*, 32. Grossman interprets the structure of Esther as a chiasm centering on 6:1-11 (The King Cannot Sleep; Episode of the Horse) (14).
101. Ibid. 34.
102. Fox, *Character and Ideology*, 185.

Similarly, Matthew Michael apparently takes it for granted that Mordecai is the main character when he sees in the books of Daniel and Esther a shared motif of royal officials conspiring to kill the main character, that is, Mordecai in the case of the book of Esther.[103]

Possibly my chapter here adds somewhat to the discussion. The motif of cloth and clothing focuses attention on Mordecai over the other main characters, Esther included. By far most of the explicit description of clothing is associated with Mordecai. Tracking Mordecai's clothing (4:1-4, 6:6-11, 8:15) reveals a structure in which his clothing alternates between the extremes of sackcloth and royal garb. Moreover, if at one time the book of Esther concluded at 8:17, as is an accepted possibility, then the book of Esther would have opened (1:6) and closed (8:15) with a matched set of passages reflecting and repeating the opulence of Ahasuerus's palace and Mordecai's exalted state. In contrast, because the two instances in which Esther's clothing is mentioned (2:17, 5:1) both relate to her transition to queenly status, they also necessarily evoke recollections of Vashti. The motif of cloth and clothing on its own provides no suggestion that Esther is the main character. Thus, for what it is worth, using the motif of cloth and clothing to determine social standing in the book of Esther identifies Mordecai, rather than the title character herself, as the main character of the book.

Tying It Up

The recurring element of feasting/banquets is unquestionably an important motif in the book of Esther, and my perception is that, to date, most scholars would identify feasting as the most prominent single motif.[104] This chapter has focused instead on the motif of cloth and clothing in Esther and on its use as a literary device that provides narrative structure, identifies social standing, and illuminates the relationship between characters. I hope that this chapter presents a convincing argument that the motif of cloth and clothing is at least as fundamental to Esther as any other.[105]

A reviewer of an early version of this chapter commented on how much would be missing in Esther if there were no invocation of the motif of dress.[106] Taking that

103. Michael, "Daniel at the Pageant," 126.

104. Fox is among many who consider feasting to be the major motif in Esther. For Fox, the major motif in Esther is feasting, and the major theme is reversal. Fox, *Character and Ideology*, 157–63.

105. A traditional element of the celebration of Purim is the dressing up of celebrants in costume. Perhaps it was the emphasis on clothing in Esther 1–8 that helped to associate Purim with the story of Mordecai and Esther and contributed to the incorporation of chapters 9 (in which Purim is introduced) and 10 to the book of Esther (A. Finitsis, personal communication). This seems quite plausible to me.

106. S. J. Parrott, personal communication.

notion to the extreme, without the motif of cloth and clothing in the book of Esther, there would be no evocative description of the luxury of Ahasuerus's palace, no headdress for Vashti to refuse to wear or to then be put on Esther, neither reaction to the unexpected catastrophe nor public mourning by Mordecai, no royally clad Esther to approach the king unbidden, no honoring ceremony designed by Haman, no honoring of Mordecai that mortifies Haman, no triumphant moment for Mordecai on behalf of his people.[107] The motif of cloth and clothing is essential to Esther.

107. And no signet ring for all the edicts.

SELECT BIBLIOGRAPHY ON DRESS

Anderson, Carol. *Ancient Egyptian Jewellery*. London: Trustees of the British Museum, British Museum Press, 1990.

Anderson, Gary A. "The Garments of Skin in Apocryphal Narrative and Biblical Commentary." Pages 101–43. In *Studies in Ancient Midrash*. Edited by James Kugel. Cambridge, MA: Harvard University Press, 2001.

Baadsgaard, Aubrey. "All the Queen's Clothes: Identifying Female Royalty at Early Dynastic Ur." *Near Eastern Archaeology* 79.3 (2016): 148–55.

Bahrani, Zainab. "Jewelry and Personal Arts in Ancient Western Asia." *CANE* 3: 1635–45.

Barber, Elizabeth J. Wayland. *Prehistoric Textiles: The Development of Cloth in the Neolithic and Bronze Ages with Special Reference to the Aegean*. Princeton, NJ: Princeton University Press, 1991.

Bari, Shahidha. *Dressed: A Philosophy of Clothes*. New York: Basic Books, 2020.

Barnes, Ruth, and Joanne B. Eicher, eds. *Dress and Gender: Making and Meaning in Cultural Contexts*. Cross-Cultural Perspectives on Women, vol. 2. Providence: Berg, 1992.

Batten, Alicia, and Antonios Finitsis. "Clothing." Pages 1–35. In *Oxford Bibliographies in Biblical Studies*. Edited by Christopher Matthews. New York: Oxford University Press, 2020.

Batten, Alicia J., and Kelly Olson, eds. *Dress in Mediterranean Antiquity: Greeks, Romans, Jews, Christians*. London: T&T Clark, 2021.

Bauks, Michaela. "Clothing and Nudity in the Noah Story (Gen 9:18-29)." Pages 379–87. In Berner et al., *Clothing and Nudity in the Hebrew Bible*.

Beeman, William O. *Language, Status and Power in Iran*. Advances in Semiotics. Bloomington: Indiana University Press, 1986.

Ben Zvi, Ehud. "Were YHWH's Clothes Worth Remembering in LPEH Yehud?" Pages 161–81. In *Dress and Clothing in the Hebrew Bible: "For All Her Household Is Clothed in Crimson."* Edited by Antonios Finitsis. New York: T&T Clark, 2019.

Bender, Claudia. *Die Sprache des Textilien: Untersuchungen zu Kleidung und Textilen im Alten Testament*. Stuttgart: Kolhammer, 2008.

Bergmann, Claudia. "We Have Seen the Enemy, and He Is Only a 'She': The Portrayal of Warriors as Women." *CBQ* 69 (2007): 651–72.

Berner, Christoph, Manuel Schäfer, Martin Schott, Sarah Schulz, and Martina Weingärtner, eds. *Clothing and Nudity in the Hebrew Bible*. London: Bloomsbury T&T Clark, 2019.

Bickart, Noah. "He Found a Hair and It Bothered Him: Female Pubic Hair Removal in the Talmud." *Nashim* 35 (2019): 128–52.

Billington, Selena. "Glorious Adornment: The Social Function of Cloth and Clothing in Israel's Tabernacle." Unpublished PhD dissertation, University of Denver, 2014.

Broby-Johansen, R. *Body and Clothes: An Illustrated History of Costume*. Translated by Erik I. Friss and Karen Rush. New York: Reinhold, 1968.

Brock, Sebastian. "Clothing Metaphors as a Means of Theological Expression in Syriac Tradition." Pages 11–38. In *Typus, Symbol, Allegorie bei den östlichen Vätern und ihren Parallelen im Mittelalter*. Edited by Margot Schmidt and Carl Friedrich Geyer. Regensburg: Friedrich Pustet, 1981.

Burgoon, Judee K., Norah E. Dunbar, and Christ Segrin. "Nonverbal Influence." Pages 445–73. In *The Persuasion Handbook: Developments in Theory and Practice*. Edited by James Price Dillard and Michael Pfau. Thousand Oaks, CA: Sage, 2002.

Cairns, Douglas L. "Clothed in Shamelessness, Shrouded in Grief: The Role of 'Garment' Metaphors in Ancient Greek Concepts of Emotion." Pages 25–41. In *Spinning Fates and the Song of the Loom: The Use of Textiles, Clothing and Cloth Production as Metaphor, Symbol and Narrative Device in Greek and Latin Literature*. Ancient Textiles Series 24. Edited by Giovanni Fanfani, Mary Harlow, and Marie-Louise Nosch. Oxford: Oxbow, 2016.

Cardon, Dominique. *Natural Dyes: Sources, Tradition, Technology and Science*. London: Archetype, 2007.

Coggins, Richard. "On Kings and Disguises." *JSOT* 50 (1991): 55–62.

Cohen, Norman J. *Masking and Unmasking Ourselves: Interpreting Biblical Texts on Clothing and Identity*. Woodstock: Jewish Lights, 2015.

Colburn, Cynthia S., and Maura K. Heyn, eds. *Reading a Dynamic Canvas: Adornment in the Ancient Mediterranean World*. Newcastle: Cambridge Scholars, 2008.

Cook, Sean. "Is Saul Among the Philistines? A Portrayal of Israel's First and Flawed King?" Pages 109–24. In *Dress and Clothing in the Hebrew Bible*. Edited by Antonios Finitsis. New York: T&T Clark, 2019.

Cordwell, Justine M., and Ronald A. Schwarz, eds. *The Fabrics of Culture: The Anthropology of Clothing and Adornment*. The Hague: Mouton, 1979.

Dalley, Stephanie. "Hebrew taḥaš, Akkadian duhšu, Faience and Beadwork." *JSS* 45 (2000): 1–19.

Dewrell, Heath. "How Tamar's Veil Became Joseph's Coat: The Meaning of *kĕtōnet (hap) passim*." *Biblica* 87 (2016): 161–74.

Dickie, Clark H. F. *The Marginal Situation: A Sociological Study of a Coloured Group*. International Library of Sociology and Social Reconstruction. London: Routledge & Kegan Paul, 1966.

Dressler, Harold. "Is the Bow of Aqhat a Symbol of Virility." *UF* 7 (1975): 217–25.

Drewal, Henry John. "Pageantry and Power in Yoruba Costuming." Pages 189–230. In *The Fabrics of Culture: The Anthropology of Clothing and Adornment*. Edited by Justine M. Cordwell and Ronald A. Schwartz. The Hague: Mouton, 1979.

Ede, Franziska. "The Garment Motif in Gen. 37-39." Pages 389–402. In Berner et al., *Clothing and Nudity in the Hebrew Bible*.

Edwards, Douglas R. "Dress and Ornamentation." Page 232–8. In *The Anchor Bible Dictionary*, vol. 2. 1st ed. Edited by David Noel Freedman. New York: Doubleday, 1992.

Eicher, Joanne B., and Sandra Lee Evenson. *The Visible Self: Global Perspectives on Dress, Culture and Society*. 4th ed. New York: Fairchild, 2015.

Eicher, Joanne B., and Mary Ellen Roach-Higgins. "Definition and Classification of Dress: Implications for Analysis of Gender Roles." Pages 8–28. In *Dress and Gender: Making and Meaning in Cultural Contexts*. Cross-Cultural Perspectives on Women, vol. 2. Edited by Ruth Barnes and Joanne B. Eicher. Providence: Berg, 1992.

Eicher, Joanne B., and Mary Ellen Roach-Higgins. "Dress and Identity." *CTRJ* 10 (1992): 1–8.

Entwistle, Joanne. "Fashion and the Fleshy Body: Dress as Embodied Practice." *FT* 4 (2000): 323–47.

Entwistle, Joanne. *The Fashioned Body: Fashion, Dress and Modern Social Theory.* Cambridge, UK: Polity, 2000.

Finitsis, Antonios, ed. *Dress and Clothing in the Hebrew Bible: "For All Her Household Are Clothed in Crimson."* LHBOTS 679. London: T&T Clark, 2019.

Fletcher-Jones, Nigel. *Ancient Egyptian Jewelry: 50 Masterpieces of Art and Design.* Cairo: American University in Cairo Press, 2020.

Flynn, Shawn W. "YHWH'S Clothing, Kingship, and Power: Origins and Vestiges in Comparative Ancient Near Eastern Contexts." Pages 11–28. In *Dress and Clothing in the Hebrew Bible: "For All Her Household Are Clothed in Crimson."* LHBOTS 679. Edited by Antonios Finitsis. London: T&T Clark, 2019.

Gansell, Amy R. "Dressing the Neo-Assyrian Queen in Identity and Ideology: Elements and Ensembles from the Royal Tombs at Nimrud." *AJA* 122 (2018): 65–100.

Garcia-Ventura, Agnès. "Clothing and Nudity in the Ancient Near East from the Perspective of Gender Studies." Pages 19–32. In Berner et al., *Clothing and Nudity in the Hebrew Bible.*

Gaspa, Salvatore. "Gold Decorations in Assyrian Textiles: An Interdisciplinary Approach." Pages 227–44. In *Prehistoric, Ancient Near Eastern and Aegean Textiles and Dress: An Interdisciplinary Anthology.* Edited by Mary Harlo, Cécile Michel, and Marie-Louise Nosch. Philadelphia, PA: Oxbow, 2014.

Giffone, Benjamin D. "'Special Forces': A Stereotype of Benjaminite Soldiers in the Deuteronomistic History and Chronicles." *SJOT* 30 (2016): 16–29.

Goebs, Katja. "Crowns." *OEAE* 1 (2001): 321–6.

Goffman, Erving. *Frame Analysis.* New York: Harper & Row, 1974.

Goffman, Erving. "The Mentally Ill and Management of Personal Front." Pages 266–8. In *Dress, Adornment and the Social Order.* Edited by Joanne B. Eicher and Mary Ellen Roach. New York: John Wiley, 1965.

Golani, Amir. "Revealed by Their Jewelry: Ethnic Identity of Israelites during the Iron Age in the Southern Levant." *PAM* 23 (2014): 269–96.

Görg, Manfred. "Der gefärbte Rock Josefs." *Biblische Notizen* 102 (2000): 9–12.

Green, J. D. M. "Anklets and the Social Construction of Gender and Age in the Late Bronze and Early Iron Age Southern Levant." Pages 283–309. In *Archaeology and Women: Ancient and Modern Issues.* Edited by Sue Hamilton, Ruth Whitehouse, and Katherine I. Wright. Publications of the Institute of Archaeology, University College London. Walnut Creek: Left Coast, 2007.

Gzella, Holger. "Nudity and Clothing in the Lexicon of the Hebrew Bible." Pages 217–35. In Berner et al., *Clothing and Nudity in the Hebrew Bible.*

Hallaschka, Martin. "Clean Garments for Joshua: The Purification of the High Priest in Zech. 3." Pages 525–40. In Berner et al., *Clothing and Nudity in the Hebrew Bible.*

Hartenstein, Friedhelm. "Clothing and Nudity in the Paradise Story (Gen. 2-3)." Pages 357–78. In Berner et al., *Clothing and Nudity in the Hebrew Bible.*

Hoffner, Harry A. "Symbols for Masculinity and Femininity: Their Use in Ancient Near Eastern Sympathetic Magic Rituals." *JBL* 85 (1966): 326–34.

Huddlestun, John. "Divestiture, Deception, and Demotion: The Garment Motif in Genesis 37–39." *JSOT* 98 (2002): 47–62.

Ilan, David. "The Crescent-Lunate Motif in the Jewelery of the Bronze and Iron Ages." Pages 137–50. In *Proceedings of the 9th International Congress on the Archaeology of the Ancient Near East*. Edited by Rolf A. Stucky, Oskar Kaelin, and Hans-Peter Mathys. Wies: Harrassowitz Verlag, 2016.

Imes, Carmen Joy. "Belonging to YHWH: Real and Imagined Inscribed Seals in Biblical Tradition." Pages 349–65. In *Write That They May Read: Studies in Literacy and Textualization in the Ancient Near East and in the Hebrew Scriptures. Essays in Honour of Professor Alan R. Millard*. Edited by D. I. Block, D. C. Deuel, C. J. Collins, and P. J. N. Lawrence. Eugene, OR: Pickwick, 2020.

Imes, Carmen Joy. "Between Two Worlds: The Functional and Symbolic Significance of the High Priestly Regalia." Pages 29–62. In *Dress and Clothing in the Hebrew Bible: "For All Her Household Are Clothed in Crimson."* LHBOTS 679. Edited by Antonios Finitsis. London: T&T Clark, 2019.

Johnstone, Janet M. "Wrapping and Tying Ancient Egyptian New Kingdom Dresses." Pages 59–82. In *Wrapping and Unwrapping Material Culture: Archaeological and Anthropological Perspectives*. Edited by Susanna Harris and Laurence Douny. Walnut Creek: Left Coast, 2014.

Joyce, Rosemary A. "Archaeology of the Body." *ARA* 34 (2005): 139–58.

Keali'inohomoku, Joann W. "You Dance What You Wear, and You Wear Your Cultural Values." Pages 77–86. In *The Fabrics of Culture: The Anthropology of Clothing and Adornment*. Edited by Justine M. Cordwell and Ronald A. Schwarz. The Hague: Mouton, 1979.

Kersken, Sabine A. *Töchter Zions, wie seid ihr gewandet? Untersuchungen zu Kleidung und Schmuck alttestamentlicher Frauen*. Münster: Ugarit-Verlag, 2008.

Kim, Chŏng-hun. *The Significance of Clothing Imagery in the Pauline Corpus*. JSNTSup 268. London: T&T Clark, 2004.

Klaus, Nathan. "The Tearing of Garments as the Main Symbol of Mourning in the Bible." *Beit Mikra* 56 (2011): 71–99.

Koenig, Sara. "Tamar and Tamar: Clothing as Deception and Defiance." Pages 87–108. In *Dress and Clothing in the Hebrew Bible: "For All Her Household Are Clothes in Crimson."* LHBOTS 679. Edited by Antonios Finitsis. New York: T&T Clark, 2019.

Köhlmoos, Melanie. "Tearing One's Clothes and Rites of Mourning." Pages 303–15. In Berner et al., *Clothing and Nudity in the Hebrew Bible*.

Krause, Joachim J. "Barefoot before God; Shoes and Sacred Space in the Hebrew Bible and Ancient Near East." Pages 315–22. In Berner et al., *Clothing and Nudity in the Hebrew Bible*.

Kruger, Paul. "The Symbolic Significance of the Hem (כנף) in 1 Samuel 15.2." Pages 105–16. In *Text and Context: Old Testament and Semitic Studies for F.C. Fensham*. Edited by W. Classen. Sheffield, England: JSOT, 1988.

LeMon, Joel M., and Richard A. Purcell. "Iconographic Case Studies from Isaiah 6:1; 59:17; and 63:1–6." Pages 269–87. In Berner et al., *Clothing and Nudity in the Hebrew Bible*.

Lennon, Sharron J., and Leslie L. Davis. "Clothing and Human Behavior from a Social Cognitive Framework Part 1: Theoretical Perspectives." *CTRJ* 7.4 (Summer 1989): 41–8.

Lennon, Sharron J., Kim P. Johnson, and Nancy A. Rudd. *Social Psychology of Dress*. New York: Fairchild, 2017.

Letourneau, Anne. "The Stain of Trauma: The Skirts of Jerusalem in Lam. 1:9." Forthcoming.

Livneh, Atar. "Garments of Shame, Garments of War: Clothing Imagery in 1 Maccabees 1:25–28, 14:9." *VT* 69.4–5 (2019): 670–81.

Low, Katherine. "Implications Surrounding Girding the Loins in Light of Gender, Body, and Power." *JSOT* 36 (2011): 3–30.

Lyell, Ellena, and Joseph Scales. "Uncovering the Dead, Dethroning the King: Divine Embodiment in 1 Samuel 28." *HS* 62 (2021): 97–115.

Lynch, Matthew J. "Neglected Physical Dimensions of 'Shame' Terminology in the Hebrew Bible." *Biblica* 91.4 (2010): 499–517.

Maier, Christl M. "Daughter Zion as Queen and the Iconography of the Female City." Pages 147–62. In *Images and Prophecy in the Ancient Eastern Mediterranean*. FRLANT 233. Edited by MarttiNissinen and Charles E.Carter. Göttingen: Vandenhoeck & Ruprecht, 2009.

Markowitz, Yvonne J. "Jewelry." *OEAE* 2 (2001): 201–7.

Matić, Uroš. "(De)Queering Hatshepsut: Binary Bind in Archaeology of Egypt and Kingship Beyond the Corporeal." *JAMT* 23 (2016): 810–31.

Matthews, Victor. "The Anthropology of Clothing in the Joseph Narrative." *JSOT* 65 (1995): 25–36.

Mauss, M. "Body Techniques." Pages 95–123. In *Sociology and Psychology: Essays by Marcel Mauss*. Trans. B. Brewster. London: Routledge & Kegan Paul, 1979.

Mauss, M. "Introduction." Pages 1–14. In *Sociology and Psychology: Essays by Marcel Mauss*. Trans. B. Brewster. London: Routledge & Kegan Paul, 1979.

Maxwell-Hyslop, K. R. *Western Asiatic Jewellery c.3000–612B.C.* Methuen's Handbooks of Archaeology. London: Methuen, 1971.

McCracken, Grant. "Clothing as Language: An Object Lesson in the Study of the Expressive Properties of Material Culture." Pages 103–28. In *Material Anthropology: Contemporary Approaches to Material Culture*. Edited by Barrie Reynolds and Margaret A. Stott. Lanham, MD: University Press of America, 1987.

McKay, Heather, A. "Clothing, Adornment and Accoutrements as Cultural and Literary Signifiers in the 'Historical' Books." Pages 238–52. In *Samuel, Kings and Chronicles I*. Edited by Athalya Brenner-Idan and Archie Lee. London: T&T Clark, 2018.

McKay, Heather, A. "Gendering the Body: Clothes Maketh the (Wo)man." Pages 84–104. In *Theology and the Body*. Edited by Robert Hannaford and J'annine Jobling. Herefordshire: Gracewing, 1999.

McKay, Heather, A. "Gendering the Discourse of Display in the Hebrew Bible." Pages 169–200. In *On Reading Prophetic Texts*. Edited by Bob Becking and Meindert Dijkstra. Leiden: Brill, 1996.

Metzler, Dieter. "Mural Crowns in the Ancient Near East and Greece." Pages 76–85. In *Yale University Art Bulletin, an Obsession with Fortune: Tyche in Greek and Roman Art*. Edited by Susan B. Matheson. New Haven, CT: Yale University Art Gallery, 1994.

Neuman, Kiersten. "Gods among Men: Fashioning the Divine Image in Assyria." Pages 5–15. In *What Shall I Say of Clothes? Theoretical and Methodological Approaches to the Study of Dress in Antiquity*. Edited by Megan Cifarelli and Laura Galinski. Boston: Archaeological Institute of America, 2017.

Noonan, Benjamin J. "Hide or Hue? Defining Hebrew תחש." *Biblica* 93 (2012): 580–9.

Ogden, Jack. *Ancient Jewellery*. Interpreting the Past. Berkeley: Trustees of the British Museum and the University of California Press, 1992.

Olson, Kelly. *Masculinity and Dress in Roman Antiquity*. Routledge Monographs in Classical Studies. London: Routledge, 2017.

Oppenheim, A. Leo. "The Golden Garments of the Gods." *JNES* 8.3 (1949): 172–93.

Ornan, Tallay. "Labor Pangs: The Revadim Plaque Type." Pages 215–35. In *Images as Sources: Studies on Ancient Near Eastern Artefacts and the Bible Inspired by the Work of Othmar Keel*. Edited by Susanne Bickel. Fribourg: Academic Press, 2007.

Oswald, Wolfgang. "Veiling Moses' Shining Face (Exodus 34:29-35)." Pages 449–57. In Berner et al., *Clothing and Nudity in the Hebrew Bible*.

Peterson, Erik. "A Theology of Dress." *Communio* 20 (Fall 1993): 558–68.

Platt, Elizabeth E. "Jewelry of Bible Times and the Catalog of Isa 3:18-23: I." *AUSS* 17 (1979): 71–84.

Platt, Elizabeth E. "Jewelry of Bible Times and the Catalog of Isa 3:18-23: II." *AUSS* 17 (1979): 189–201.

Platt, Elizabeth E. "Jewelry, Ancient Israelite." *ABD* 3: 823–34.

Prouser, Ora Horn. "Suited to the Throne: The Symbolic Use of Clothing in the David and Saul Narratives." *JSOT* 71 (1996): 27–37.

Quick, Laura. "Clothed in Curses: Ritual, Curse and Story in the Deir 'Alla Plaster Inscription." Pages 95–109. In *To Gaul, to Greece and into Noah's Ark: Essays in Honour of Kevin J. Cathcart on the Occasion of His Eightieth Birthday*. Journal of Semitic Studies Supplement. Edited by Laura Quick, Ekaterina E. Kozlova, Sonja Noll, and Philip Y. Yoo. Oxford: Oxford University Press, 2019.

Quick, Laura. "Decorated Women: A Sociological Approach to the Function of Cosmetics in the Books of Esther and Ruth." *Biblical Interpretation* 27 (2019): 354–71.

Quick, Laura. *Dress, Adornment, and the Body in the Hebrew Bible*. Oxford: Oxford University Press, 2021.

Quick, Laura. "'Like a Garment Eaten by Moths' (Job 13:28): Clothing, Nudity and Illness in the Book of Job." *BibInt* (2020): 1–20.

Quick, Laura. "'She Made Herself Up Provocatively for the Charming of the Eyes of Men' (Jdt. 10.4): Cosmetics and Body Adornment in the Stories of Judith and Susanna." *JSP* 28 (2019): 215–36.

Quick, Laura, and Ellena Lyell. "Clothing, Conformity and Power: Garment Imagery in the Book of Esther." *VT* (forthcoming).

Rees, Susannah. "The נזם and Navigating Power Structures." *BibInt* (forthcoming).

Roach, Mary Ellen, and Joanne B. Eicher. *The Visible Self: Perspectives on Dress*. Englewood Cliff, NJ: Prentice Hall, 1973.

Roach, Mary Ellen, and Joanne Bubolz Eicher. *Dress, Adornment and the Social Order*. New York: John Wiley, 1965.

Roach-Higgins, Mary Ellen, and Joanne B. Eicher. "Dress and Identity." *Clothing and Textiles Research Journal* 10 (1992): 1–8.

Roach-Higgins, Mary Ellen, Joanne B. Eicher, and Kim K. P. Johnson, eds. *Dress and Identity*. New York: Fairchild, 1995.

Roach-Higgins, Mary Ellen, Joanne B. Eicher, and Kim K. P. Johnson, eds. "The Language of Personal Adornment." Pages 7–22. In *The Fabrics of Culture: The Anthropology of Clothing and Adornment*. Edited by Justine M. Cordwell and Ronald A. Schwarz. The Hague: Mouton, 1979.

Rooke, Deborah W. "Breeches of the Covenant: Gender, Garments and the Priesthood." Pages 19–37. In *Embroidered Garments: Priests and Gender in Biblical Israel*. Hebrew Bible Monographs. Edited by Deborah W. Rooke. Sheffield, England: Sheffield Phoenix Press, 2009.

Rooker, Mark F. "חגר." Pages 22–3. In *New International Dictionary of Old Testament Theology and Exegesis*, vol. 2. Edited by Willem VanGemeren. Grand Rapids, MI: Zondervan, 1997.

Ross, Robert. *Clothing: A Global History*. Cambridge: Polity, 2008.

Ryan, Mary Shaw. *Clothing: A Study in Human Behaviour*. New York: Holt, Rinehart & Winston. 1966.

Salvesen, Alison. "כֶּתֶר (Esther 1:11; 2:17; 6:8): 'Something to do with a Camel?'" *JSS* 44 (1999): 35–46.

Sass, Benjamin. "Jewelry." *OEANE* 3 (2001): 238–46.

Schmitt, Jean-Claude. "The Ethics of Gesture." Pages 129–47. In *Fragments for a History of the Human Body*, part 2. Edited by Michel Feher, Ramona Naddaf and Nadia Tazi. New York: Urzone, 1989.

Schneider, Jane, and Annette B. Weiner. "Introduction." Pages 1–29. In *Cloth and Human Experience*. Smithsonian Series in Ethnographic Inquiry. Edited by Annette B. Weiner and Jane Schneider. Washington, DC: Smithsonian Institution, 1989.

Schwarz, Ronald A., and J. M.Cordwell, eds. *The Fabrics of Culture: The Anthropology of Clothing and Adornment*. The Hague: Mouton, 1979.

Schwarz, Ronald A., and J. M.Cordwell, eds. "Uncovering the Secret Vice: Towards an Anthropology of Clothing and Adornment." Pages 23–46. In *The Fabrics of Culture: The Anthropology of Clothing and Adornment*. Edited byJustine M. Cordwell and Ronald A. Schwarz. The Hague: Mouton, 1979.

Seidler, Ayelet. "'Fasting,' 'Sackcloth,' and 'Ashes'—From Nineveh to Shushan." *VT* 69 (2019): 117–34.

Serova, Dina. "Stripped Bare: Communicating Rank and Status in Old Kingdom Egypt." Pages 163–84. In Berner et al., *Clothing and Nudity in the Hebrew Bible*.

Shukla, Pravina. *Costume: Performing Identities through Dress*. Indianapolis: Indiana University Press, 2015.

Siebert-Hommes, Jopie. "'On the Third Day Esther Put On her Queen's Robes' (Esther 5:1): The Symbolic Function of Clothing in the Book of Esther." *Lectio Difficilior* 1 (2002): 1–9.

Spoelstra, Joshua Joel. "Mordecai's Royal Vestments: Princely and/or Priestly." *Old Testament Essays* 32 (2019): 174–96.

Spoelstra, Joshua Joel. "Apotropaic Accessories: The People's Tassels and the High Priest's Rosette." Pages 63–86. In *Dress and Clothing in the Hebrew Bible: "For All Her Household Are Clothed in Crimson."* LHBOTS 679. Edited by Antonios Finitsis. New York: T&T Clark, 2019.

Starbuck, Scott R. A. "Disrobing an Isaianic Metaphor מְעִיל צְדָקָה (MEʾÎL SEDĀQÂ 'Robe of Righteousness') as Power Transfer in Isaiah 61:10." Pages 143–60. In *Dress and Clothing in the Hebrew Bible: "For All Her Household Are Clothed in Crimson."* LHBOTS 679. Edited by Antonios Finitsis. London: T&T Clark, 2019.

Staubli, Thomas. *Kleider in biblischer Zeit*. Freiburg: Katholisches Bibelwerk, 2013.

Stone, Gregory P. "Appearance and the Self." Pages 86–118. In *Human Behavior and Social Processes: An Interactionist Approach*. Edited by Arnold M. Rose. Boston, MA: Houghton Mifflin, 1962.

Stulman, Louis. "Reading the Bible through the Lens of Trauma and Art." Pages 177–92. In *Trauma and Traumatization in Individual and Collective Dimensions: Insights from Biblical Studies and Beyond*. Edited by Eve-Marie Becker, Jan Dochhorn, and Else Kragelund Holt. Göttingen: Vandenhoeck & Ruprecht, 2014.

Swartz, Michael D. "The Semiotics of the Priestly Vestments in Ancient Judaism." Pages 57–80. In *Sacrifice in Religious Experience*. Studies in the History of Religions 93. Edited by Albert I. Baumgarten. Boston, MA: Brill, 2018.

Tait, Hugh, ed. *Seven Thousand Years of Jewellery*. London: Trustees of the British Museum, British Museum Publications, 1986.

Thomas, D. Winton. "A Note on Zechariah III 4." Article. *JTS* 33 (1932): 279–80.

Tidwell, Neville L. A. "Linen Ephod: 1 Sam 2:18 and 2 Sam 6:14." *VT* 24.4 (1974): 505–7.

Turner, Terence S. "The Social Skin." *HAU: Journal of Ethnographic Theory* 2.2 (2012): 486–504.

van der Toorn, Karel. "The Significance of the Veil in the Ancient Near East." Pages 327–39. In *Pomegranates and Golden Bells: Studies in Biblical, Jewish, and Near Eastern Ritual, Law, and Literature in Honor of Jacob Milgrom*. Edited by David P. Wright, David Noel Freedom, and Avi Hurvitz. Winona Lake, IN: Eisenbrauns, 1995.

van Oorschot, Jürgen. "Nudity and Clothing in the Hebrew Bible: Theological and Anthropological Aspects." Pages 237–49. In Berner et al., *Clothing and Nudity in the Hebrew Bible*.

VanPool, Christine S., and Elizabeth Newsome. "The Spirit in the Material: A Case Study of Animism in the American Southwest." *American Antiquity* 77.2 (2012): 243–62.

Vedeler, Harold Torger. "Reconstructing Meaning in Deuteronomy 22:5: Gender, Society, and Transvestitism in Israel and the Ancient near East." *JBL* 127 (2008): 459–76.

Verduci, Josephine A. "Early Iron Age Adornment within Southern Levantine Mortuary Contexts: An Argument for Existential Significance in Understanding Material Culture." Pages 25–46. In *What Shall I Say of Clothes? Theoretical and Methodological Approaches to the Study of Dress in Antiquity*. Edited by Megan Cifarelli and Laura Galinski. Boston, MA: Archaeological Institute of America, 2017.

Verduci, Josephine A. *Metal Jewellery of the Southern Levant and Its Western Neighbours: Cross-Cultural Influences in the Early Iron Age Eastern Mediterranean*. Ancient Near Eastern Studies Supplement 53. Louvain, Belgium: Peeters, 2018.

Verman, Mark. "Royalty, Robes and the Art of Biblical Narrative." *SJOT* 30 (2016): 30–43.

Viberg, Åke. "Covering a Woman with the Mantle." Pages 136–44. In *Symbols of Law: A Contextual Analysis of Legal Symbolic Acts in the Old Testament*. Sweden: Almqvist & Wiksell International, 1992.

Wagstaff, Bethany Joy. *Redressing Clothing in the Hebrew Bible: Material-Cultural Approaches*. University of Exeter Dissertation, 2017.

Weingärtner, Martina. "The Symbolism of Vestimentary Acts in Gen. 27, Gen. 38, and 1 Sam. 17." Pages 403–16. In Berner et al., *Clothing and Nudity in the Hebrew Bible*.

Wilson, Ian D. "The Emperor and His Clothing: David Robed and Unrobed Before the Ark and Michal." Pages 125–42. In *Dress and Clothing in the Hebrew Bible: "For All Her Household Are Clothed in Crimson."* LHBOTS 679. Edited by Antonios Finitsis. London: T&T Clark, 2019.

Yamauchi, Edwin M., and Marvin R. Wilson. "Mourning and Weeping." Pages 1232–45. In *Dictionary of Daily Life: In Biblical & Post-Biblical Antiquity*. Edited by Edwin M. Yamauchi and Marvin R. Wilson. Peabody, MA: Hendrickson, 2017.

Zwickel, Wolfgang. "Fabrication, Functions, and Uses of Textiles in the Hebrew Bible." Pages 187–215. In Berner et al., *Clothing and Nudity in the Hebrew Bible*.

CONTRIBUTORS

Brady Alan Beard
ABD
Emory University
Atlanta, Georgia

Selena Billington
PhD
Independent scholar
Boulder, CO

Antonios Finitsis
Professor of Hebrew Bible
Pacific Lutheran University
Tacoma, Washington

Carmen Joy Imes
Associate Professor of Old Testament
Talbot School of Theology
Biola University
La Mirada, California

Jennifer Brown Jones
Instructor
Liberty University
Lynchburg, Virginia

Sara M. Koenig
Professor of Biblical Studies
Seattle Pacific University
Seattle, Washington

Ellena Lyell
PhD
Honorary Research Fellow
University of Exeter
United Kingdom

Jennifer M. Matheny
Assistant Professor
Nazarene Theological Seminary
Kansas City, Missouri

Heather A. McKay
Professor
Edge Hill University
Ormskirk, Lancashire
United Kingdom

S. J. Parrott
ABD
Oxford University
Oxford, United Kingdom

Susannah Rees
ABD
King's College, London
United Kingdom

Scott R. A. Starbuck
Senior Lecturer of Religious Studies
Gonzaga University
Spokane, Washington

Martina Weingärtner
PhD
Collège de France
Paris, France

INDEX OF SUBJECTS

INDEX OF PRIMARY SOURCES

Printed in the USA
CPSIA information can be obtained
at www.ICGtesting.com
LVHW020314201023
761647LV00005B/50